DA BRUDDERHOOD OF
Zeeba Zeeba Eata

Other *Pearls Before Swine* Books

The Ratvolution Will Not Be Televised
Nighthogs
This Little Piggy Stayed Home
BLTs Taste So Darn Good

Treasuries

Lions and Tigers and Crocs, Oh My!
Sgt. Piggy's Lonely Hearts Club Comic

DA BRUDDERHOOD OF
Zeeba Zeeba Eata

A *Pearls Before Swine* Collection by Stephan Pastis

**Andrews McMeel
Publishing, LLC**

Kansas City

Pearls Before Swine is distributed internationally by United Feature Syndicate.

Da Brudderhood of Zeeba Zeeba Eata copyright © 2007 by Stephan Pastis. All rights reserved. Printed in the United States of America. No part of this book may be used or reproduced in any manner whatsoever without written permission except in the case of reprints in the context of reviews. For information, write Andrews McMeel Publishing, LLC, an Andrews McMeel Universal company, 4520 Main Street, Kansas City, Missouri 64111.

07 08 09 10 11 BBG 10 9 8 7 6 5 4 3 2 1

ISBN-13: 978-0-7407-6801-9
ISBN-10: 0-7407-6801-8

Library of Congress Control Number: 2006937278

Pearls Before Swine can be viewed on the Internet at
www.comics.com/comics/pearls.

www.andrewsmcmeel.com

These strips appeared in newspapers from January 24, 2005 to October 30, 2005.

Introduction

It was the summer of 1996 and I had had it with being a lawyer.

I was in the midst of a case I absolutely hated. The hours were long. And my incessant worrying about work kept me up too many nights. All I had ever wanted to be was a cartoonist, but somehow I had taken a detour into a San Francisco law firm and a life I really didn't want.

So I decided to do something I almost never did, which was to take a day off work. But this wouldn't be just any day off work. I decided I was going to drive an hour north and try to meet my idol, Charles "Sparky" Schulz, the legendary creator of the comic strip *Peanuts*.

I had very little information to go on. I knew he lived in Santa Rosa. I knew that he owned an ice arena. And I knew from something I had read that part of his morning routine was to eat an English muffin in a café somewhere near that ice arena.

In short, not enough information to find him, but probably enough to qualify as a stalker.

So the next morning, I woke up early, got into my trusty Honda Accord, and headed north.

Thanks to my wife (who had grown up in Santa Rosa and had given me directions), I was able to find the arena rather easily. I saw that it was attached to a café called the Warm Puppy Café. I parked the car and walked inside.

There were a few skaters out on the ice, but the café itself was empty. So I sat at one of the many unoccupied tables and waited. And waited. Which is about when the thought hit me.

This was ridiculous.

I had taken a day off of work in the midst of a difficult case that demanded I work at least ten hours a day, all for the chance of meeting someone who probably wouldn't show up. I didn't even know for sure that he came to this café. Or if he did, what time he came. Moreover, what if he was on vacation? What if he just didn't feel like eating an English muffin that day? People can tire of English muffins, you know.

It was futile. It had been a stupid idea all along. I was Linus in the Pumpkin Patch, waiting in vain for the Great Pumpkin that would never arrive.

And then the door opened.

And there in his light blue sweater and khaki pants was Sparky.

I couldn't believe my luck. Against all odds, my stupid spontaneous plan had worked. I immediately wanted to rush over to him and introduce myself and tell him how much *Peanuts* had meant to me. But I knew I had to play it cool. I couldn't startle him. Had to let him eat his breakfast and read his newspaper.

So I ordered some coffee and sat back down and tried to act cool. Ho hum. Don't mind me. I'm just here to watch the skaters.

But every now and then, I snuck a glance. There, just over my shoulder, was the Greatest Cartoonist on the Planet, humbly eating his English muffin. I knew it would be rude to interrupt him while he was eating, so I waited for him to finish. When he was done, I walked slowly over to the table and knelt down.

"Hi, Sparky, I'm Stephan Pastis. I'm an attorney."

Absolute silence. No return greeting. "Oh, Lord," I realized. "He thinks I'm going to serve him with a subpoena."

I changed course quickly. "But I also draw a comic strip, and I took the day off work to try and meet you." And the moment I said that, he cleared away the newspapers from the seat next to him and invited me to sit down.

It was unbelievable. My heart was racing and I could barely speak, but there I was, sitting across the table from Charles Schulz.

"You must enjoy the challenge of being an attorney," he said as soon as I sat down. "Would you want to give that up to be a cartoonist?"

"In a heartbeat," I replied.

He seemed surprised at that. I could tell that he thought being an attorney was an exciting job. I tried to tell him a little about what made it bad, but in my nervousness, I'm sure I didn't make any sense. When I was done babbling, he asked me if I had brought any cartoons with me. I told him that I had, but that they were in the car. He told me to go out and get them.

Panic set in. Here I was, an absolute novice whose only "skill" was having the gumption to interrupt the creator of Charlie Brown during his breakfast and now I was going to have to show him my strips. This was Frank Lloyd Wright asking to see my blueprints, Beethoven asking me to play a few notes, Ted Williams asking me to take a couple swings.

As it turned out, the strip I had brought with me was called *The Infirm*, and it was about a struggling attorney at a large law firm. Looking back at it, I can see what a bad strip it was. But with trembling hands, I walked back into the arena and handed it to Sparky.

He read six of the strips and smiled, but never laughed. When he was finished reading them, he said, "Well, you can draw. You've got the package down." I wasn't entirely sure what he meant by that, but I didn't ask. He suggested a few changes, such as eliminating the narrator I was using in the strip (I used a narrator to move the action, rather than speech balloons) and changing my pen (he didn't like the marker I was using).

I told him what a huge influence he had had on me. I described a couple of my favorite *Peanuts* strips, both of which were from the 1950s. He seemed pleased, but at the same time somewhat upset that I hadn't cited any of his recent strips. He said, "I think in the past few years, I've done some of the best strips I've ever drawn."

He then began discussing some of the strips that were in the newspapers. As it turned out, the comic section from the *San Francisco Chronicle* was on the table in front of us. I remember he praised both *Mutts* and *Rose is Rose*. He also said that he really missed *The Far Side*.

We talked about his influences, his deadlines, his workload, how long it took him to draw a strip, and on and on. Before long, an entire hour had passed.

I felt bad about taking so much of his time and began gathering my stuff. Amazingly, he told me that if I made the changes he suggested to the strip, I should bring it back up and he would take me over to his studio. I couldn't believe his generosity.

I asked whether it would be too "touristy" to have my picture taken with him. He said, "No, that's fine. People ask me all the time." So we stood in front of the fireplace in the café and I handed my camera to one of the café employees. As we stood there side by side for the photo, he put his arm around me and I put my arm around him. It was as though we were old buddies.

I knew right then that I was the luckiest guy alive.

The Great Pumpkin had arrived.

—Stephan Pastis
March 2007

In memory of Sparky.

And for the hour he didn't
have to give me.

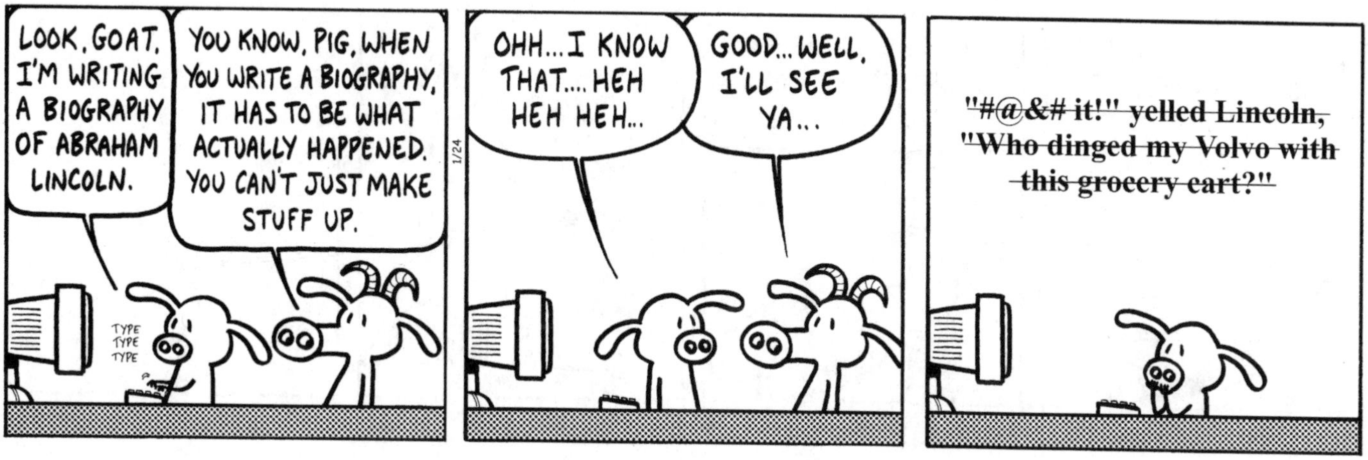
LOOK, GOAT, I'M WRITING A BIOGRAPHY OF ABRAHAM LINCOLN.
TYPE TYPE TYPE
YOU KNOW, PIG, WHEN YOU WRITE A BIOGRAPHY, IT HAS TO BE WHAT ACTUALLY HAPPENED. YOU CAN'T JUST MAKE STUFF UP.
1/24
OHH...I KNOW THAT.... HEH HEH HEH...
GOOD... WELL, I'LL SEE YA...
"#@&# it!" yelled Lincoln, "Who dinged my Volvo with this grocery cart?"

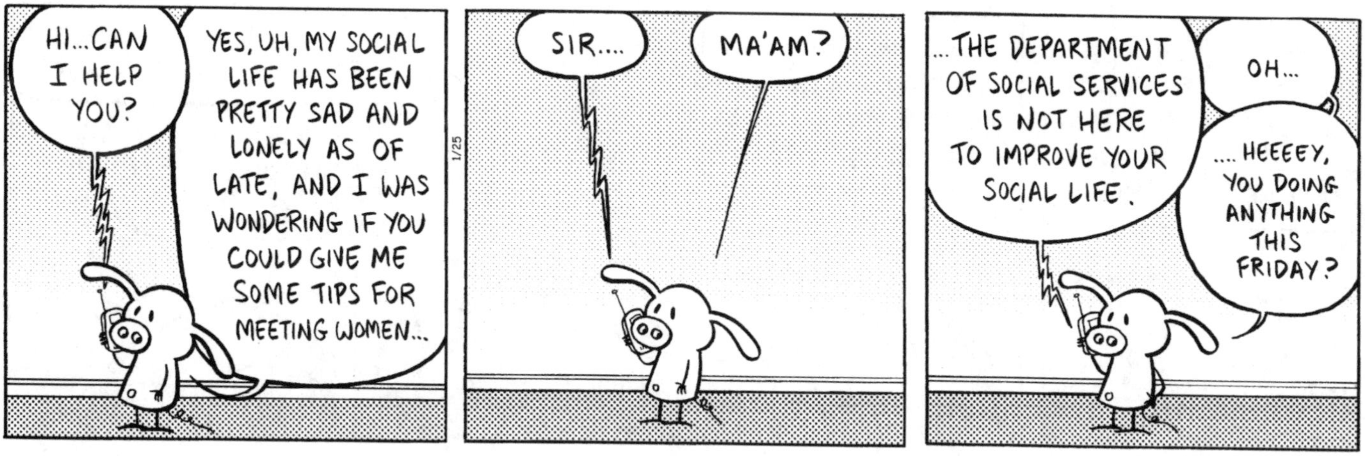
HI...CAN I HELP YOU?
YES, UH, MY SOCIAL LIFE HAS BEEN PRETTY SAD AND LONELY AS OF LATE, AND I WAS WONDERING IF YOU COULD GIVE ME SOME TIPS FOR MEETING WOMEN...
1/25
SIR....
MA'AM?
...THE DEPARTMENT OF SOCIAL SERVICES IS NOT HERE TO IMPROVE YOUR SOCIAL LIFE.
OH...
....HEEEEY, YOU DOING ANYTHING THIS FRIDAY?

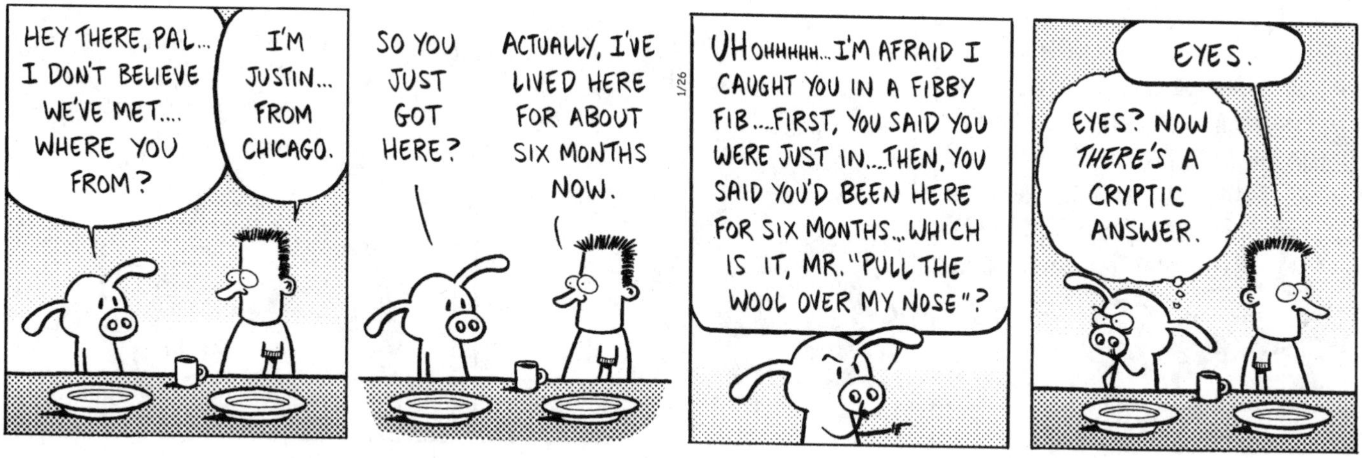
HEY THERE, PAL... I DON'T BELIEVE WE'VE MET.... WHERE YOU FROM?
I'M JUSTIN... FROM CHICAGO.
SO YOU JUST GOT HERE?
ACTUALLY, I'VE LIVED HERE FOR ABOUT SIX MONTHS NOW.
1/26
UH OHHHHHH...I'M AFRAID I CAUGHT YOU IN A FIBBY FIB....FIRST, YOU SAID YOU WERE JUST IN....THEN, YOU SAID YOU'D BEEN HERE FOR SIX MONTHS... WHICH IS IT, MR. "PULL THE WOOL OVER MY NOSE"?
EYES.
EYES? NOW *THERE'S* A CRYPTIC ANSWER.

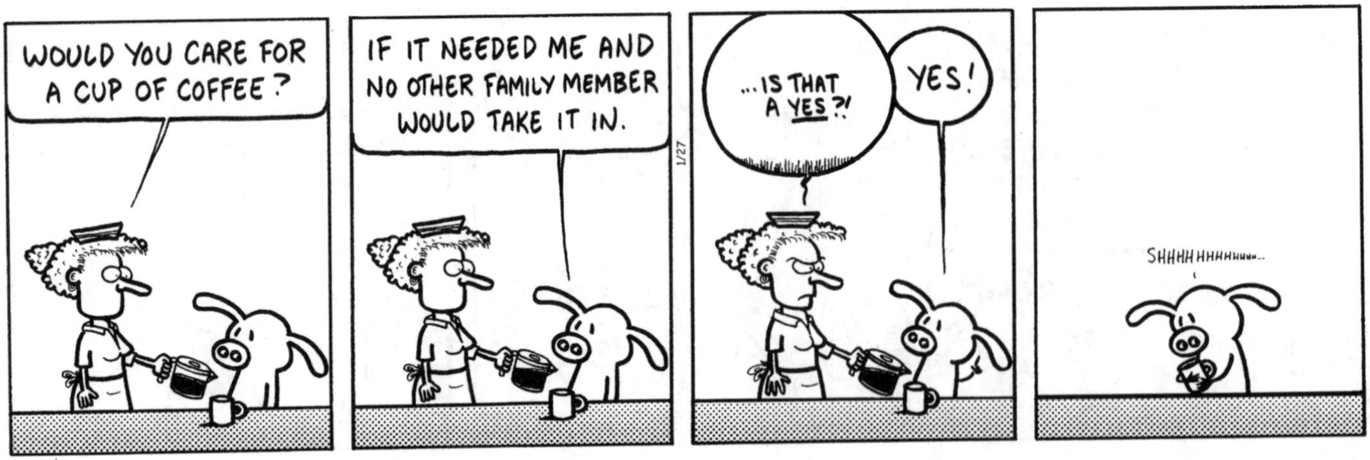
WOULD YOU CARE FOR A CUP OF COFFEE?
IF IT NEEDED ME AND NO OTHER FAMILY MEMBER WOULD TAKE IT IN.
1/27
...IS THAT A YES?!
YES!
SHHHHHHHHHhhhh...

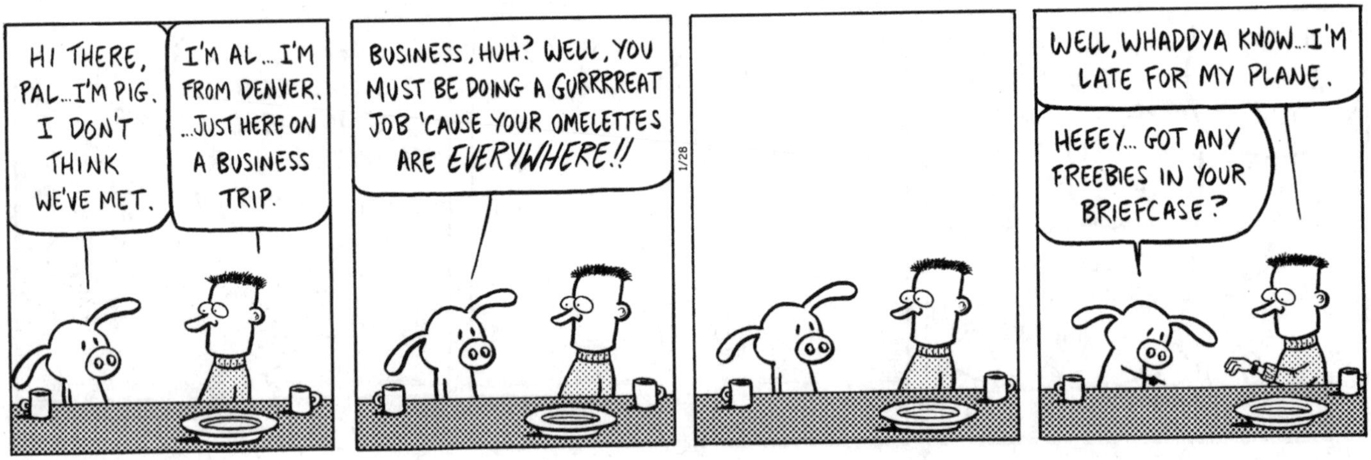
HI THERE, PAL...I'M PIG. I DON'T THINK WE'VE MET.
I'M AL...I'M FROM DENVER. ...JUST HERE ON A BUSINESS TRIP.
BUSINESS, HUH? WELL, YOU MUST BE DOING A GURRRREAT JOB 'CAUSE YOUR OMELETTES ARE EVERYWHERE!!
1/28
WELL, WHADDYA KNOW...I'M LATE FOR MY PLANE.
HEEEY... GOT ANY FREEBIES IN YOUR BRIEFCASE?

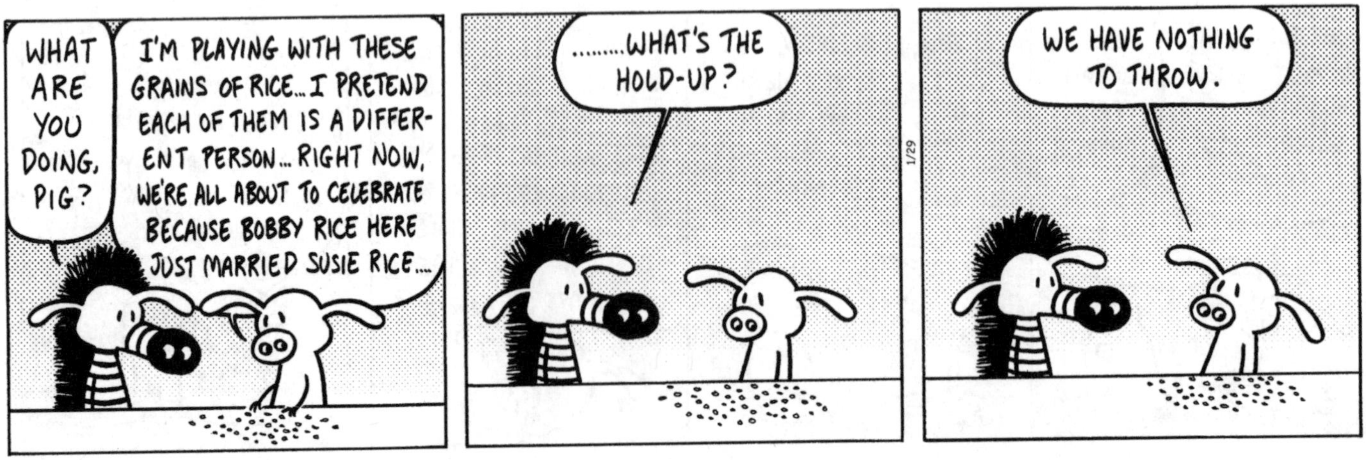
WHAT ARE YOU DOING, PIG?
I'M PLAYING WITH THESE GRAINS OF RICE...I PRETEND EACH OF THEM IS A DIFFER-ENT PERSON... RIGHT NOW, WE'RE ALL ABOUT TO CELEBRATE BECAUSE BOBBY RICE HERE JUST MARRIED SUSIE RICE....
.........WHAT'S THE HOLD-UP?
1/29
WE HAVE NOTHING TO THROW.

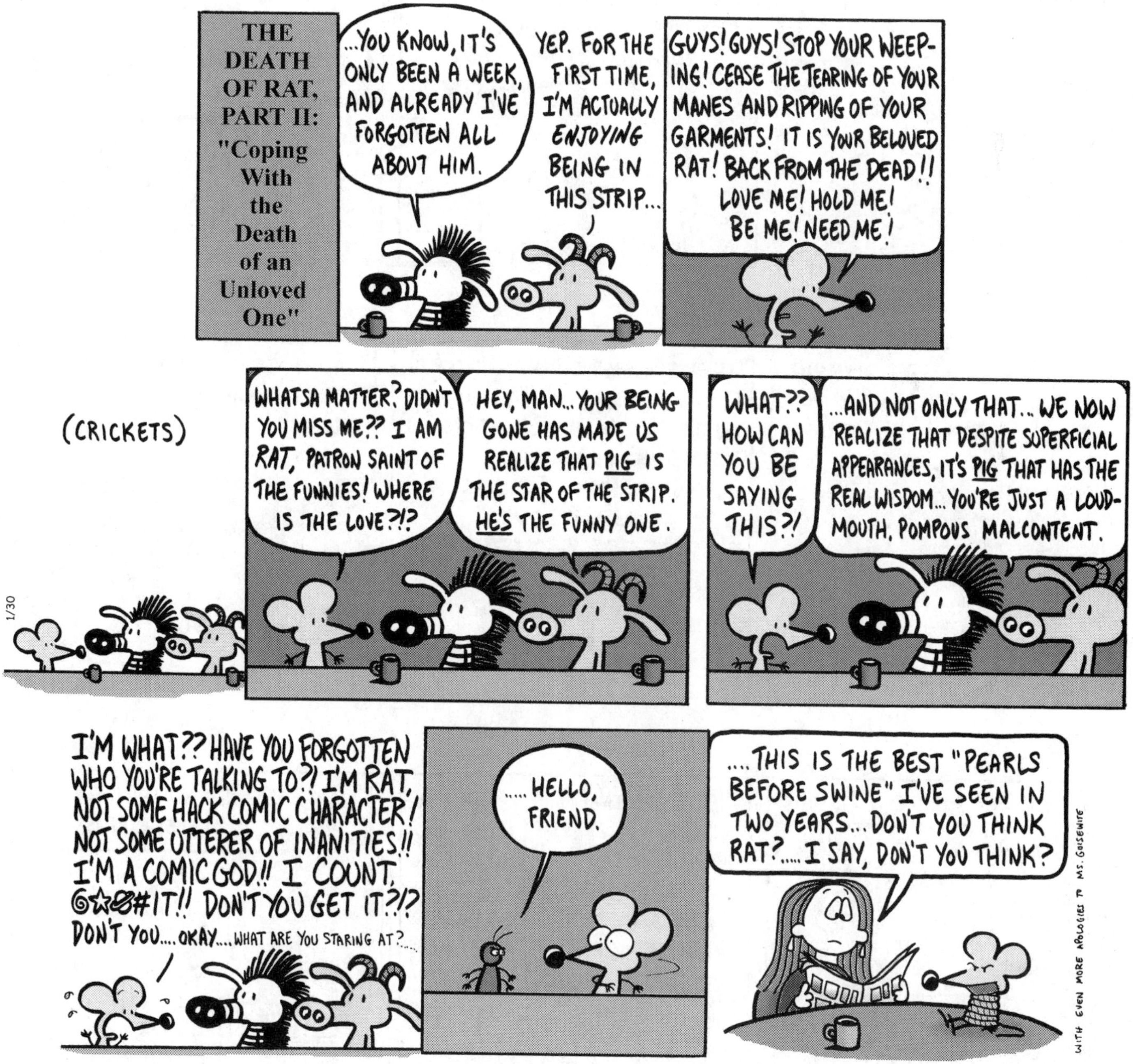
THE DEATH OF RAT, PART II: "Coping With the Death of an Unloved One"
...YOU KNOW, IT'S ONLY BEEN A WEEK, AND ALREADY I'VE FORGOTTEN ALL ABOUT HIM.
YEP. FOR THE FIRST TIME, I'M ACTUALLY ENJOYING BEING IN THIS STRIP...
GUYS! GUYS! STOP YOUR WEEPING! CEASE THE TEARING OF YOUR MANES AND RIPPING OF YOUR GARMENTS! IT IS YOUR BELOVED RAT! BACK FROM THE DEAD!! LOVE ME! HOLD ME! BE ME! NEED ME!
(CRICKETS)
1/30
WHATSA MATTER? DIDN'T YOU MISS ME?? I AM RAT, PATRON SAINT OF THE FUNNIES! WHERE IS THE LOVE?!?
HEY, MAN... YOUR BEING GONE HAS MADE US REALIZE THAT PIG IS THE STAR OF THE STRIP. HE'S THE FUNNY ONE.
WHAT?? HOW CAN YOU BE SAYING THIS?!
...AND NOT ONLY THAT... WE NOW REALIZE THAT DESPITE SUPERFICIAL APPEARANCES, IT'S PIG THAT HAS THE REAL WISDOM... YOU'RE JUST A LOUDMOUTH, POMPOUS MALCONTENT.
I'M WHAT?? HAVE YOU FORGOTTEN WHO YOU'RE TALKING TO?! I'M RAT, NOT SOME HACK COMIC CHARACTER! NOT SOME UTTERER OF INANITIES!! I'M A COMIC GOD!! I COUNT, @☆&#IT!! DON'T YOU GET IT?!? DON'T YOU.... OKAY.... WHAT ARE YOU STARING AT?....
.....HELLO, FRIEND.
....THIS IS THE BEST "PEARLS BEFORE SWINE" I'VE SEEN IN TWO YEARS... DON'T YOU THINK RAT?..... I SAY, DON'T YOU THINK?
WITH EVEN MORE APOLOGIES TO MS. GUISEWITE

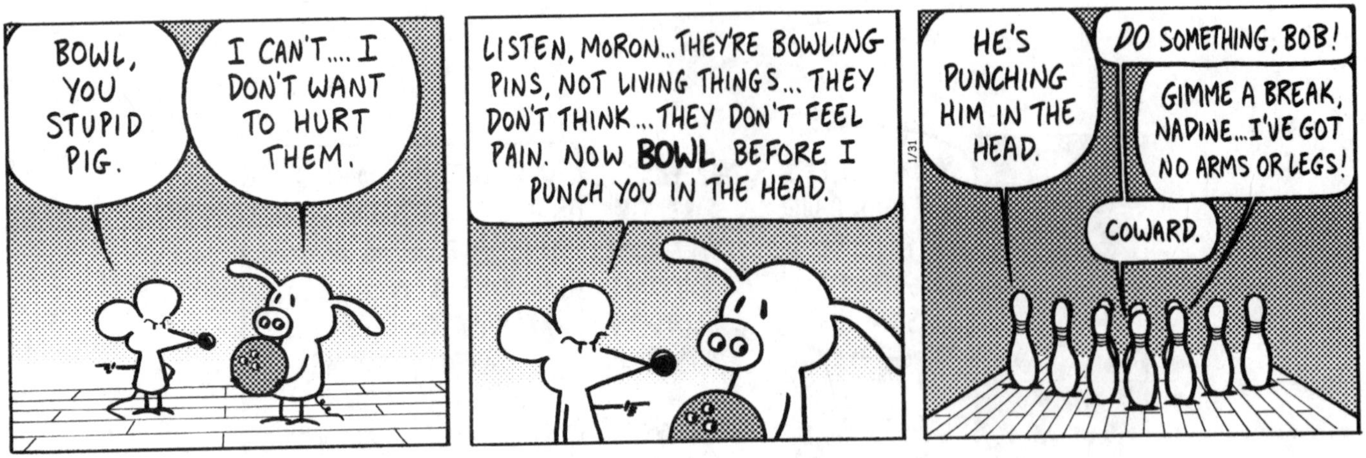
BOWL, YOU STUPID PIG.
I CAN'T.... I DON'T WANT TO HURT THEM.
LISTEN, MORON...THEY'RE BOWLING PINS, NOT LIVING THINGS... THEY DON'T THINK... THEY DON'T FEEL PAIN. NOW **BOWL**, BEFORE I PUNCH YOU IN THE HEAD.
1/31
HE'S PUNCHING HIM IN THE HEAD.
DO SOMETHING, BOB!
GIMME A BREAK, NADINE...I'VE GOT NO ARMS OR LEGS!
COWARD.

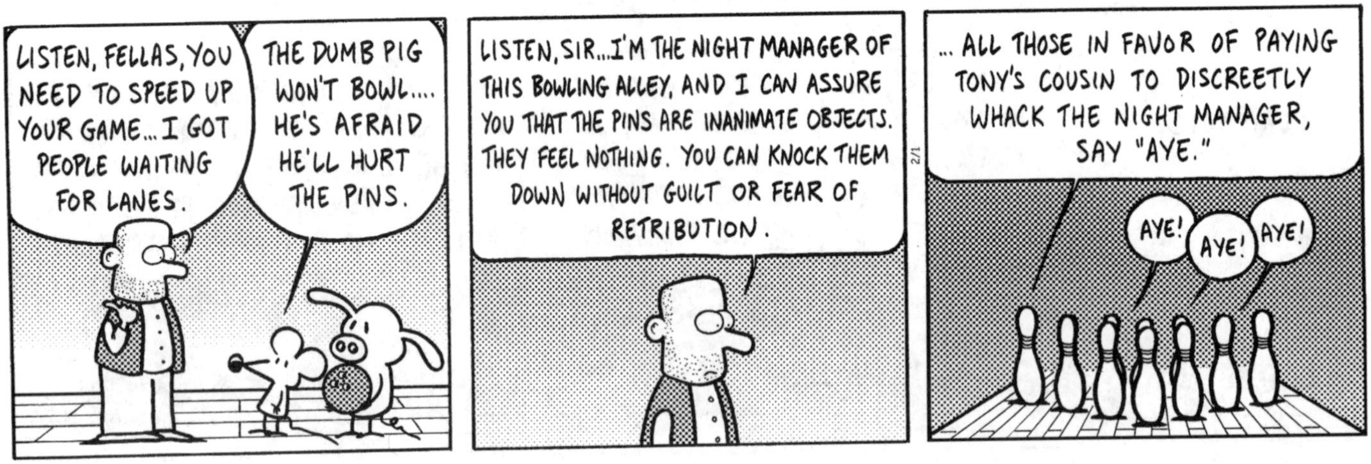
LISTEN, FELLAS, YOU NEED TO SPEED UP YOUR GAME... I GOT PEOPLE WAITING FOR LANES.
THE DUMB PIG WON'T BOWL.... HE'S AFRAID HE'LL HURT THE PINS.
LISTEN, SIR...I'M THE NIGHT MANAGER OF THIS BOWLING ALLEY, AND I CAN ASSURE YOU THAT THE PINS ARE INANIMATE OBJECTS. THEY FEEL NOTHING. YOU CAN KNOCK THEM DOWN WITHOUT GUILT OR FEAR OF RETRIBUTION.
2/1
... ALL THOSE IN FAVOR OF PAYING TONY'S COUSIN TO DISCREETLY WHACK THE NIGHT MANAGER, SAY "AYE."
AYE!
AYE!
AYE!

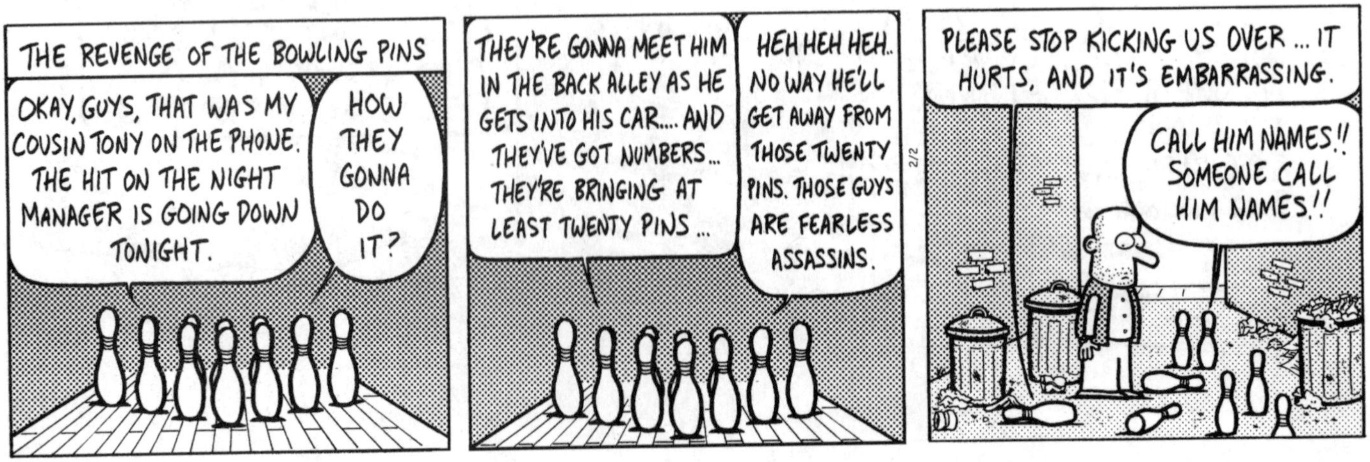
THE REVENGE OF THE BOWLING PINS
OKAY, GUYS, THAT WAS MY COUSIN TONY ON THE PHONE. THE HIT ON THE NIGHT MANAGER IS GOING DOWN TONIGHT.
HOW THEY GONNA DO IT?
THEY'RE GONNA MEET HIM IN THE BACK ALLEY AS HE GETS INTO HIS CAR.... AND THEY'VE GOT NUMBERS... THEY'RE BRINGING AT LEAST TWENTY PINS ...
HEH HEH HEH.. NO WAY HE'LL GET AWAY FROM THOSE TWENTY PINS. THOSE GUYS ARE FEARLESS ASSASSINS.
2/2
PLEASE STOP KICKING US OVER ... IT HURTS, AND IT'S EMBARRASSING.
CALL HIM NAMES!! SOMEONE CALL HIM NAMES!!

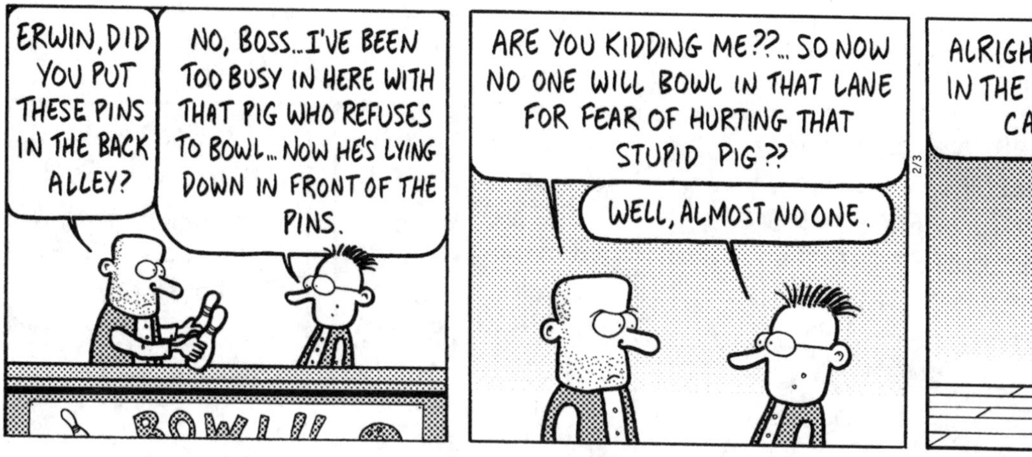
ERWIN, DID YOU PUT THESE PINS IN THE BACK ALLEY?
NO, BOSS... I'VE BEEN TOO BUSY IN HERE WITH THAT PIG WHO REFUSES TO BOWL... NOW HE'S LYING DOWN IN FRONT OF THE PINS.
BOWL!!!
ARE YOU KIDDING ME??... SO NOW NO ONE WILL BOWL IN THAT LANE FOR FEAR OF HURTING THAT STUPID PIG??
WELL, ALMOST NO ONE.
2/3
ALRIGHT, NOW.... IF I NAIL YOU IN THE BACK OF THE HEAD, WE'RE CALLING IT A SPARE.

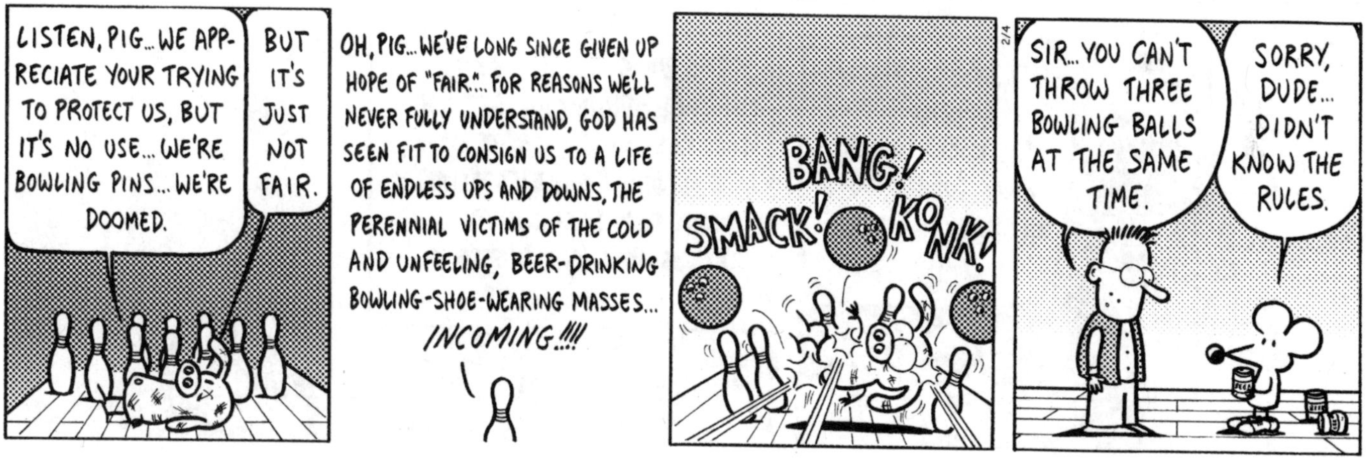
LISTEN, PIG... WE APPRECIATE YOUR TRYING TO PROTECT US, BUT IT'S NO USE... WE'RE BOWLING PINS... WE'RE DOOMED.
BUT IT'S JUST NOT FAIR.
OH, PIG... WE'VE LONG SINCE GIVEN UP HOPE OF "FAIR."... FOR REASONS WE'LL NEVER FULLY UNDERSTAND, GOD HAS SEEN FIT TO CONSIGN US TO A LIFE OF ENDLESS UPS AND DOWNS, THE PERENNIAL VICTIMS OF THE COLD AND UNFEELING, BEER-DRINKING BOWLING-SHOE-WEARING MASSES...
INCOMING!!!!
2/4
BANG!
SMACK!
KONK!
SIR... YOU CAN'T THROW THREE BOWLING BALLS AT THE SAME TIME.
SORRY, DUDE... DIDN'T KNOW THE RULES.

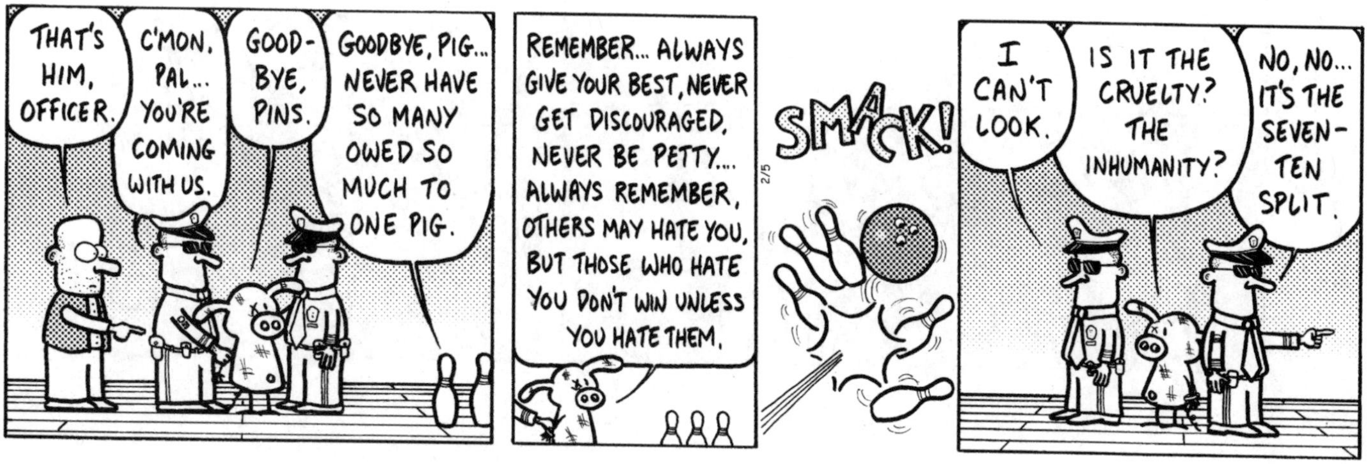
THAT'S HIM, OFFICER.
C'MON, PAL... YOU'RE COMING WITH US.
GOOD-BYE, PINS.
GOODBYE, PIG... NEVER HAVE SO MANY OWED SO MUCH TO ONE PIG.
REMEMBER... ALWAYS GIVE YOUR BEST, NEVER GET DISCOURAGED, NEVER BE PETTY.... ALWAYS REMEMBER, OTHERS MAY HATE YOU, BUT THOSE WHO HATE YOU DON'T WIN UNLESS YOU HATE THEM.
2/5
SMACK!
I CAN'T LOOK.
IS IT THE CRUELTY? THE INHUMANITY?
NO, NO... IT'S THE SEVEN-TEN SPLIT.

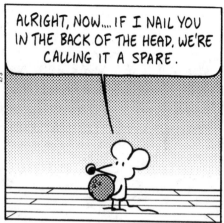

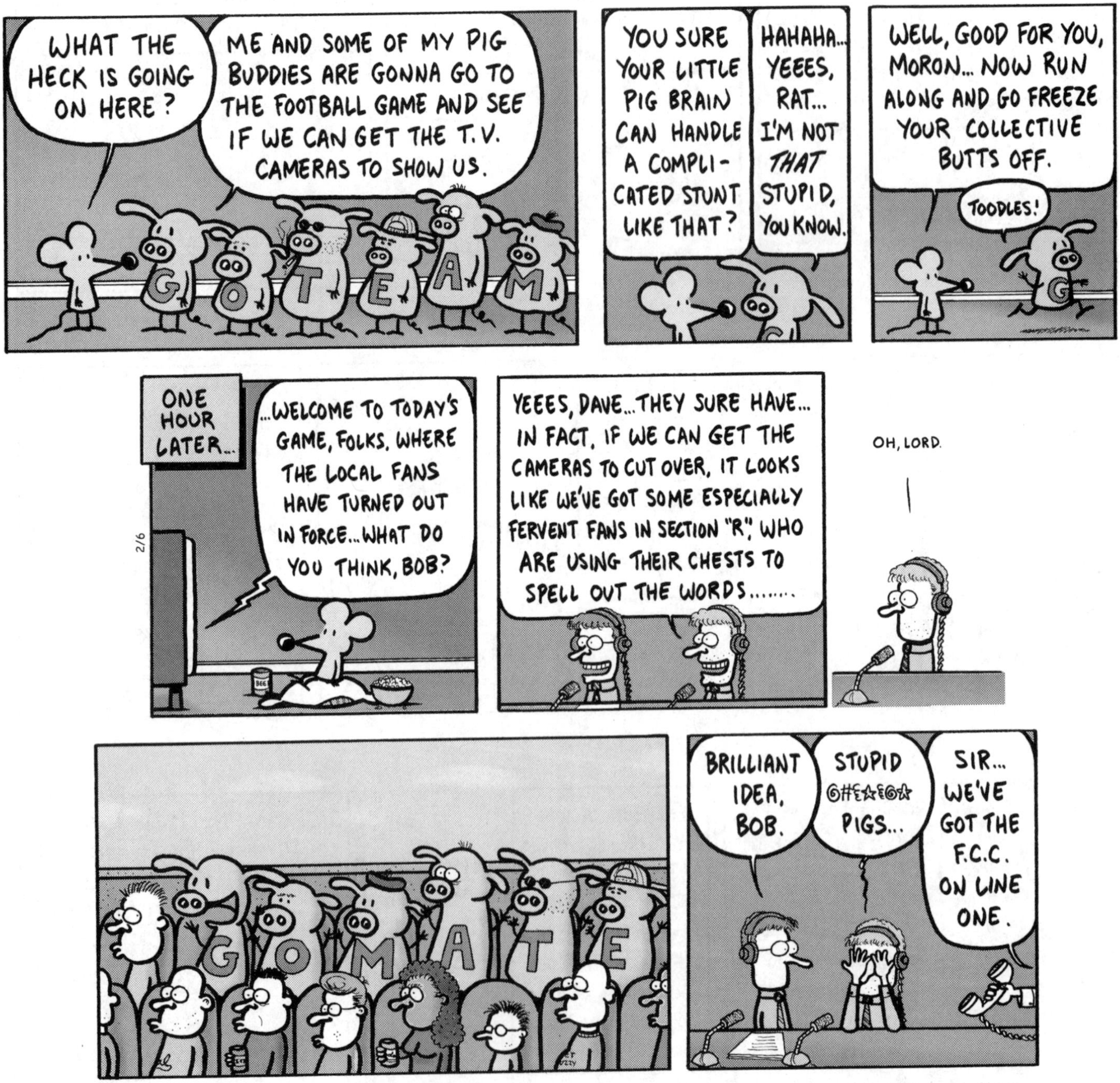
WHAT THE HECK IS GOING ON HERE?
ME AND SOME OF MY PIG BUDDIES ARE GONNA GO TO THE FOOTBALL GAME AND SEE IF WE CAN GET THE T.V. CAMERAS TO SHOW US.
GOTEAM
YOU SURE YOUR LITTLE PIG BRAIN CAN HANDLE A COMPLI-CATED STUNT LIKE THAT?
HAHAHA... YEEES, RAT... I'M NOT *THAT* STUPID, YOU KNOW.
WELL, GOOD FOR YOU, MORON... NOW RUN ALONG AND GO FREEZE YOUR COLLECTIVE BUTTS OFF.
TOODLES!
ONE HOUR LATER...
2/6
...WELCOME TO TODAY'S GAME, FOLKS, WHERE THE LOCAL FANS HAVE TURNED OUT IN FORCE...WHAT DO YOU THINK, BOB?
YEEES, DAVE...THEY SURE HAVE... IN FACT, IF WE CAN GET THE CAMERAS TO CUT OVER, IT LOOKS LIKE WE'VE GOT SOME ESPECIALLY FERVENT FANS IN SECTION "R," WHO ARE USING THEIR CHESTS TO SPELL OUT THE WORDS.......
OH, LORD.
GOMATE
BRILLIANT IDEA, BOB.
STUPID @#€☆€@☆ PIGS...
SIR... WE'VE GOT THE F.C.C. ON LINE ONE.

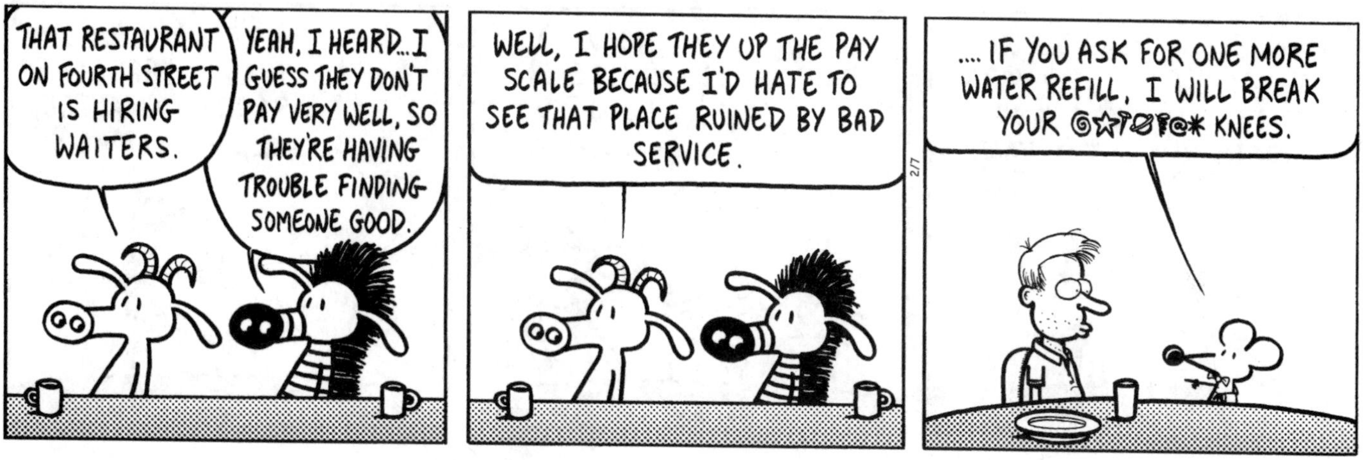
THAT RESTAURANT ON FOURTH STREET IS HIRING WAITERS.
YEAH, I HEARD...I GUESS THEY DON'T PAY VERY WELL, SO THEY'RE HAVING TROUBLE FINDING SOMEONE GOOD.
WELL, I HOPE THEY UP THE PAY SCALE BECAUSE I'D HATE TO SEE THAT PLACE RUINED BY BAD SERVICE.
2/7
.... IF YOU ASK FOR ONE MORE WATER REFILL, I WILL BREAK YOUR @☆?@?@* KNEES.

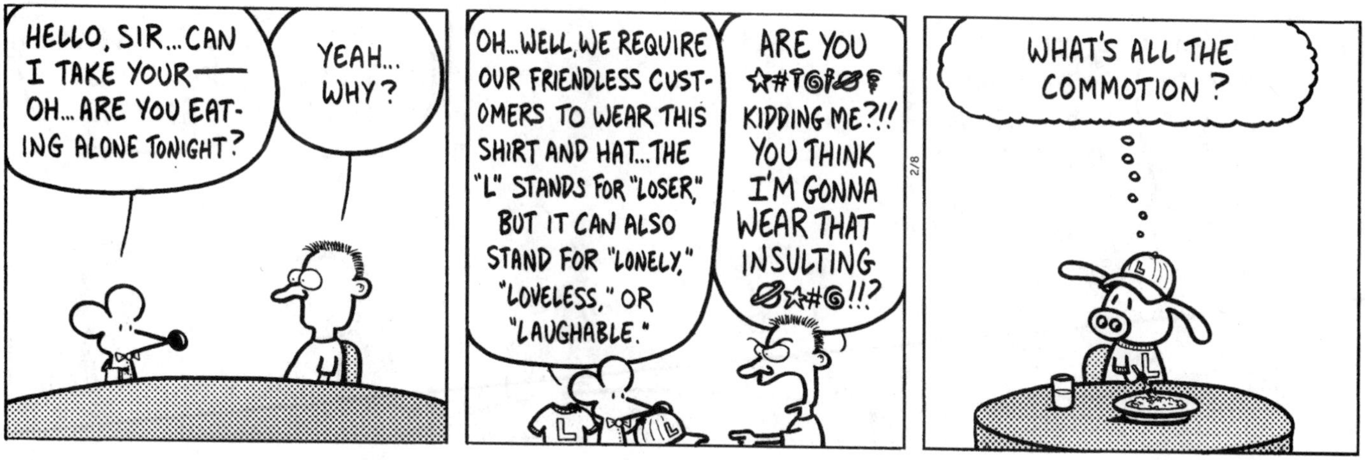
HELLO, SIR...CAN I TAKE YOUR— OH...ARE YOU EATING ALONE TONIGHT?
YEAH... WHY?
OH...WELL, WE REQUIRE OUR FRIENDLESS CUSTOMERS TO WEAR THIS SHIRT AND HAT...THE "L" STANDS FOR "LOSER," BUT IT CAN ALSO STAND FOR "LONELY," "LOVELESS," OR "LAUGHABLE."
ARE YOU ☆#?@?@? KIDDING ME?!! YOU THINK I'M GONNA WEAR THAT INSULTING @☆#@!!?
2/8
WHAT'S ALL THE COMMOTION?

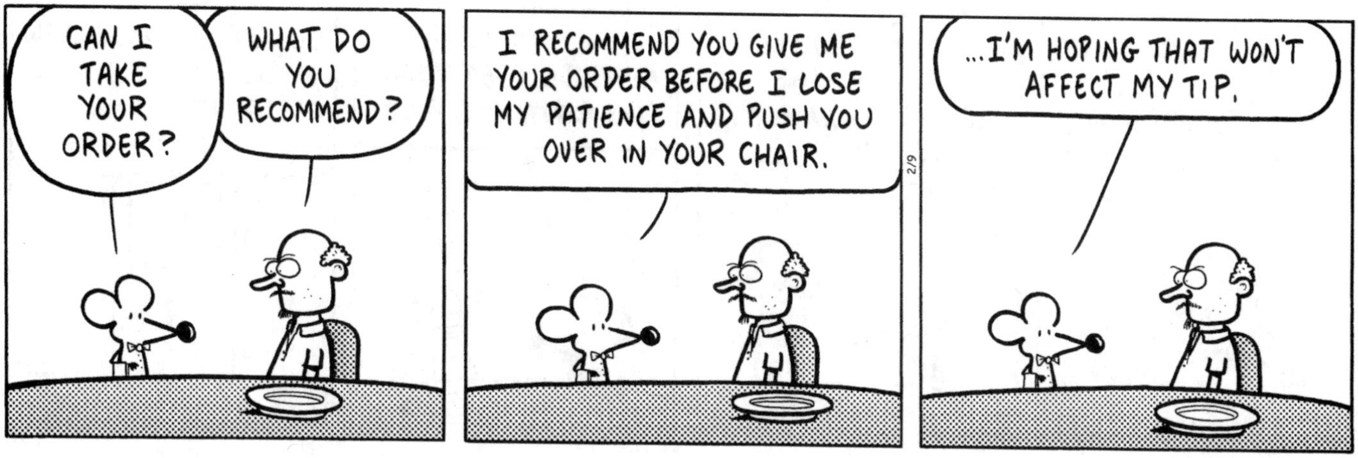
CAN I TAKE YOUR ORDER?
WHAT DO YOU RECOMMEND?
I RECOMMEND YOU GIVE ME YOUR ORDER BEFORE I LOSE MY PATIENCE AND PUSH YOU OVER IN YOUR CHAIR.
2/9
...I'M HOPING THAT WON'T AFFECT MY TIP.

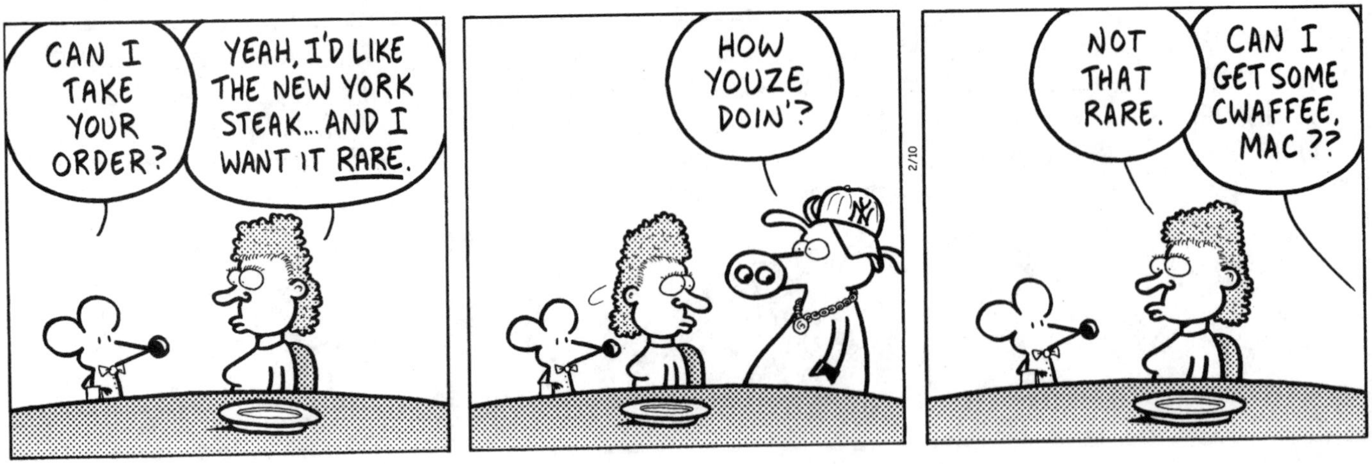
CAN I TAKE YOUR ORDER?
YEAH, I'D LIKE THE NEW YORK STEAK... AND I WANT IT RARE.
HOW YOUZE DOIN'?
2/10
NOT THAT RARE.
CAN I GET SOME CWAFFEE, MAC??

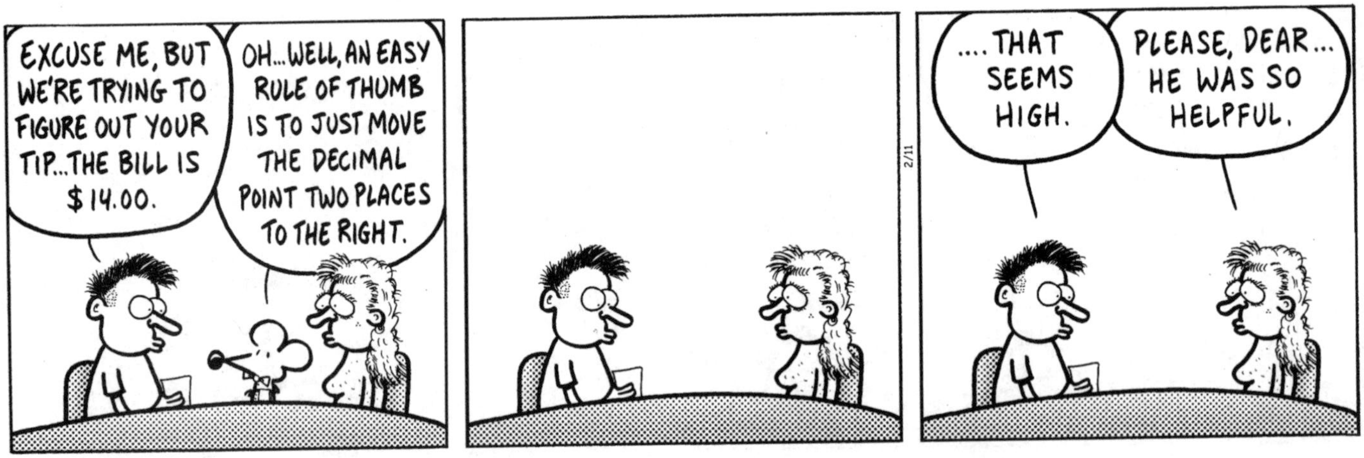
EXCUSE ME, BUT WE'RE TRYING TO FIGURE OUT YOUR TIP...THE BILL IS $14.00.
OH...WELL, AN EASY RULE OF THUMB IS TO JUST MOVE THE DECIMAL POINT TWO PLACES TO THE RIGHT.
2/11
....THAT SEEMS HIGH.
PLEASE, DEAR... HE WAS SO HELPFUL.

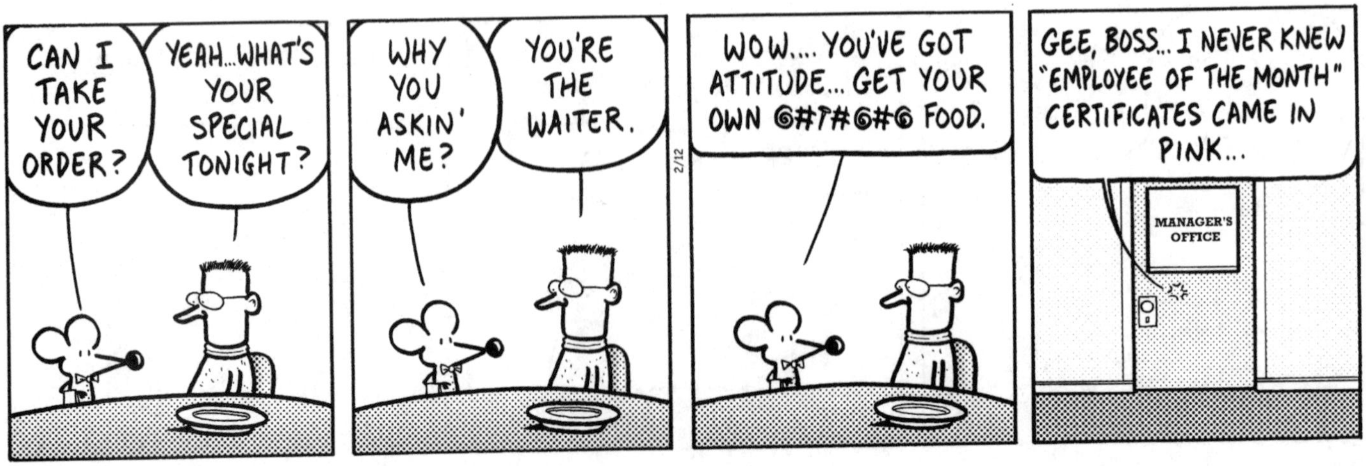
CAN I TAKE YOUR ORDER?
YEAH...WHAT'S YOUR SPECIAL TONIGHT?
WHY YOU ASKIN' ME?
YOU'RE THE WAITER.
2/12
WOW.... YOU'VE GOT ATTITUDE... GET YOUR OWN @#?#@#@ FOOD.
GEE, BOSS... I NEVER KNEW "EMPLOYEE OF THE MONTH" CERTIFICATES CAME IN PINK...
MANAGER'S OFFICE

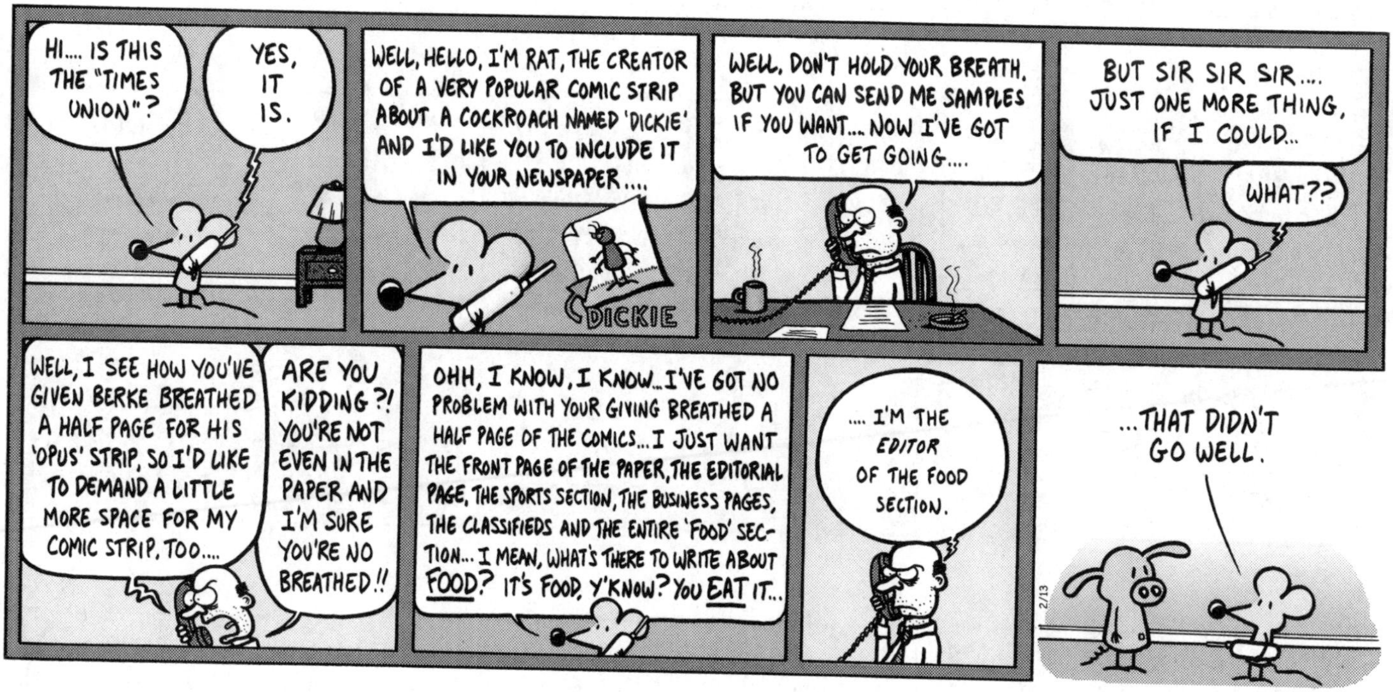

HI.... IS THIS THE "TIMES UNION"?
YES, IT IS.
WELL, HELLO, I'M RAT, THE CREATOR OF A VERY POPULAR COMIC STRIP ABOUT A COCKROACH NAMED 'DICKIE' AND I'D LIKE YOU TO INCLUDE IT IN YOUR NEWSPAPER....
DICKIE
WELL, DON'T HOLD YOUR BREATH. BUT YOU CAN SEND ME SAMPLES IF YOU WANT.... NOW I'VE GOT TO GET GOING....
BUT SIR SIR SIR.... JUST ONE MORE THING, IF I COULD...
WHAT??
WELL, I SEE HOW YOU'VE GIVEN BERKE BREATHED A HALF PAGE FOR HIS 'OPUS' STRIP, SO I'D LIKE TO DEMAND A LITTLE MORE SPACE FOR MY COMIC STRIP, TOO....
ARE YOU KIDDING?! YOU'RE NOT EVEN IN THE PAPER AND I'M SURE YOU'RE NO BREATHED!!
OHH, I KNOW, I KNOW... I'VE GOT NO PROBLEM WITH YOUR GIVING BREATHED A HALF PAGE OF THE COMICS... I JUST WANT THE FRONT PAGE OF THE PAPER, THE EDITORIAL PAGE, THE SPORTS SECTION, THE BUSINESS PAGES, THE CLASSIFIEDS AND THE ENTIRE 'FOOD' SECTION... I MEAN, WHAT'S THERE TO WRITE ABOUT FOOD? IT'S FOOD, Y'KNOW? YOU EAT IT...
.... I'M THE EDITOR OF THE FOOD SECTION.
2/13
...THAT DIDN'T GO WELL.

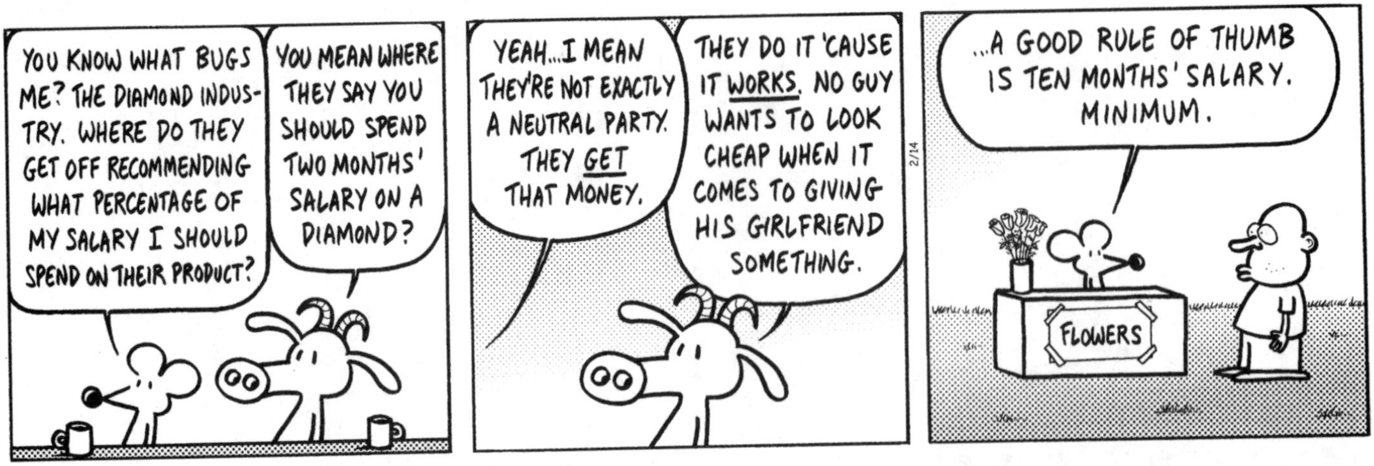
YOU KNOW WHAT BUGS ME? THE DIAMOND INDUSTRY. WHERE DO THEY GET OFF RECOMMENDING WHAT PERCENTAGE OF MY SALARY I SHOULD SPEND ON THEIR PRODUCT?
YOU MEAN WHERE THEY SAY YOU SHOULD SPEND TWO MONTHS' SALARY ON A DIAMOND?
YEAH...I MEAN THEY'RE NOT EXACTLY A NEUTRAL PARTY. THEY GET THAT MONEY.
THEY DO IT 'CAUSE IT WORKS. NO GUY WANTS TO LOOK CHEAP WHEN IT COMES TO GIVING HIS GIRLFRIEND SOMETHING.
2/14
...A GOOD RULE OF THUMB IS TEN MONTHS' SALARY. MINIMUM.
FLOWERS

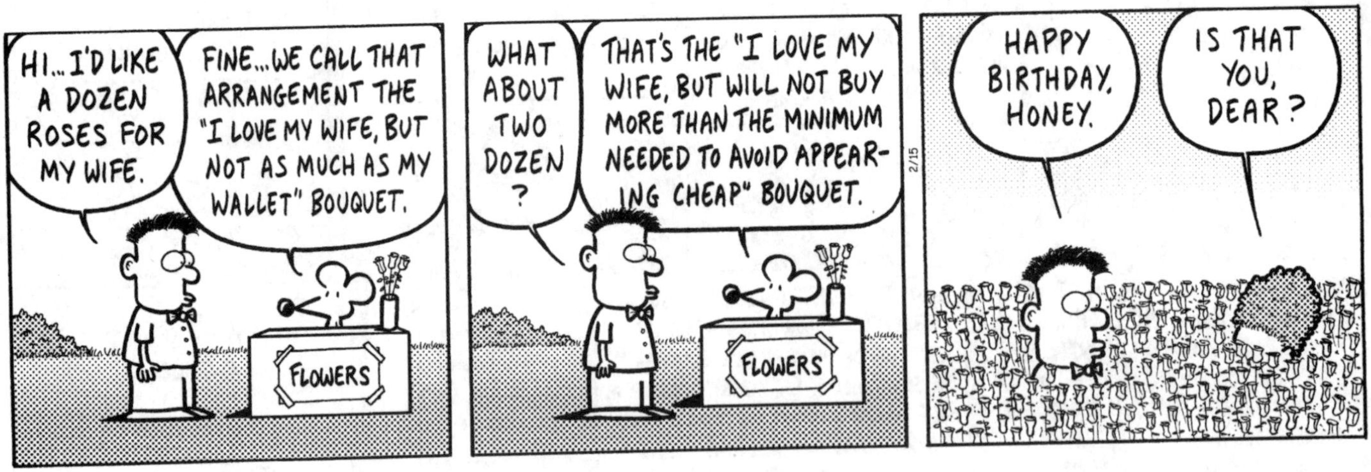
HI...I'D LIKE A DOZEN ROSES FOR MY WIFE.
FINE...WE CALL THAT ARRANGEMENT THE "I LOVE MY WIFE, BUT NOT AS MUCH AS MY WALLET" BOUQUET.
FLOWERS
WHAT ABOUT TWO DOZEN?
THAT'S THE "I LOVE MY WIFE, BUT WILL NOT BUY MORE THAN THE MINIMUM NEEDED TO AVOID APPEARING CHEAP" BOUQUET.
FLOWERS
2/15
HAPPY BIRTHDAY, HONEY.
IS THAT YOU, DEAR?

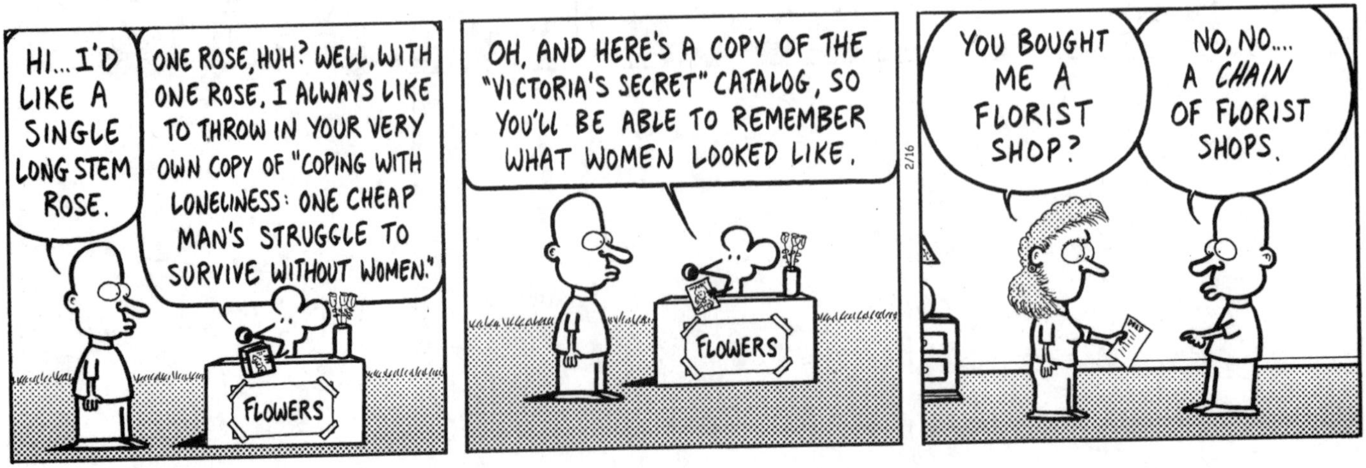
HI...I'D LIKE A SINGLE LONG STEM ROSE.
ONE ROSE, HUH? WELL, WITH ONE ROSE, I ALWAYS LIKE TO THROW IN YOUR VERY OWN COPY OF "COPING WITH LONELINESS: ONE CHEAP MAN'S STRUGGLE TO SURVIVE WITHOUT WOMEN."
FLOWERS
OH, AND HERE'S A COPY OF THE "VICTORIA'S SECRET" CATALOG, SO YOU'LL BE ABLE TO REMEMBER WHAT WOMEN LOOKED LIKE.
FLOWERS
2/16
YOU BOUGHT ME A FLORIST SHOP?
NO, NO.... A CHAIN OF FLORIST SHOPS.

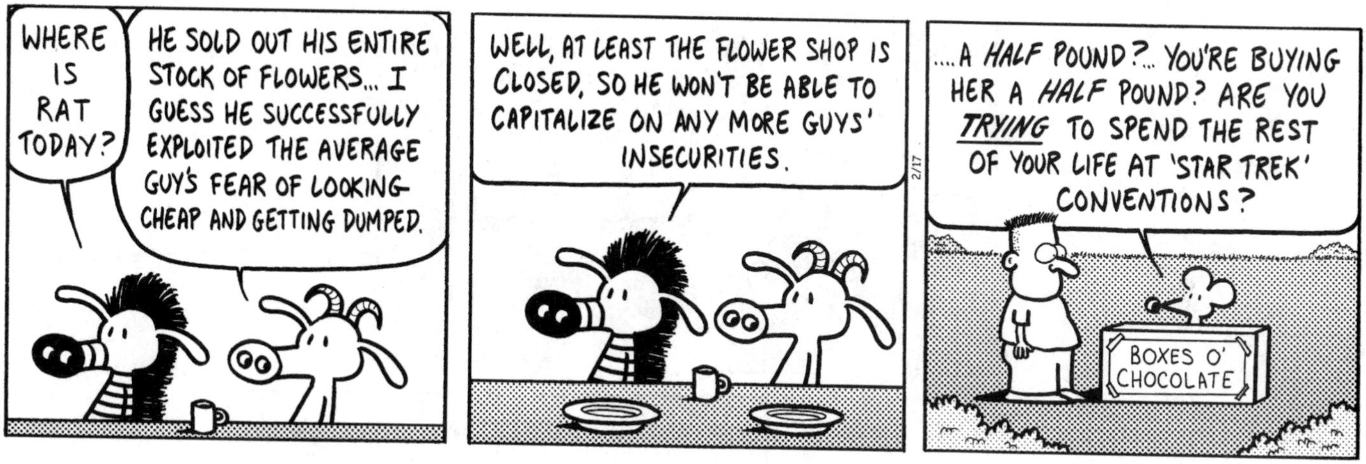
WHERE IS RAT TODAY?
HE SOLD OUT HIS ENTIRE STOCK OF FLOWERS... I GUESS HE SUCCESSFULLY EXPLOITED THE AVERAGE GUY'S FEAR OF LOOKING CHEAP AND GETTING DUMPED.
WELL, AT LEAST THE FLOWER SHOP IS CLOSED, SO HE WON'T BE ABLE TO CAPITALIZE ON ANY MORE GUYS' INSECURITIES.
2/17
....A *HALF* POUND?... YOU'RE BUYING HER A *HALF* POUND? ARE YOU *TRYING* TO SPEND THE REST OF YOUR LIFE AT 'STAR TREK' CONVENTIONS?
BOXES O' CHOCOLATE

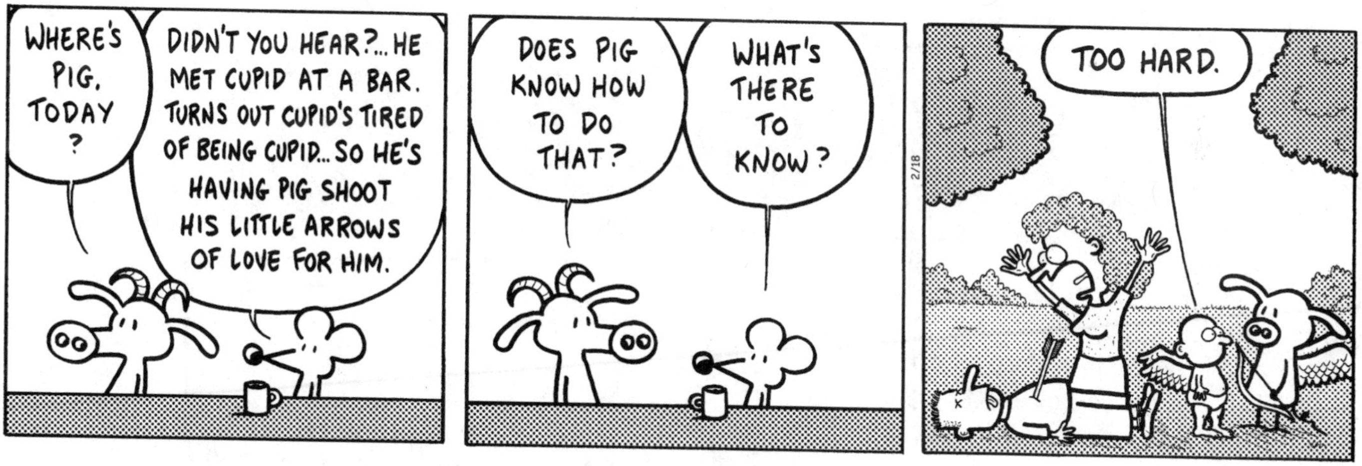
WHERE'S PIG, TODAY?
DIDN'T YOU HEAR?... HE MET CUPID AT A BAR. TURNS OUT CUPID'S TIRED OF BEING CUPID... SO HE'S HAVING PIG SHOOT HIS LITTLE ARROWS OF LOVE FOR HIM.
DOES PIG KNOW HOW TO DO THAT?
WHAT'S THERE TO KNOW?
2/18
TOO HARD.

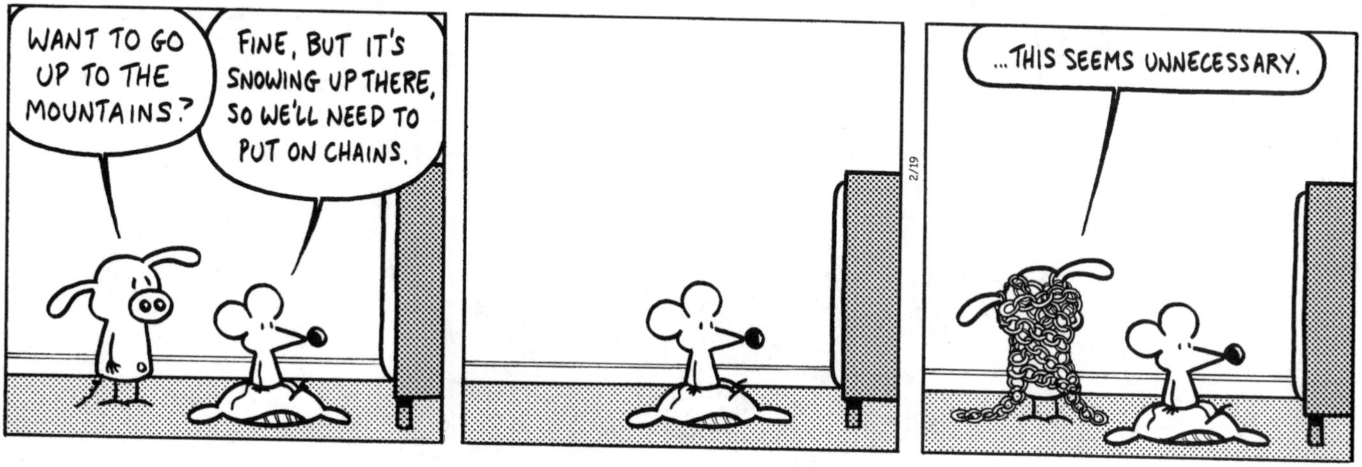
WANT TO GO UP TO THE MOUNTAINS?
FINE, BUT IT'S SNOWING UP THERE, SO WE'LL NEED TO PUT ON CHAINS.
2/19
...THIS SEEMS UNNECESSARY.

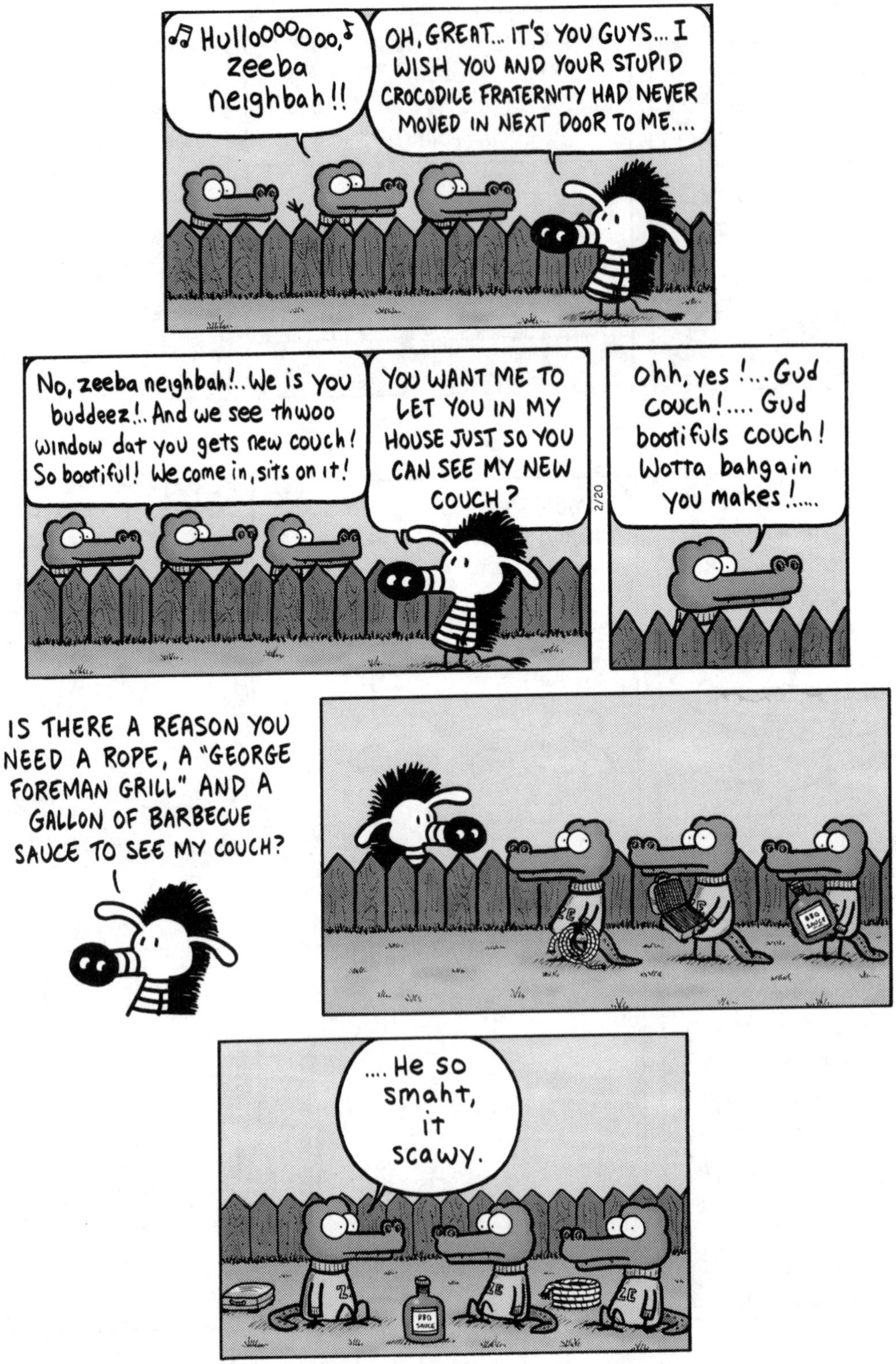
♫ Hulloooooo,♪ zeeba neighbah!!
OH, GREAT... IT'S YOU GUYS... I WISH YOU AND YOUR STUPID CROCODILE FRATERNITY HAD NEVER MOVED IN NEXT DOOR TO ME....
No, zeeba neighbah!.. We is you buddeez!.. And we see thwoo window dat you gets new couch! So bootiful! We come in, sits on it!
YOU WANT ME TO LET YOU IN MY HOUSE JUST SO YOU CAN SEE MY NEW COUCH?
2/20
Ohh, yes!... Gud couch!.... Gud bootifuls couch! Wotta bahgain you makes!.....
IS THERE A REASON YOU NEED A ROPE, A "GEORGE FOREMAN GRILL" AND A GALLON OF BARBECUE SAUCE TO SEE MY COUCH?
ZE
BBQ SAUCE
.... He so smaht, it scawy.

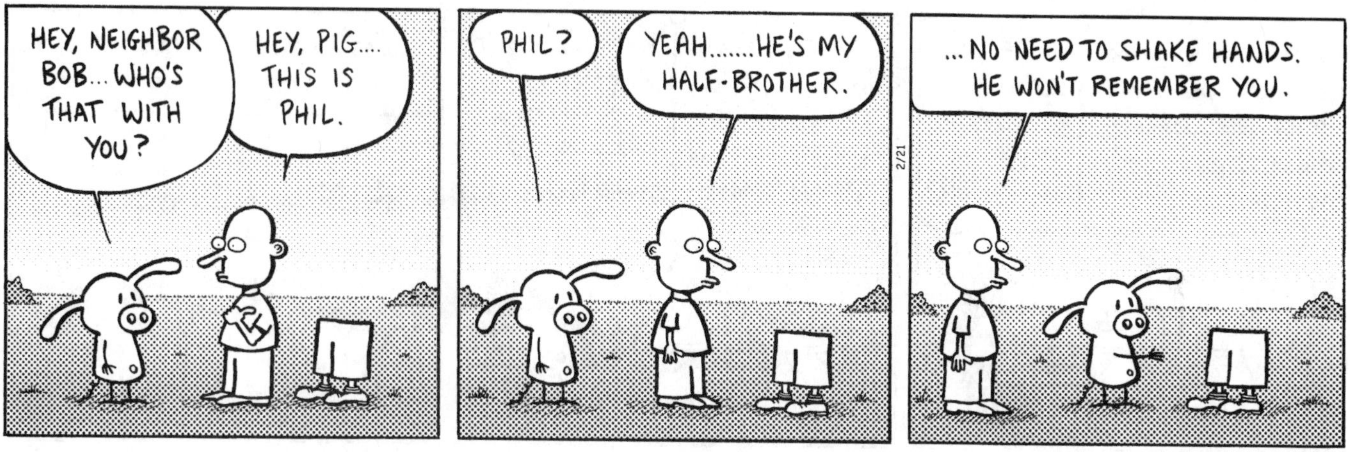
HEY, NEIGHBOR BOB... WHO'S THAT WITH YOU?
HEY, PIG.... THIS IS PHIL.
PHIL?
YEAH.......HE'S MY HALF-BROTHER.
2/21
...NO NEED TO SHAKE HANDS. HE WON'T REMEMBER YOU.

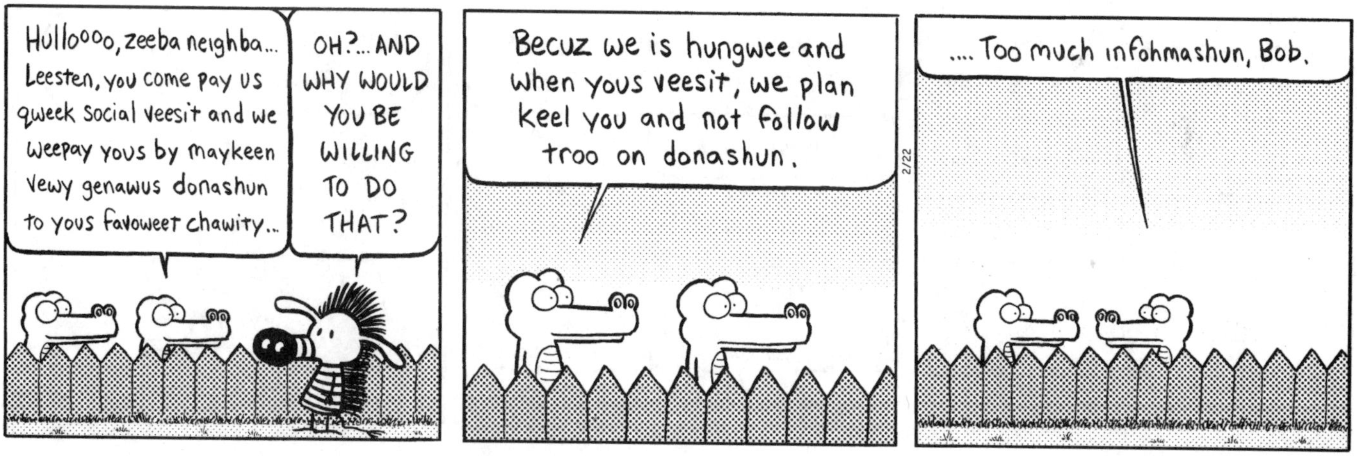
Hulloooo, zeeba neighba... Leesten, you come pay us qweek social veesit and we weepay yous by maykeen vewy genawus donashun to yous favoweet chawity...
OH?... AND WHY WOULD YOU BE WILLING TO DO THAT?
Becuz we is hungwee and when yous veesit, we plan keel you and not follow troo on donashun.
2/22
.... Too much infohmashun, Bob.

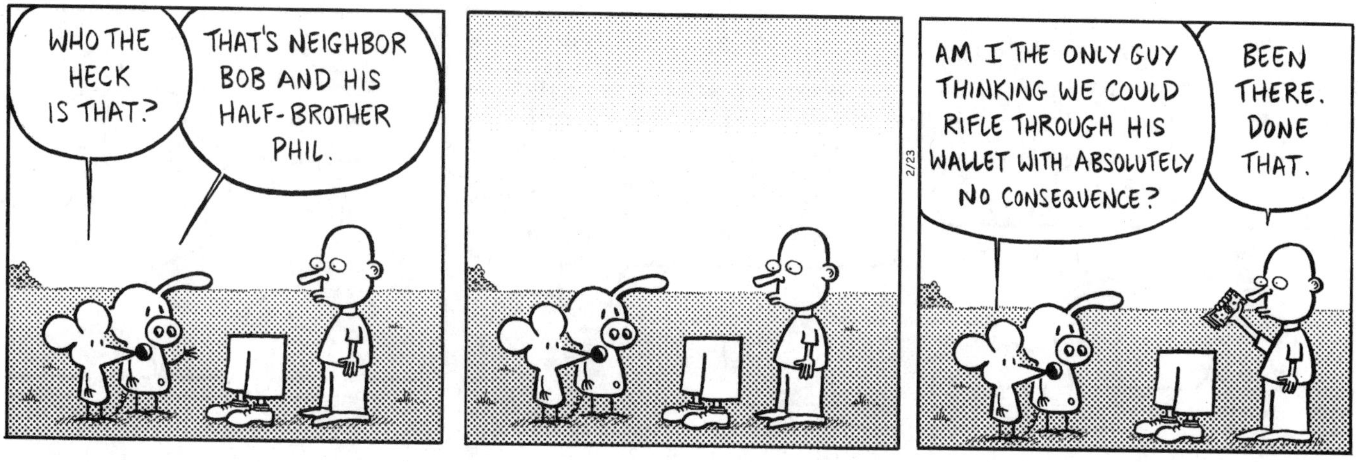
WHO THE HECK IS THAT?
THAT'S NEIGHBOR BOB AND HIS HALF-BROTHER PHIL.
2/23
AM I THE ONLY GUY THINKING WE COULD RIFLE THROUGH HIS WALLET WITH ABSOLUTELY NO CONSEQUENCE?
BEEN THERE. DONE THAT.

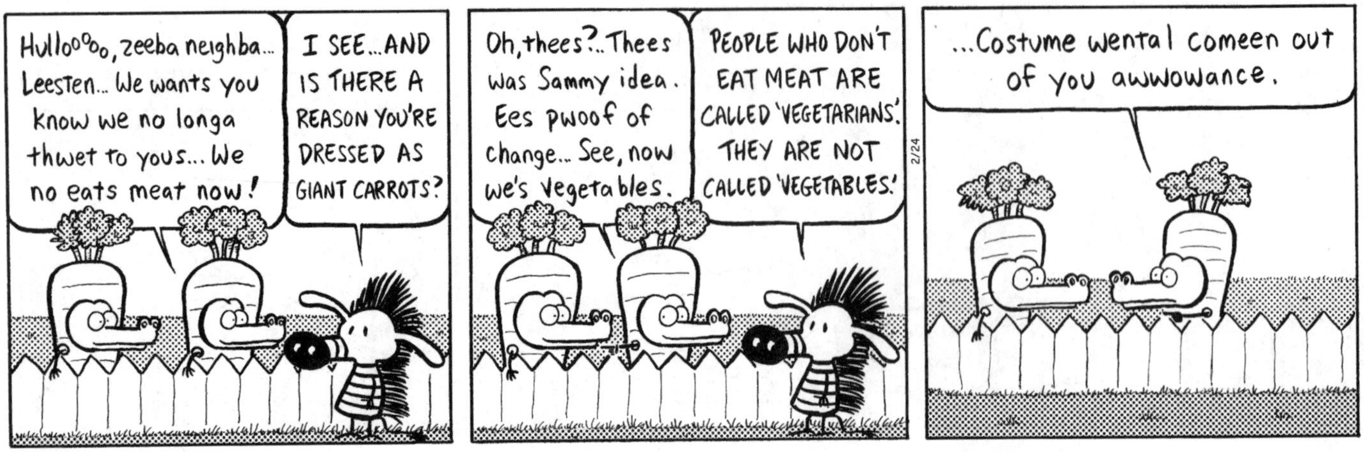
Hulloo°°o, zeeba neighba... Leesten... We wants you know we no longa thwet to yous... We no eats meat now!
I SEE...AND IS THERE A REASON YOU'RE DRESSED AS GIANT CARROTS?
Oh, thees?.. Thees was Sammy idea. Ees pwoof of change... See, now we's vegetables.
PEOPLE WHO DON'T EAT MEAT ARE CALLED 'VEGETARIANS.' THEY ARE NOT CALLED 'VEGETABLES.'
2/24
...Costume wental comeen out of you awwowance.

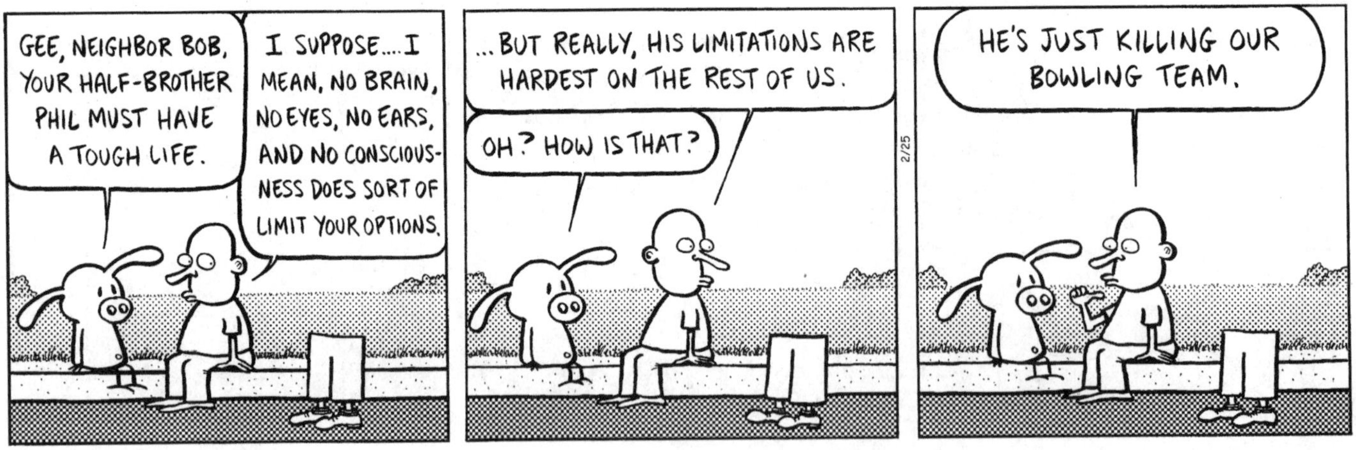
GEE, NEIGHBOR BOB, YOUR HALF-BROTHER PHIL MUST HAVE A TOUGH LIFE.
I SUPPOSE....I MEAN, NO BRAIN, NO EYES, NO EARS, AND NO CONSCIOUSNESS DOES SORT OF LIMIT YOUR OPTIONS.
...BUT REALLY, HIS LIMITATIONS ARE HARDEST ON THE REST OF US.
OH? HOW IS THAT?
2/25
HE'S JUST KILLING OUR BOWLING TEAM.

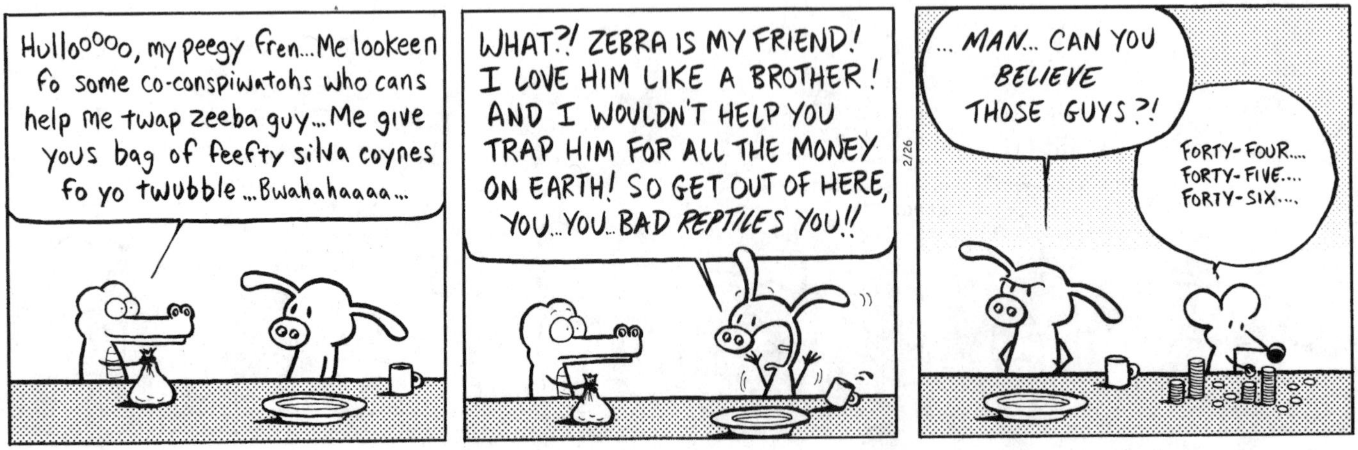
Hulloo°°o, my peegy fren... Me lookeen fo some co-conspiwatohs who cans help me twap zeeba guy... Me give yous bag of feefty silva coynes fo yo twubble ...Bwahahaaaa...
WHAT?! ZEBRA IS MY FRIEND! I LOVE HIM LIKE A BROTHER! AND I WOULDN'T HELP YOU TRAP HIM FOR ALL THE MONEY ON EARTH! SO GET OUT OF HERE, YOU...YOU...BAD *REPTILES* YOU!!
2/26
...*MAN*... CAN YOU *BELIEVE* THOSE GUYS?!
FORTY-FOUR.... FORTY-FIVE.... FORTY-SIX....

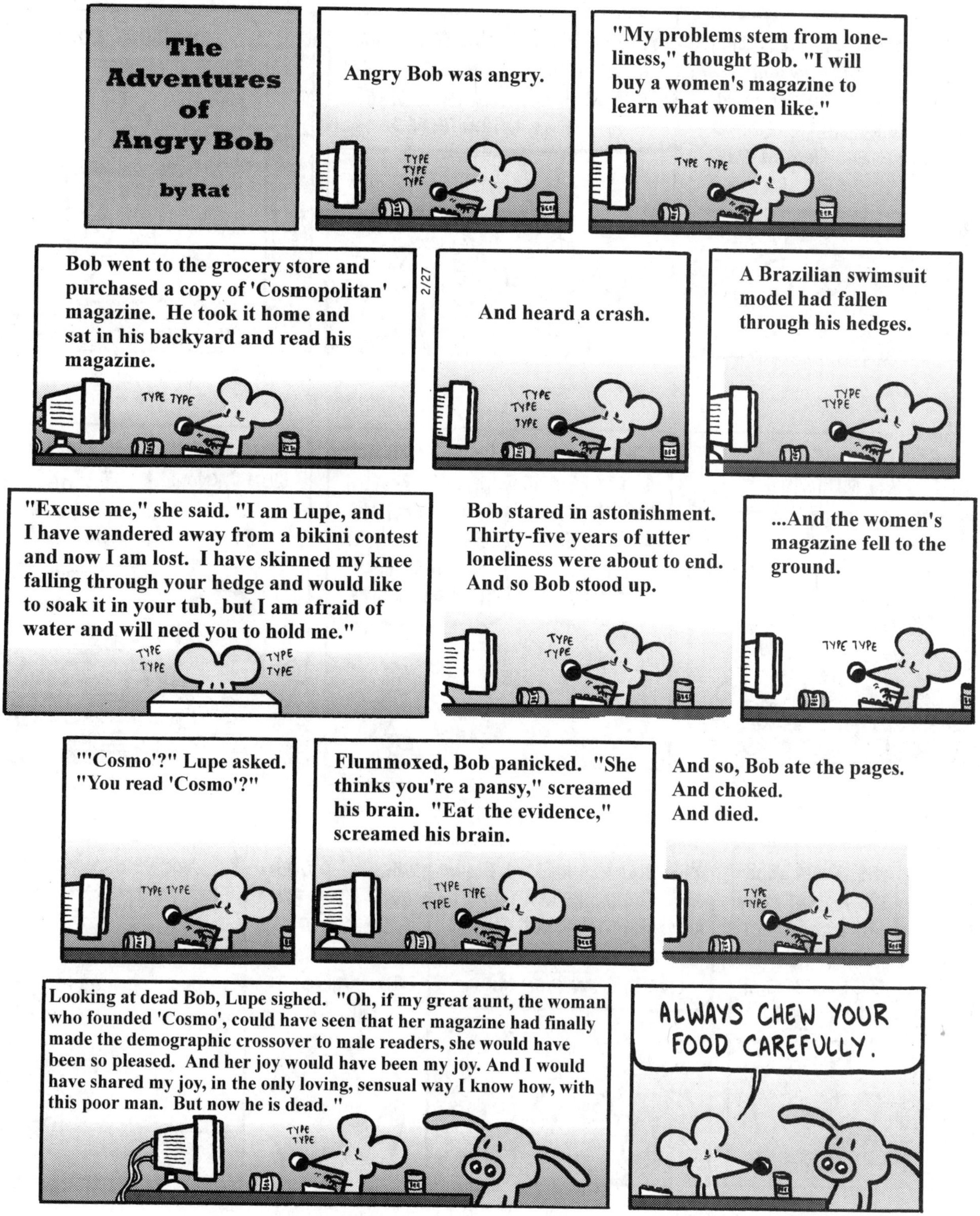
The Adventures of Angry Bob
by Rat
Angry Bob was angry.
TYPE TYPE TYPE
"My problems stem from loneliness," thought Bob. "I will buy a women's magazine to learn what women like."
TYPE TYPE
Bob went to the grocery store and purchased a copy of 'Cosmopolitan' magazine. He took it home and sat in his backyard and read his magazine.
TYPE TYPE
2/27
And heard a crash.
TYPE TYPE TYPE
A Brazilian swimsuit model had fallen through his hedges.
TYPE TYPE
"Excuse me," she said. "I am Lupe, and I have wandered away from a bikini contest and now I am lost. I have skinned my knee falling through your hedge and would like to soak it in your tub, but I am afraid of water and will need you to hold me."
TYPE TYPE TYPE TYPE
Bob stared in astonishment. Thirty-five years of utter loneliness were about to end. And so Bob stood up.
TYPE TYPE
...And the women's magazine fell to the ground.
TYPE TYPE
"'Cosmo'?" Lupe asked. "You read 'Cosmo'?"
TYPE TYPE
Flummoxed, Bob panicked. "She thinks you're a pansy," screamed his brain. "Eat the evidence," screamed his brain.
TYPE TYPE TYPE
And so, Bob ate the pages.
And choked.
And died.
TYPE TYPE
Looking at dead Bob, Lupe sighed. "Oh, if my great aunt, the woman who founded 'Cosmo', could have seen that her magazine had finally made the demographic crossover to male readers, she would have been so pleased. And her joy would have been my joy. And I would have shared my joy, in the only loving, sensual way I know how, with this poor man. But now he is dead."
TYPE TYPE
ALWAYS CHEW YOUR FOOD CAREFULLY.

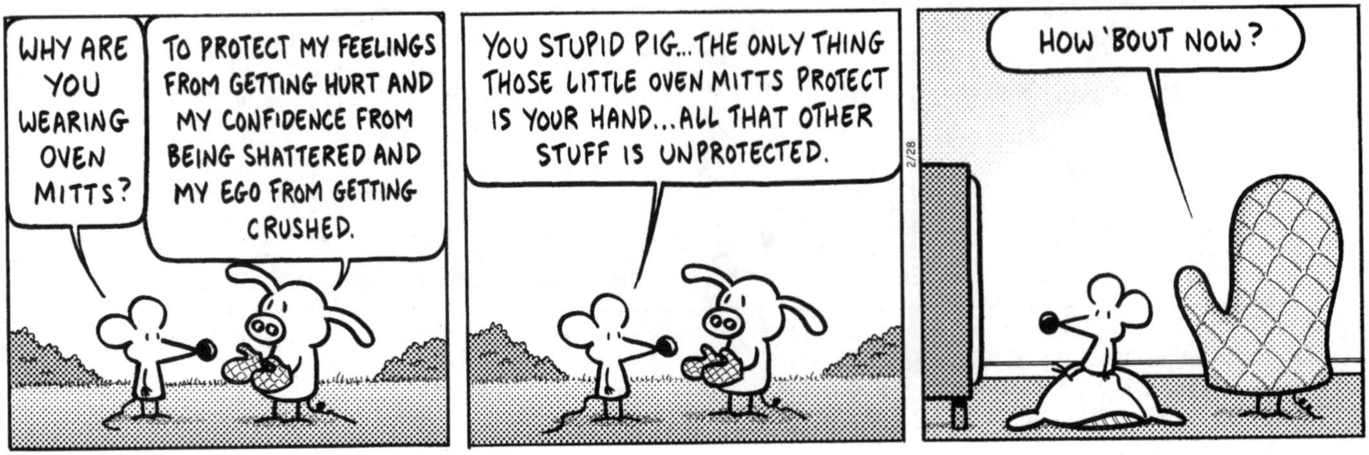
WHY ARE YOU WEARING OVEN MITTS?
TO PROTECT MY FEELINGS FROM GETTING HURT AND MY CONFIDENCE FROM BEING SHATTERED AND MY EGO FROM GETTING CRUSHED.
YOU STUPID PIG...THE ONLY THING THOSE LITTLE OVEN MITTS PROTECT IS YOUR HAND...ALL THAT OTHER STUFF IS UNPROTECTED.
2/28
HOW 'BOUT NOW?

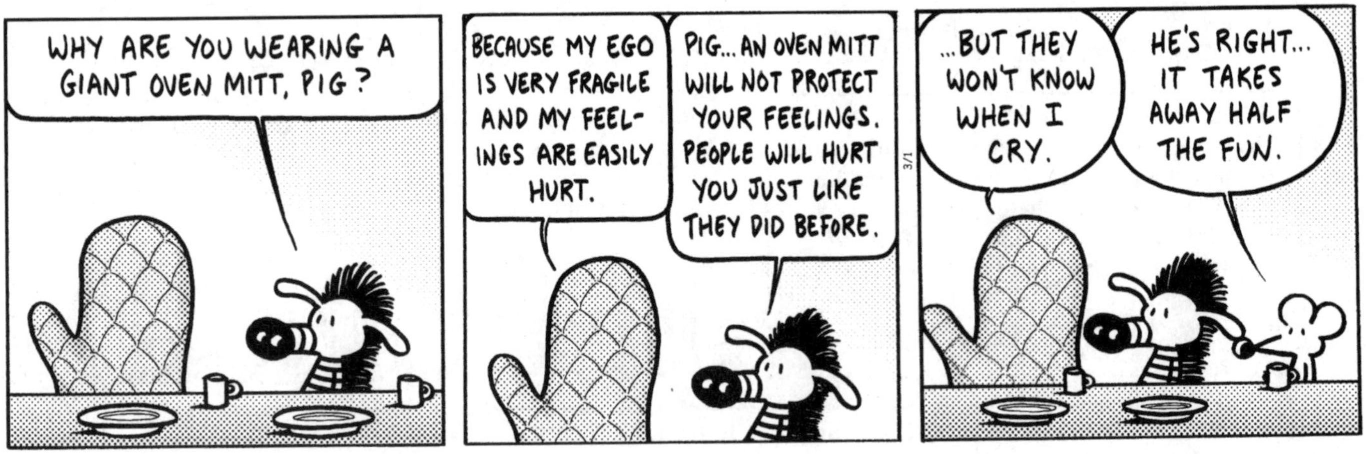
WHY ARE YOU WEARING A GIANT OVEN MITT, PIG?
BECAUSE MY EGO IS VERY FRAGILE AND MY FEELINGS ARE EASILY HURT.
PIG...AN OVEN MITT WILL NOT PROTECT YOUR FEELINGS. PEOPLE WILL HURT YOU JUST LIKE THEY DID BEFORE.
3/1
...BUT THEY WON'T KNOW WHEN I CRY.
HE'S RIGHT... IT TAKES AWAY HALF THE FUN.

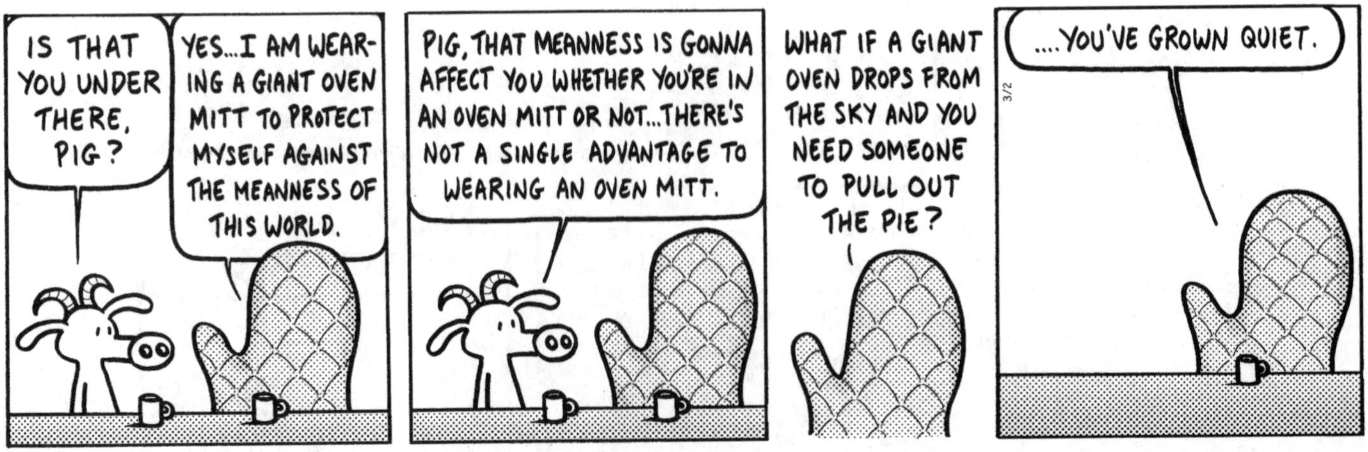
IS THAT YOU UNDER THERE, PIG?
YES...I AM WEARING A GIANT OVEN MITT TO PROTECT MYSELF AGAINST THE MEANNESS OF THIS WORLD.
PIG, THAT MEANNESS IS GONNA AFFECT YOU WHETHER YOU'RE IN AN OVEN MITT OR NOT...THERE'S NOT A SINGLE ADVANTAGE TO WEARING AN OVEN MITT.
WHAT IF A GIANT OVEN DROPS FROM THE SKY AND YOU NEED SOMEONE TO PULL OUT THE PIE?
3/2
....YOU'VE GROWN QUIET.

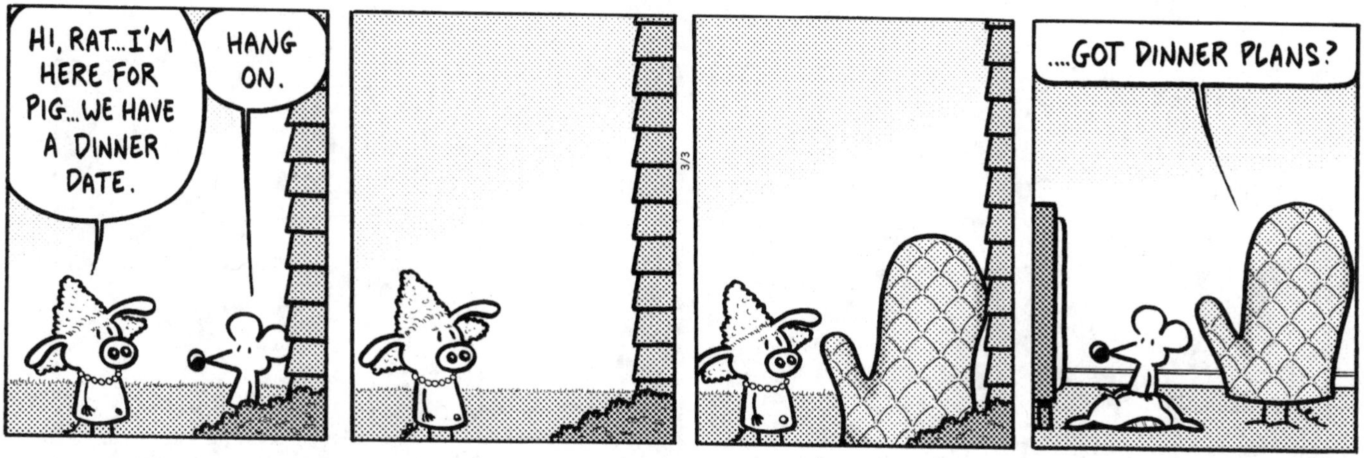
HI, RAT...I'M HERE FOR PIG...WE HAVE A DINNER DATE.
HANG ON.
3/3
....GOT DINNER PLANS?

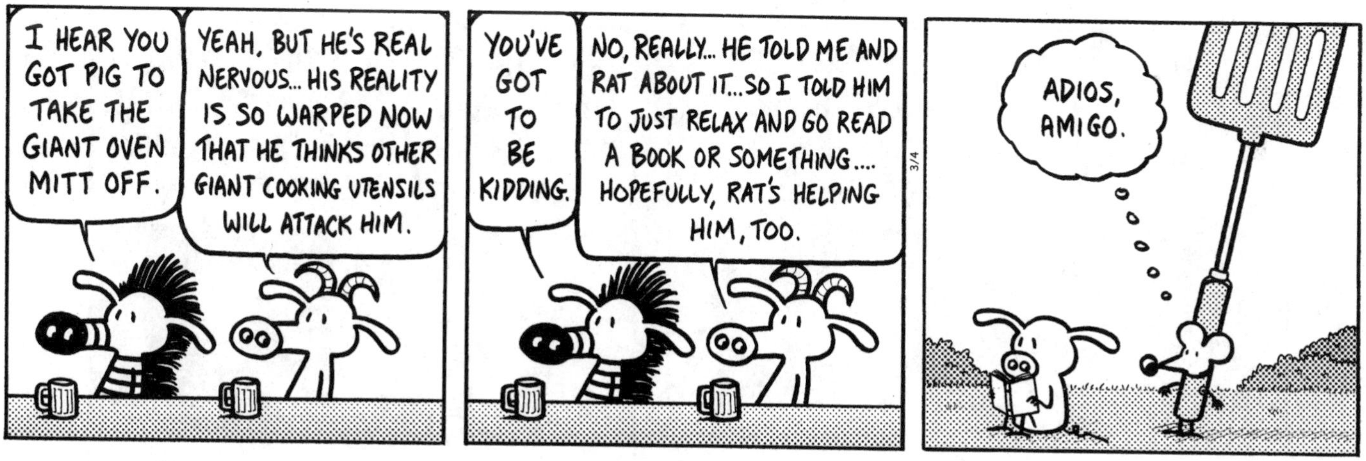
I HEAR YOU GOT PIG TO TAKE THE GIANT OVEN MITT OFF.
YEAH, BUT HE'S REAL NERVOUS... HIS REALITY IS SO WARPED NOW THAT HE THINKS OTHER GIANT COOKING UTENSILS WILL ATTACK HIM.
YOU'VE GOT TO BE KIDDING.
NO, REALLY... HE TOLD ME AND RAT ABOUT IT...SO I TOLD HIM TO JUST RELAX AND GO READ A BOOK OR SOMETHING.... HOPEFULLY, RAT'S HELPING HIM, TOO.
3/4
ADIOS, AMIGO.

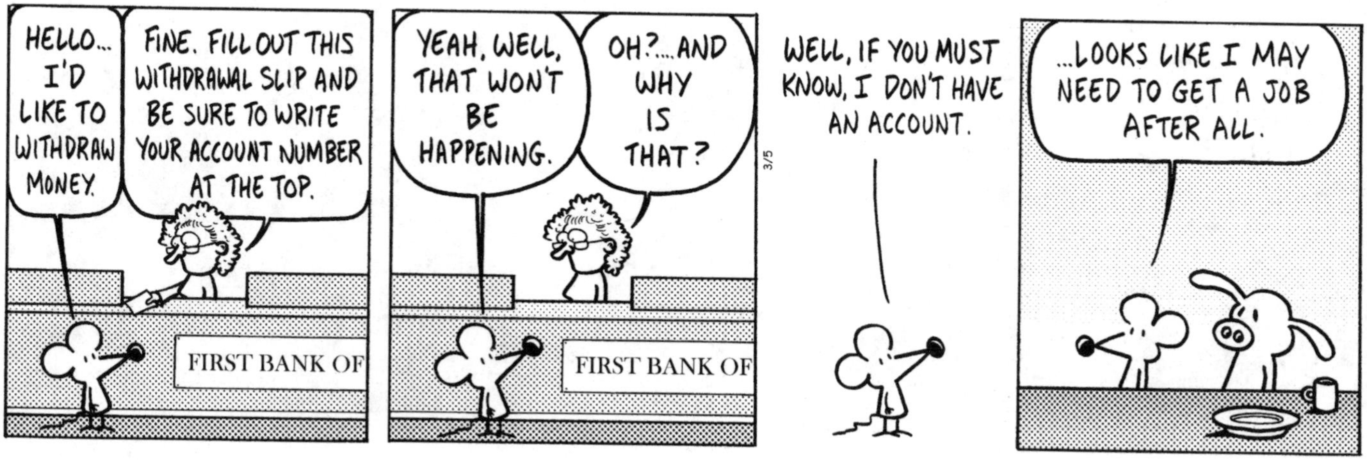
HELLO... I'D LIKE TO WITHDRAW MONEY.
FINE. FILL OUT THIS WITHDRAWAL SLIP AND BE SURE TO WRITE YOUR ACCOUNT NUMBER AT THE TOP.
FIRST BANK OF
YEAH, WELL, THAT WON'T BE HAPPENING.
OH?....AND WHY IS THAT?
FIRST BANK OF
3/5
WELL, IF YOU MUST KNOW, I DON'T HAVE AN ACCOUNT.
...LOOKS LIKE I MAY NEED TO GET A JOB AFTER ALL.

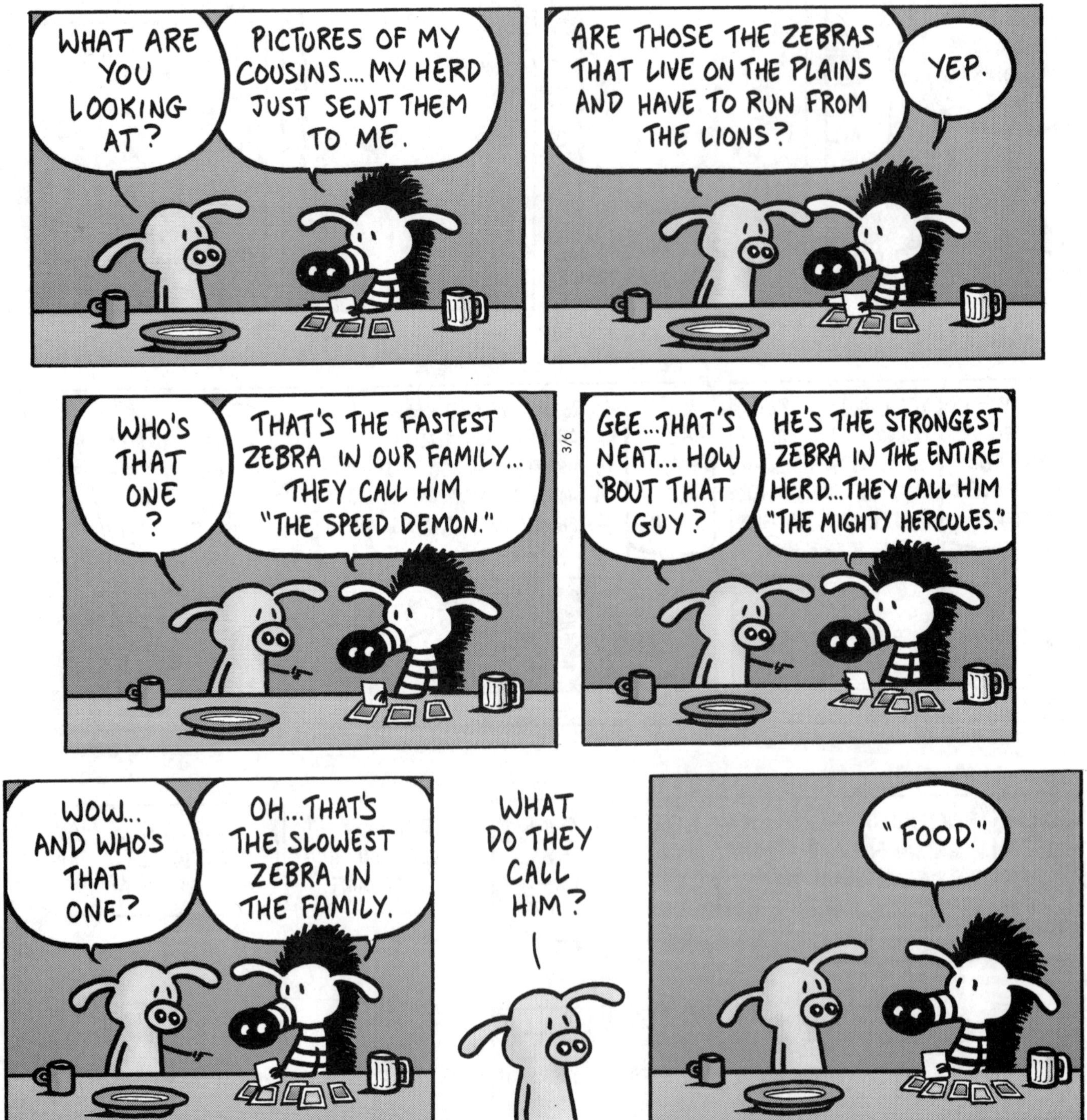
WHAT ARE YOU LOOKING AT?
PICTURES OF MY COUSINS.... MY HERD JUST SENT THEM TO ME.
ARE THOSE THE ZEBRAS THAT LIVE ON THE PLAINS AND HAVE TO RUN FROM THE LIONS?
YEP.
WHO'S THAT ONE ?
THAT'S THE FASTEST ZEBRA IN OUR FAMILY... THEY CALL HIM "THE SPEED DEMON."
GEE...THAT'S NEAT... HOW 'BOUT THAT GUY?
HE'S THE STRONGEST ZEBRA IN THE ENTIRE HERD...THEY CALL HIM "THE MIGHTY HERCULES."
WOW... AND WHO'S THAT ONE?
OH...THAT'S THE SLOWEST ZEBRA IN THE FAMILY.
WHAT DO THEY CALL HIM?
"FOOD."

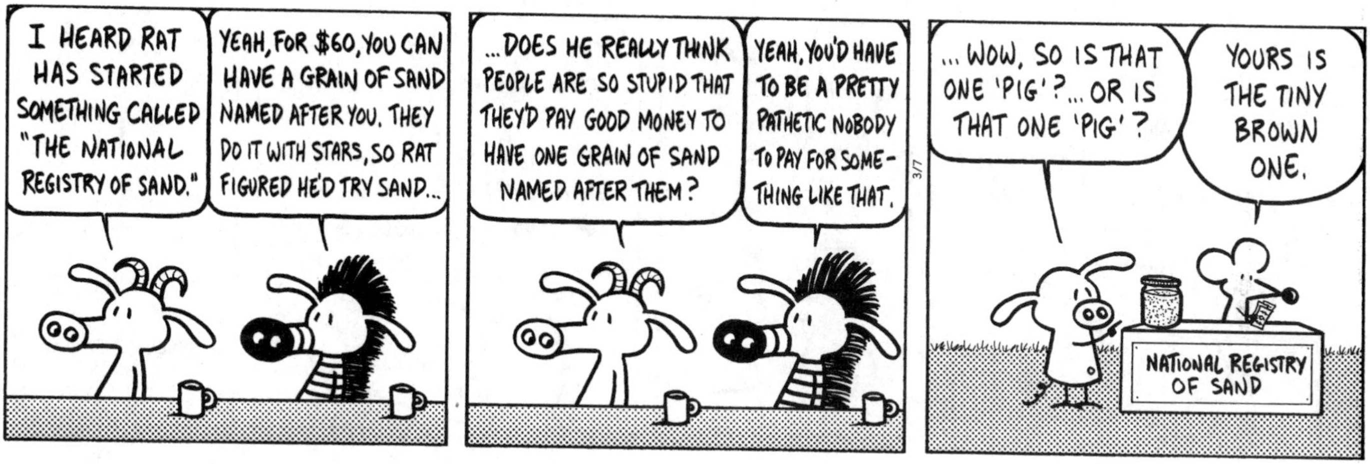
I HEARD RAT HAS STARTED SOMETHING CALLED "THE NATIONAL REGISTRY OF SAND."
YEAH, FOR $60, YOU CAN HAVE A GRAIN OF SAND NAMED AFTER YOU. THEY DO IT WITH STARS, SO RAT FIGURED HE'D TRY SAND...
...DOES HE REALLY THINK PEOPLE ARE SO STUPID THAT THEY'D PAY GOOD MONEY TO HAVE ONE GRAIN OF SAND NAMED AFTER THEM?
YEAH, YOU'D HAVE TO BE A PRETTY PATHETIC NOBODY TO PAY FOR SOMETHING LIKE THAT.
... WOW, SO IS THAT ONE 'PIG'?... OR IS THAT ONE 'PIG'?
YOURS IS THE TINY BROWN ONE.
NATIONAL REGISTRY OF SAND

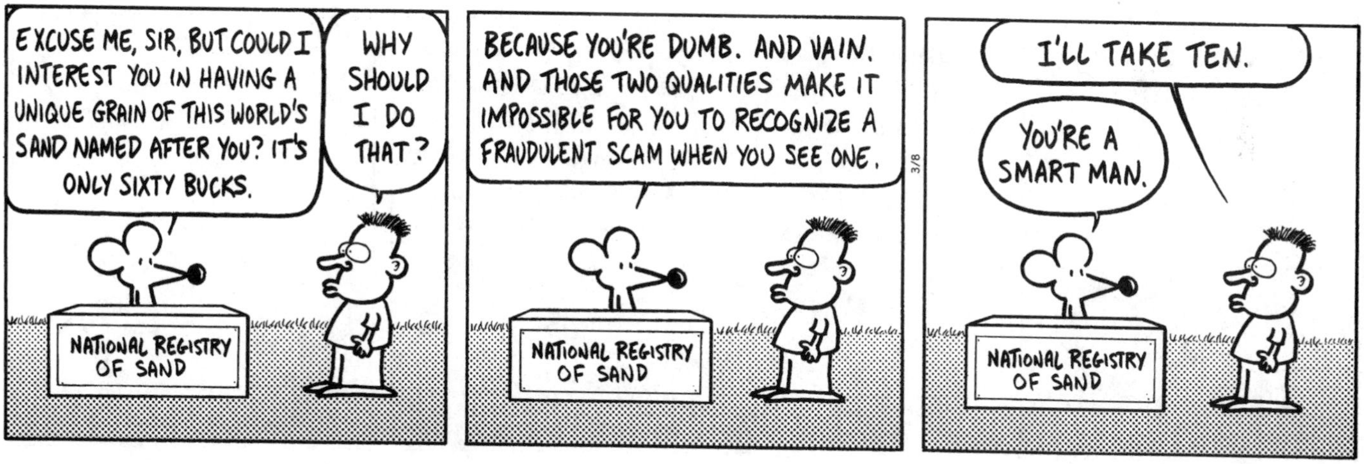
EXCUSE ME, SIR, BUT COULD I INTEREST YOU IN HAVING A UNIQUE GRAIN OF THIS WORLD'S SAND NAMED AFTER YOU? IT'S ONLY SIXTY BUCKS.
WHY SHOULD I DO THAT?
NATIONAL REGISTRY OF SAND
BECAUSE YOU'RE DUMB. AND VAIN. AND THOSE TWO QUALITIES MAKE IT IMPOSSIBLE FOR YOU TO RECOGNIZE A FRAUDULENT SCAM WHEN YOU SEE ONE.
NATIONAL REGISTRY OF SAND
I'LL TAKE TEN.
YOU'RE A SMART MAN.
NATIONAL REGISTRY OF SAND

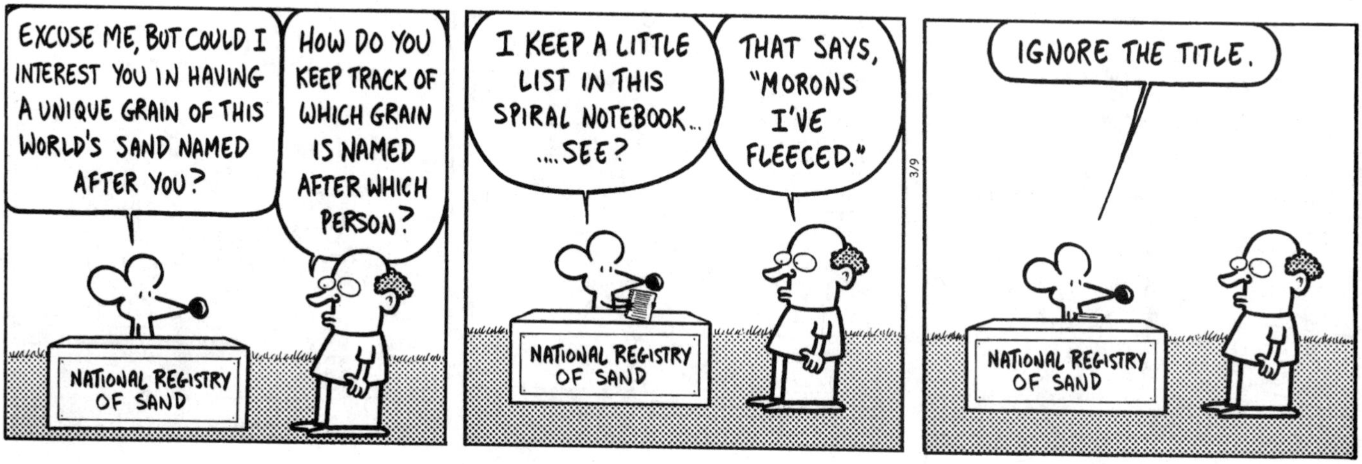
EXCUSE ME, BUT COULD I INTEREST YOU IN HAVING A UNIQUE GRAIN OF THIS WORLD'S SAND NAMED AFTER YOU?
HOW DO YOU KEEP TRACK OF WHICH GRAIN IS NAMED AFTER WHICH PERSON?
NATIONAL REGISTRY OF SAND
I KEEP A LITTLE LIST IN THIS SPIRAL NOTEBOOK... ....SEE?
THAT SAYS, "MORONS I'VE FLEECED."
NATIONAL REGISTRY OF SAND
IGNORE THE TITLE.
NATIONAL REGISTRY OF SAND

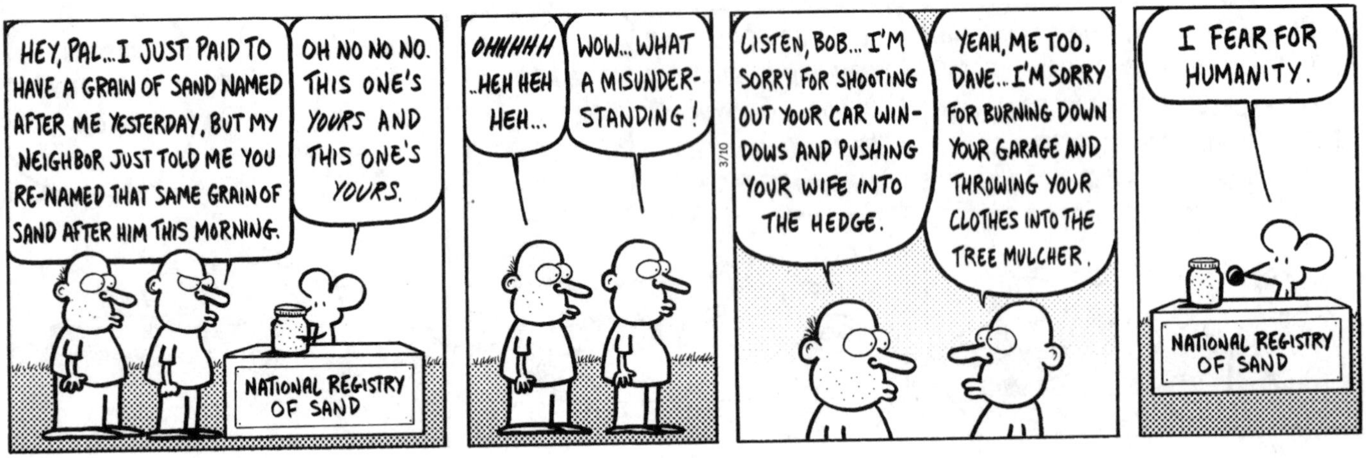
HEY, PAL... I JUST PAID TO HAVE A GRAIN OF SAND NAMED AFTER ME YESTERDAY, BUT MY NEIGHBOR JUST TOLD ME YOU RE-NAMED THAT SAME GRAIN OF SAND AFTER HIM THIS MORNING.
OH NO NO NO. THIS ONE'S *YOURS* AND THIS ONE'S *YOURS*.
NATIONAL REGISTRY OF SAND
OHHHHH ..HEH HEH HEH...
WOW... WHAT A MISUNDERSTANDING!
3/10
LISTEN, BOB... I'M SORRY FOR SHOOTING OUT YOUR CAR WINDOWS AND PUSHING YOUR WIFE INTO THE HEDGE.
YEAH, ME TOO, DAVE... I'M SORRY FOR BURNING DOWN YOUR GARAGE AND THROWING YOUR CLOTHES INTO THE TREE MULCHER.
I FEAR FOR HUMANITY.
NATIONAL REGISTRY OF SAND

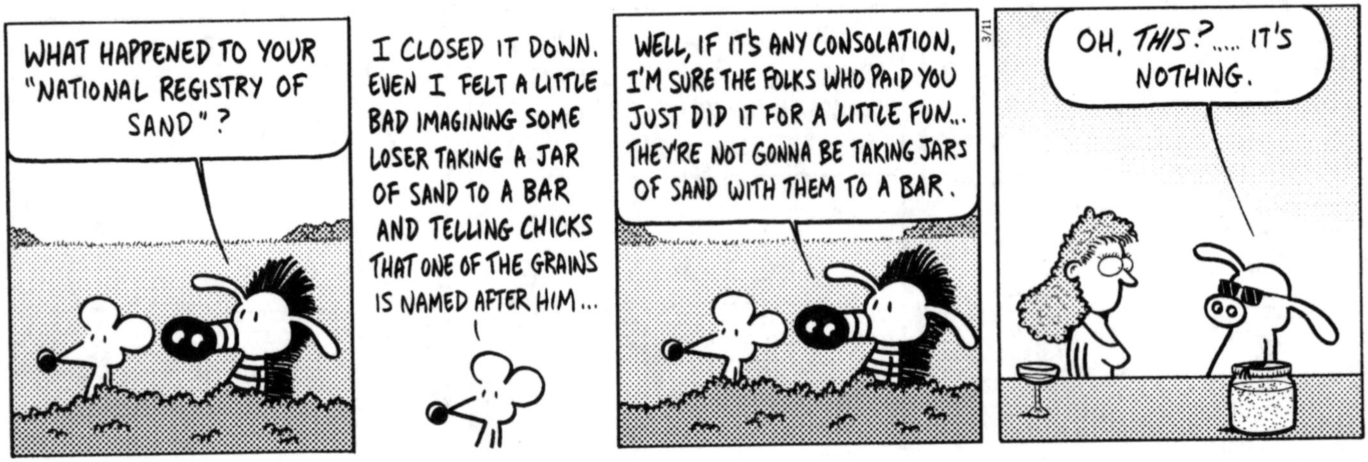
WHAT HAPPENED TO YOUR "NATIONAL REGISTRY OF SAND"?
I CLOSED IT DOWN. EVEN I FELT A LITTLE BAD IMAGINING SOME LOSER TAKING A JAR OF SAND TO A BAR AND TELLING CHICKS THAT ONE OF THE GRAINS IS NAMED AFTER HIM...
WELL, IF IT'S ANY CONSOLATION, I'M SURE THE FOLKS WHO PAID YOU JUST DID IT FOR A LITTLE FUN... THEY'RE NOT GONNA BE TAKING JARS OF SAND WITH THEM TO A BAR.
3/11
OH, *THIS?*..... IT'S NOTHING.

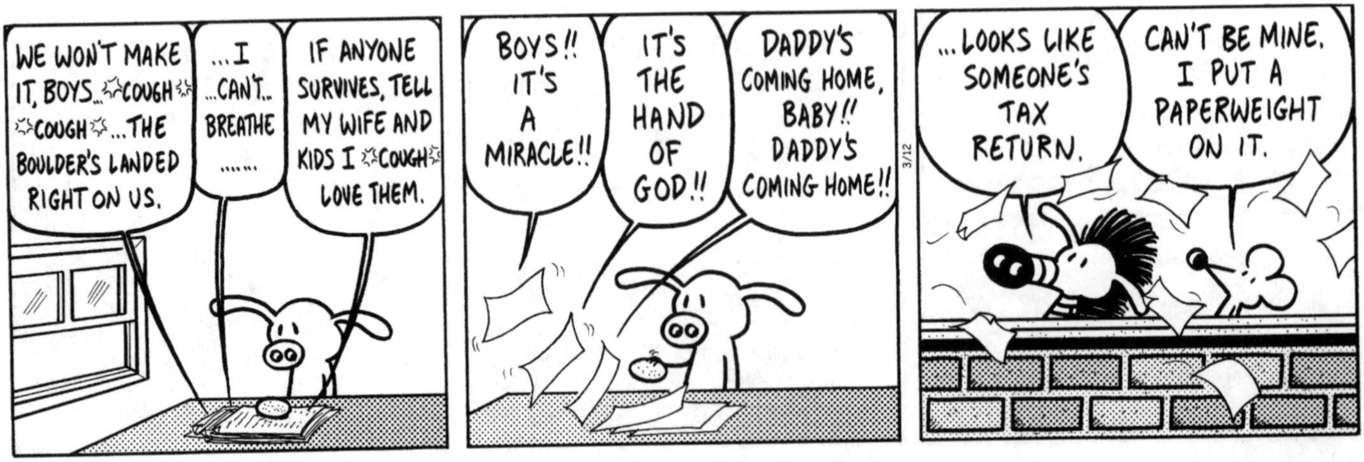
WE WON'T MAKE IT, BOYS... ☼COUGH☼ ☼COUGH☼ ...THE BOULDER'S LANDED RIGHT ON US.
...I ...CAN'T.. BREATHE ......
IF ANYONE SURVIVES, TELL MY WIFE AND KIDS I ☼COUGH☼ LOVE THEM.
BOYS!! IT'S A MIRACLE!!
IT'S THE HAND OF GOD!!
DADDY'S COMING HOME, BABY!! DADDY'S COMING HOME!!
3/12
...LOOKS LIKE SOMEONE'S TAX RETURN.
CAN'T BE MINE. I PUT A PAPERWEIGHT ON IT.

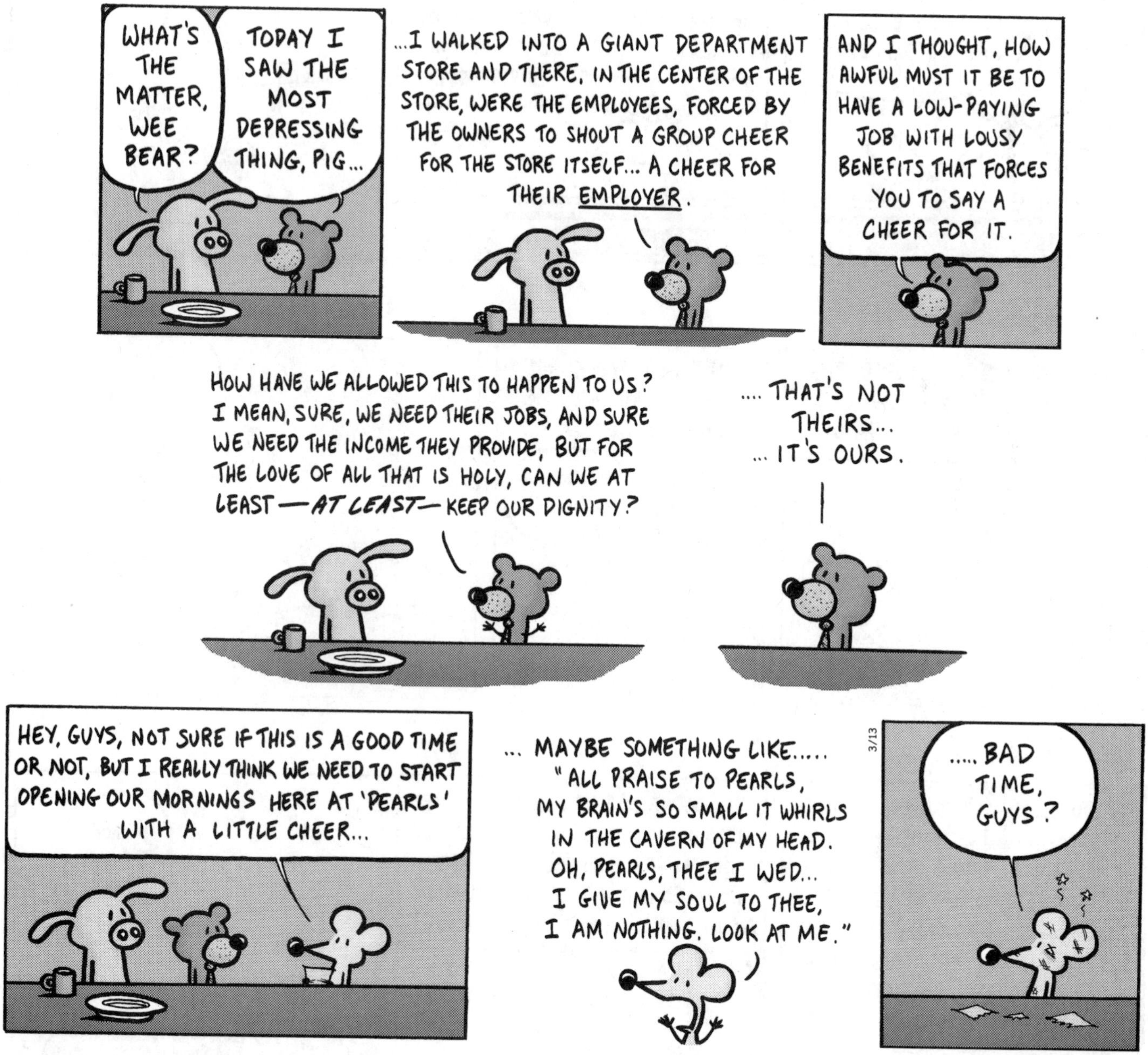
WHAT'S THE MATTER, WEE BEAR?
TODAY I SAW THE MOST DEPRESSING THING, PIG...
...I WALKED INTO A GIANT DEPARTMENT STORE AND THERE, IN THE CENTER OF THE STORE, WERE THE EMPLOYEES, FORCED BY THE OWNERS TO SHOUT A GROUP CHEER FOR THE STORE ITSELF... A CHEER FOR THEIR EMPLOYER.
AND I THOUGHT, HOW AWFUL MUST IT BE TO HAVE A LOW-PAYING JOB WITH LOUSY BENEFITS THAT FORCES YOU TO SAY A CHEER FOR IT.
HOW HAVE WE ALLOWED THIS TO HAPPEN TO US? I MEAN, SURE, WE NEED THEIR JOBS, AND SURE WE NEED THE INCOME THEY PROVIDE, BUT FOR THE LOVE OF ALL THAT IS HOLY, CAN WE AT LEAST —AT LEAST— KEEP OUR DIGNITY?
.... THAT'S NOT THEIRS... ... IT'S OURS.
HEY, GUYS, NOT SURE IF THIS IS A GOOD TIME OR NOT, BUT I REALLY THINK WE NEED TO START OPENING OUR MORNINGS HERE AT 'PEARLS' WITH A LITTLE CHEER...
... MAYBE SOMETHING LIKE..... "ALL PRAISE TO PEARLS, MY BRAIN'S SO SMALL IT WHIRLS IN THE CAVERN OF MY HEAD. OH, PEARLS, THEE I WED... I GIVE MY SOUL TO THEE, I AM NOTHING. LOOK AT ME."
3/13
..... BAD TIME, GUYS?

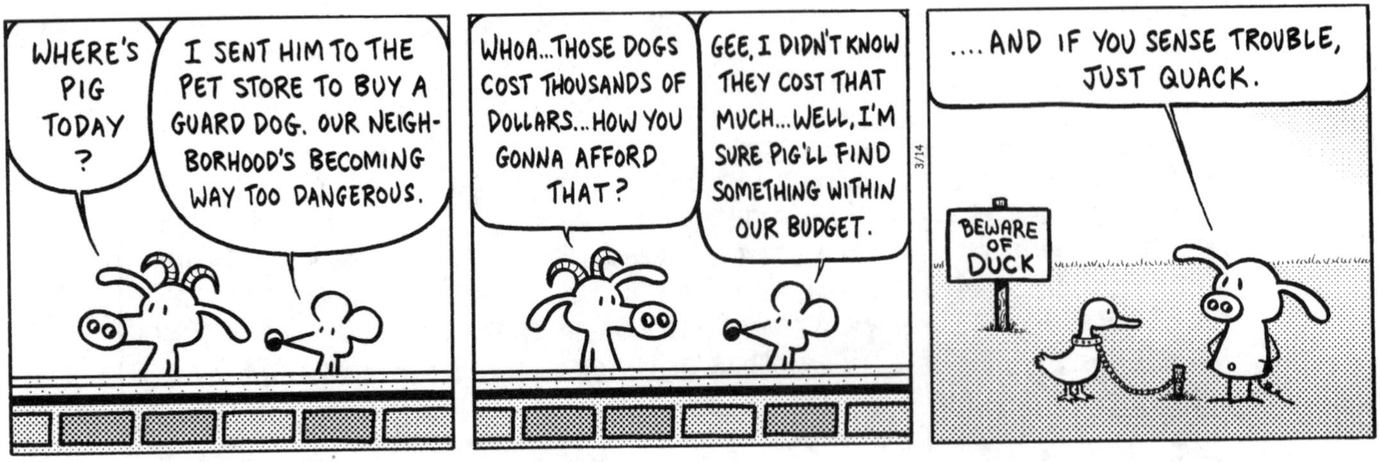
WHERE'S PIG TODAY ?
I SENT HIM TO THE PET STORE TO BUY A GUARD DOG. OUR NEIGHBORHOOD'S BECOMING WAY TOO DANGEROUS.
WHOA...THOSE DOGS COST THOUSANDS OF DOLLARS...HOW YOU GONNA AFFORD THAT?
GEE, I DIDN'T KNOW THEY COST THAT MUCH...WELL, I'M SURE PIG'LL FIND SOMETHING WITHIN OUR BUDGET.
3/14
BEWARE OF DUCK
....AND IF YOU SENSE TROUBLE, JUST QUACK.

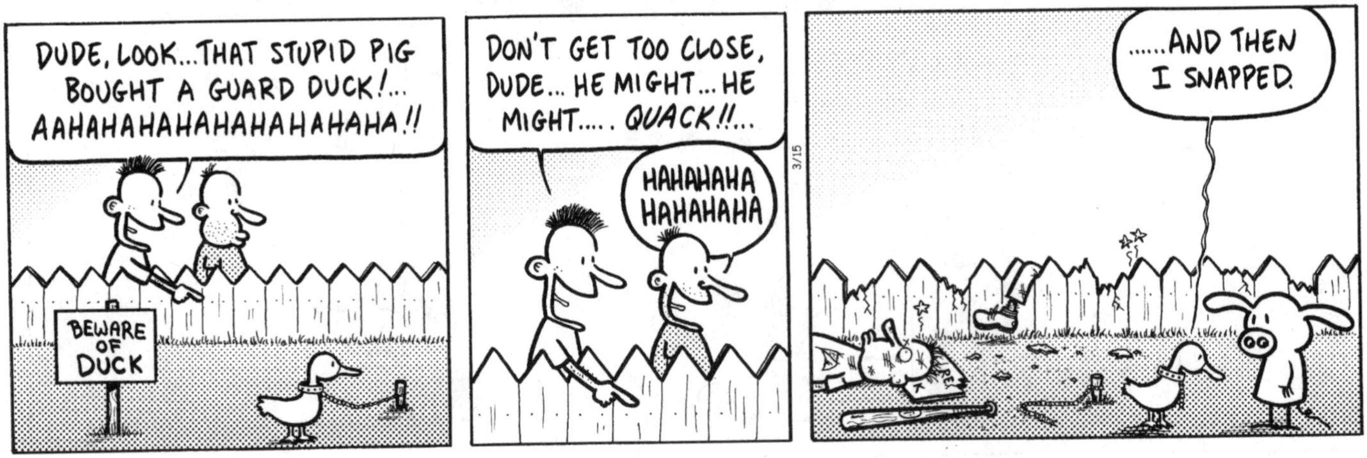
DUDE, LOOK...THAT STUPID PIG BOUGHT A GUARD DUCK!... AAHAHAHAHAHAHAHAHAHAHA!!
BEWARE OF DUCK
DON'T GET TOO CLOSE, DUDE... HE MIGHT... HE MIGHT..... *QUACK!!*...
HAHAHAHA HAHAHAHA
3/15
......AND THEN I SNAPPED.

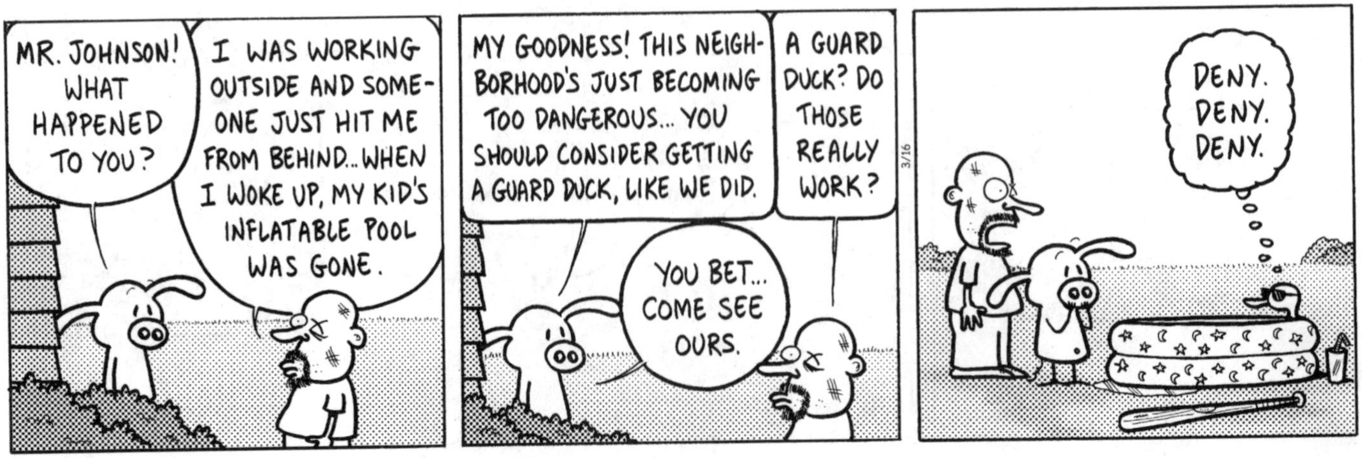
MR. JOHNSON! WHAT HAPPENED TO YOU?
I WAS WORKING OUTSIDE AND SOMEONE JUST HIT ME FROM BEHIND...WHEN I WOKE UP, MY KID'S INFLATABLE POOL WAS GONE.
MY GOODNESS! THIS NEIGHBORHOOD'S JUST BECOMING TOO DANGEROUS... YOU SHOULD CONSIDER GETTING A GUARD DUCK, LIKE WE DID.
A GUARD DUCK? DO THOSE REALLY WORK?
YOU BET... COME SEE OURS.
3/16
DENY. DENY. DENY.

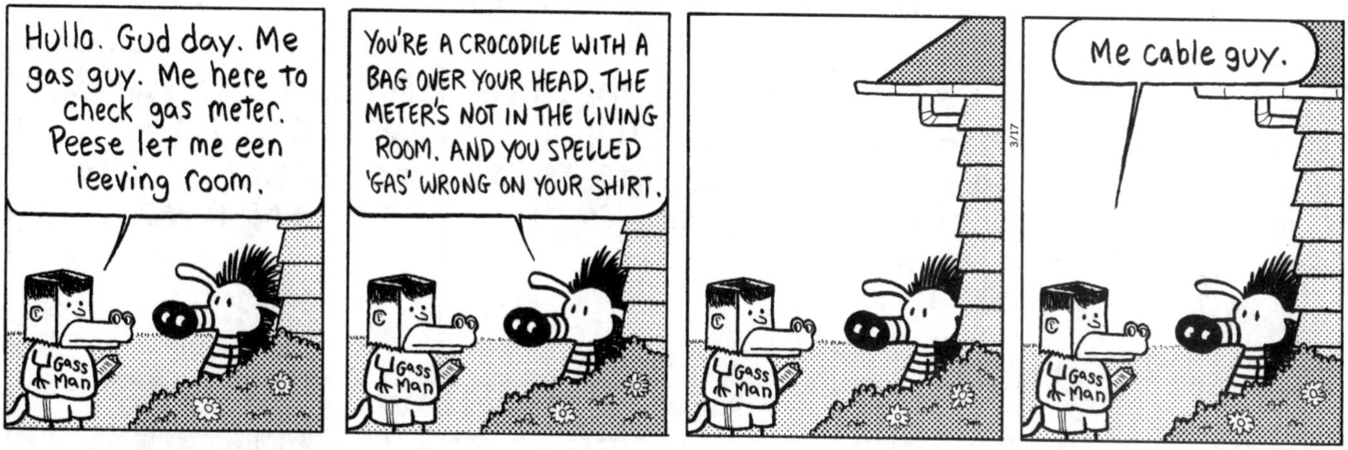
Hullo. Gud day. Me gas guy. Me here to check gas meter. Peese let me een leeving room.
Gass Man
YOU'RE A CROCODILE WITH A BAG OVER YOUR HEAD. THE METER'S NOT IN THE LIVING ROOM. AND YOU SPELLED 'GAS' WRONG ON YOUR SHIRT.
3/17
Me cable guy.

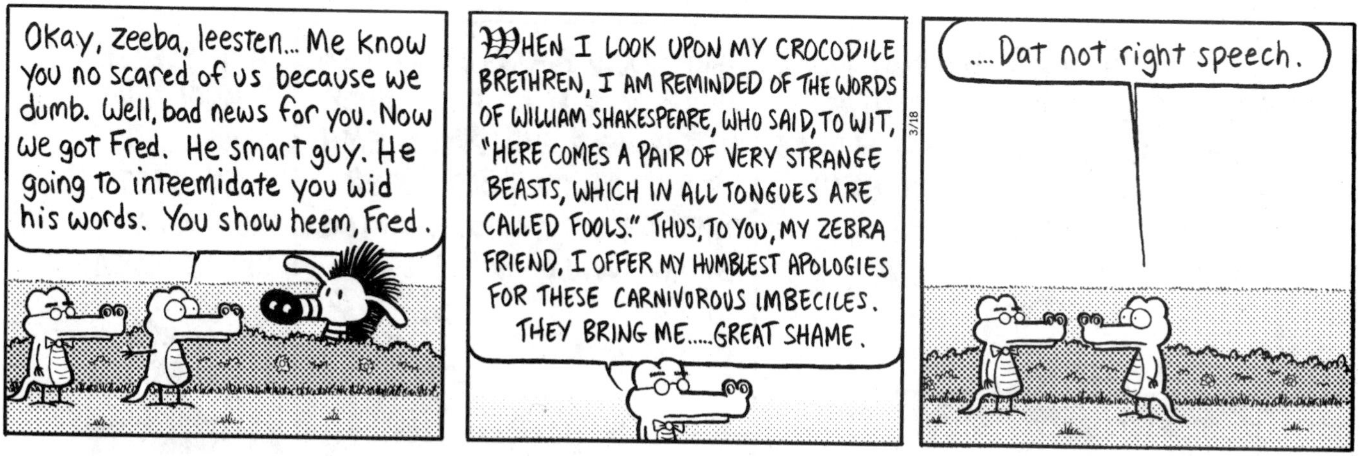
Okay, zeeba, leesten... Me know you no scared of us because we dumb. Well, bad news for you. Now we got Fred. He smart guy. He going to inteemidate you wid his words. You show heem, Fred.
WHEN I LOOK UPON MY CROCODILE BRETHREN, I AM REMINDED OF THE WORDS OF WILLIAM SHAKESPEARE, WHO SAID, TO WIT, "HERE COMES A PAIR OF VERY STRANGE BEASTS, WHICH IN ALL TONGUES ARE CALLED FOOLS." THUS, TO YOU, MY ZEBRA FRIEND, I OFFER MY HUMBLEST APOLOGIES FOR THESE CARNIVOROUS IMBECILES. THEY BRING ME.....GREAT SHAME.
3/18
....Dat not right speech.

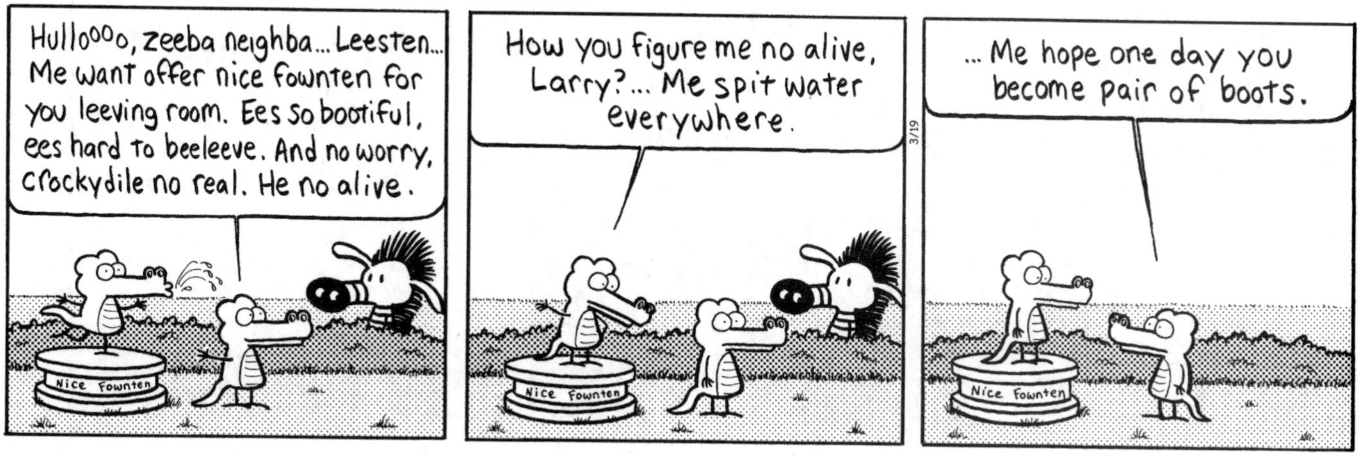
Hulloooo, zeeba neighba... Leesten... Me want offer nice fownten for you leeving room. Ees so bootiful, ees hard to beeleeve. And no worry, crockydile no real. He no alive.
Nice Fownten
How you figure me no alive, Larry?... Me spit water everywhere.
3/19
... Me hope one day you become pair of boots.

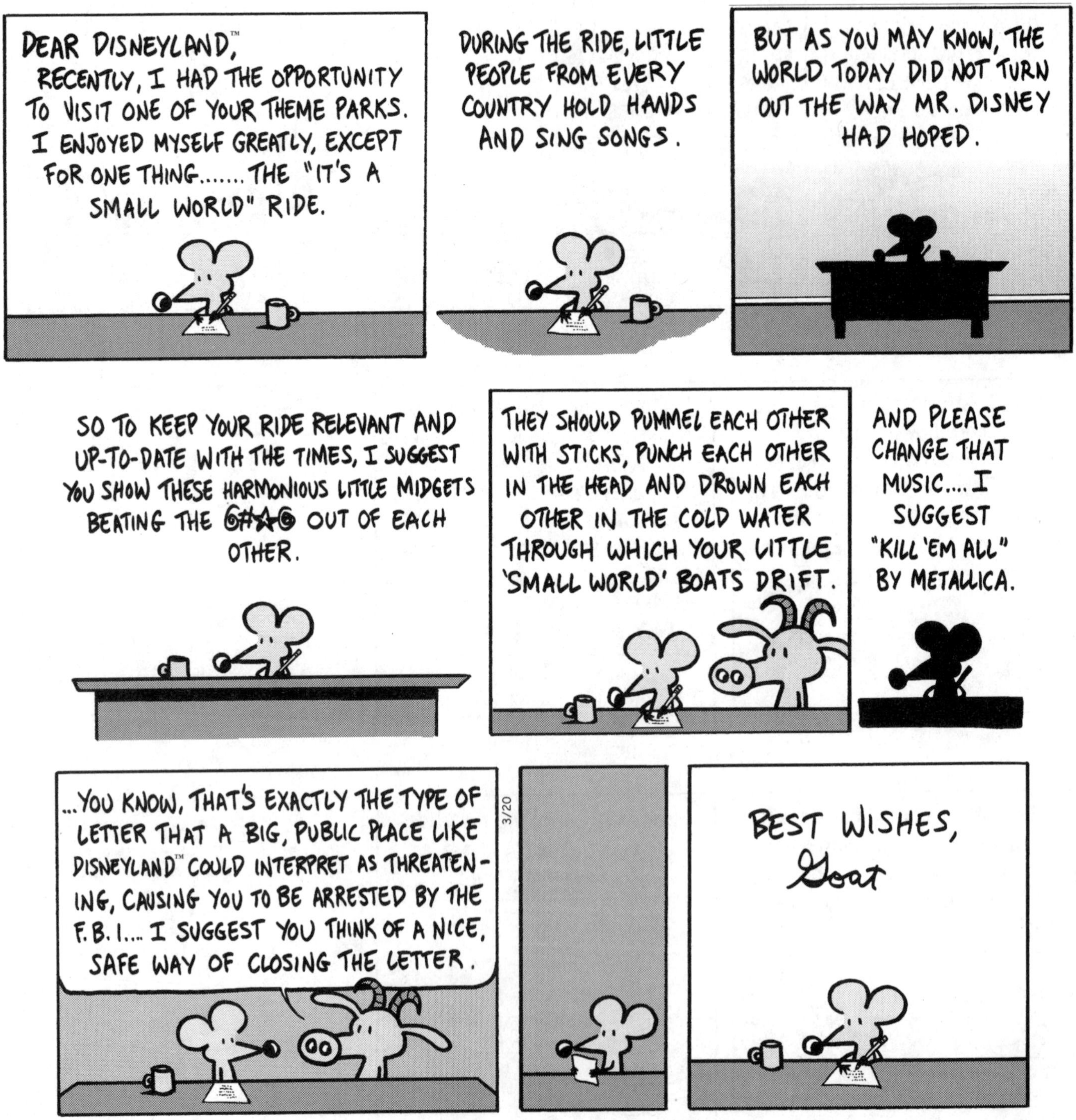
DEAR DISNEYLAND™,
RECENTLY, I HAD THE OPPORTUNITY TO VISIT ONE OF YOUR THEME PARKS. I ENJOYED MYSELF GREATLY, EXCEPT FOR ONE THING....... THE "IT'S A SMALL WORLD" RIDE.
DURING THE RIDE, LITTLE PEOPLE FROM EVERY COUNTRY HOLD HANDS AND SING SONGS.
BUT AS YOU MAY KNOW, THE WORLD TODAY DID NOT TURN OUT THE WAY MR. DISNEY HAD HOPED.
SO TO KEEP YOUR RIDE RELEVANT AND UP-TO-DATE WITH THE TIMES, I SUGGEST YOU SHOW THESE HARMONIOUS LITTLE MIDGETS BEATING THE G#★G OUT OF EACH OTHER.
THEY SHOULD PUMMEL EACH OTHER WITH STICKS, PUNCH EACH OTHER IN THE HEAD AND DROWN EACH OTHER IN THE COLD WATER THROUGH WHICH YOUR LITTLE 'SMALL WORLD' BOATS DRIFT.
AND PLEASE CHANGE THAT MUSIC.... I SUGGEST "KILL 'EM ALL" BY METALLICA.
...YOU KNOW, THAT'S EXACTLY THE TYPE OF LETTER THAT A BIG, PUBLIC PLACE LIKE DISNEYLAND™ COULD INTERPRET AS THREATENING, CAUSING YOU TO BE ARRESTED BY THE F.B.I.... I SUGGEST YOU THINK OF A NICE, SAFE WAY OF CLOSING THE LETTER.
3/20
BEST WISHES,
Goat

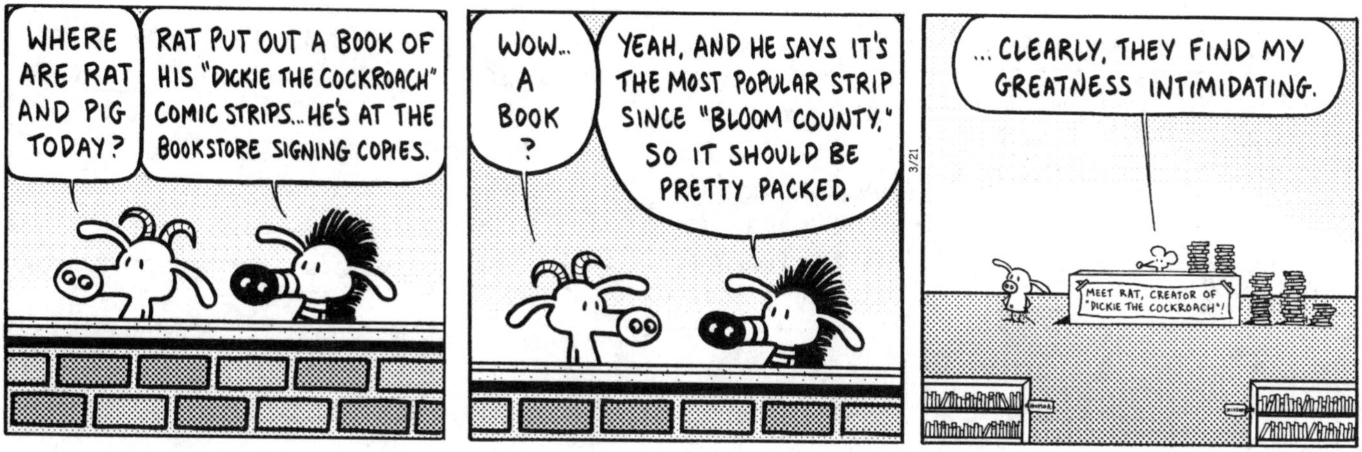
WHERE ARE RAT AND PIG TODAY?
RAT PUT OUT A BOOK OF HIS "DICKIE THE COCKROACH" COMIC STRIPS... HE'S AT THE BOOKSTORE SIGNING COPIES.
WOW... A BOOK?
YEAH, AND HE SAYS IT'S THE MOST POPULAR STRIP SINCE "BLOOM COUNTY," SO IT SHOULD BE PRETTY PACKED.
3/21
...CLEARLY, THEY FIND MY GREATNESS INTIMIDATING.
MEET RAT, CREATOR OF "DICKIE THE COCKROACH"!

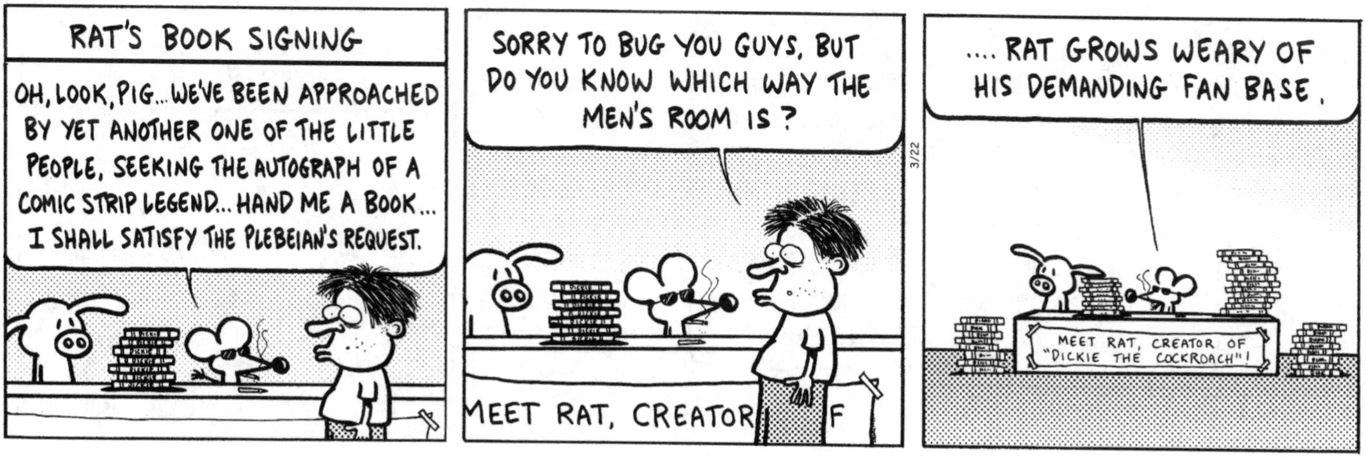
RAT'S BOOK SIGNING
OH, LOOK, PIG... WE'VE BEEN APPROACHED BY YET ANOTHER ONE OF THE LITTLE PEOPLE, SEEKING THE AUTOGRAPH OF A COMIC STRIP LEGEND... HAND ME A BOOK... I SHALL SATISFY THE PLEBEIAN'S REQUEST.
SORRY TO BUG YOU GUYS, BUT DO YOU KNOW WHICH WAY THE MEN'S ROOM IS?
MEET RAT, CREATOR F
3/22
.... RAT GROWS WEARY OF HIS DEMANDING FAN BASE.
MEET RAT, CREATOR OF "DICKIE THE COCKROACH"!

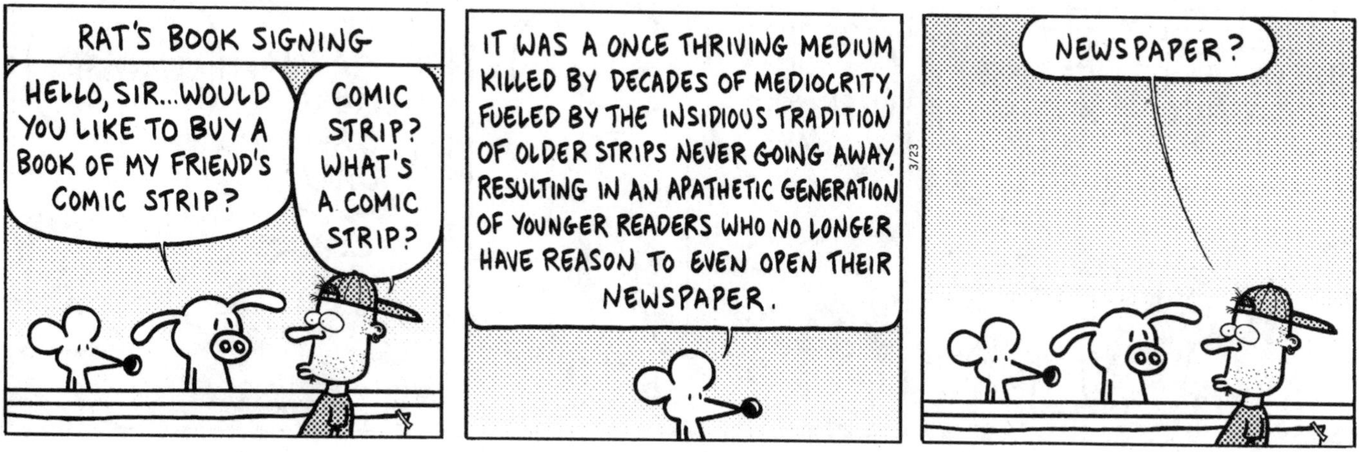
RAT'S BOOK SIGNING
HELLO, SIR... WOULD YOU LIKE TO BUY A BOOK OF MY FRIEND'S COMIC STRIP?
COMIC STRIP? WHAT'S A COMIC STRIP?
IT WAS A ONCE THRIVING MEDIUM KILLED BY DECADES OF MEDIOCRITY, FUELED BY THE INSIDIOUS TRADITION OF OLDER STRIPS NEVER GOING AWAY, RESULTING IN AN APATHETIC GENERATION OF YOUNGER READERS WHO NO LONGER HAVE REASON TO EVEN OPEN THEIR NEWSPAPER.
3/23
NEWSPAPER?

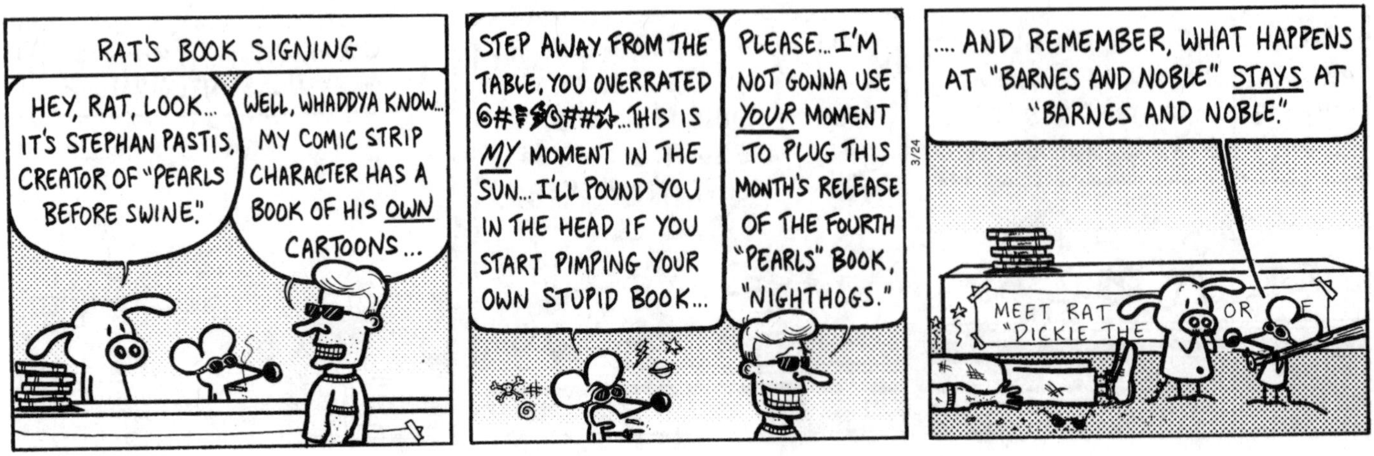
RAT'S BOOK SIGNING
HEY, RAT, LOOK... IT'S STEPHAN PASTIS, CREATOR OF "PEARLS BEFORE SWINE."
WELL, WHADDYA KNOW... MY COMIC STRIP CHARACTER HAS A BOOK OF HIS OWN CARTOONS...
STEP AWAY FROM THE TABLE, YOU OVERRATED 6#✵$@##✩...THIS IS MY MOMENT IN THE SUN... I'LL POUND YOU IN THE HEAD IF YOU START PIMPING YOUR OWN STUPID BOOK...
PLEASE... I'M NOT GONNA USE YOUR MOMENT TO PLUG THIS MONTH'S RELEASE OF THE FOURTH "PEARLS" BOOK, "NIGHTHOGS."
3/24
.... AND REMEMBER, WHAT HAPPENS AT "BARNES AND NOBLE" STAYS AT "BARNES AND NOBLE."
MEET RAT
"DICKIE THE
OR

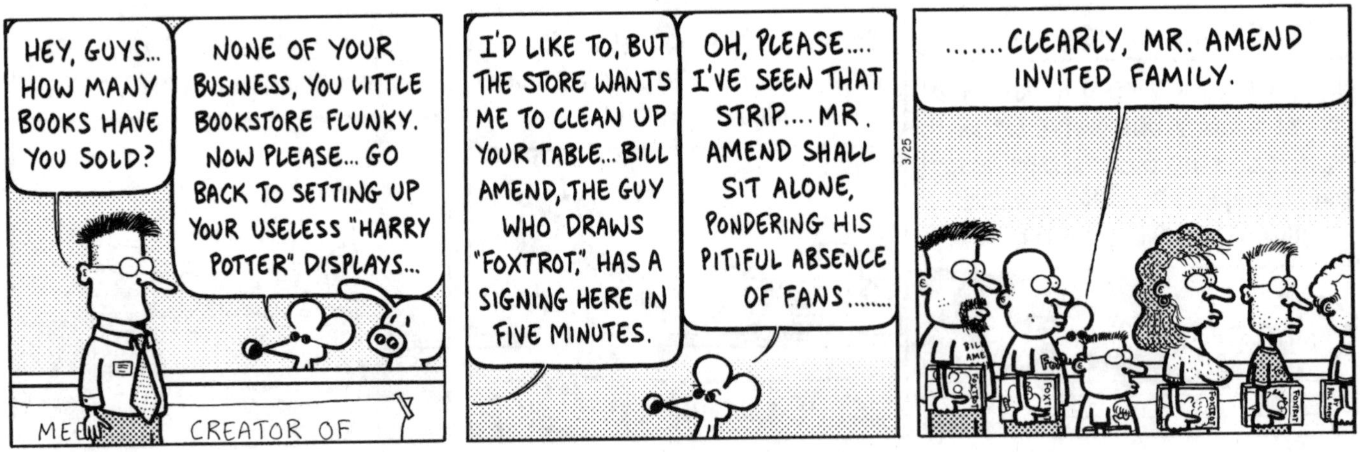
HEY, GUYS... HOW MANY BOOKS HAVE YOU SOLD?
NONE OF YOUR BUSINESS, YOU LITTLE BOOKSTORE FLUNKY. NOW PLEASE... GO BACK TO SETTING UP YOUR USELESS "HARRY POTTER" DISPLAYS...
MEE
CREATOR OF
I'D LIKE TO, BUT THE STORE WANTS ME TO CLEAN UP YOUR TABLE... BILL AMEND, THE GUY WHO DRAWS "FOXTROT," HAS A SIGNING HERE IN FIVE MINUTES.
OH, PLEASE.... I'VE SEEN THAT STRIP.... MR. AMEND SHALL SIT ALONE, PONDERING HIS PITIFUL ABSENCE OF FANS.......
3/25
.......CLEARLY, MR. AMEND INVITED FAMILY.

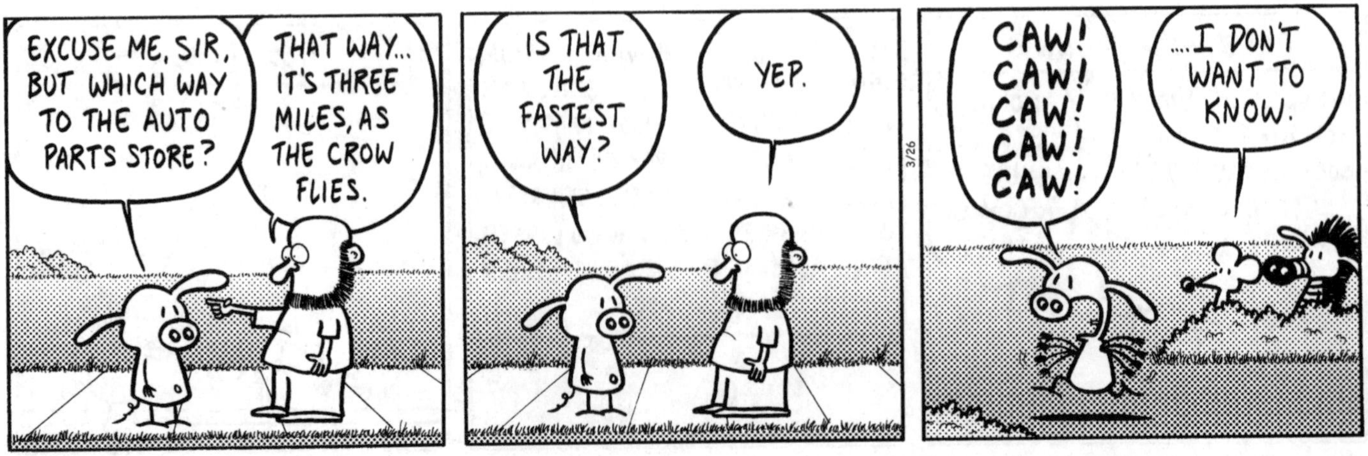
EXCUSE ME, SIR, BUT WHICH WAY TO THE AUTO PARTS STORE?
THAT WAY... IT'S THREE MILES, AS THE CROW FLIES.
IS THAT THE FASTEST WAY?
YEP.
3/26
CAW! CAW! CAW! CAW! CAW!
....I DON'T WANT TO KNOW.

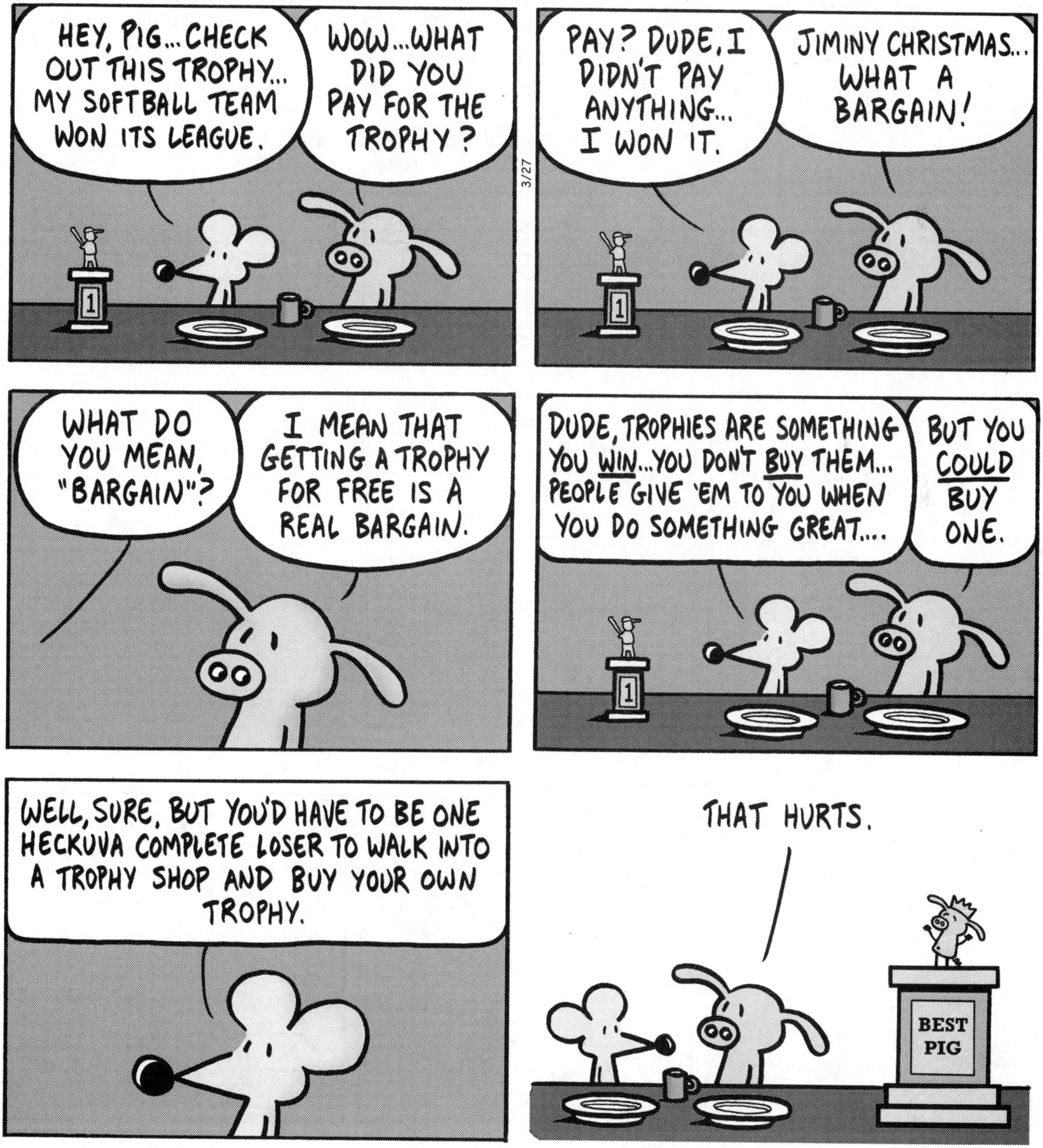
HEY, PIG... CHECK OUT THIS TROPHY... MY SOFTBALL TEAM WON ITS LEAGUE.
WOW... WHAT DID YOU PAY FOR THE TROPHY?
3/27
PAY? DUDE, I DIDN'T PAY ANYTHING... I WON IT.
JIMINY CHRISTMAS... WHAT A BARGAIN!
1
WHAT DO YOU MEAN, "BARGAIN"?
I MEAN THAT GETTING A TROPHY FOR FREE IS A REAL BARGAIN.
DUDE, TROPHIES ARE SOMETHING YOU WIN... YOU DON'T BUY THEM... PEOPLE GIVE 'EM TO YOU WHEN YOU DO SOMETHING GREAT....
BUT YOU COULD BUY ONE.
WELL, SURE, BUT YOU'D HAVE TO BE ONE HECKUVA COMPLETE LOSER TO WALK INTO A TROPHY SHOP AND BUY YOUR OWN TROPHY.
THAT HURTS.
BEST PIG

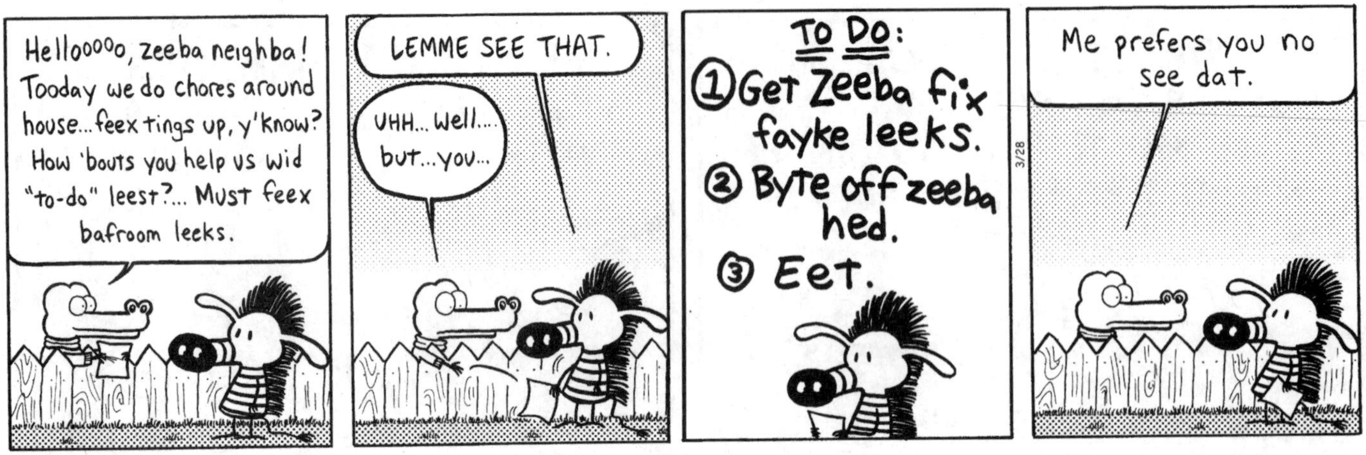
Hellooooo, zeeba neighba! Tooday we do chores around house...feex tings up, y'know? How 'bouts you help us wid "to-do" leest?... Must feex bafroom leeks.
LEMME SEE THAT.
UHH... well.... but...you...
TO DO:
① Get Zeeba fix fayke leeks.
② Byte off zeeba hed.
③ Eet.
3/28
Me prefers you no see dat.

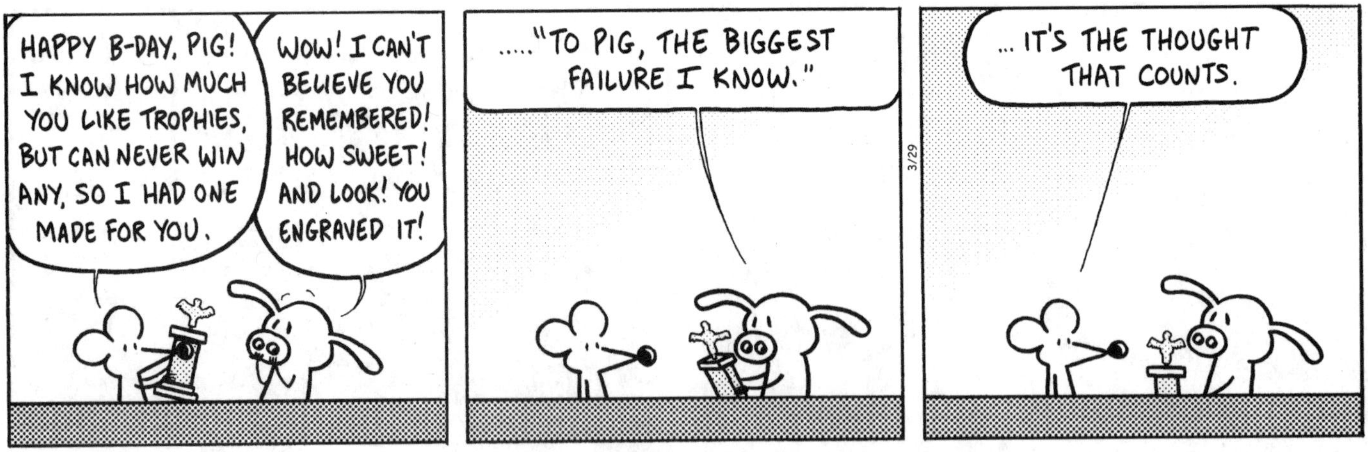
HAPPY B-DAY, PIG! I KNOW HOW MUCH YOU LIKE TROPHIES, BUT CAN NEVER WIN ANY, SO I HAD ONE MADE FOR YOU.
WOW! I CAN'T BELIEVE YOU REMEMBERED! HOW SWEET! AND LOOK! YOU ENGRAVED IT!
....."TO PIG, THE BIGGEST FAILURE I KNOW."
3/29
... IT'S THE THOUGHT THAT COUNTS.

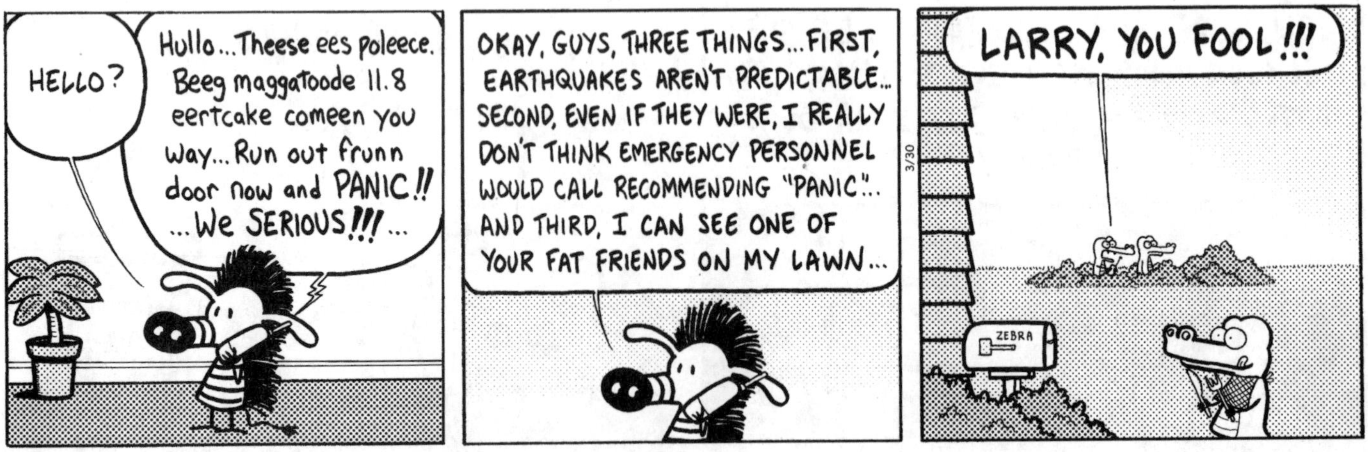
HELLO?
Hullo...Theese ees poleece. Beeg maggatoode 11.8 eertcake comeen you way...Run out frunn door now and PANIC!! ...We SERIOUS!!!...
OKAY, GUYS, THREE THINGS...FIRST, EARTHQUAKES AREN'T PREDICTABLE... SECOND, EVEN IF THEY WERE, I REALLY DON'T THINK EMERGENCY PERSONNEL WOULD CALL RECOMMENDING "PANIC"... AND THIRD, I CAN SEE ONE OF YOUR FAT FRIENDS ON MY LAWN...
3/30
LARRY, YOU FOOL!!!
ZEBRA

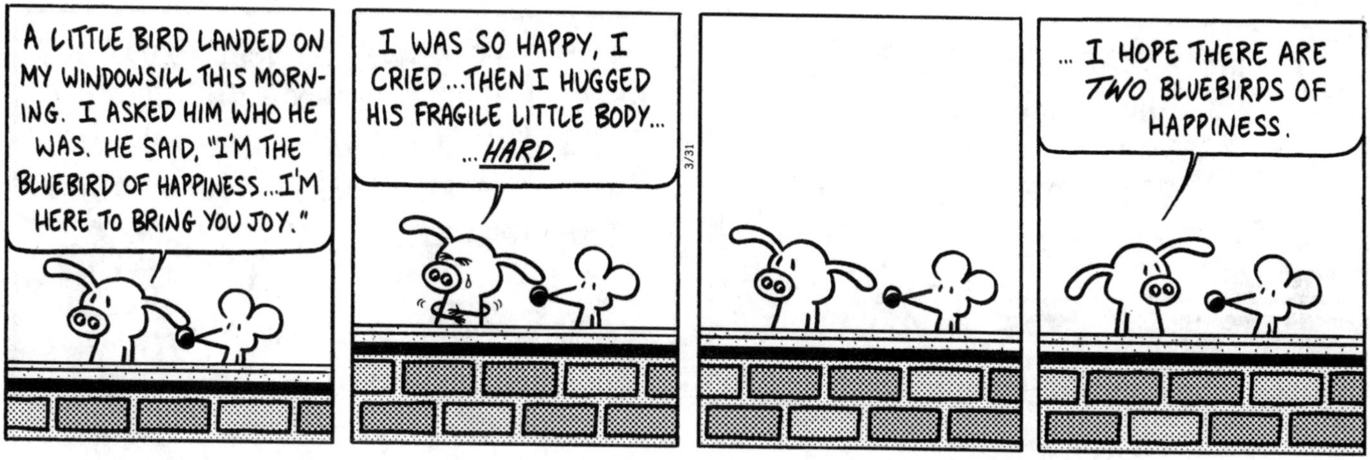
A LITTLE BIRD LANDED ON MY WINDOWSILL THIS MORNING. I ASKED HIM WHO HE WAS. HE SAID, "I'M THE BLUEBIRD OF HAPPINESS...I'M HERE TO BRING YOU JOY."
I WAS SO HAPPY, I CRIED...THEN I HUGGED HIS FRAGILE LITTLE BODY... ...HARD.
3/31
... I HOPE THERE ARE TWO BLUEBIRDS OF HAPPINESS.

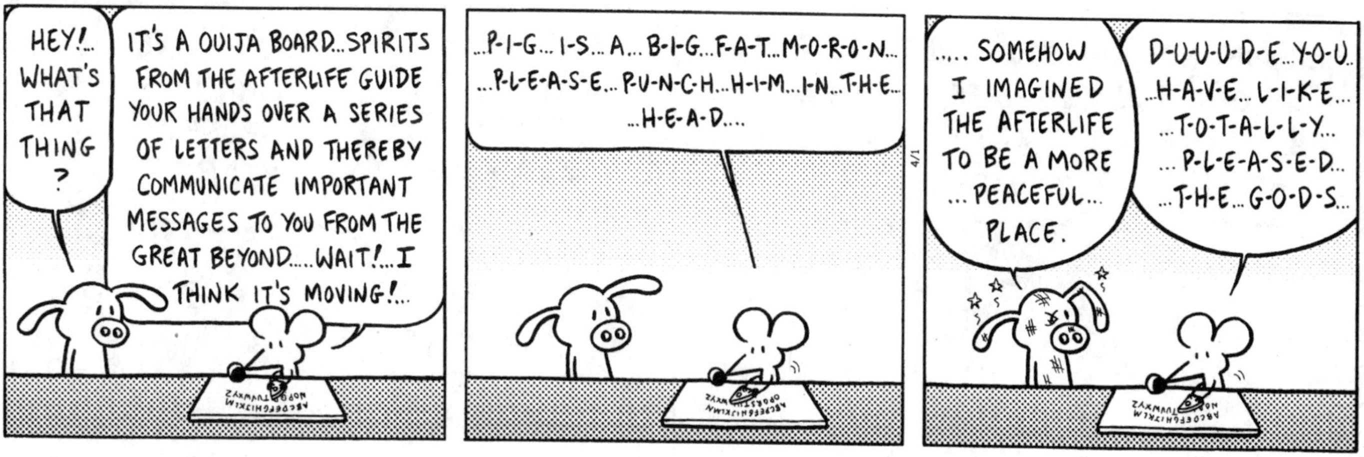
HEY!... WHAT'S THAT THING?
IT'S A OUIJA BOARD...SPIRITS FROM THE AFTERLIFE GUIDE YOUR HANDS OVER A SERIES OF LETTERS AND THEREBY COMMUNICATE IMPORTANT MESSAGES TO YOU FROM THE GREAT BEYOND.....WAIT!...I THINK IT'S MOVING!...
...P-I-G... I-S... A... B-I-G...F-A-T...M-O-R-O-N... ...P-L-E-A-S-E... P-U-N-C-H...H-I-M...I-N...T-H-E... ...H-E-A-D....
4/1
..... SOMEHOW I IMAGINED THE AFTERLIFE TO BE A MORE ... PEACEFUL... PLACE.
D-U-U-U-D-E...Y-O-U... H-A-V-E... L-I-K-E... ...T-O-T-A-L-L-Y... ... P-L-E-A-S-E-D... ...T-H-E... G-O-D-S...

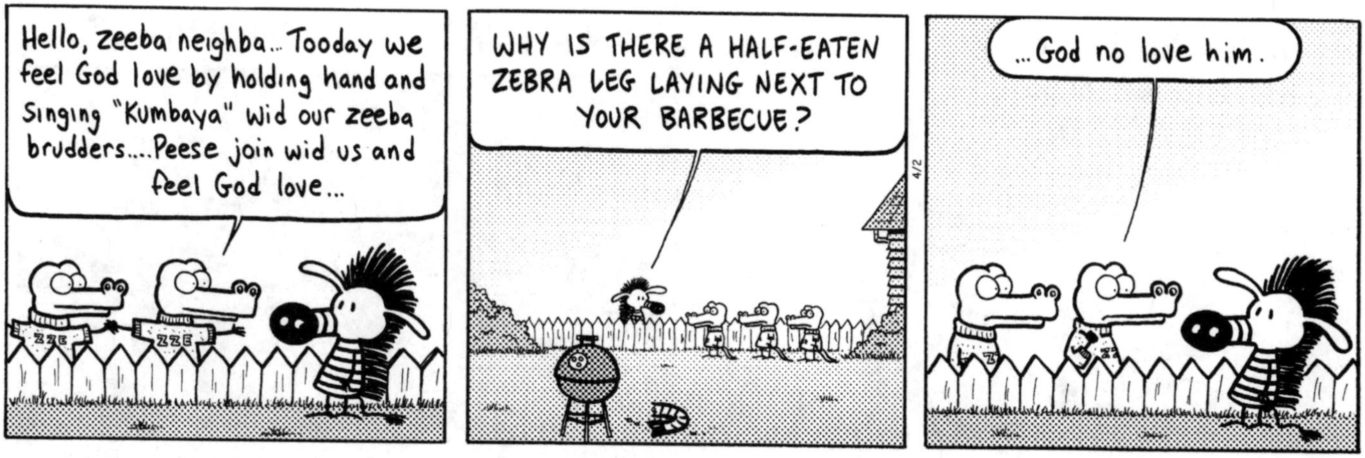
Hello, zeeba neighba... Tooday we feel God love by holding hand and Singing "Kumbaya" wid our zeeba brudders....Peese join wid us and feel God love...
WHY IS THERE A HALF-EATEN ZEBRA LEG LAYING NEXT TO YOUR BARBECUE?
4/2
...God no love him.

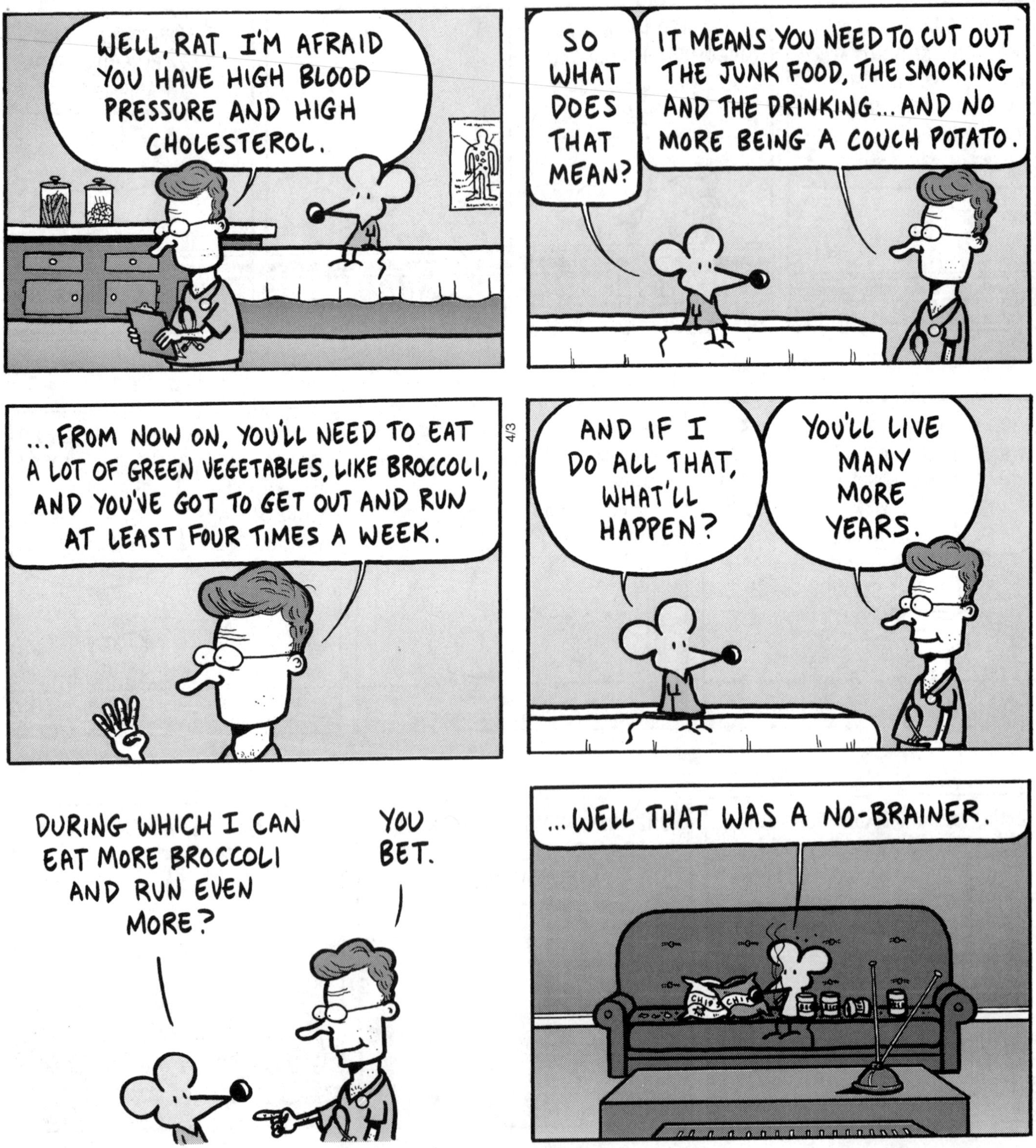
WELL, RAT, I'M AFRAID YOU HAVE HIGH BLOOD PRESSURE AND HIGH CHOLESTEROL.
SO WHAT DOES THAT MEAN?
IT MEANS YOU NEED TO CUT OUT THE JUNK FOOD, THE SMOKING AND THE DRINKING... AND NO MORE BEING A COUCH POTATO.
...FROM NOW ON, YOU'LL NEED TO EAT A LOT OF GREEN VEGETABLES, LIKE BROCCOLI, AND YOU'VE GOT TO GET OUT AND RUN AT LEAST FOUR TIMES A WEEK.
4/3
AND IF I DO ALL THAT, WHAT'LL HAPPEN?
YOU'LL LIVE MANY MORE YEARS.
DURING WHICH I CAN EAT MORE BROCCOLI AND RUN EVEN MORE?
YOU BET.
...WELL THAT WAS A NO-BRAINER.
CHIPS
CHIP

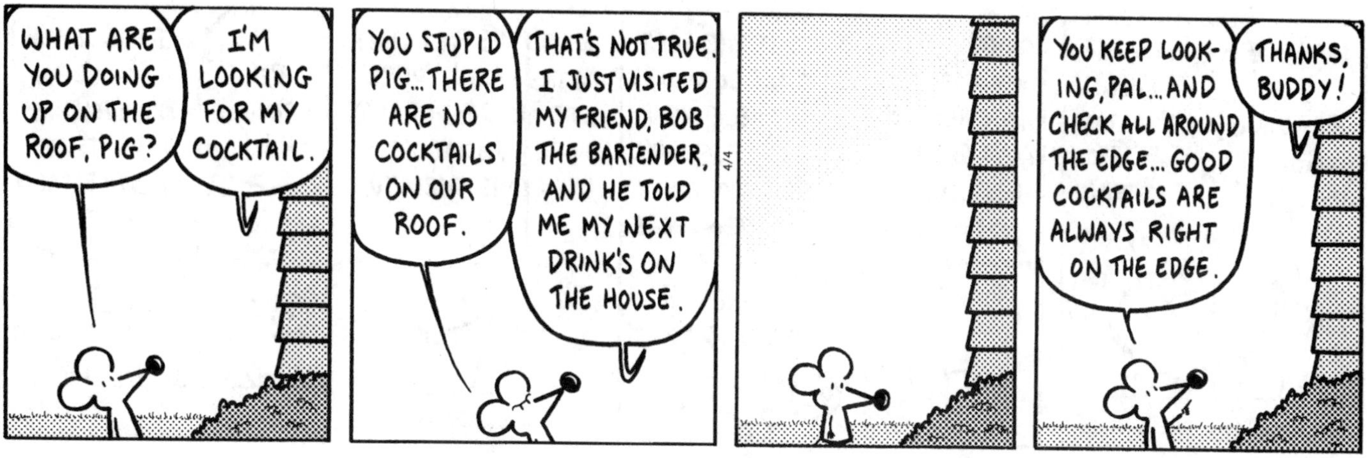
WHAT ARE YOU DOING UP ON THE ROOF, PIG?
I'M LOOKING FOR MY COCKTAIL.
YOU STUPID PIG... THERE ARE NO COCKTAILS ON OUR ROOF.
THAT'S NOT TRUE. I JUST VISITED MY FRIEND, BOB THE BARTENDER, AND HE TOLD ME MY NEXT DRINK'S ON THE HOUSE.
4/4
YOU KEEP LOOKING, PAL... AND CHECK ALL AROUND THE EDGE... GOOD COCKTAILS ARE ALWAYS RIGHT ON THE EDGE.
THANKS, BUDDY!

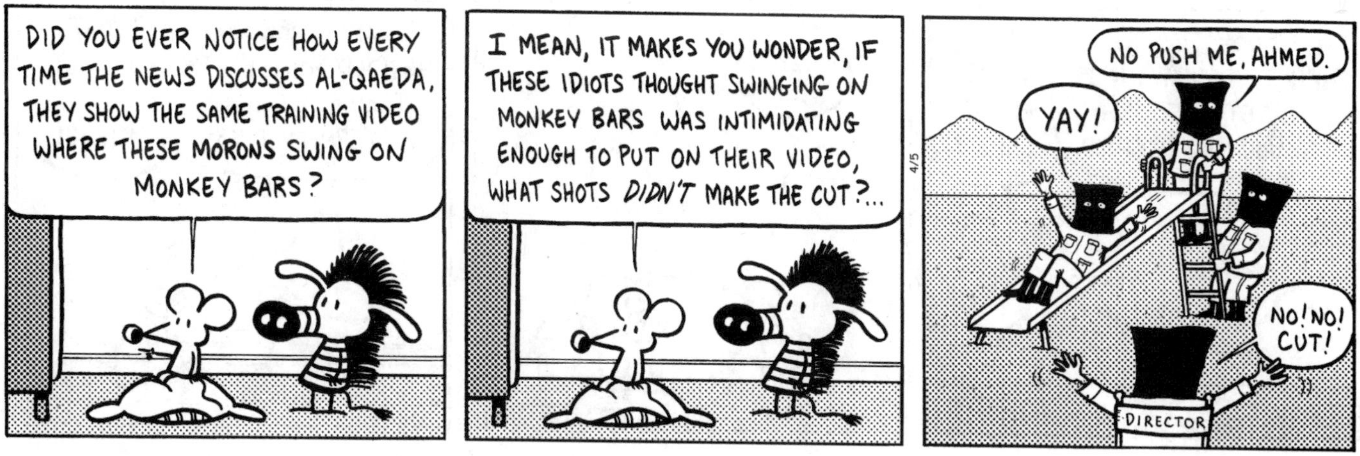
DID YOU EVER NOTICE HOW EVERY TIME THE NEWS DISCUSSES AL-QAEDA, THEY SHOW THE SAME TRAINING VIDEO WHERE THESE MORONS SWING ON MONKEY BARS?
I MEAN, IT MAKES YOU WONDER, IF THESE IDIOTS THOUGHT SWINGING ON MONKEY BARS WAS INTIMIDATING ENOUGH TO PUT ON THEIR VIDEO, WHAT SHOTS *DIDN'T* MAKE THE CUT?...
4/5
NO PUSH ME, AHMED.
YAY!
NO! NO! CUT!
DIRECTOR

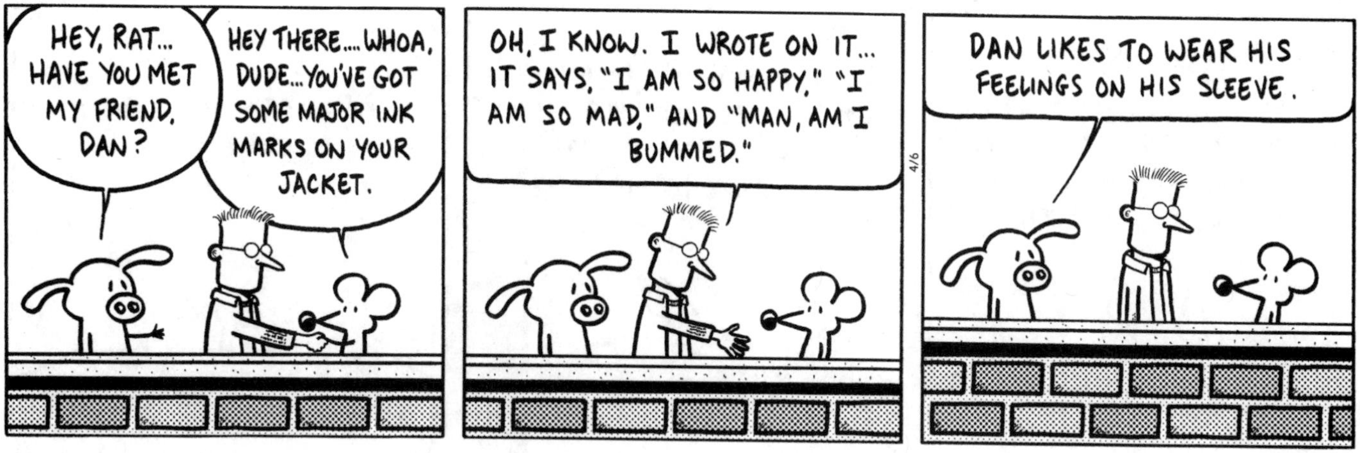
HEY, RAT... HAVE YOU MET MY FRIEND, DAN?
HEY THERE.... WHOA, DUDE... YOU'VE GOT SOME MAJOR INK MARKS ON YOUR JACKET.
OH, I KNOW. I WROTE ON IT... IT SAYS, "I AM SO HAPPY," "I AM SO MAD," AND "MAN, AM I BUMMED."
4/6
DAN LIKES TO WEAR HIS FEELINGS ON HIS SLEEVE.

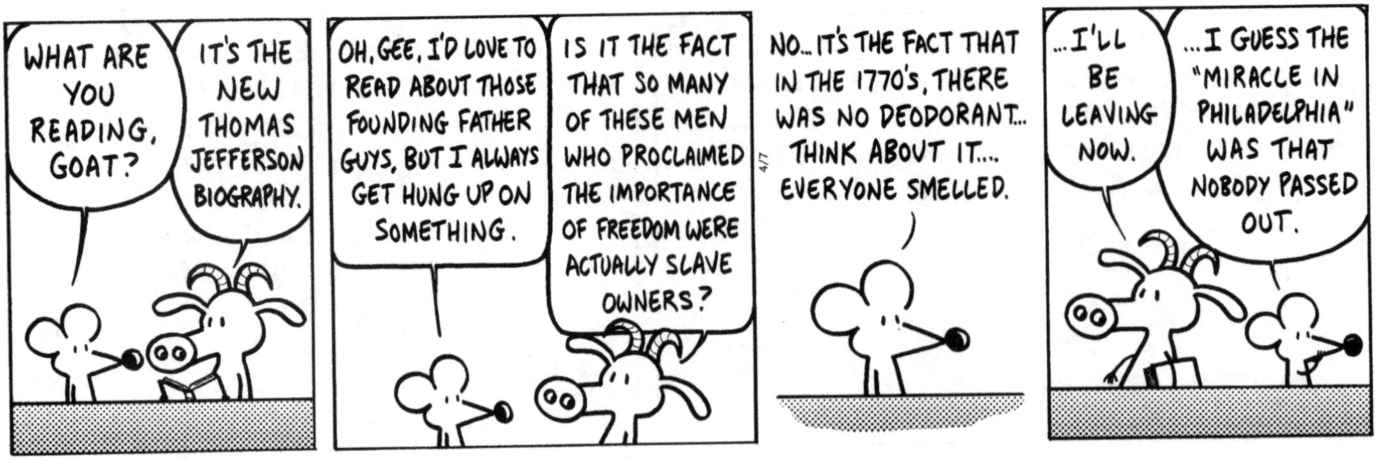
WHAT ARE YOU READING, GOAT?
IT'S THE NEW THOMAS JEFFERSON BIOGRAPHY.
OH, GEE, I'D LOVE TO READ ABOUT THOSE FOUNDING FATHER GUYS, BUT I ALWAYS GET HUNG UP ON SOMETHING.
IS IT THE FACT THAT SO MANY OF THESE MEN WHO PROCLAIMED THE IMPORTANCE OF FREEDOM WERE ACTUALLY SLAVE OWNERS?
NO... IT'S THE FACT THAT IN THE 1770'S, THERE WAS NO DEODORANT... THINK ABOUT IT.... EVERYONE SMELLED.
...I'LL BE LEAVING NOW.
...I GUESS THE "MIRACLE IN PHILADELPHIA" WAS THAT NOBODY PASSED OUT.

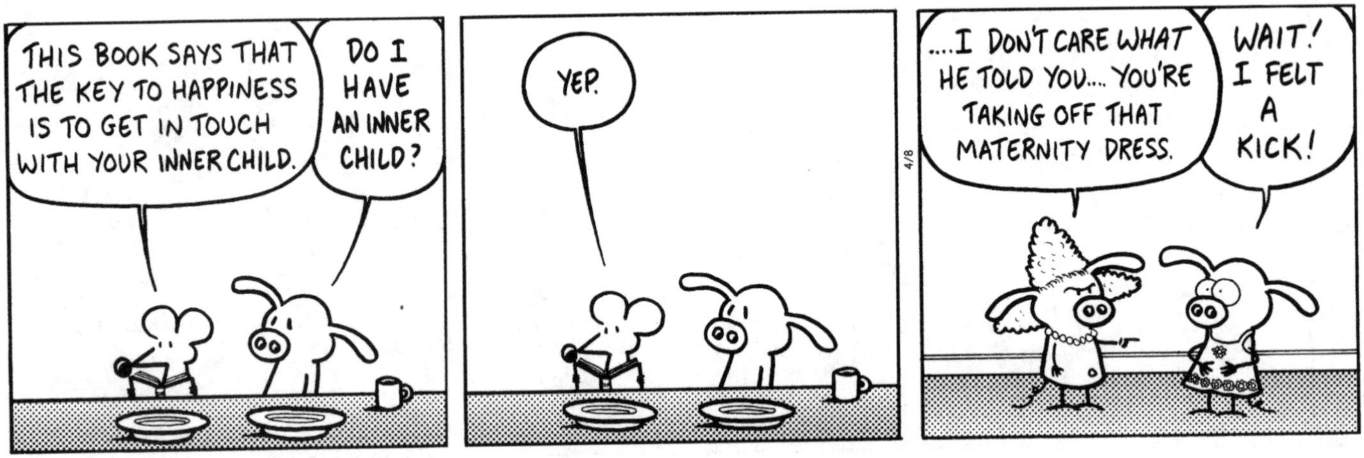
THIS BOOK SAYS THAT THE KEY TO HAPPINESS IS TO GET IN TOUCH WITH YOUR INNER CHILD.
DO I HAVE AN INNER CHILD?
YEP.
....I DON'T CARE WHAT HE TOLD YOU.... YOU'RE TAKING OFF THAT MATERNITY DRESS.
WAIT! I FELT A KICK!

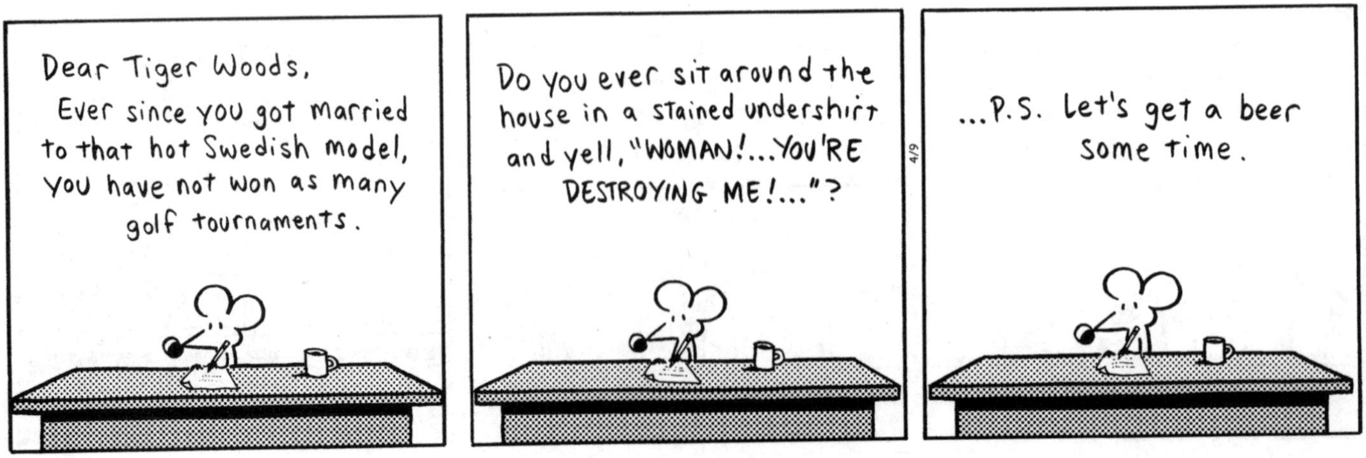
Dear Tiger Woods,
Ever since you got married to that hot Swedish model, you have not won as many golf tournaments.
Do you ever sit around the house in a stained undershirt and yell, "WOMAN!... YOU'RE DESTROYING ME!..."?
...P.S. Let's get a beer some time.

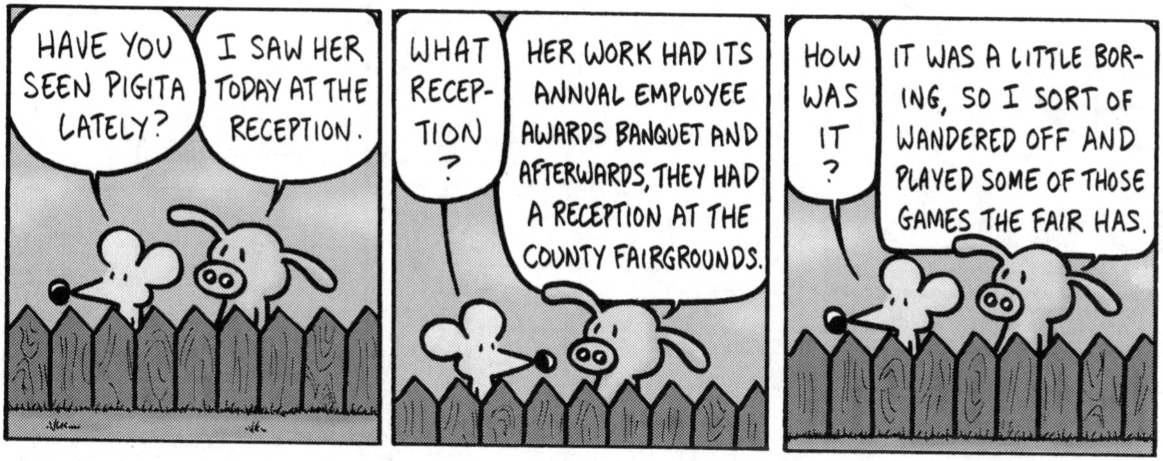
HAVE YOU SEEN PIGITA LATELY?
I SAW HER TODAY AT THE RECEPTION.
WHAT RECEPTION?
HER WORK HAD ITS ANNUAL EMPLOYEE AWARDS BANQUET AND AFTERWARDS, THEY HAD A RECEPTION AT THE COUNTY FAIRGROUNDS.
HOW WAS IT?
IT WAS A LITTLE BORING, SO I SORT OF WANDERED OFF AND PLAYED SOME OF THOSE GAMES THE FAIR HAS.

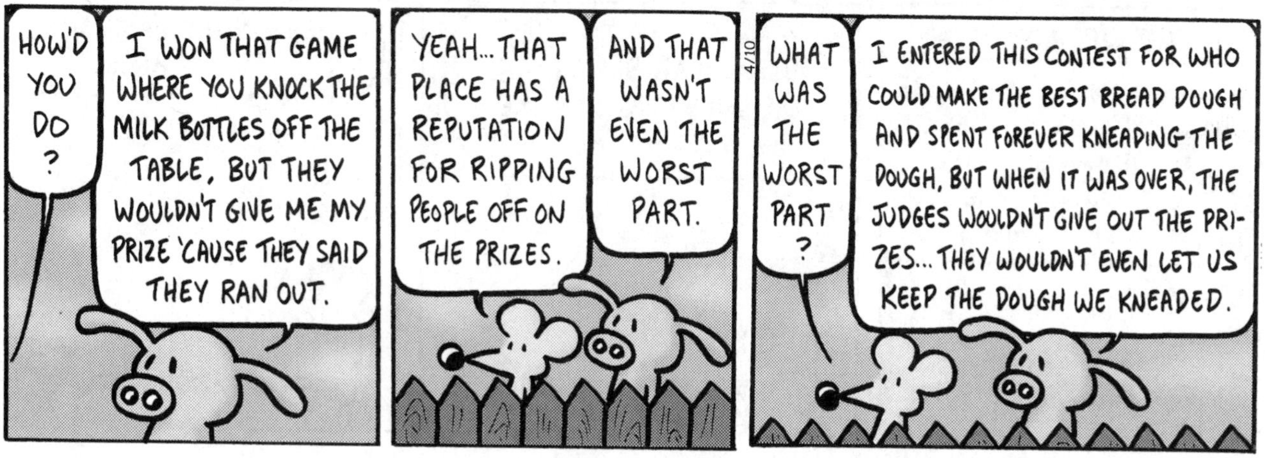
HOW'D YOU DO?
I WON THAT GAME WHERE YOU KNOCK THE MILK BOTTLES OFF THE TABLE, BUT THEY WOULDN'T GIVE ME MY PRIZE 'CAUSE THEY SAID THEY RAN OUT.
YEAH... THAT PLACE HAS A REPUTATION FOR RIPPING PEOPLE OFF ON THE PRIZES.
AND THAT WASN'T EVEN THE WORST PART.
4/10
WHAT WAS THE WORST PART?
I ENTERED THIS CONTEST FOR WHO COULD MAKE THE BEST BREAD DOUGH AND SPENT FOREVER KNEADING THE DOUGH, BUT WHEN IT WAS OVER, THE JUDGES WOULDN'T GIVE OUT THE PRIZES... THEY WOULDN'T EVEN LET US KEEP THE DOUGH WE KNEADED.

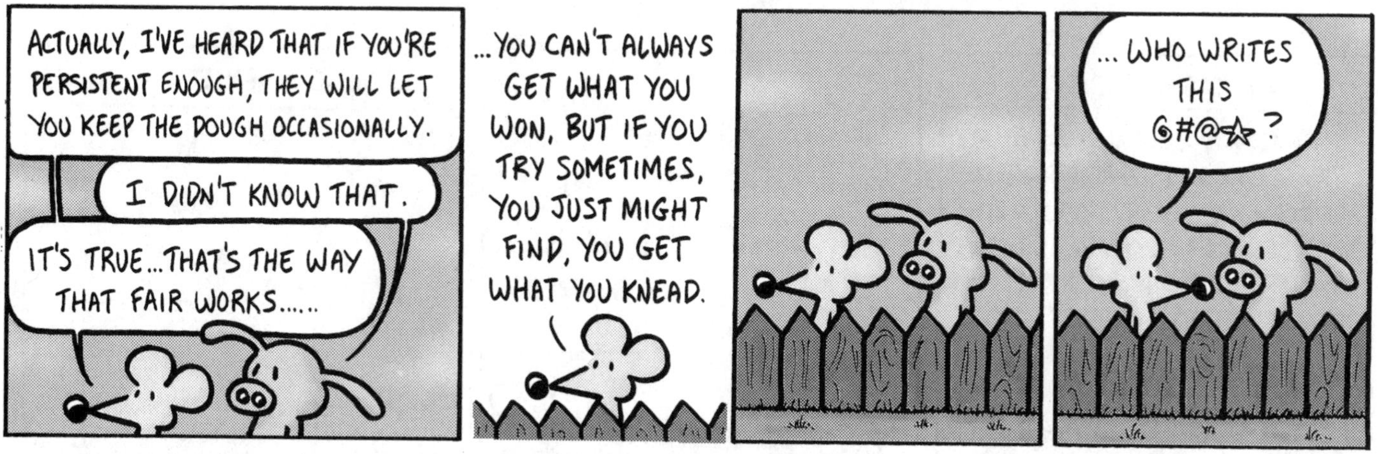
ACTUALLY, I'VE HEARD THAT IF YOU'RE PERSISTENT ENOUGH, THEY WILL LET YOU KEEP THE DOUGH OCCASIONALLY.
I DIDN'T KNOW THAT.
IT'S TRUE... THAT'S THE WAY THAT FAIR WORKS.....
...YOU CAN'T ALWAYS GET WHAT YOU WON, BUT IF YOU TRY SOMETIMES, YOU JUST MIGHT FIND, YOU GET WHAT YOU KNEAD.
...WHO WRITES THIS 6#@☆?

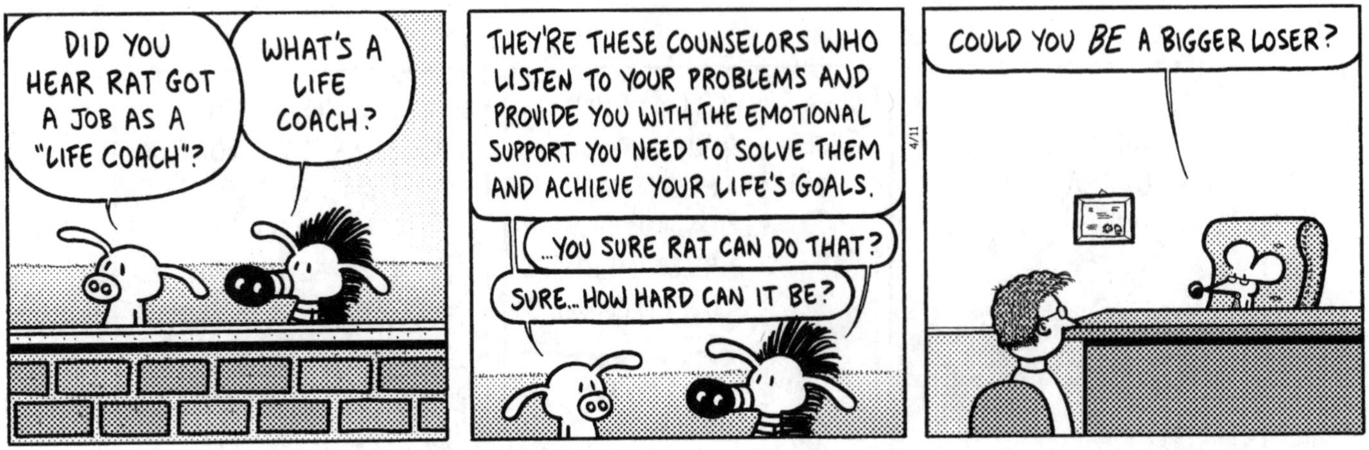
DID YOU HEAR RAT GOT A JOB AS A "LIFE COACH"?
WHAT'S A LIFE COACH?
THEY'RE THESE COUNSELORS WHO LISTEN TO YOUR PROBLEMS AND PROVIDE YOU WITH THE EMOTIONAL SUPPORT YOU NEED TO SOLVE THEM AND ACHIEVE YOUR LIFE'S GOALS.
...YOU SURE RAT CAN DO THAT?
SURE... HOW HARD CAN IT BE?
4/11
COULD YOU *BE* A BIGGER LOSER?

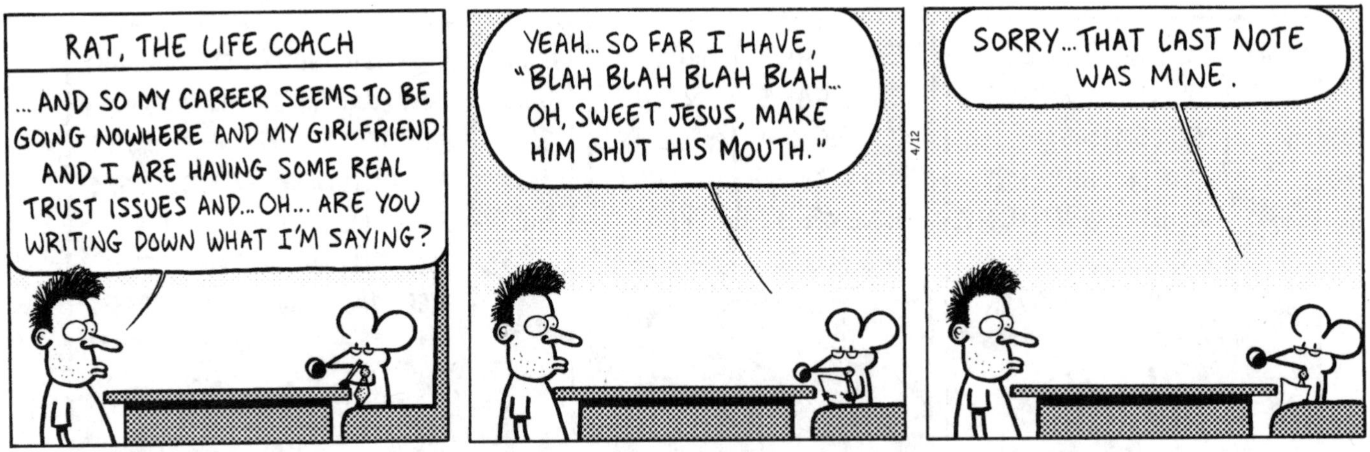
RAT, THE LIFE COACH
...AND SO MY CAREER SEEMS TO BE GOING NOWHERE AND MY GIRLFRIEND AND I ARE HAVING SOME REAL TRUST ISSUES AND... OH... ARE YOU WRITING DOWN WHAT I'M SAYING?
YEAH... SO FAR I HAVE, "BLAH BLAH BLAH BLAH... OH, SWEET JESUS, MAKE HIM SHUT HIS MOUTH."
4/12
SORRY... THAT LAST NOTE WAS MINE.

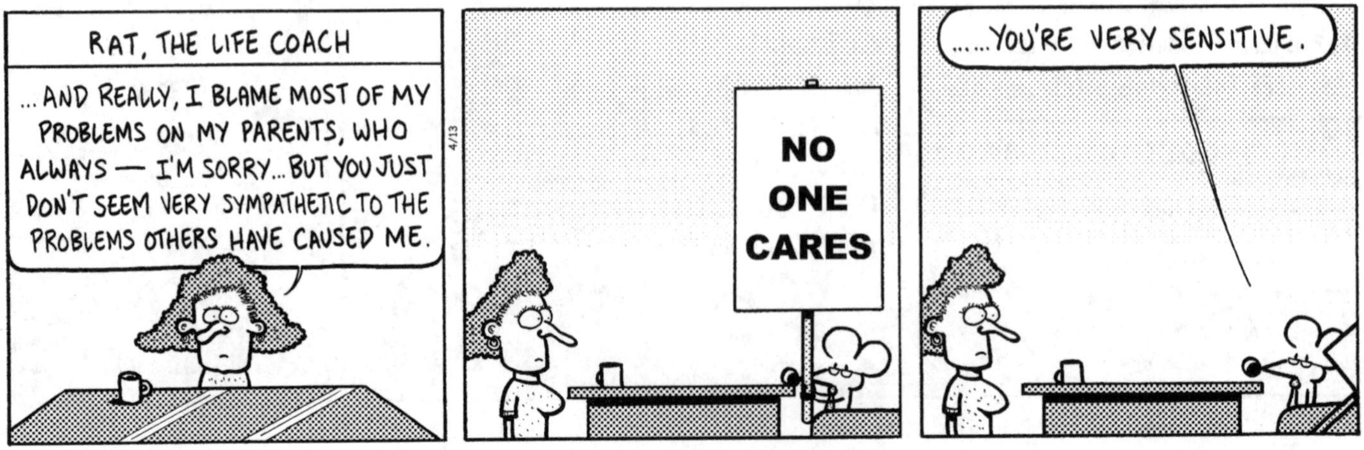
RAT, THE LIFE COACH
...AND REALLY, I BLAME MOST OF MY PROBLEMS ON MY PARENTS, WHO ALWAYS — I'M SORRY... BUT YOU JUST DON'T SEEM VERY SYMPATHETIC TO THE PROBLEMS OTHERS HAVE CAUSED ME.
4/13
NO ONE CARES
......YOU'RE VERY SENSITIVE.

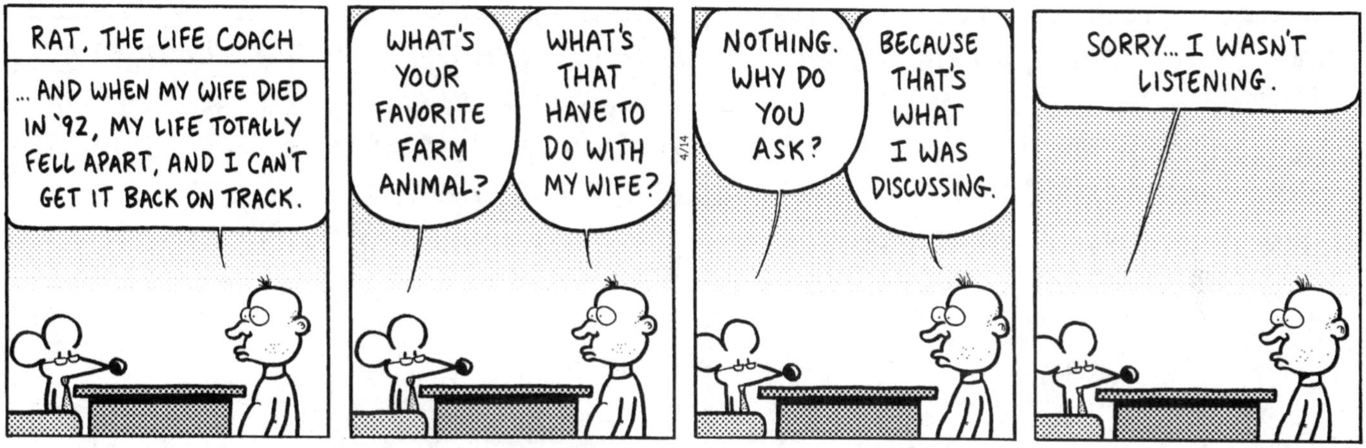
RAT, THE LIFE COACH
...AND WHEN MY WIFE DIED IN '92, MY LIFE TOTALLY FELL APART, AND I CAN'T GET IT BACK ON TRACK.
WHAT'S YOUR FAVORITE FARM ANIMAL?
WHAT'S THAT HAVE TO DO WITH MY WIFE?
4/14
NOTHING. WHY DO YOU ASK?
BECAUSE THAT'S WHAT I WAS DISCUSSING.
SORRY... I WASN'T LISTENING.

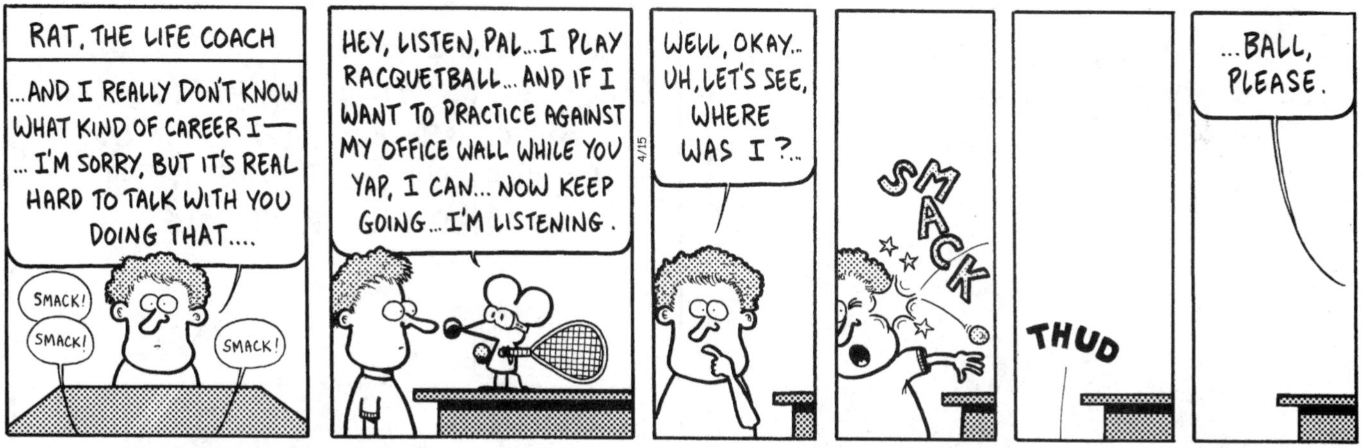
RAT, THE LIFE COACH
...AND I REALLY DON'T KNOW WHAT KIND OF CAREER I— ...I'M SORRY, BUT IT'S REAL HARD TO TALK WITH YOU DOING THAT....
SMACK!
SMACK!
SMACK!
HEY, LISTEN, PAL... I PLAY RACQUETBALL... AND IF I WANT TO PRACTICE AGAINST MY OFFICE WALL WHILE YOU YAP, I CAN... NOW KEEP GOING... I'M LISTENING.
4/15
WELL, OKAY.. UH, LET'S SEE, WHERE WAS I?..
SMACK
THUD
...BALL, PLEASE.

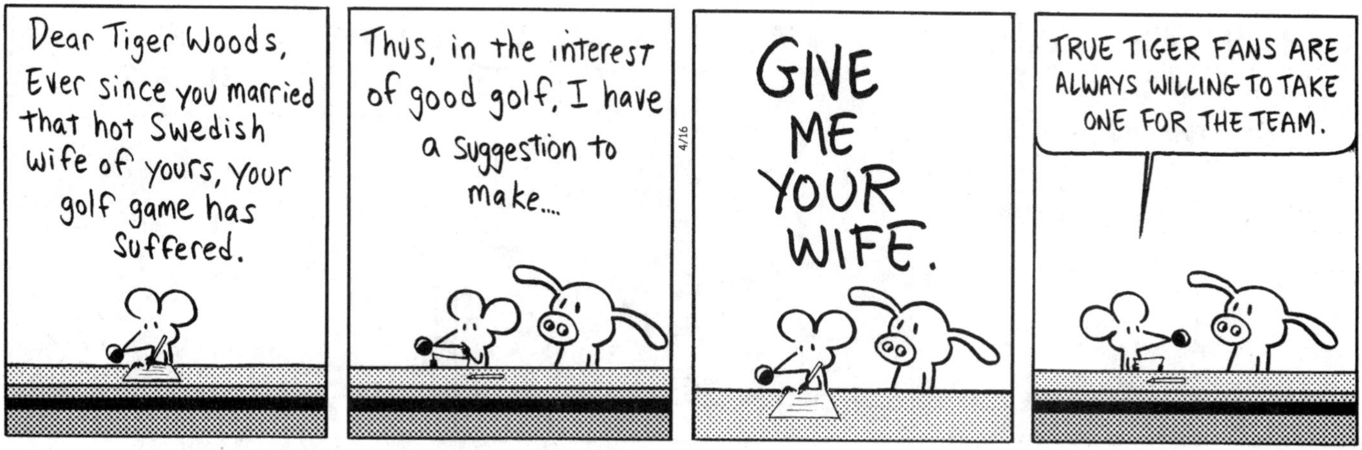
Dear Tiger Woods, Ever since you married that hot Swedish wife of yours, your golf game has suffered.
Thus, in the interest of good golf, I have a suggestion to make....
4/16
GIVE ME YOUR WIFE.
TRUE TIGER FANS ARE ALWAYS WILLING TO TAKE ONE FOR THE TEAM.

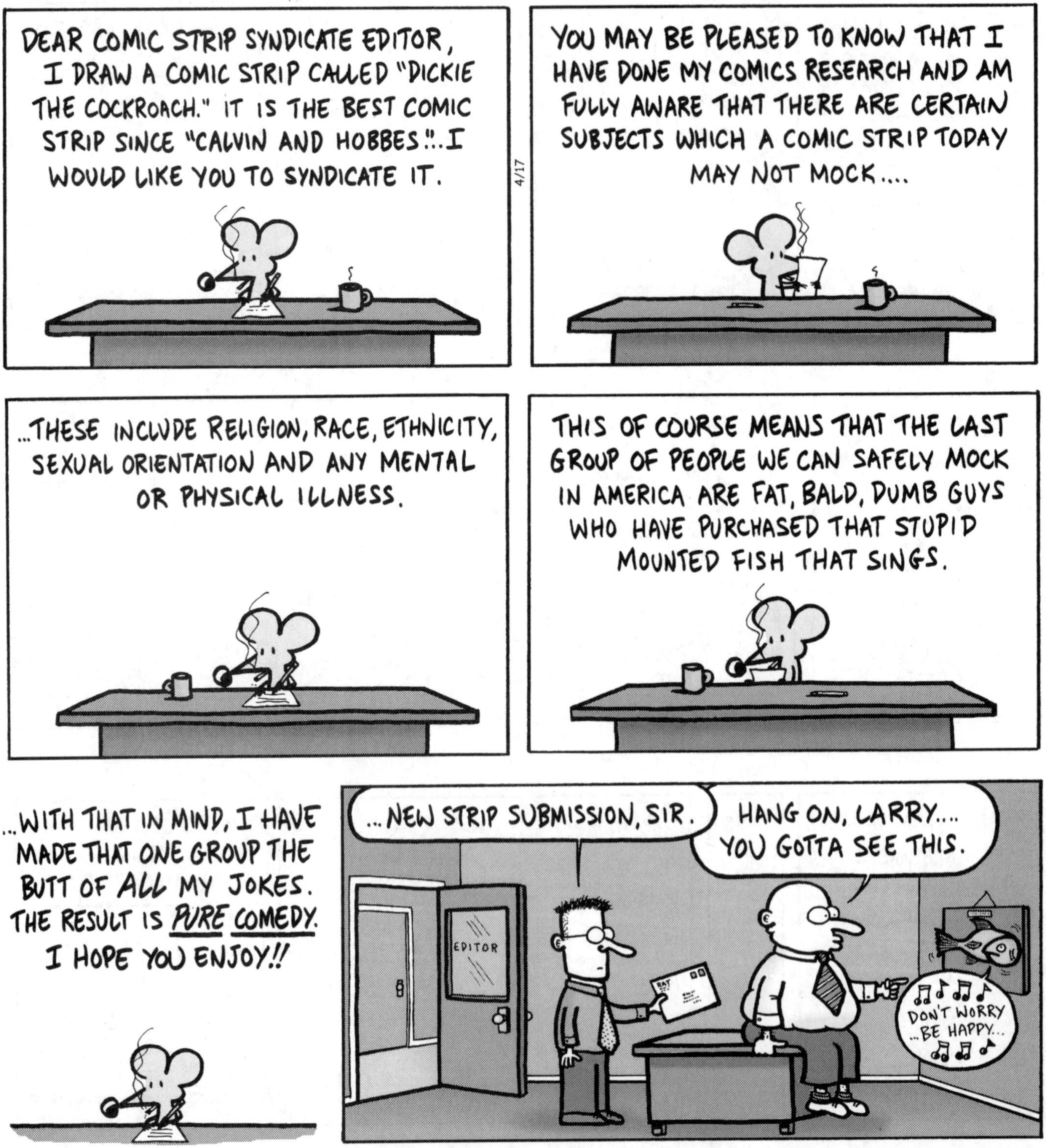
DEAR COMIC STRIP SYNDICATE EDITOR,
I DRAW A COMIC STRIP CALLED "DICKIE THE COCKROACH." IT IS THE BEST COMIC STRIP SINCE "CALVIN AND HOBBES."..I WOULD LIKE YOU TO SYNDICATE IT.
4/17
YOU MAY BE PLEASED TO KNOW THAT I HAVE DONE MY COMICS RESEARCH AND AM FULLY AWARE THAT THERE ARE CERTAIN SUBJECTS WHICH A COMIC STRIP TODAY MAY NOT MOCK....
...THESE INCLUDE RELIGION, RACE, ETHNICITY, SEXUAL ORIENTATION AND ANY MENTAL OR PHYSICAL ILLNESS.
THIS OF COURSE MEANS THAT THE LAST GROUP OF PEOPLE WE CAN SAFELY MOCK IN AMERICA ARE FAT, BALD, DUMB GUYS WHO HAVE PURCHASED THAT STUPID MOUNTED FISH THAT SINGS.
...WITH THAT IN MIND, I HAVE MADE THAT ONE GROUP THE BUTT OF ALL MY JOKES. THE RESULT IS PURE COMEDY. I HOPE YOU ENJOY!!
...NEW STRIP SUBMISSION, SIR.
HANG ON, LARRY.... YOU GOTTA SEE THIS.
EDITOR
RAT
DON'T WORRY ...BE HAPPY...

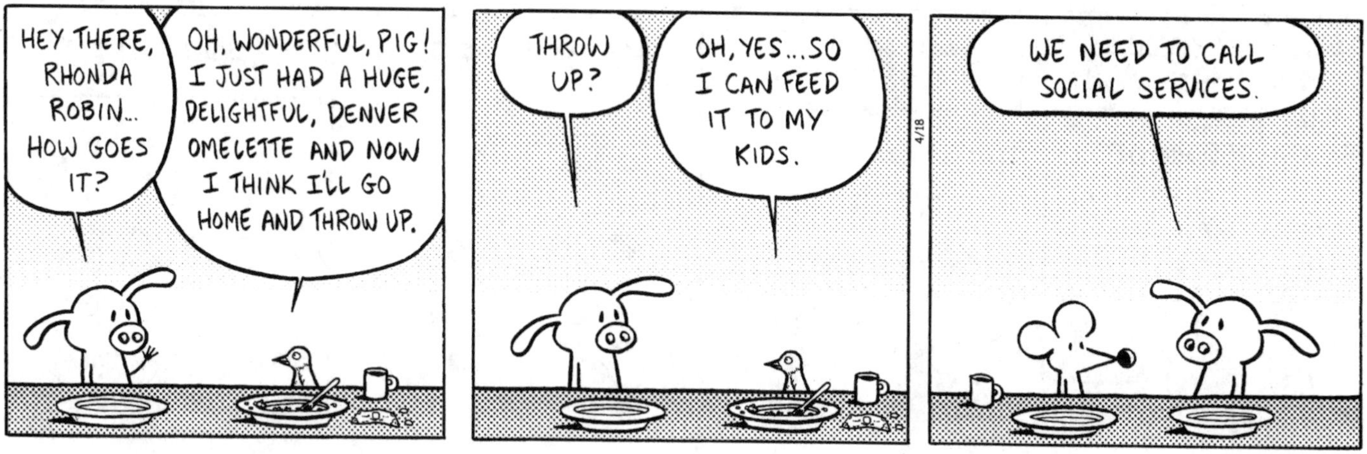
HEY THERE, RHONDA ROBIN... HOW GOES IT?
OH, WONDERFUL, PIG! I JUST HAD A HUGE, DELIGHTFUL, DENVER OMELETTE AND NOW I THINK I'LL GO HOME AND THROW UP.
THROW UP?
OH, YES...SO I CAN FEED IT TO MY KIDS.
4/18
WE NEED TO CALL SOCIAL SERVICES.

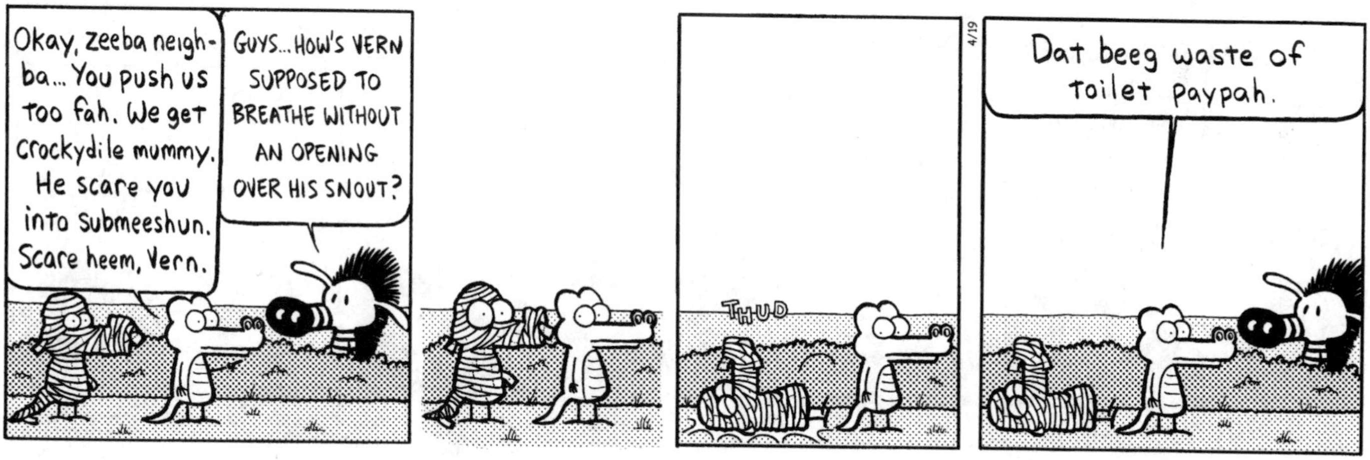
Okay, zeeba neigh-ba... You push us too fah. We get crockydile mummy. He scare you into submeeshun. Scare heem, Vern.
GUYS...HOW'S VERN SUPPOSED TO BREATHE WITHOUT AN OPENING OVER HIS SNOUT?
THUD
4/19
Dat beeg waste of toilet paypah.

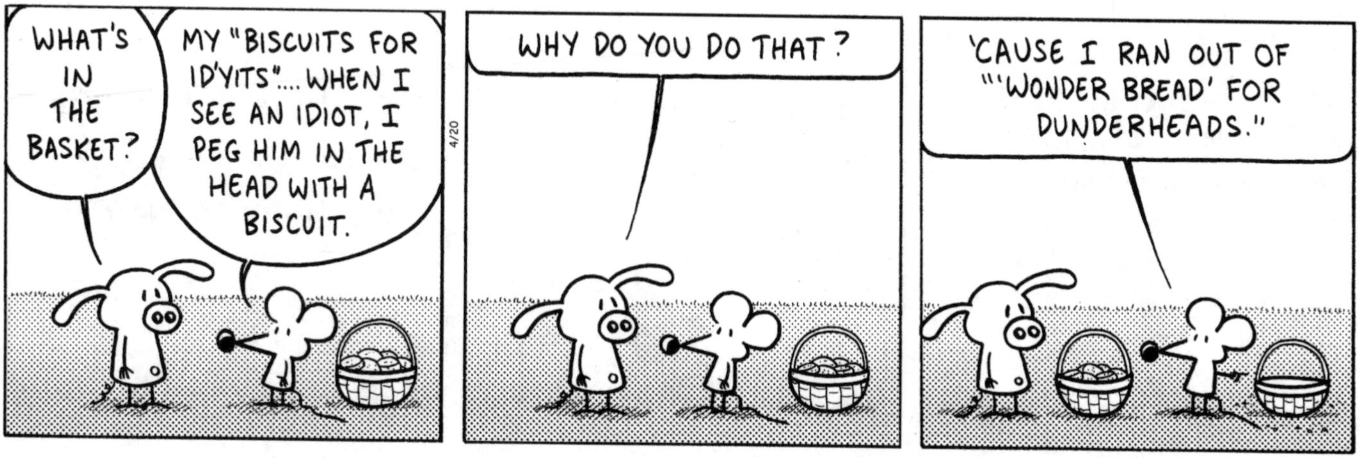
WHAT'S IN THE BASKET?
MY "BISCUITS FOR ID'YITS"... WHEN I SEE AN IDIOT, I PEG HIM IN THE HEAD WITH A BISCUIT.
4/20
WHY DO YOU DO THAT?
'CAUSE I RAN OUT OF "'WONDER BREAD' FOR DUNDERHEADS."

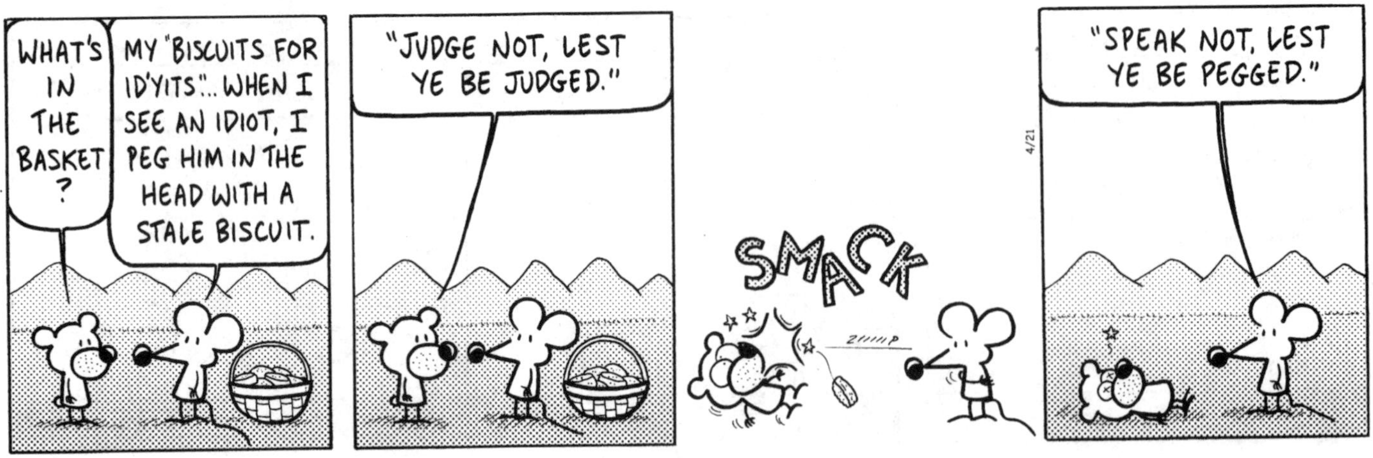
WHAT'S IN THE BASKET?
MY "BISCUITS FOR ID'YITS"... WHEN I SEE AN IDIOT, I PEG HIM IN THE HEAD WITH A STALE BISCUIT.
"JUDGE NOT, LEST YE BE JUDGED."
SMACK
ZIIIIIP
4/21
"SPEAK NOT, LEST YE BE PEGGED."

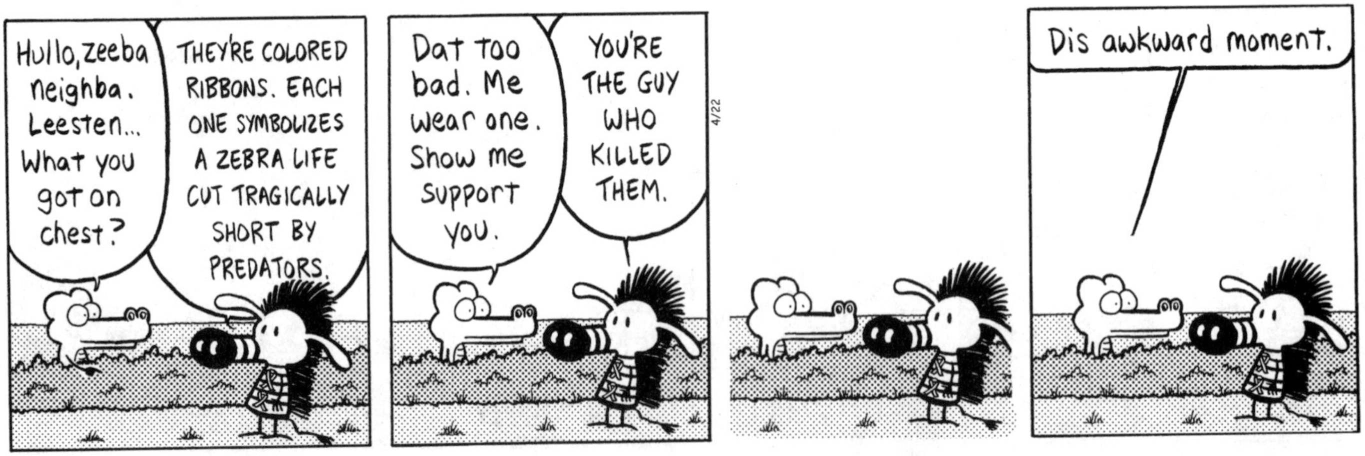
Hullo, zeeba neighba. Leesten... What you got on chest?
THEY'RE COLORED RIBBONS. EACH ONE SYMBOLIZES A ZEBRA LIFE CUT TRAGICALLY SHORT BY PREDATORS.
Dat too bad. Me wear one. Show me support you.
YOU'RE THE GUY WHO KILLED THEM.
4/22
Dis awkward moment.

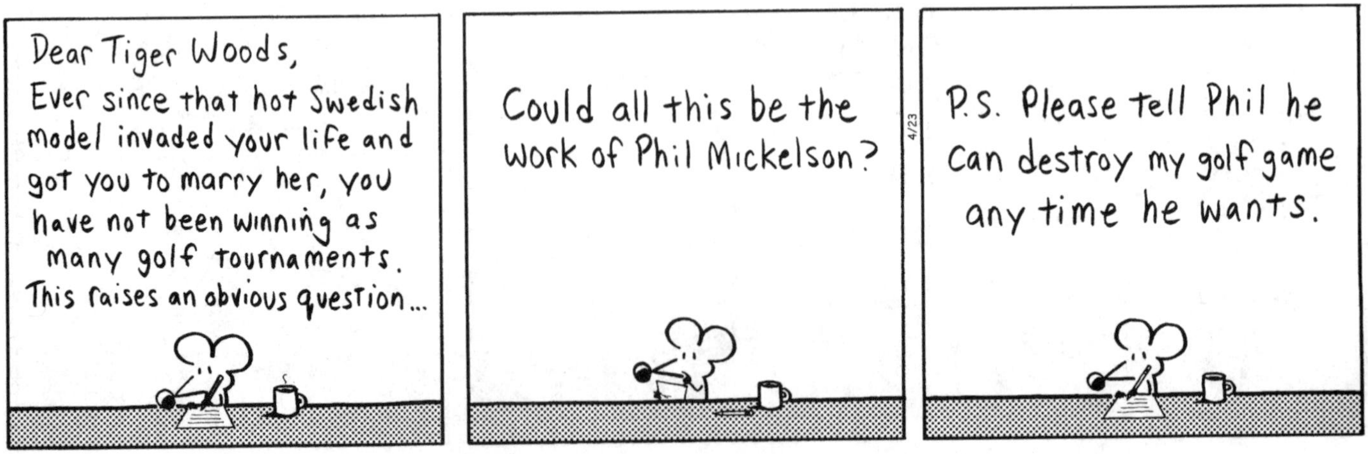
Dear Tiger Woods,
Ever since that hot Swedish model invaded your life and got you to marry her, you have not been winning as many golf tournaments. This raises an obvious question...
Could all this be the work of Phil Mickelson?
4/23
P.S. Please tell Phil he can destroy my golf game any time he wants.

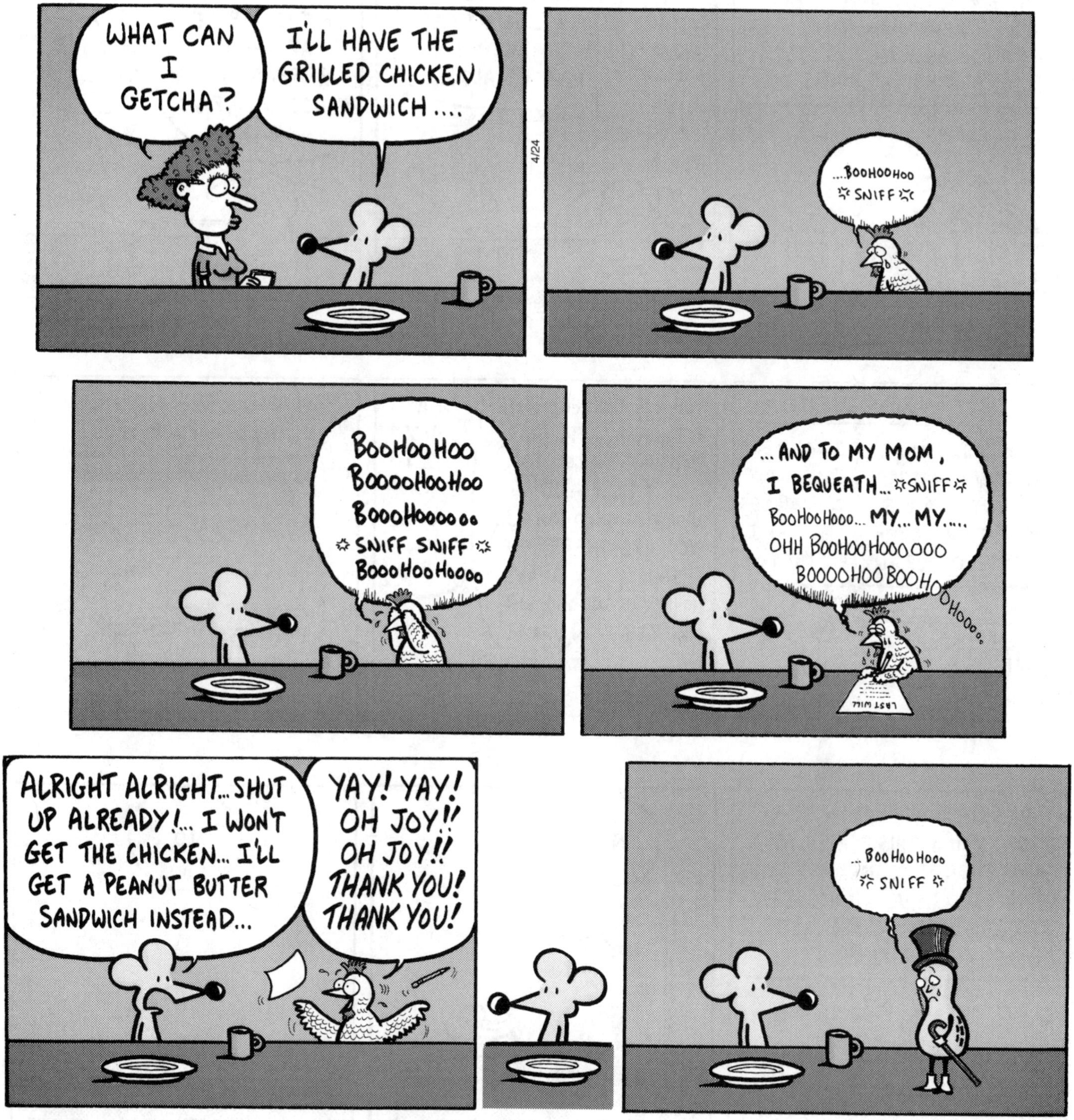

WHAT CAN I GETCHA?
I'LL HAVE THE GRILLED CHICKEN SANDWICH....
4/24
....BOOHOOHOO SNIFF
BOOHOOHOO BOOOOHOOHOO BOOOHOOOOOOO SNIFF SNIFF BOOOHOOHOOOO
...AND TO MY MOM, I BEQUEATH... SNIFF BOOHOOHOOO... MY... MY..... OHH BOOHOOHOOOOOO BOOOOHOO BOOHOOHOOOOO
LAST WILL
ALRIGHT ALRIGHT... SHUT UP ALREADY!... I WON'T GET THE CHICKEN... I'LL GET A PEANUT BUTTER SANDWICH INSTEAD...
YAY! YAY! OH JOY!! OH JOY!! THANK YOU! THANK YOU!
...BOOHOOHOOO SNIFF

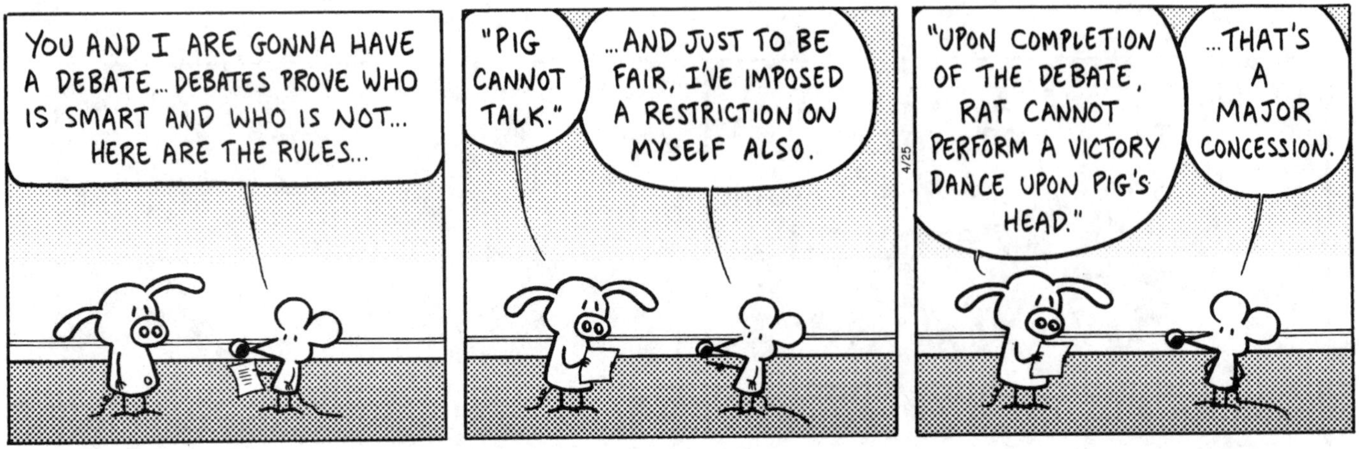
YOU AND I ARE GONNA HAVE A DEBATE... DEBATES PROVE WHO IS SMART AND WHO IS NOT... HERE ARE THE RULES...
"PIG CANNOT TALK."
...AND JUST TO BE FAIR, I'VE IMPOSED A RESTRICTION ON MYSELF ALSO.
4/25
"UPON COMPLETION OF THE DEBATE, RAT CANNOT PERFORM A VICTORY DANCE UPON PIG'S HEAD."
...THAT'S A MAJOR CONCESSION.

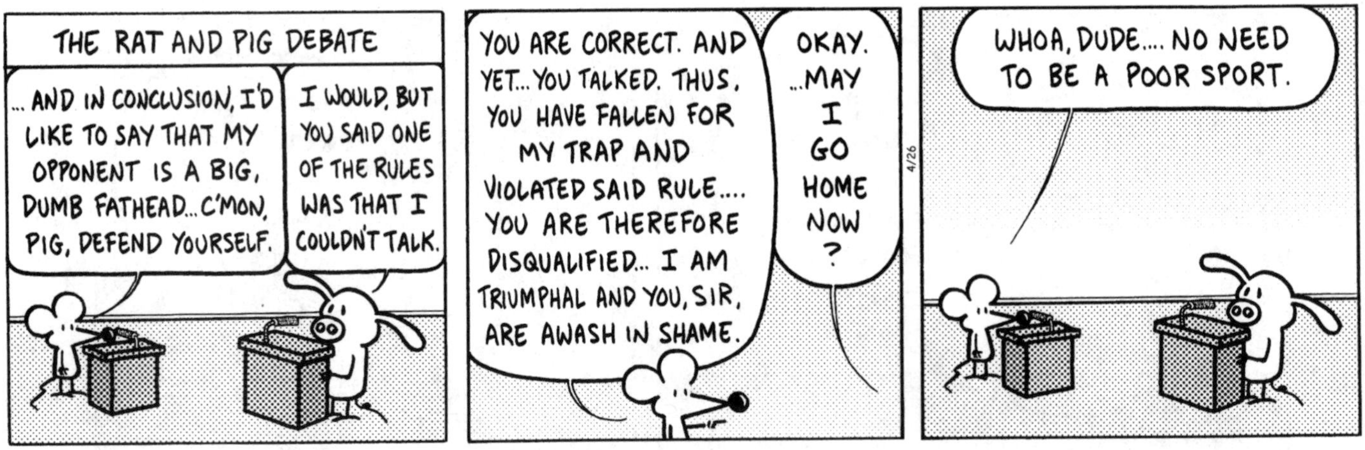
THE RAT AND PIG DEBATE
... AND IN CONCLUSION, I'D LIKE TO SAY THAT MY OPPONENT IS A BIG, DUMB FATHEAD... C'MON, PIG, DEFEND YOURSELF.
I WOULD, BUT YOU SAID ONE OF THE RULES WAS THAT I COULDN'T TALK.
YOU ARE CORRECT. AND YET... YOU TALKED. THUS, YOU HAVE FALLEN FOR MY TRAP AND VIOLATED SAID RULE.... YOU ARE THEREFORE DISQUALIFIED... I AM TRIUMPHAL AND YOU, SIR, ARE AWASH IN SHAME.
OKAY. ...MAY I GO HOME NOW ?
4/26
WHOA, DUDE.... NO NEED TO BE A POOR SPORT.

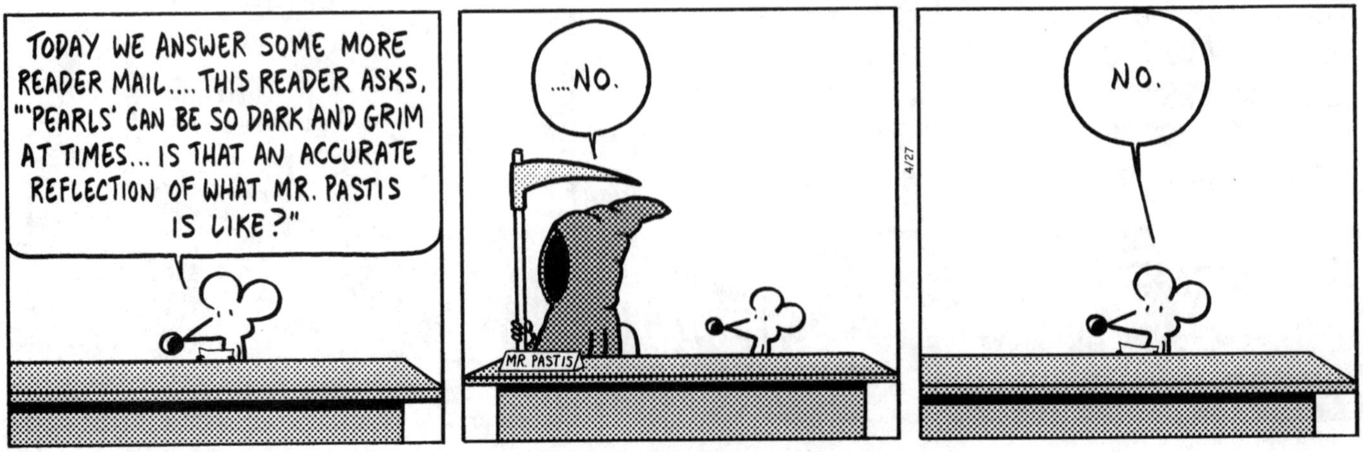
TODAY WE ANSWER SOME MORE READER MAIL.... THIS READER ASKS, "'PEARLS' CAN BE SO DARK AND GRIM AT TIMES... IS THAT AN ACCURATE REFLECTION OF WHAT MR. PASTIS IS LIKE?"
....NO.
MR. PASTIS
4/27
NO.

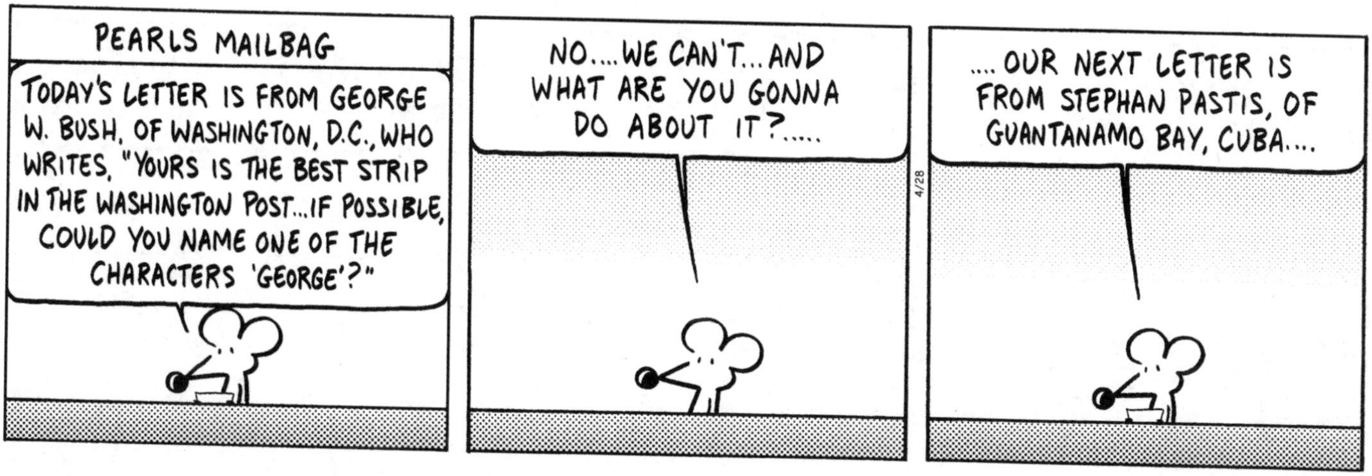
PEARLS MAILBAG
TODAY'S LETTER IS FROM GEORGE W. BUSH, OF WASHINGTON, D.C., WHO WRITES, "YOURS IS THE BEST STRIP IN THE WASHINGTON POST...IF POSSIBLE, COULD YOU NAME ONE OF THE CHARACTERS 'GEORGE'?"
NO....WE CAN'T...AND WHAT ARE YOU GONNA DO ABOUT IT?.....
4/28
....OUR NEXT LETTER IS FROM STEPHAN PASTIS, OF GUANTANAMO BAY, CUBA....

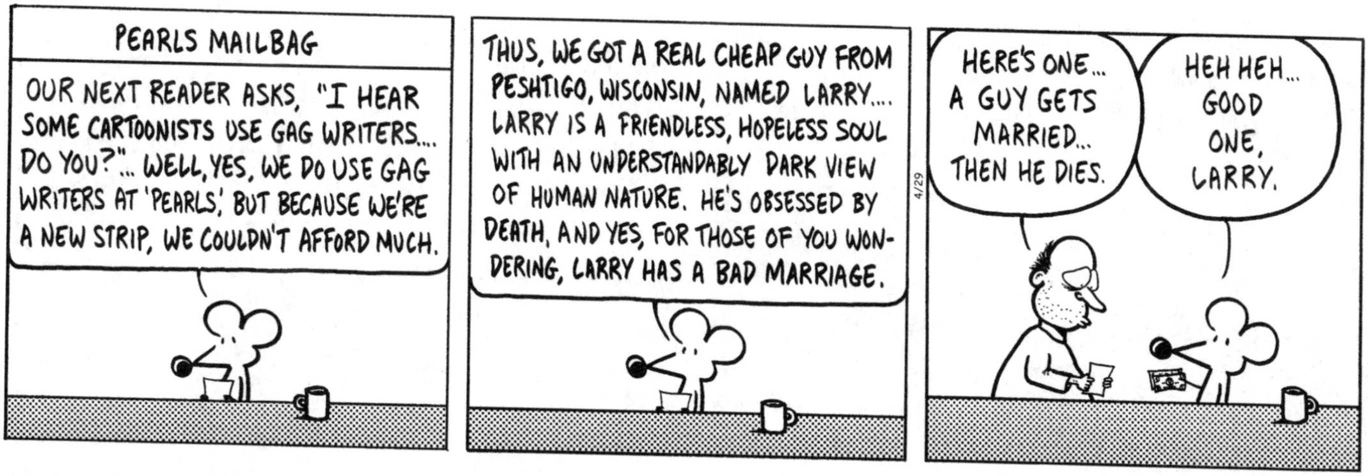
PEARLS MAILBAG
OUR NEXT READER ASKS, "I HEAR SOME CARTOONISTS USE GAG WRITERS... DO YOU?"... WELL, YES, WE DO USE GAG WRITERS AT 'PEARLS,' BUT BECAUSE WE'RE A NEW STRIP, WE COULDN'T AFFORD MUCH.
THUS, WE GOT A REAL CHEAP GUY FROM PESHTIGO, WISCONSIN, NAMED LARRY.... LARRY IS A FRIENDLESS, HOPELESS SOUL WITH AN UNDERSTANDABLY DARK VIEW OF HUMAN NATURE. HE'S OBSESSED BY DEATH, AND YES, FOR THOSE OF YOU WONDERING, LARRY HAS A BAD MARRIAGE.
4/29
HERE'S ONE... A GUY GETS MARRIED... THEN HE DIES.
HEH HEH... GOOD ONE, LARRY.

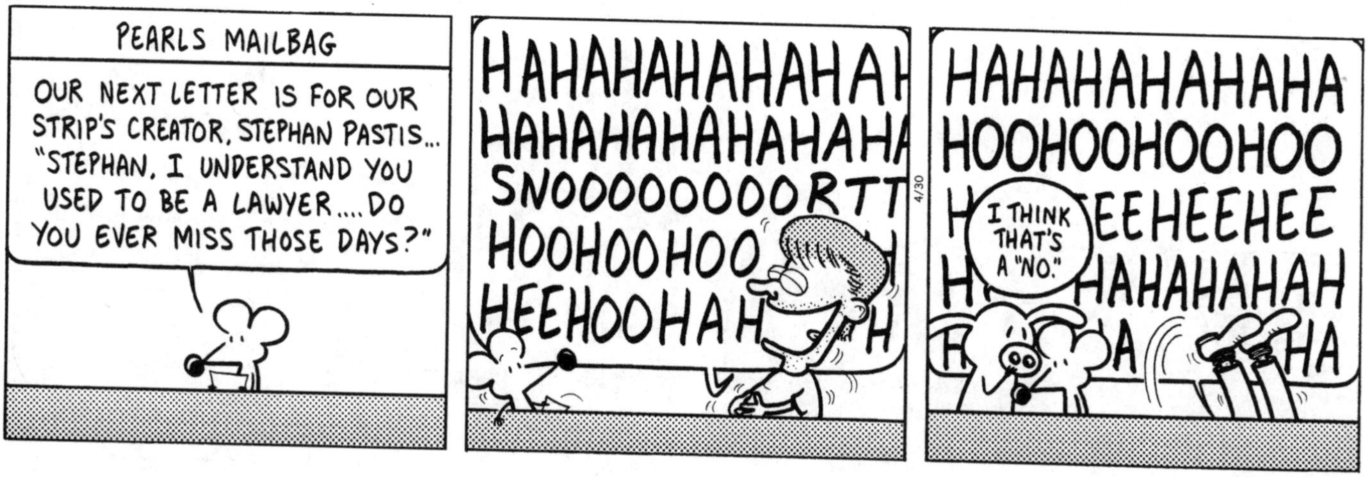
PEARLS MAILBAG
OUR NEXT LETTER IS FOR OUR STRIP'S CREATOR, STEPHAN PASTIS... "STEPHAN, I UNDERSTAND YOU USED TO BE A LAWYER....DO YOU EVER MISS THOSE DAYS?"
HAHAHAHAHAHAH
HAHAHAHAHAHAHA
SNOOOOOOOOORTT
HOOHOOHOO
HEEHOOHAH
4/30
HAHAHAHAHAHA
HOOHOOHOOHOO
EEHEEHEE
I THINK THAT'S A "NO."
HAHAHAHAH
HA

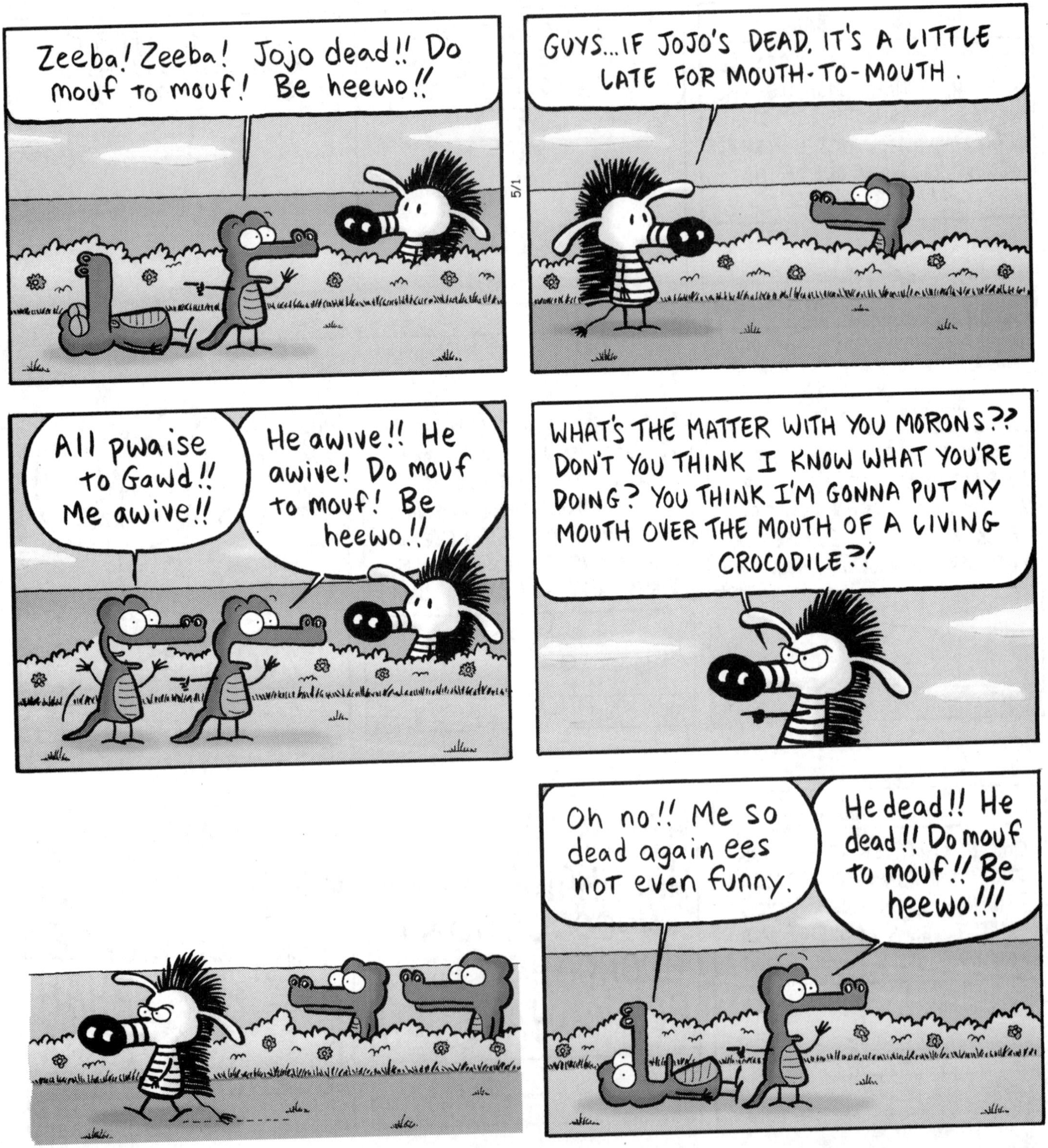
Zeeba! Zeeba! Jojo dead!! Do mouf to mouf! Be heewo!!
5/1
GUYS...IF JOJO'S DEAD, IT'S A LITTLE LATE FOR MOUTH-TO-MOUTH.
All pwaise to Gawd!! Me awive!!
He awive!! He awive! Do mouf to mouf! Be heewo!!
WHAT'S THE MATTER WITH YOU MORONS?? DON'T YOU THINK I KNOW WHAT YOU'RE DOING? YOU THINK I'M GONNA PUT MY MOUTH OVER THE MOUTH OF A LIVING CROCODILE?!
Oh no!! Me so dead again ees not even funny.
He dead!! He dead!! Do mouf to mouf!! Be heewo!!!

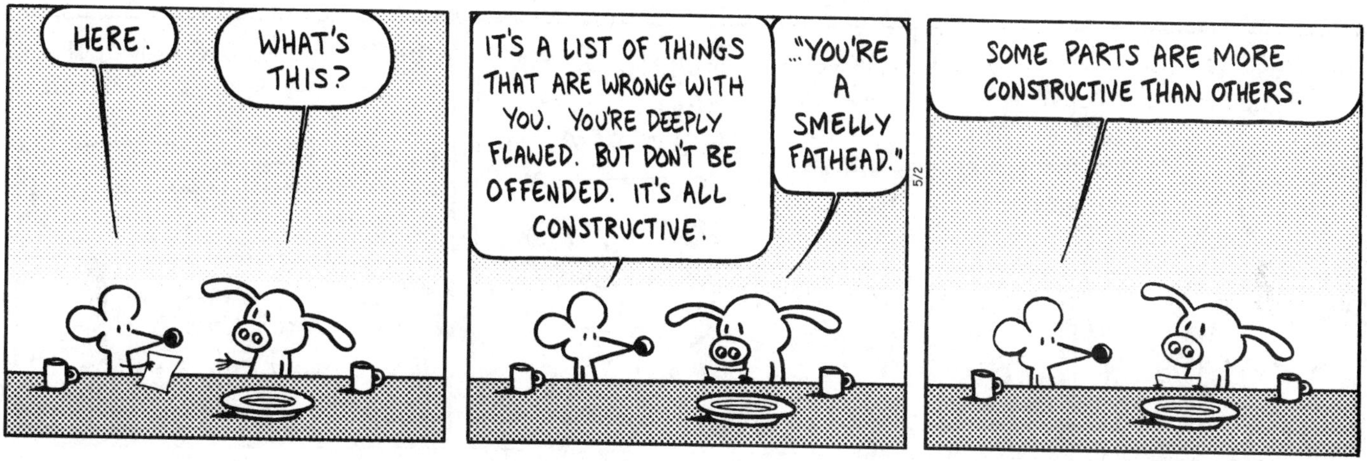
HERE.
WHAT'S THIS?
IT'S A LIST OF THINGS THAT ARE WRONG WITH YOU. YOU'RE DEEPLY FLAWED. BUT DON'T BE OFFENDED. IT'S ALL CONSTRUCTIVE.
..."YOU'RE A SMELLY FATHEAD."
5/2
SOME PARTS ARE MORE CONSTRUCTIVE THAN OTHERS.

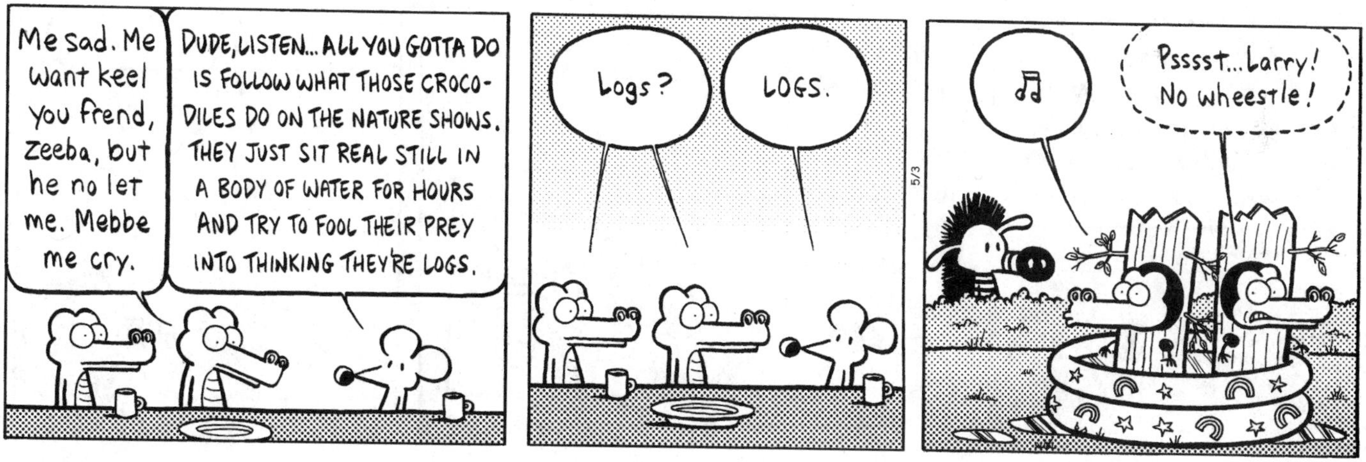
Me sad. Me want keel you frend, zeeba, but he no let me. Mebbe me cry.
DUDE, LISTEN... ALL YOU GOTTA DO IS FOLLOW WHAT THOSE CROCODILES DO ON THE NATURE SHOWS. THEY JUST SIT REAL STILL IN A BODY OF WATER FOR HOURS AND TRY TO FOOL THEIR PREY INTO THINKING THEY'RE LOGS.
Logs?
LOGS.
5/3
♫
Psssst... Larry! No wheestle!

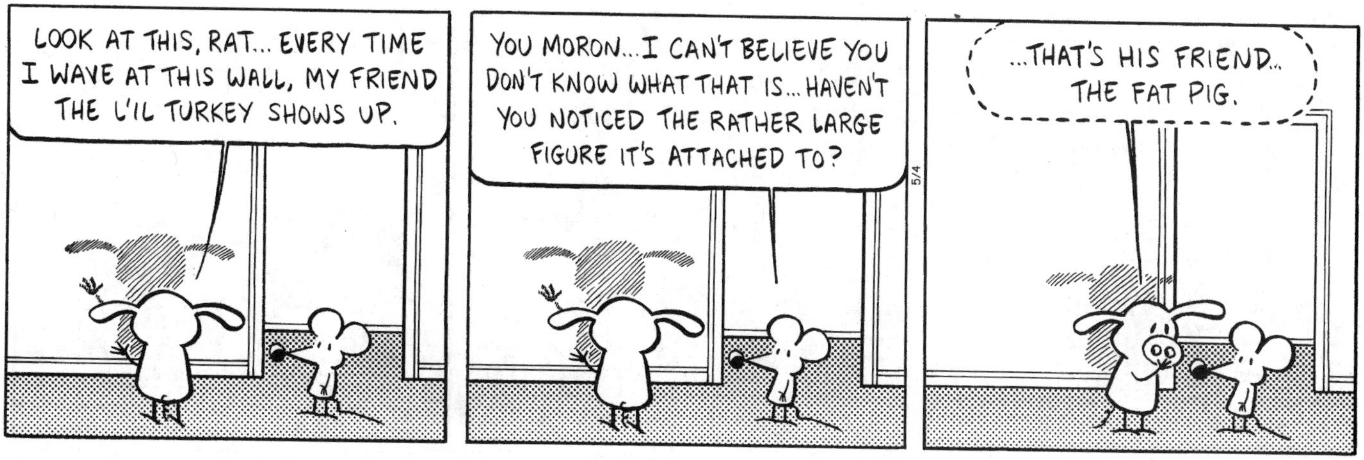
LOOK AT THIS, RAT... EVERY TIME I WAVE AT THIS WALL, MY FRIEND THE L'IL TURKEY SHOWS UP.
YOU MORON... I CAN'T BELIEVE YOU DON'T KNOW WHAT THAT IS... HAVEN'T YOU NOTICED THE RATHER LARGE FIGURE IT'S ATTACHED TO?
5/4
...THAT'S HIS FRIEND.. THE FAT PIG.

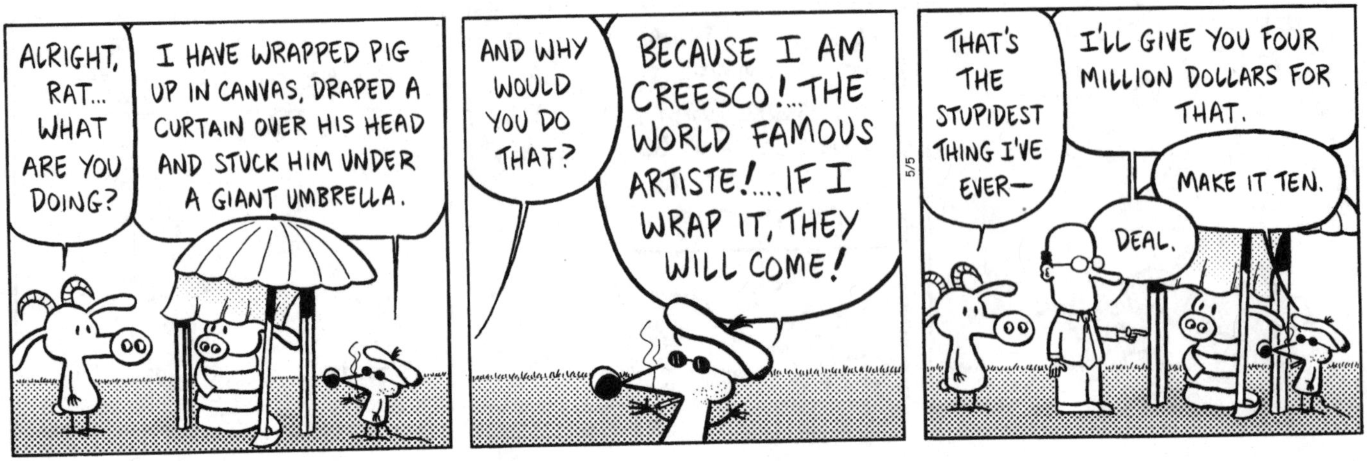
ALRIGHT, RAT... WHAT ARE YOU DOING?
I HAVE WRAPPED PIG UP IN CANVAS, DRAPED A CURTAIN OVER HIS HEAD AND STUCK HIM UNDER A GIANT UMBRELLA.
AND WHY WOULD YOU DO THAT?
BECAUSE I AM CREESCO!...THE WORLD FAMOUS ARTISTE!....IF I WRAP IT, THEY WILL COME!
5/5
THAT'S THE STUPIDEST THING I'VE EVER—
I'LL GIVE YOU FOUR MILLION DOLLARS FOR THAT.
DEAL.
MAKE IT TEN.

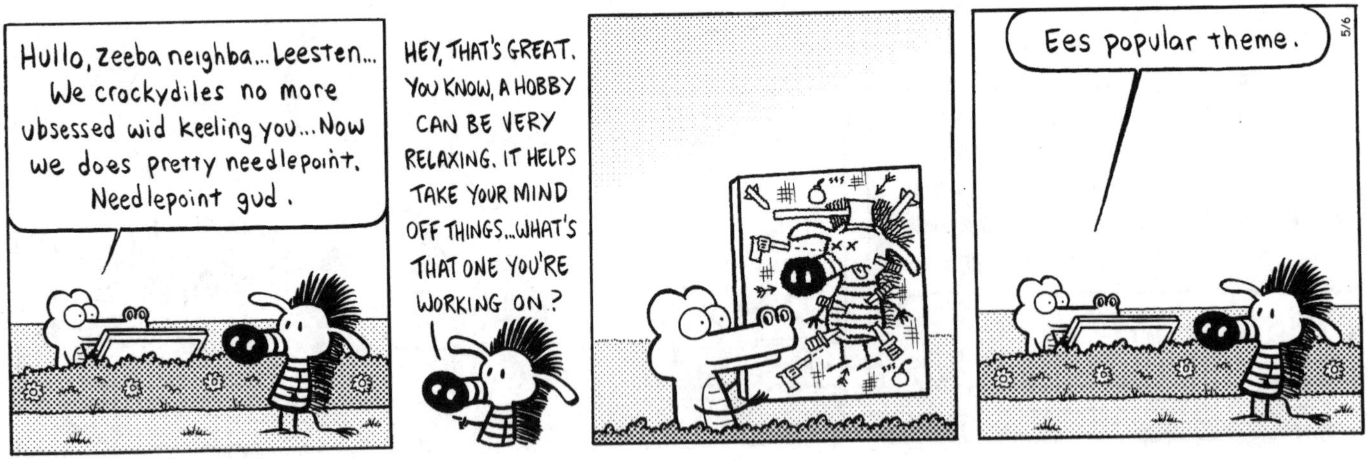
Hullo, zeeba neighba... Leesten... We crockydiles no more ubsessed wid keeling you... Now we does pretty needlepoint. Needlepoint gud.
HEY, THAT'S GREAT. YOU KNOW, A HOBBY CAN BE VERY RELAXING. IT HELPS TAKE YOUR MIND OFF THINGS...WHAT'S THAT ONE YOU'RE WORKING ON?
Ees popular theme.
5/6

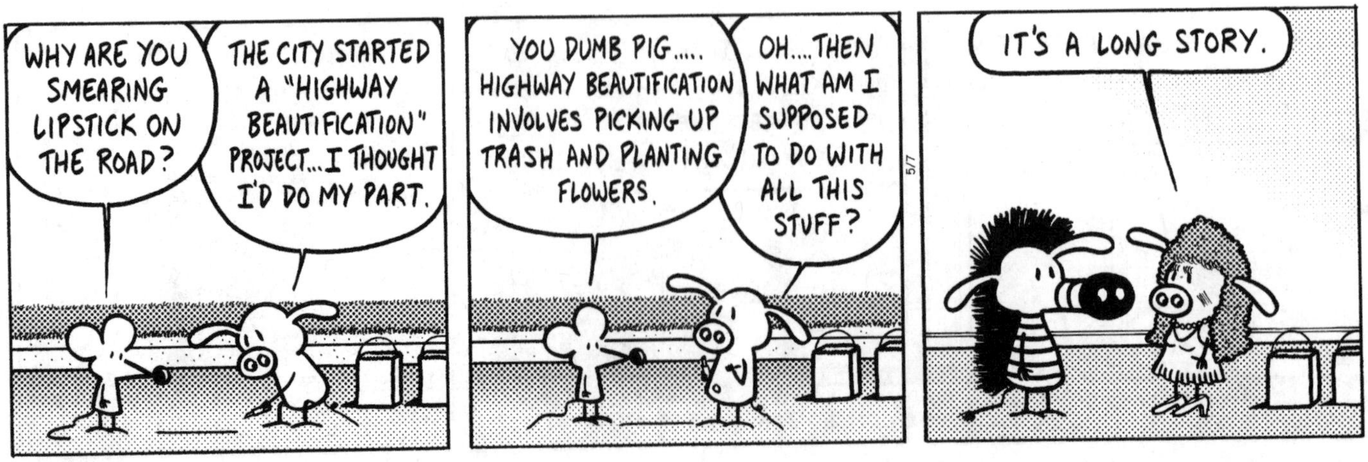
WHY ARE YOU SMEARING LIPSTICK ON THE ROAD?
THE CITY STARTED A "HIGHWAY BEAUTIFICATION" PROJECT...I THOUGHT I'D DO MY PART.
YOU DUMB PIG..... HIGHWAY BEAUTIFICATION INVOLVES PICKING UP TRASH AND PLANTING FLOWERS.
OH....THEN WHAT AM I SUPPOSED TO DO WITH ALL THIS STUFF?
5/7
IT'S A LONG STORY.

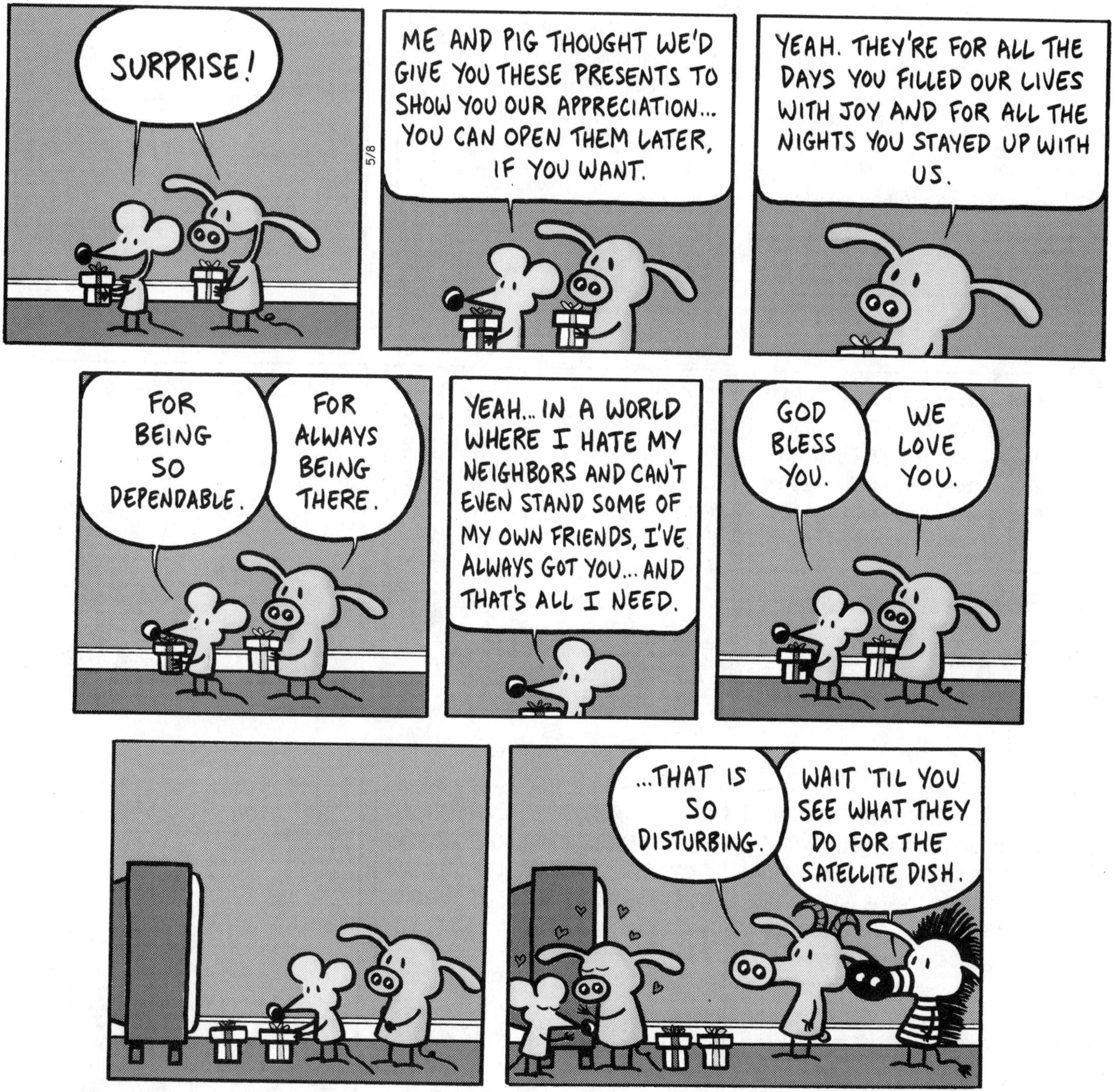
SURPRISE!
5/8
ME AND PIG THOUGHT WE'D GIVE YOU THESE PRESENTS TO SHOW YOU OUR APPRECIATION... YOU CAN OPEN THEM LATER, IF YOU WANT.
YEAH. THEY'RE FOR ALL THE DAYS YOU FILLED OUR LIVES WITH JOY AND FOR ALL THE NIGHTS YOU STAYED UP WITH US.
FOR BEING SO DEPENDABLE.
FOR ALWAYS BEING THERE.
YEAH... IN A WORLD WHERE I HATE MY NEIGHBORS AND CAN'T EVEN STAND SOME OF MY OWN FRIENDS, I'VE ALWAYS GOT YOU... AND THAT'S ALL I NEED.
GOD BLESS YOU.
WE LOVE YOU.
...THAT IS SO DISTURBING.
WAIT 'TIL YOU SEE WHAT THEY DO FOR THE SATELLITE DISH.

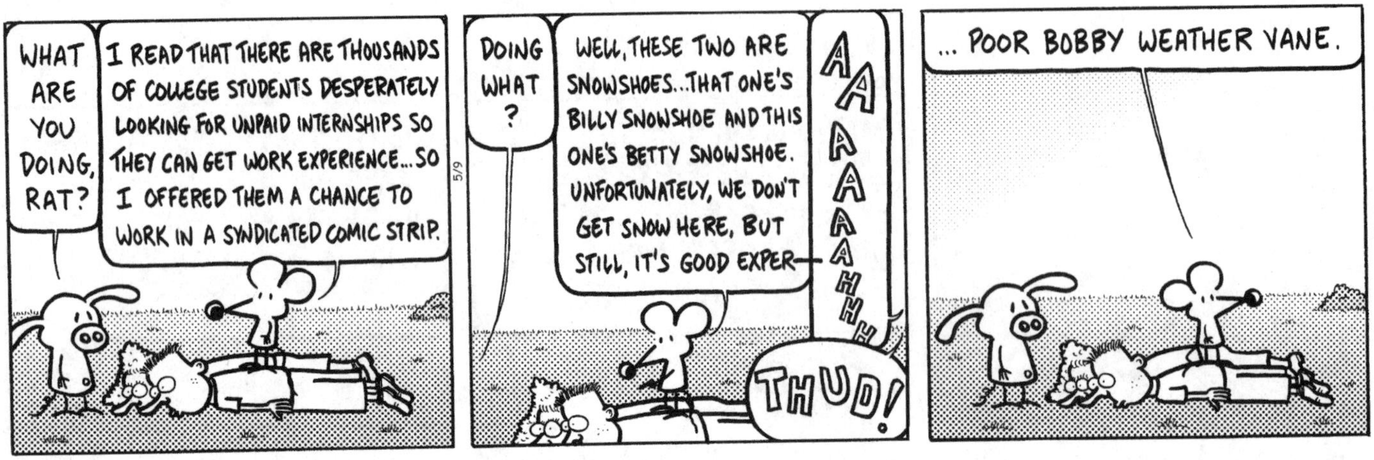
WHAT ARE YOU DOING, RAT?
I READ THAT THERE ARE THOUSANDS OF COLLEGE STUDENTS DESPERATELY LOOKING FOR UNPAID INTERNSHIPS SO THEY CAN GET WORK EXPERIENCE... SO I OFFERED THEM A CHANCE TO WORK IN A SYNDICATED COMIC STRIP.
5/9
DOING WHAT ?
WELL, THESE TWO ARE SNOWSHOES... THAT ONE'S BILLY SNOWSHOE AND THIS ONE'S BETTY SNOWSHOE. UNFORTUNATELY, WE DON'T GET SNOW HERE, BUT STILL, IT'S GOOD EXPER–
AAAAAAAHHH
THUD!
... POOR BOBBY WEATHER VANE.

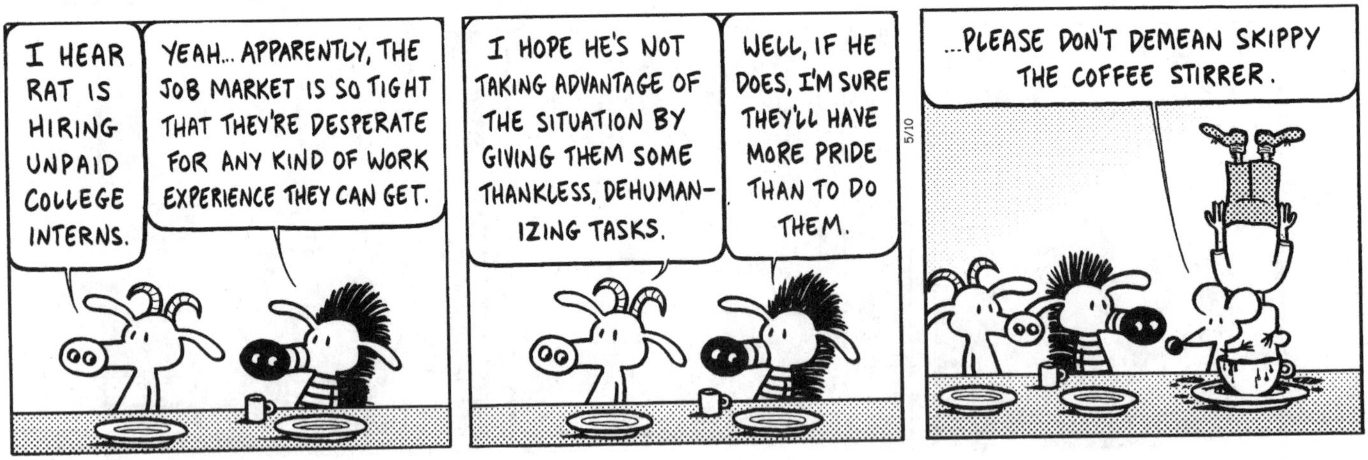
I HEAR RAT IS HIRING UNPAID COLLEGE INTERNS.
YEAH... APPARENTLY, THE JOB MARKET IS SO TIGHT THAT THEY'RE DESPERATE FOR ANY KIND OF WORK EXPERIENCE THEY CAN GET.
5/10
I HOPE HE'S NOT TAKING ADVANTAGE OF THE SITUATION BY GIVING THEM SOME THANKLESS, DEHUMANIZING TASKS.
WELL, IF HE DOES, I'M SURE THEY'LL HAVE MORE PRIDE THAN TO DO THEM.
...PLEASE DON'T DEMEAN SKIPPY THE COFFEE STIRRER.

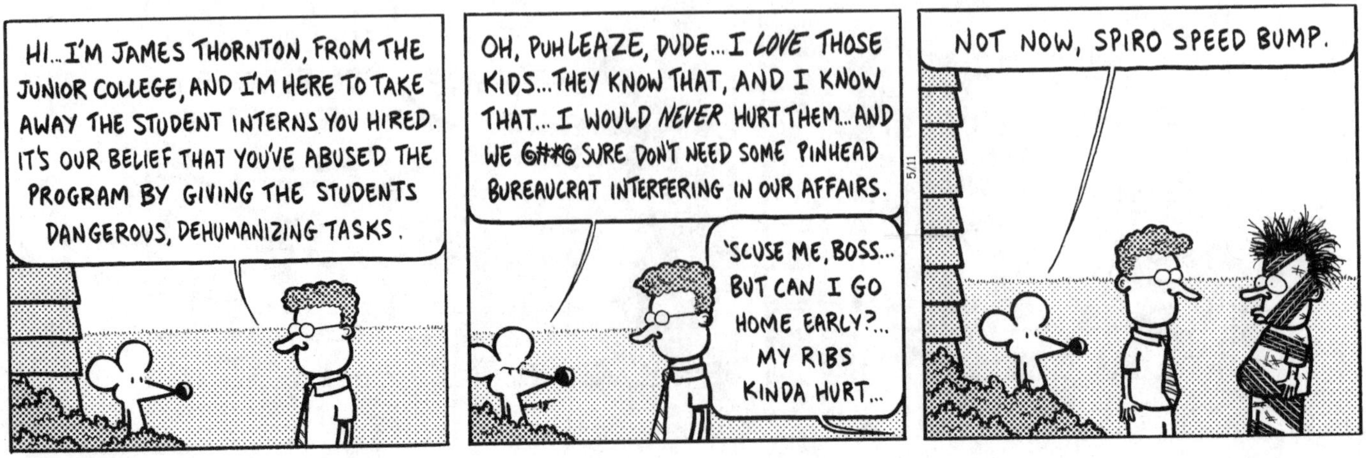
HI... I'M JAMES THORNTON, FROM THE JUNIOR COLLEGE, AND I'M HERE TO TAKE AWAY THE STUDENT INTERNS YOU HIRED. IT'S OUR BELIEF THAT YOU'VE ABUSED THE PROGRAM BY GIVING THE STUDENTS DANGEROUS, DEHUMANIZING TASKS.
5/11
OH, PUHLEAZE, DUDE... I LOVE THOSE KIDS... THEY KNOW THAT, AND I KNOW THAT... I WOULD NEVER HURT THEM... AND WE @#*@ SURE DON'T NEED SOME PINHEAD BUREAUCRAT INTERFERING IN OUR AFFAIRS.
'SCUSE ME, BOSS... BUT CAN I GO HOME EARLY?... MY RIBS KINDA HURT...
NOT NOW, SPIRO SPEED BUMP.

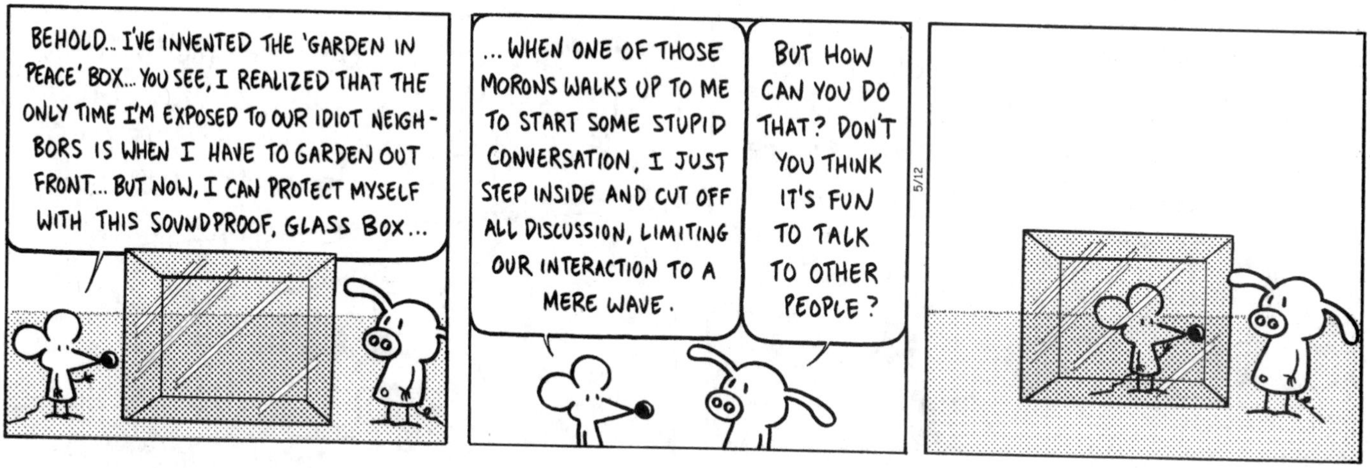
BEHOLD.. I'VE INVENTED THE 'GARDEN IN PEACE' BOX... YOU SEE, I REALIZED THAT THE ONLY TIME I'M EXPOSED TO OUR IDIOT NEIGH-BORS IS WHEN I HAVE TO GARDEN OUT FRONT... BUT NOW, I CAN PROTECT MYSELF WITH THIS SOUNDPROOF, GLASS BOX...
...WHEN ONE OF THOSE MORONS WALKS UP TO ME TO START SOME STUPID CONVERSATION, I JUST STEP INSIDE AND CUT OFF ALL DISCUSSION, LIMITING OUR INTERACTION TO A MERE WAVE.
BUT HOW CAN YOU DO THAT? DON'T YOU THINK IT'S FUN TO TALK TO OTHER PEOPLE?
5/12

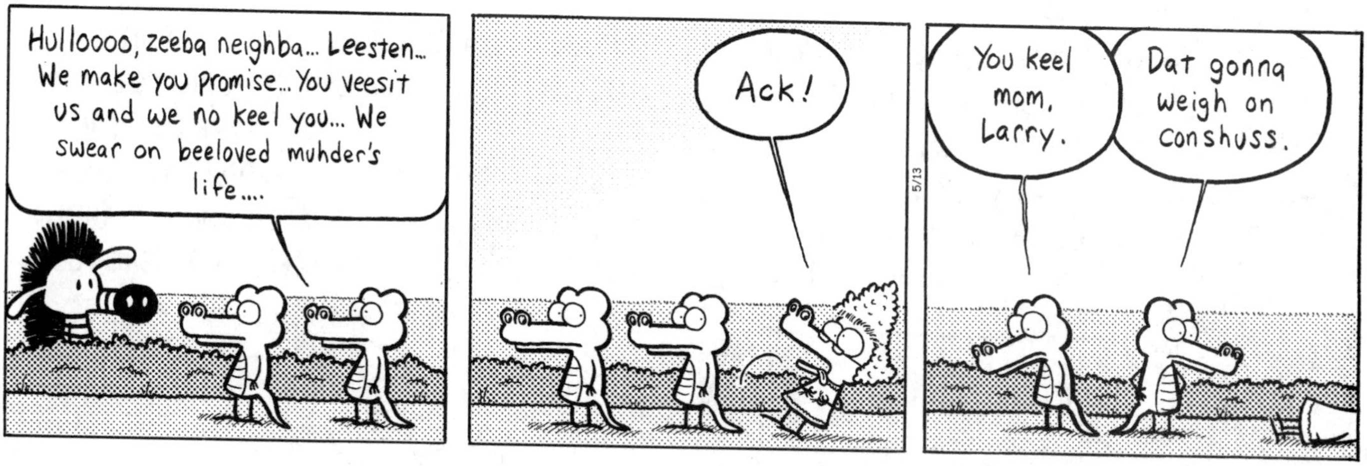
Hulloooo, zeeba neighba... Leesten... We make you promise... You veesit us and we no keel you... We swear on beeloved muhder's life....
Ack!
5/13
You keel mom, Larry.
Dat gonna weigh on conshuss.

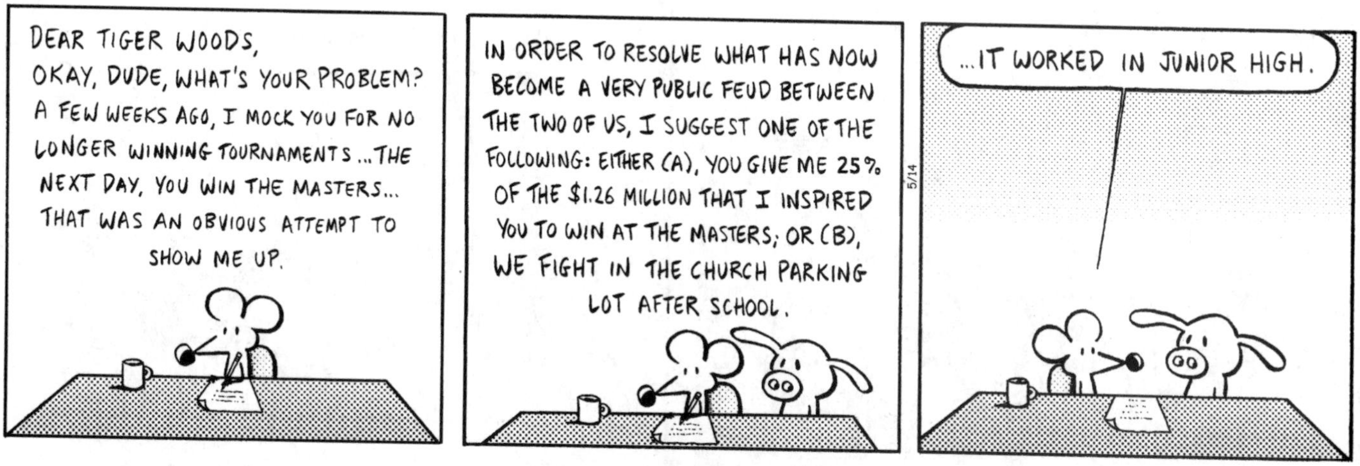
DEAR TIGER WOODS,
OKAY, DUDE, WHAT'S YOUR PROBLEM? A FEW WEEKS AGO, I MOCK YOU FOR NO LONGER WINNING TOURNAMENTS ...THE NEXT DAY, YOU WIN THE MASTERS... THAT WAS AN OBVIOUS ATTEMPT TO SHOW ME UP.
IN ORDER TO RESOLVE WHAT HAS NOW BECOME A VERY PUBLIC FEUD BETWEEN THE TWO OF US, I SUGGEST ONE OF THE FOLLOWING: EITHER (A), YOU GIVE ME 25% OF THE $1.26 MILLION THAT I INSPIRED YOU TO WIN AT THE MASTERS; OR (B), WE FIGHT IN THE CHURCH PARKING LOT AFTER SCHOOL.
5/14
...IT WORKED IN JUNIOR HIGH.

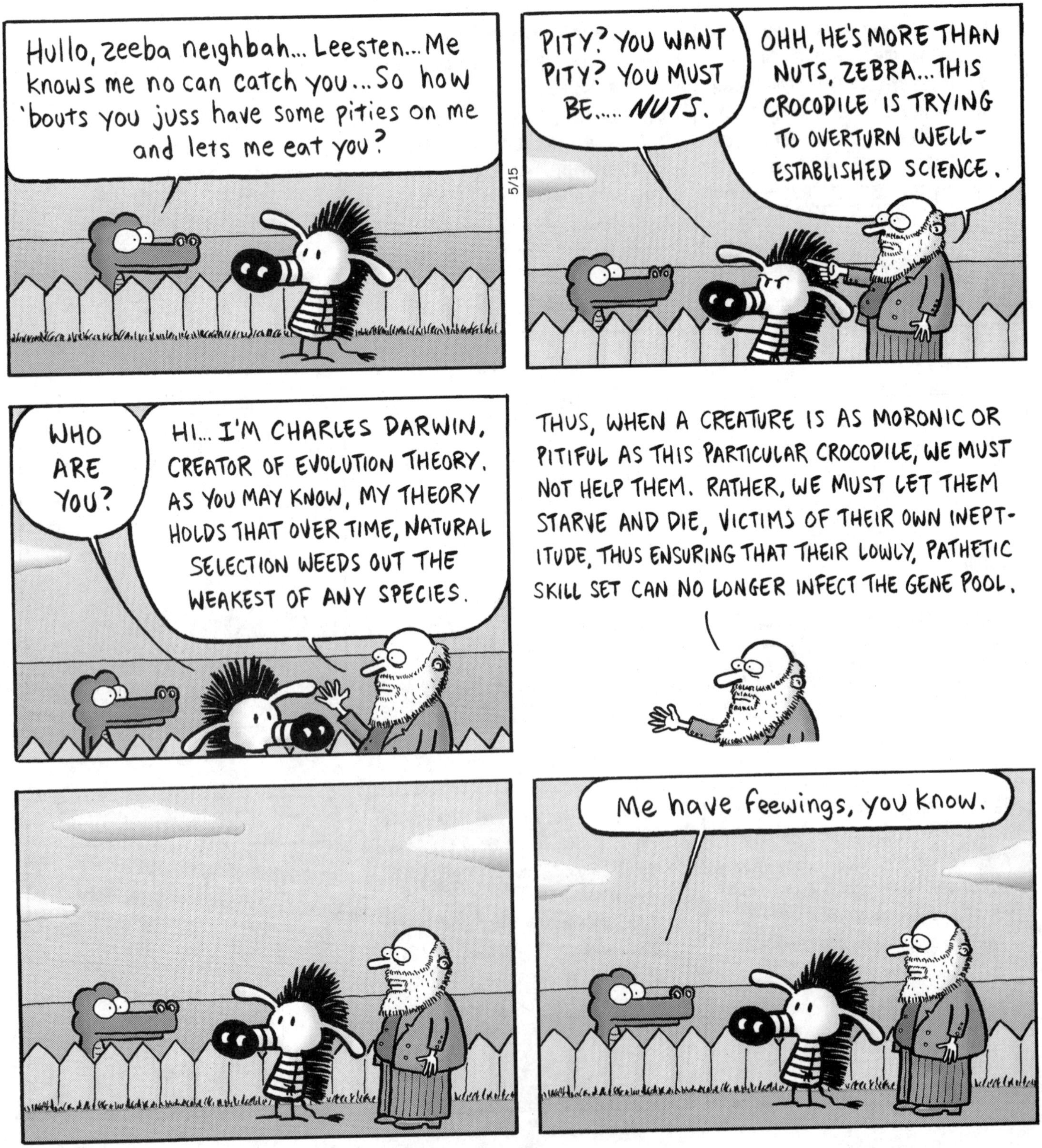
Hullo, zeeba neighbah... Leesten... Me knows me no can catch you... So how 'bouts you juss have some pities on me and lets me eat you?
5/15
PITY? YOU WANT PITY? YOU MUST BE..... NUTS.
OHH, HE'S MORE THAN NUTS, ZEBRA...THIS CROCODILE IS TRYING TO OVERTURN WELL-ESTABLISHED SCIENCE.
WHO ARE YOU?
HI... I'M CHARLES DARWIN, CREATOR OF EVOLUTION THEORY. AS YOU MAY KNOW, MY THEORY HOLDS THAT OVER TIME, NATURAL SELECTION WEEDS OUT THE WEAKEST OF ANY SPECIES.
THUS, WHEN A CREATURE IS AS MORONIC OR PITIFUL AS THIS PARTICULAR CROCODILE, WE MUST NOT HELP THEM. RATHER, WE MUST LET THEM STARVE AND DIE, VICTIMS OF THEIR OWN INEPT-ITUDE, THUS ENSURING THAT THEIR LOWLY, PATHETIC SKILL SET CAN NO LONGER INFECT THE GENE POOL.
Me have feewings, you know.

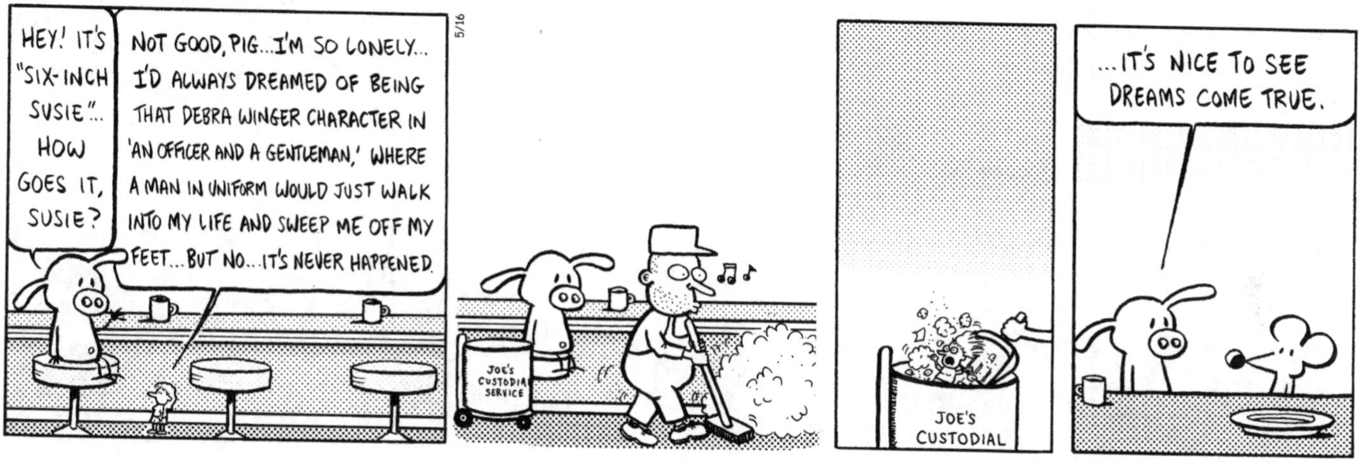
HEY! IT'S "SIX-INCH SUSIE"... HOW GOES IT, SUSIE?
NOT GOOD, PIG...I'M SO LONELY... I'D ALWAYS DREAMED OF BEING THAT DEBRA WINGER CHARACTER IN 'AN OFFICER AND A GENTLEMAN,' WHERE A MAN IN UNIFORM WOULD JUST WALK INTO MY LIFE AND SWEEP ME OFF MY FEET...BUT NO...IT'S NEVER HAPPENED.
5/16
JOE'S CUSTODIAL SERVICE
JOE'S CUSTODIAL
...IT'S NICE TO SEE DREAMS COME TRUE.

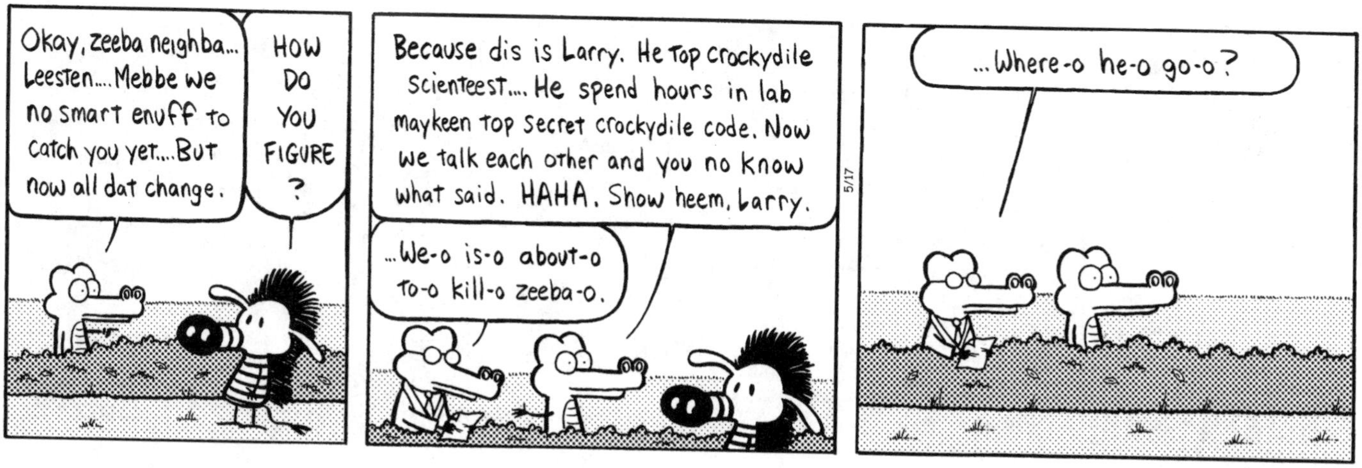
Okay, zeeba neighba... Leesten.... Mebbe we no smart enuff to catch you yet....But now all dat change.
HOW DO YOU FIGURE?
Because dis is Larry. He top crockydile Scienteest.... He spend hours in lab maykeen top secret crockydile code. Now we talk each other and you no know what said. HAHA. Show heem, Larry.
...We-o is-o about-o to-o kill-o zeeba-o.
5/17
...Where-o he-o go-o?

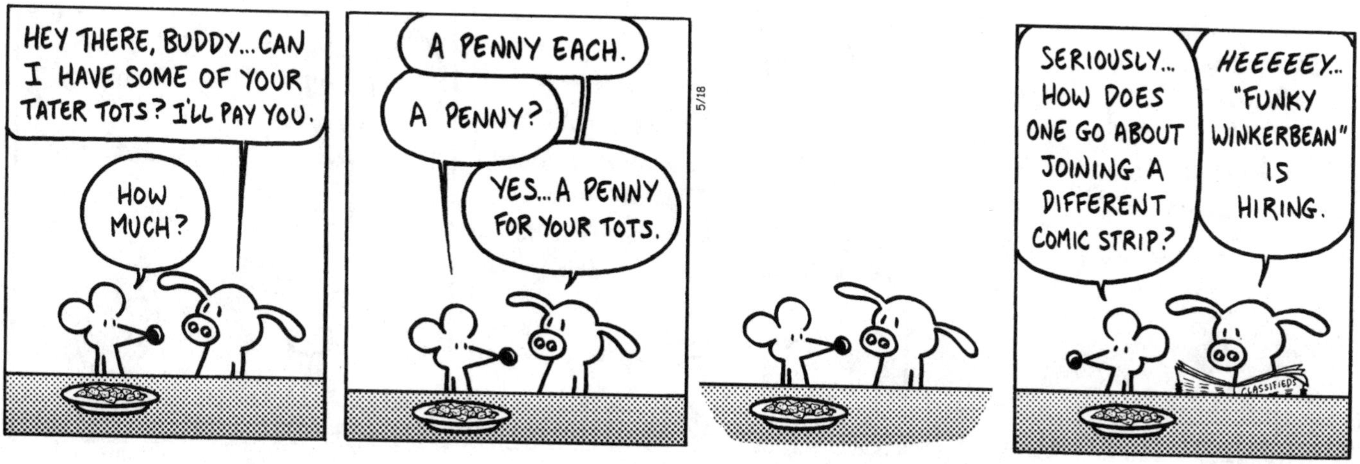
HEY THERE, BUDDY...CAN I HAVE SOME OF YOUR TATER TOTS? I'LL PAY YOU.
HOW MUCH?
A PENNY EACH.
A PENNY?
YES...A PENNY FOR YOUR TOTS.
5/18
SERIOUSLY... HOW DOES ONE GO ABOUT JOINING A DIFFERENT COMIC STRIP?
HEEEEEY... "FUNKY WINKERBEAN" IS HIRING.
CLASSIFIEDS

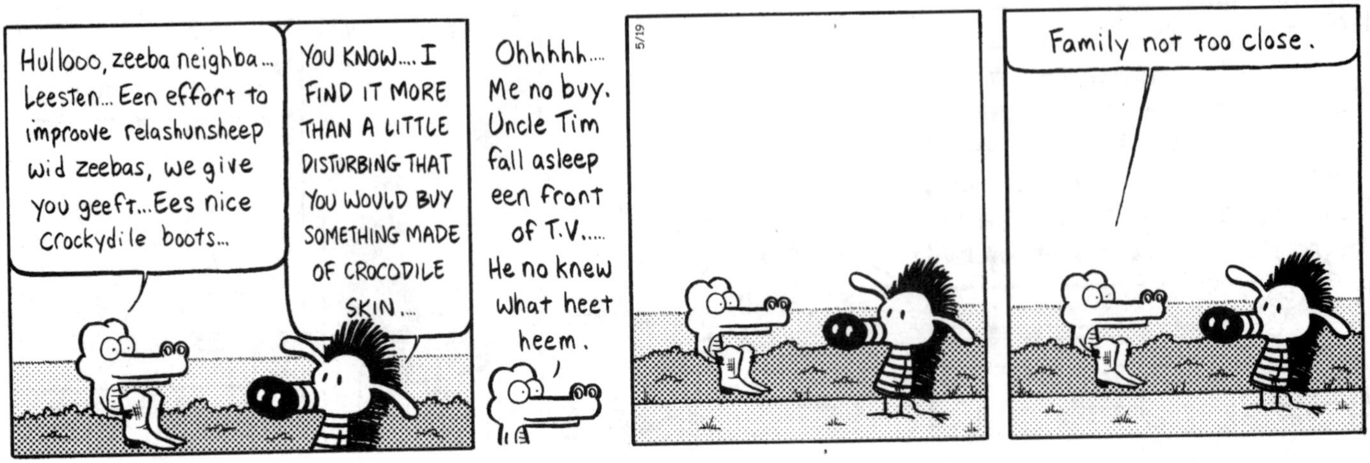
Hulloo, zeeba neighba... Leesten... Een effort to improove relashunsheep wid zeebas, we give you geeft...Ees nice Crockydile boots...
YOU KNOW.... I FIND IT MORE THAN A LITTLE DISTURBING THAT YOU WOULD BUY SOMETHING MADE OF CROCODILE SKIN....
Ohhhhh.... Me no buy. Uncle Tim fall asleep een front of T.V..... He no knew what heet heem.
5/19
Family not too close.

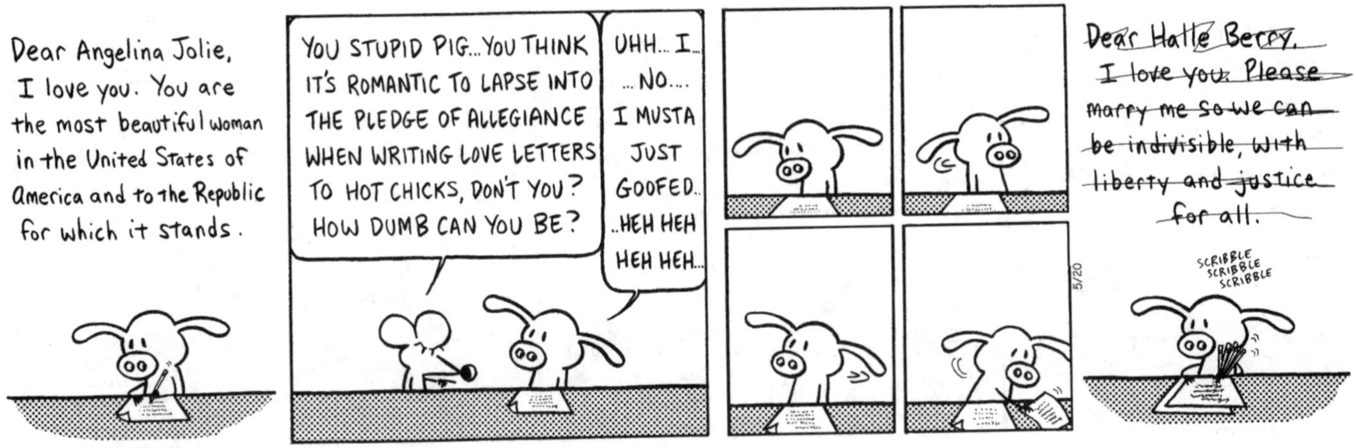
Dear Angelina Jolie, I love you. You are the most beautiful woman in the United States of America and to the Republic for which it stands.
YOU STUPID PIG...YOU THINK IT'S ROMANTIC TO LAPSE INTO THE PLEDGE OF ALLEGIANCE WHEN WRITING LOVE LETTERS TO HOT CHICKS, DON'T YOU? HOW DUMB CAN YOU BE?
UHH... I... ...NO.... I MUSTA JUST GOOFED.. ..HEH HEH HEH HEH...
5/20
Dear Halle Berry, I love you. Please marry me so we can be indivisible, with liberty and justice for all.
SCRIBBLE SCRIBBLE SCRIBBLE

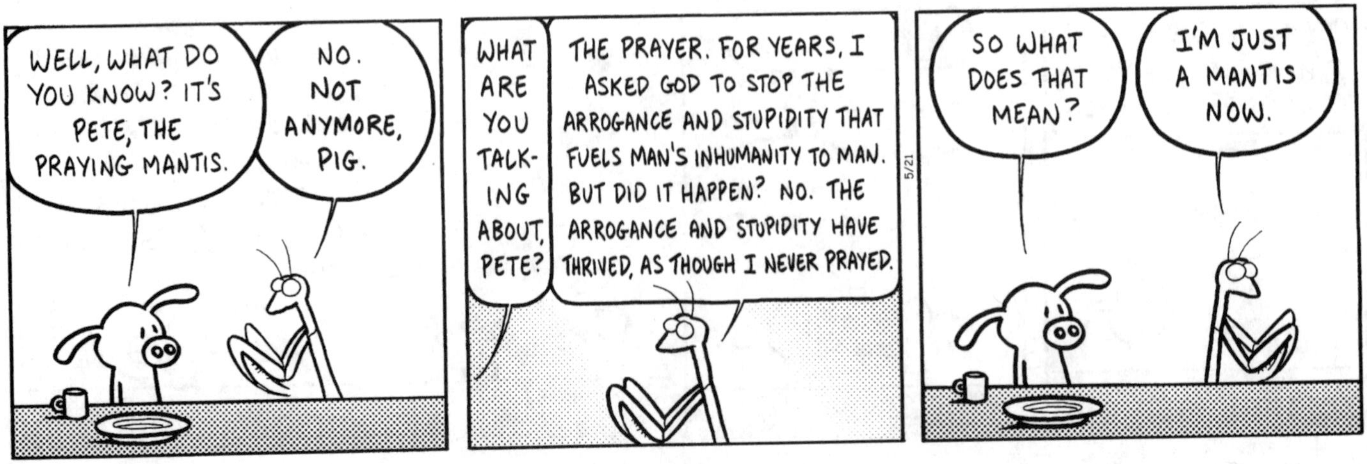
WELL, WHAT DO YOU KNOW? IT'S PETE, THE PRAYING MANTIS.
NO. NOT ANYMORE, PIG.
WHAT ARE YOU TALK-ING ABOUT, PETE?
THE PRAYER. FOR YEARS, I ASKED GOD TO STOP THE ARROGANCE AND STUPIDITY THAT FUELS MAN'S INHUMANITY TO MAN. BUT DID IT HAPPEN? NO. THE ARROGANCE AND STUPIDITY HAVE THRIVED, AS THOUGH I NEVER PRAYED.
5/21
SO WHAT DOES THAT MEAN?
I'M JUST A MANTIS NOW.

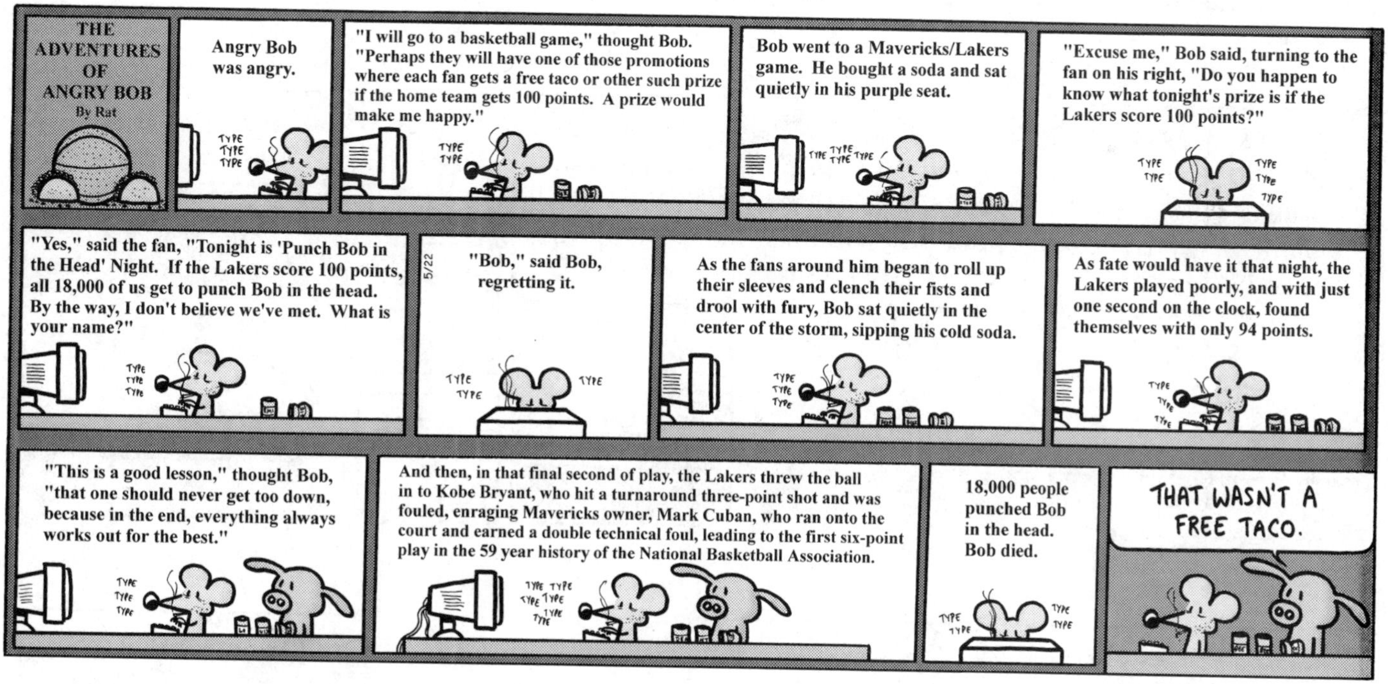
THE ADVENTURES OF ANGRY BOB
By Rat
Angry Bob was angry.
TYPE TYPE TYPE
"I will go to a basketball game," thought Bob. "Perhaps they will have one of those promotions where each fan gets a free taco or other such prize if the home team gets 100 points. A prize would make me happy."
TYPE TYPE
Bob went to a Mavericks/Lakers game. He bought a soda and sat quietly in his purple seat.
TYPE TYPE TYPE TYPE
"Excuse me," Bob said, turning to the fan on his right, "Do you happen to know what tonight's prize is if the Lakers score 100 points?"
TYPE TYPE TYPE TYPE TYPE
"Yes," said the fan, "Tonight is 'Punch Bob in the Head' Night. If the Lakers score 100 points, all 18,000 of us get to punch Bob in the head. By the way, I don't believe we've met. What is your name?"
TYPE TYPE TYPE
5/22
"Bob," said Bob, regretting it.
TYPE TYPE TYPE
As the fans around him began to roll up their sleeves and clench their fists and drool with fury, Bob sat quietly in the center of the storm, sipping his cold soda.
TYPE TYPE TYPE
As fate would have it that night, the Lakers played poorly, and with just one second on the clock, found themselves with only 94 points.
TYPE TYPE TYPE
"This is a good lesson," thought Bob, "that one should never get too down, because in the end, everything always works out for the best."
TYPE TYPE TYPE
And then, in that final second of play, the Lakers threw the ball in to Kobe Bryant, who hit a turnaround three-point shot and was fouled, enraging Mavericks owner, Mark Cuban, who ran onto the court and earned a double technical foul, leading to the first six-point play in the 59 year history of the National Basketball Association.
TYPE TYPE TYPE TYPE TYPE TYPE
18,000 people punched Bob in the head. Bob died.
TYPE TYPE TYPE TYPE
THAT WASN'T A FREE TACO.

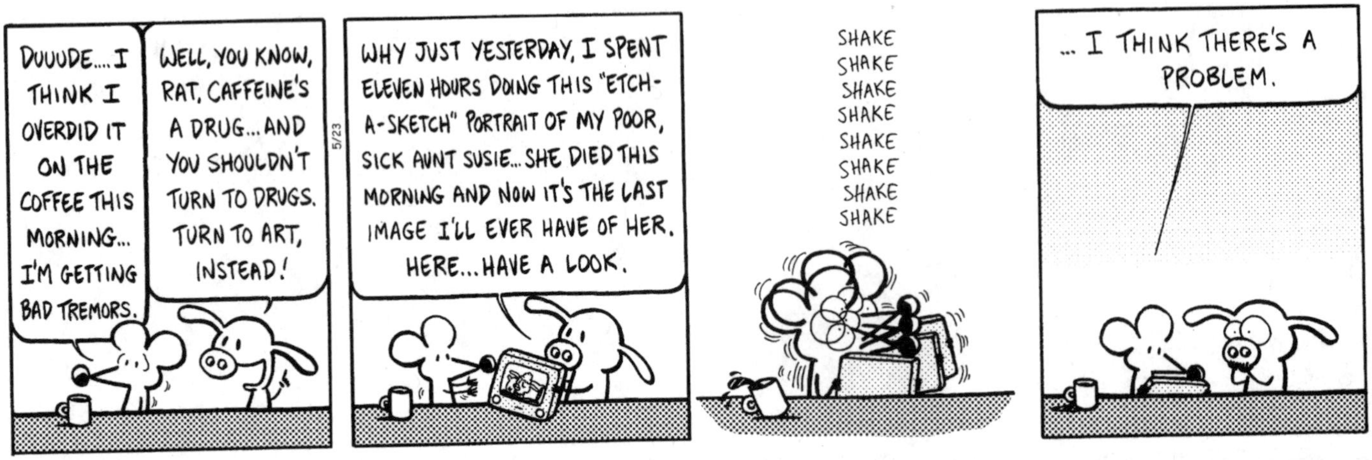
DUUUDE.... I THINK I OVERDID IT ON THE COFFEE THIS MORNING... I'M GETTING BAD TREMORS.
WELL, YOU KNOW, RAT, CAFFEINE'S A DRUG... AND YOU SHOULDN'T TURN TO DRUGS. TURN TO ART, INSTEAD!
5/23
WHY JUST YESTERDAY, I SPENT ELEVEN HOURS DOING THIS "ETCH-A-SKETCH" PORTRAIT OF MY POOR, SICK AUNT SUSIE... SHE DIED THIS MORNING AND NOW IT'S THE LAST IMAGE I'LL EVER HAVE OF HER. HERE... HAVE A LOOK.
SHAKE SHAKE SHAKE SHAKE SHAKE SHAKE SHAKE SHAKE
... I THINK THERE'S A PROBLEM.

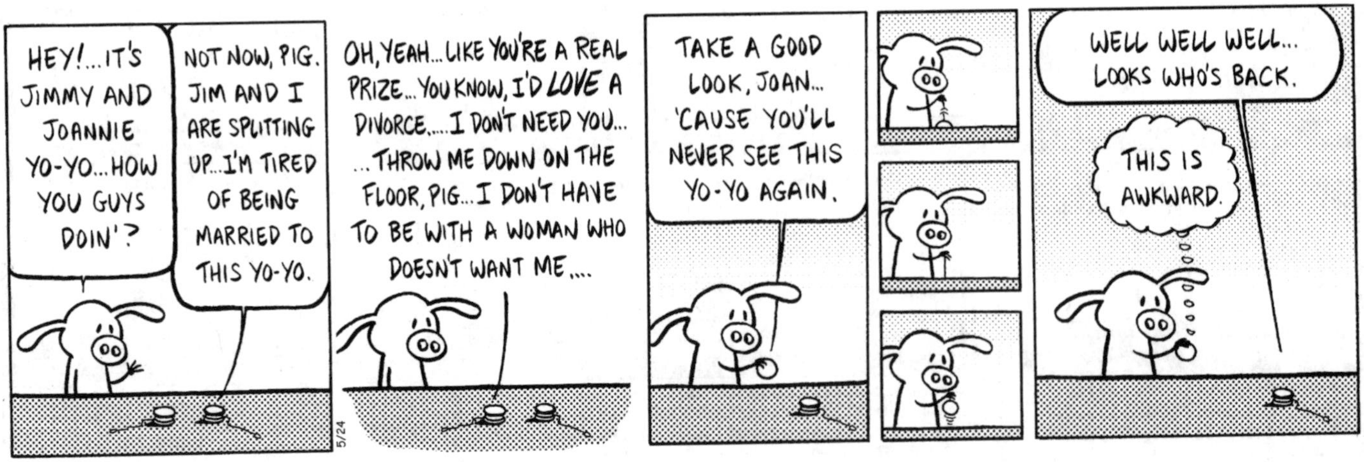
HEY!... IT'S JIMMY AND JOANNIE YO-YO... HOW YOU GUYS DOIN'?
NOT NOW, PIG. JIM AND I ARE SPLITTING UP... I'M TIRED OF BEING MARRIED TO THIS YO-YO.
OH, YEAH... LIKE YOU'RE A REAL PRIZE... YOU KNOW, I'D *LOVE* A DIVORCE..... I DON'T NEED YOU... ...THROW ME DOWN ON THE FLOOR, PIG... I DON'T HAVE TO BE WITH A WOMAN WHO DOESN'T WANT ME....
5/24
TAKE A GOOD LOOK, JOAN... 'CAUSE YOU'LL NEVER SEE THIS YO-YO AGAIN.
WELL WELL WELL... LOOKS WHO'S BACK.
THIS IS AWKWARD.

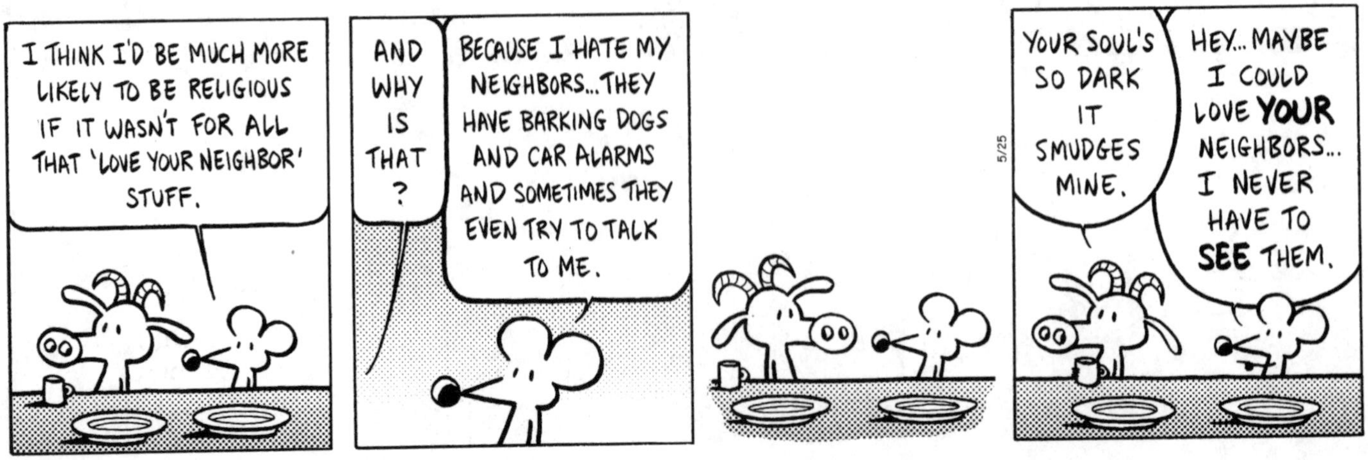
I THINK I'D BE MUCH MORE LIKELY TO BE RELIGIOUS IF IT WASN'T FOR ALL THAT 'LOVE YOUR NEIGHBOR' STUFF.
AND WHY IS THAT?
BECAUSE I HATE MY NEIGHBORS... THEY HAVE BARKING DOGS AND CAR ALARMS AND SOMETIMES THEY EVEN TRY TO TALK TO ME.
5/25
YOUR SOUL'S SO DARK IT SMUDGES MINE.
HEY... MAYBE I COULD LOVE **YOUR** NEIGHBORS... I NEVER HAVE TO **SEE** THEM.

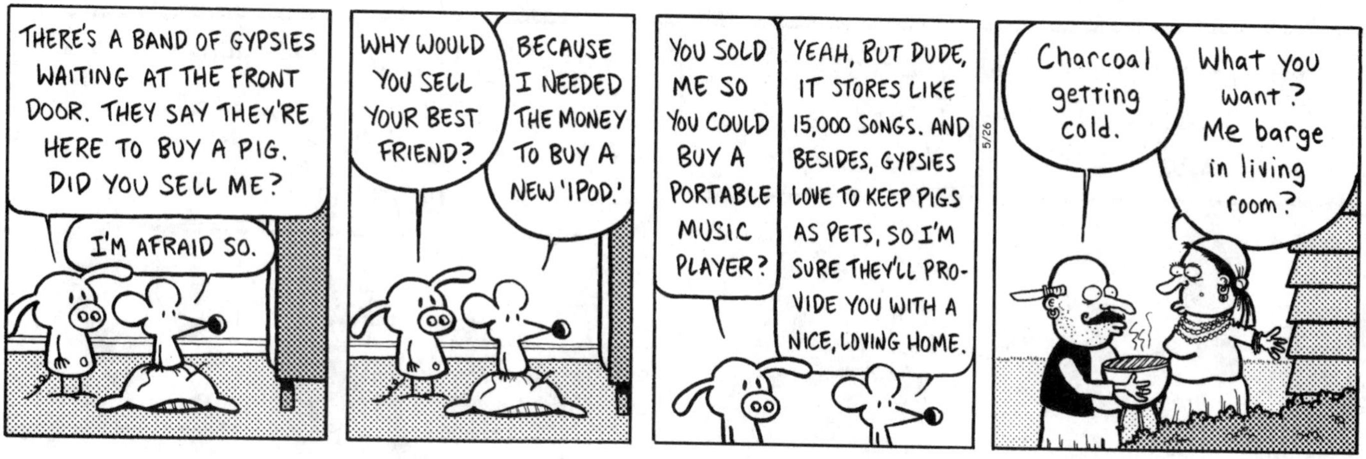
THERE'S A BAND OF GYPSIES WAITING AT THE FRONT DOOR. THEY SAY THEY'RE HERE TO BUY A PIG. DID YOU SELL ME?
I'M AFRAID SO.
WHY WOULD YOU SELL YOUR BEST FRIEND?
BECAUSE I NEEDED THE MONEY TO BUY A NEW 'IPOD.'
YOU SOLD ME SO YOU COULD BUY A PORTABLE MUSIC PLAYER?
YEAH, BUT DUDE, IT STORES LIKE 15,000 SONGS. AND BESIDES, GYPSIES LOVE TO KEEP PIGS AS PETS, SO I'M SURE THEY'LL PROVIDE YOU WITH A NICE, LOVING HOME.
5/26
Charcoal getting cold.
What you want? Me barge in living room?

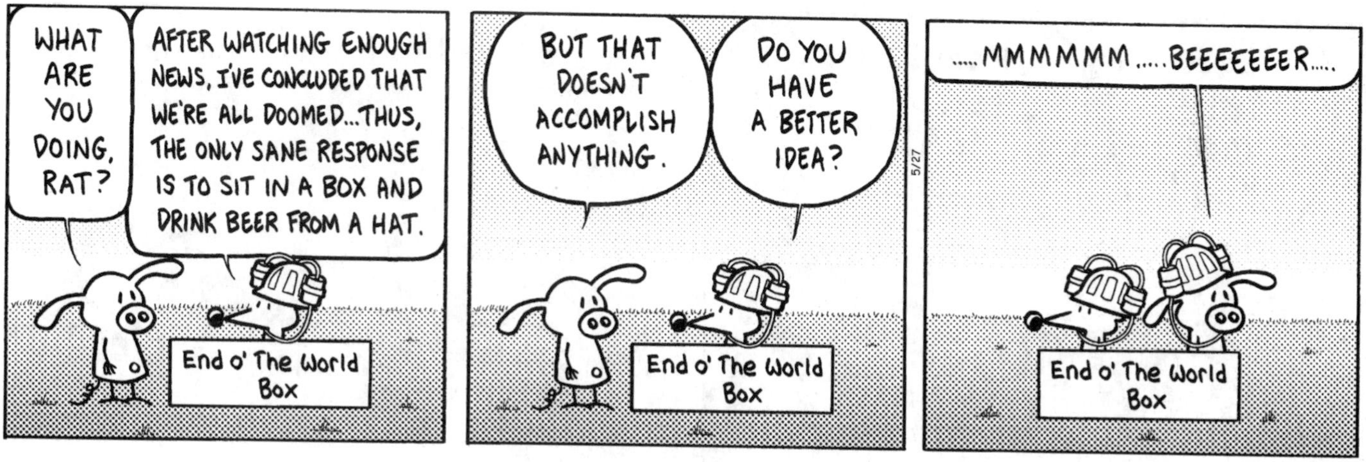
WHAT ARE YOU DOING, RAT?
AFTER WATCHING ENOUGH NEWS, I'VE CONCLUDED THAT WE'RE ALL DOOMED...THUS, THE ONLY SANE RESPONSE IS TO SIT IN A BOX AND DRINK BEER FROM A HAT.
End o' The World Box
BUT THAT DOESN'T ACCOMPLISH ANYTHING.
DO YOU HAVE A BETTER IDEA?
End o' The World Box
5/27
.....MMMMMM.....BEEEEEEER.....
End o' The World Box

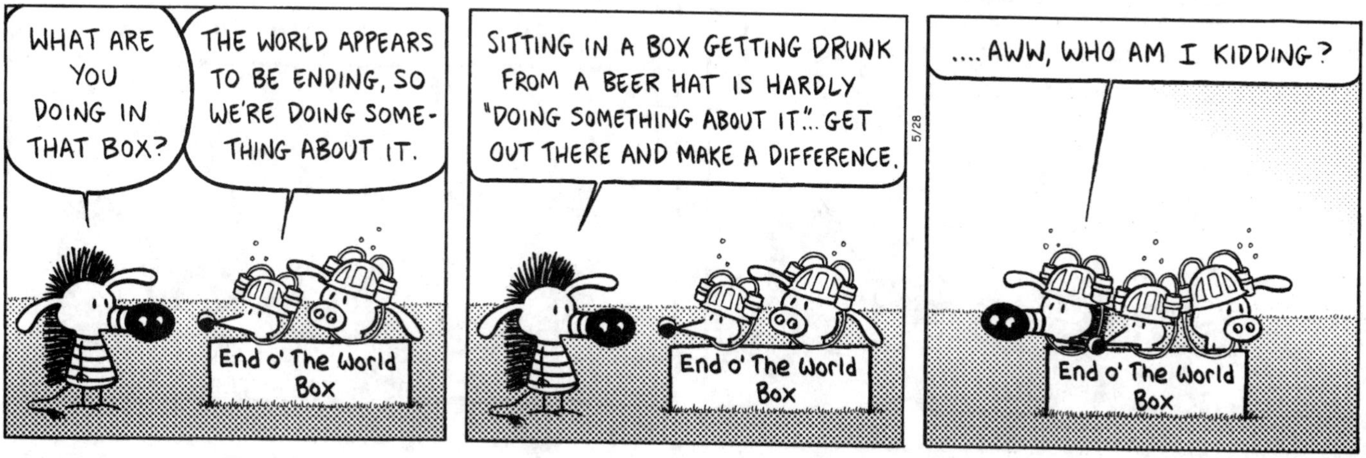
WHAT ARE YOU DOING IN THAT BOX?
THE WORLD APPEARS TO BE ENDING, SO WE'RE DOING SOMETHING ABOUT IT.
End o' The World Box
SITTING IN A BOX GETTING DRUNK FROM A BEER HAT IS HARDLY "DOING SOMETHING ABOUT IT"... GET OUT THERE AND MAKE A DIFFERENCE.
End o' The World Box
5/28
....AWW, WHO AM I KIDDING?
End o' The World Box

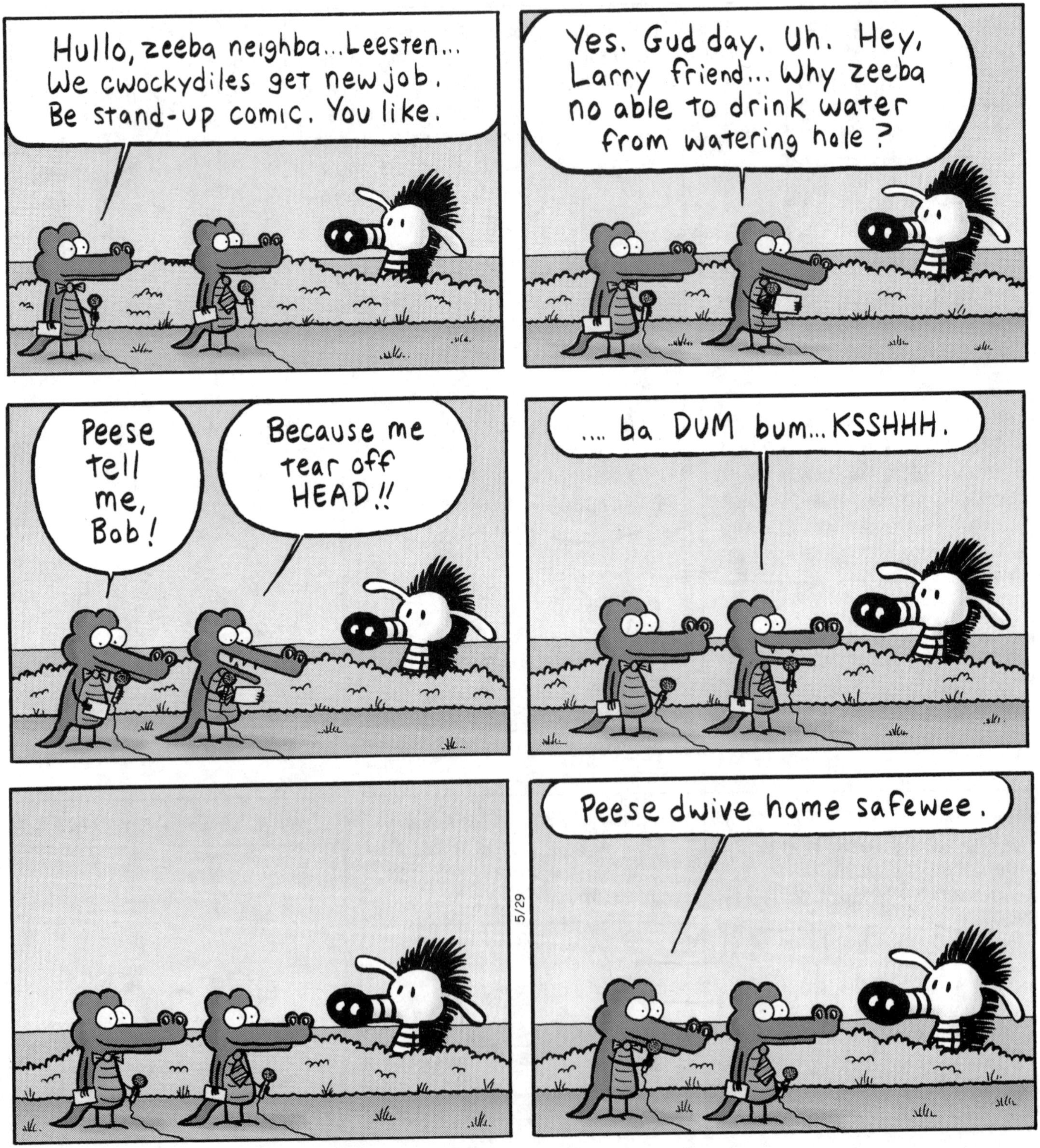
Hullo, zeeba neighba...Leesten... We cwockydiles get new job. Be stand-up comic. You like.
Yes. Gud day. Uh. Hey, Larry friend... Why zeeba no able to drink water from watering hole?
Peese tell me, Bob!
Because me tear off HEAD!!
.... ba DUM bum... KSSHHH.
5/29
Peese dwive home safewee.

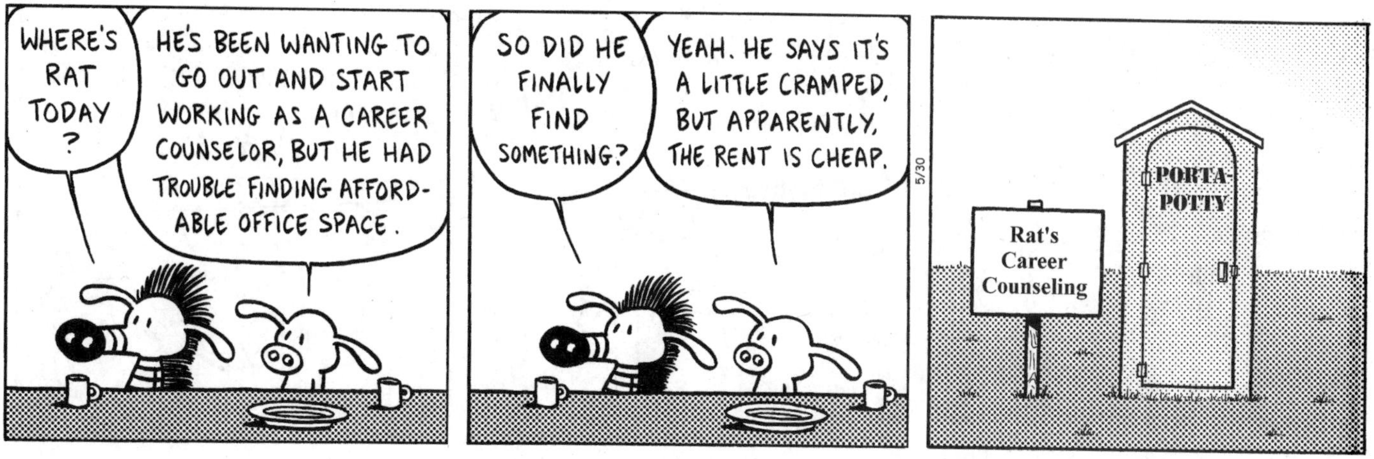
WHERE'S RAT TODAY?
HE'S BEEN WANTING TO GO OUT AND START WORKING AS A CAREER COUNSELOR, BUT HE HAD TROUBLE FINDING AFFORDABLE OFFICE SPACE.
SO DID HE FINALLY FIND SOMETHING?
YEAH. HE SAYS IT'S A LITTLE CRAMPED, BUT APPARENTLY, THE RENT IS CHEAP.
5/30
PORTA-POTTY
Rat's Career Counseling

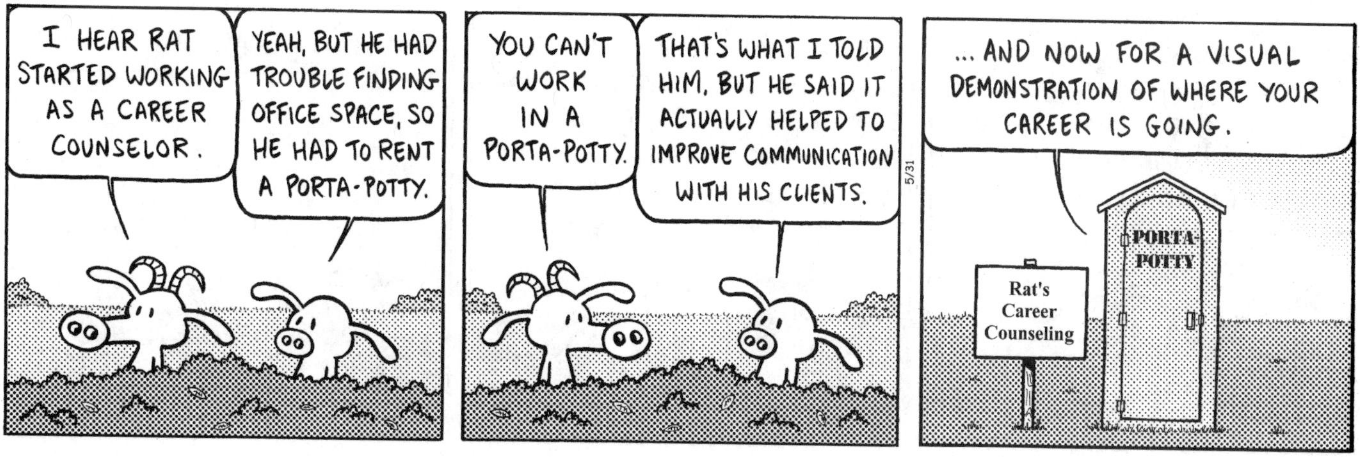
I HEAR RAT STARTED WORKING AS A CAREER COUNSELOR.
YEAH, BUT HE HAD TROUBLE FINDING OFFICE SPACE, SO HE HAD TO RENT A PORTA-POTTY.
YOU CAN'T WORK IN A PORTA-POTTY.
THAT'S WHAT I TOLD HIM, BUT HE SAID IT ACTUALLY HELPED TO IMPROVE COMMUNICATION WITH HIS CLIENTS.
5/31
...AND NOW FOR A VISUAL DEMONSTRATION OF WHERE YOUR CAREER IS GOING.
PORTA-POTTY
Rat's Career Counseling

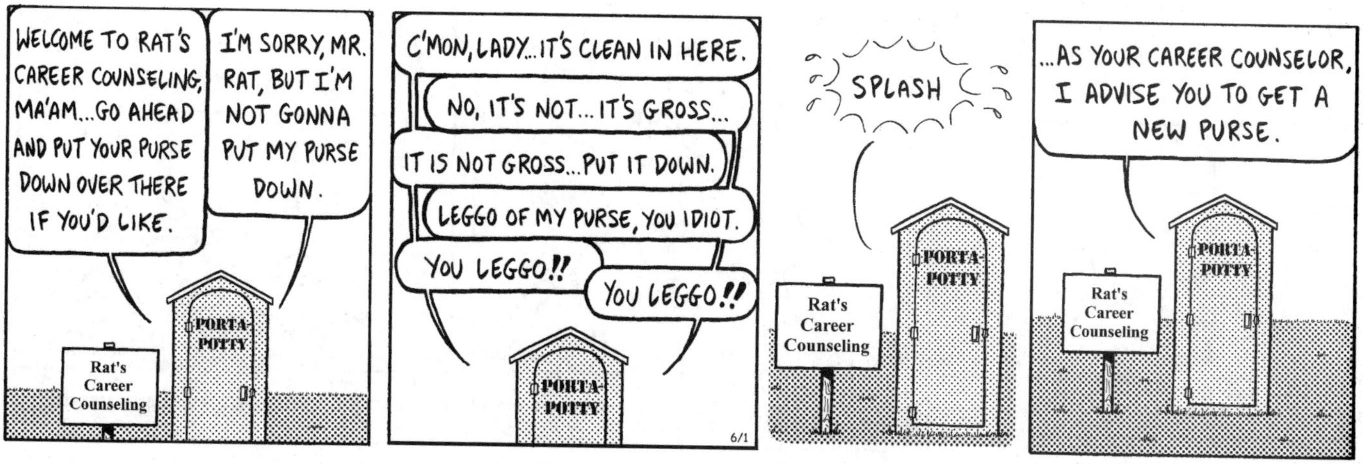
WELCOME TO RAT'S CAREER COUNSELING, MA'AM...GO AHEAD AND PUT YOUR PURSE DOWN OVER THERE IF YOU'D LIKE.
I'M SORRY, MR. RAT, BUT I'M NOT GONNA PUT MY PURSE DOWN.
PORTA-POTTY
Rat's Career Counseling
C'MON, LADY...IT'S CLEAN IN HERE.
NO, IT'S NOT...IT'S GROSS...
IT IS NOT GROSS...PUT IT DOWN.
LEGGO OF MY PURSE, YOU IDIOT.
YOU LEGGO!!
YOU LEGGO!!
PORTA-POTTY
6/1
SPLASH
Rat's Career Counseling
PORTA-POTTY
...AS YOUR CAREER COUNSELOR, I ADVISE YOU TO GET A NEW PURSE.
Rat's Career Counseling
PORTA-POTTY

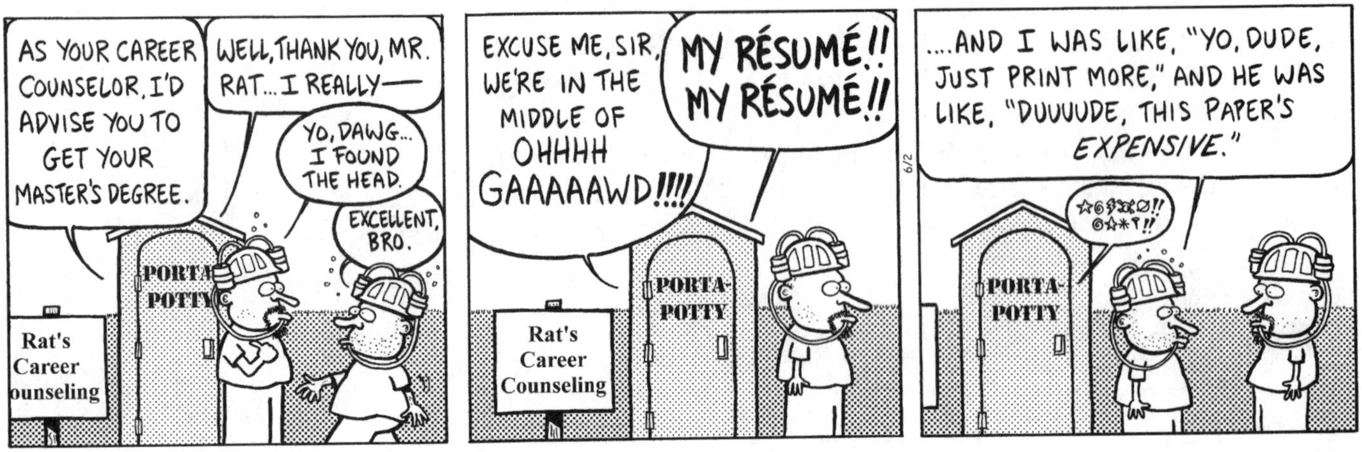
AS YOUR CAREER COUNSELOR, I'D ADVISE YOU TO GET YOUR MASTER'S DEGREE.
WELL, THANK YOU, MR. RAT... I REALLY—
YO, DAWG... I FOUND THE HEAD.
EXCELLENT, BRO.
PORTA POTTY
Rat's Career ounseling
EXCUSE ME, SIR, WE'RE IN THE MIDDLE OF OHHHH GAAAAAWD!!!!
MY RÉSUMÉ!! MY RÉSUMÉ!!
PORTA-POTTY
Rat's Career Counseling
....AND I WAS LIKE, "YO, DUDE, JUST PRINT MORE," AND HE WAS LIKE, "DUUUUDE, THIS PAPER'S *EXPENSIVE*."
PORTA-POTTY

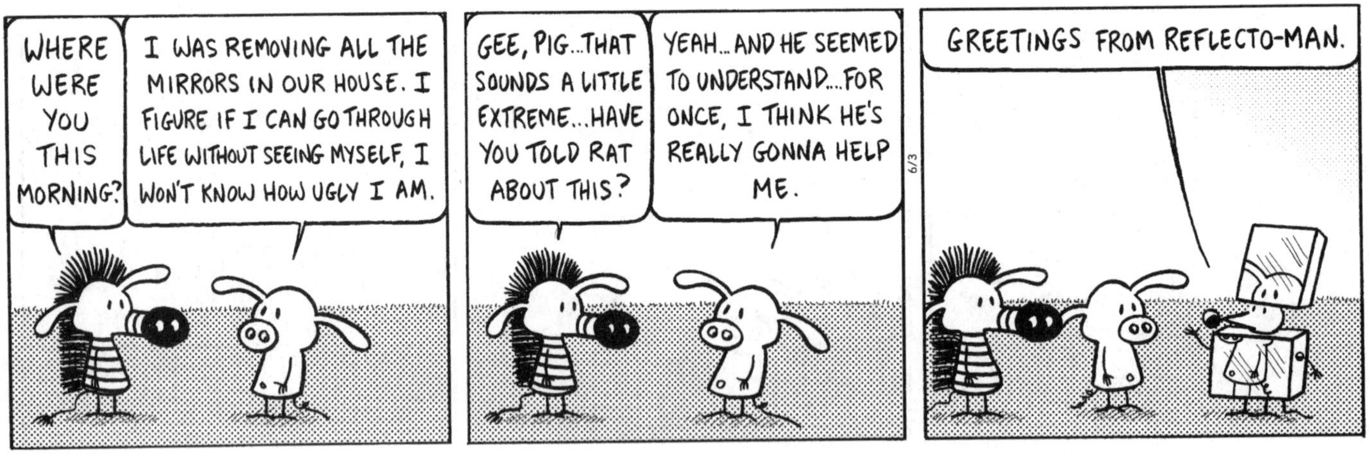
WHERE WERE YOU THIS MORNING?
I WAS REMOVING ALL THE MIRRORS IN OUR HOUSE. I FIGURE IF I CAN GO THROUGH LIFE WITHOUT SEEING MYSELF, I WON'T KNOW HOW UGLY I AM.
GEE, PIG...THAT SOUNDS A LITTLE EXTREME...HAVE YOU TOLD RAT ABOUT THIS?
YEAH... AND HE SEEMED TO UNDERSTAND....FOR ONCE, I THINK HE'S REALLY GONNA HELP ME.
GREETINGS FROM REFLECTO-MAN.

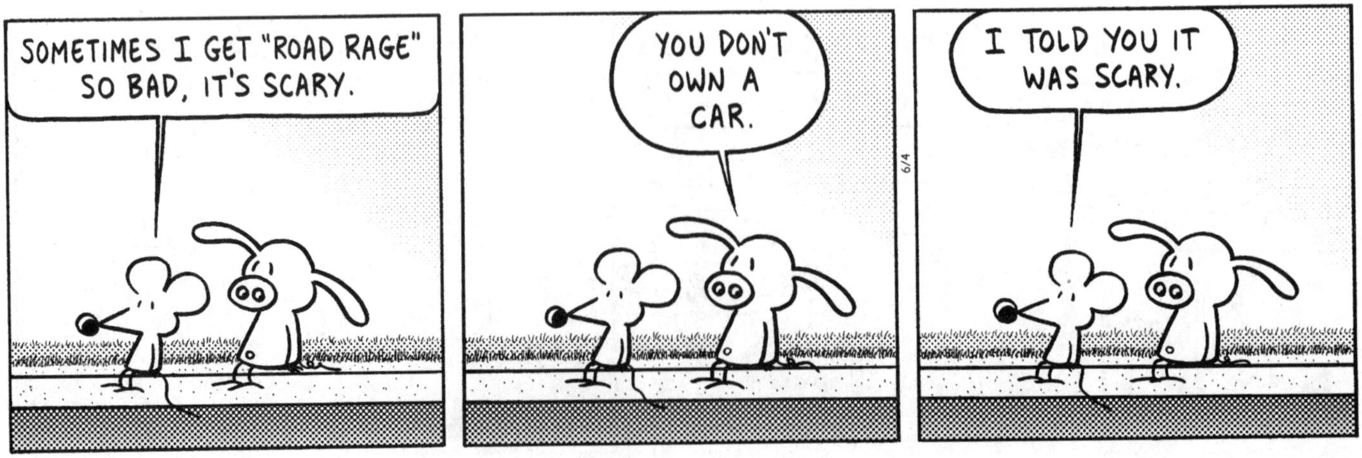
SOMETIMES I GET "ROAD RAGE" SO BAD, IT'S SCARY.
YOU DON'T OWN A CAR.
I TOLD YOU IT WAS SCARY.

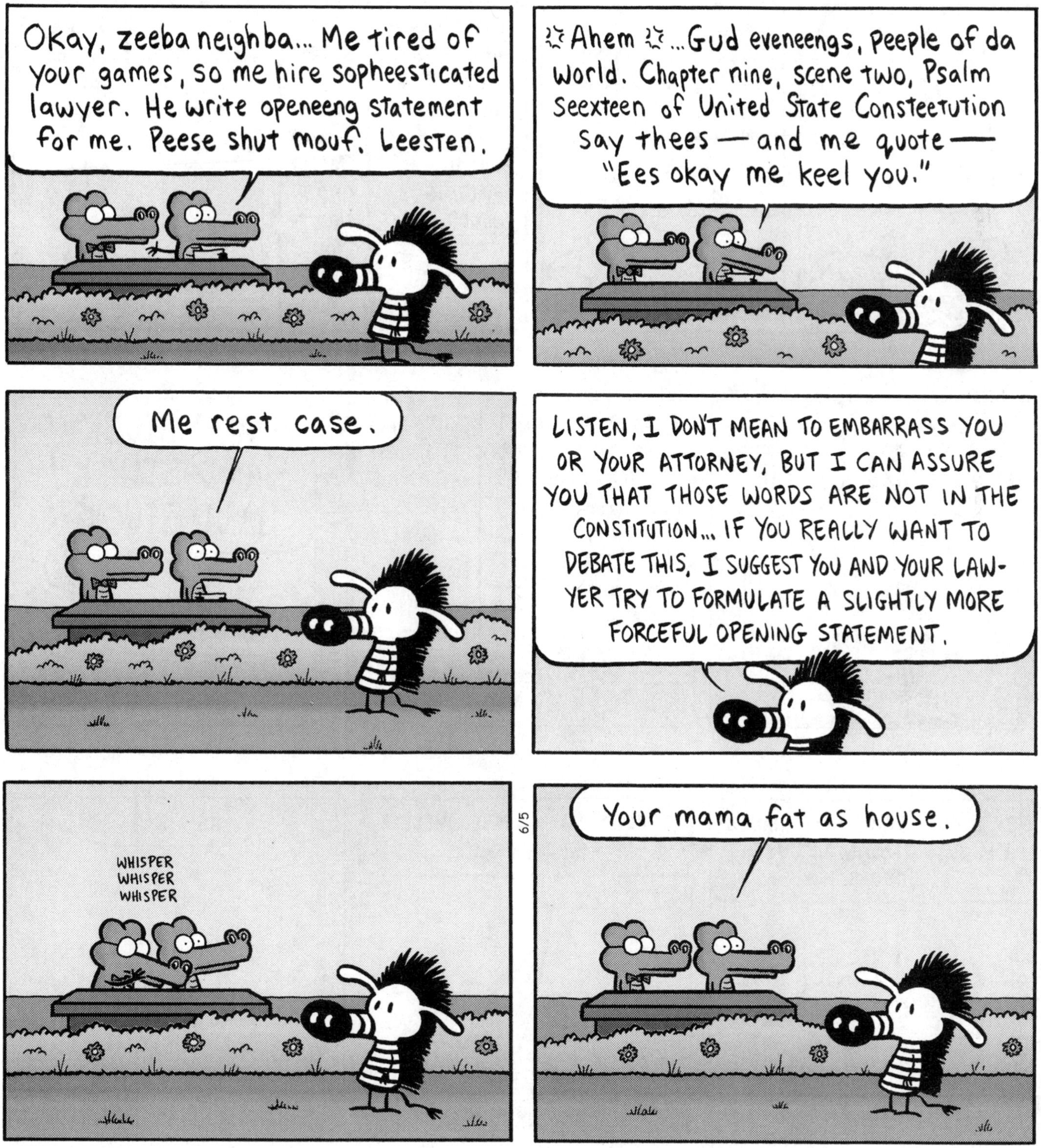
Okay, zeeba neighba... Me tired of your games, so me hire sopheesticated lawyer. He write openeeng statement for me. Peese shut mouf. Leesten.
Ahem ...Gud eveneengs, peeple of da world. Chapter nine, scene two, Psalm seexteen of United State Consteetution say thees — and me quote — "Ees okay me keel you."
Me rest case.
LISTEN, I DON'T MEAN TO EMBARRASS YOU OR YOUR ATTORNEY, BUT I CAN ASSURE YOU THAT THOSE WORDS ARE NOT IN THE CONSTITUTION... IF YOU REALLY WANT TO DEBATE THIS, I SUGGEST YOU AND YOUR LAWYER TRY TO FORMULATE A SLIGHTLY MORE FORCEFUL OPENING STATEMENT.
WHISPER WHISPER WHISPER
6/5
Your mama fat as house.

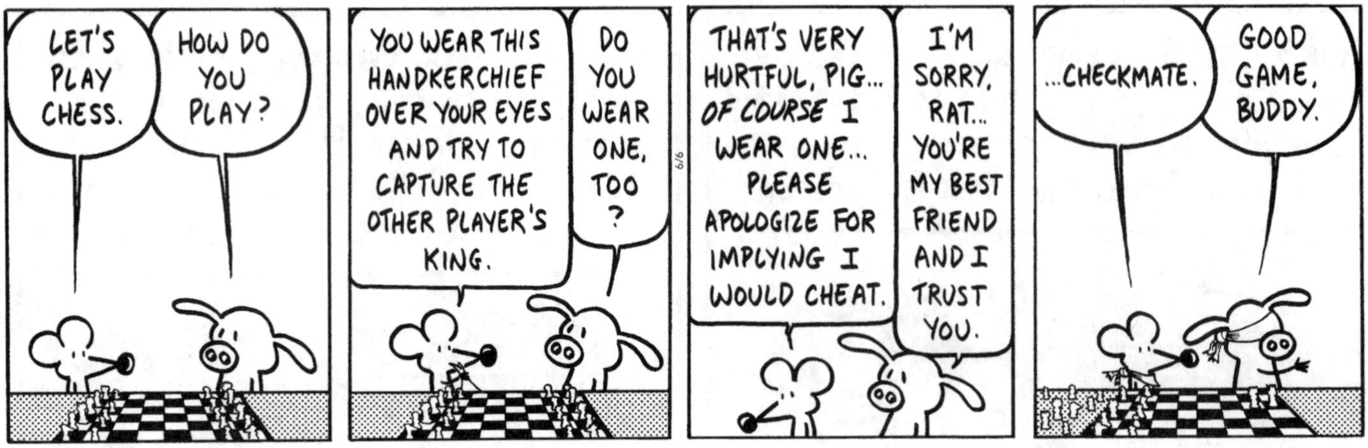
LET'S PLAY CHESS.
HOW DO YOU PLAY?
YOU WEAR THIS HANDKERCHIEF OVER YOUR EYES AND TRY TO CAPTURE THE OTHER PLAYER'S KING.
DO YOU WEAR ONE, TOO?
6/6
THAT'S VERY HURTFUL, PIG... *OF COURSE* I WEAR ONE... PLEASE APOLOGIZE FOR IMPLYING I WOULD CHEAT.
I'M SORRY, RAT... YOU'RE MY BEST FRIEND AND I TRUST YOU.
...CHECKMATE.
GOOD GAME, BUDDY.

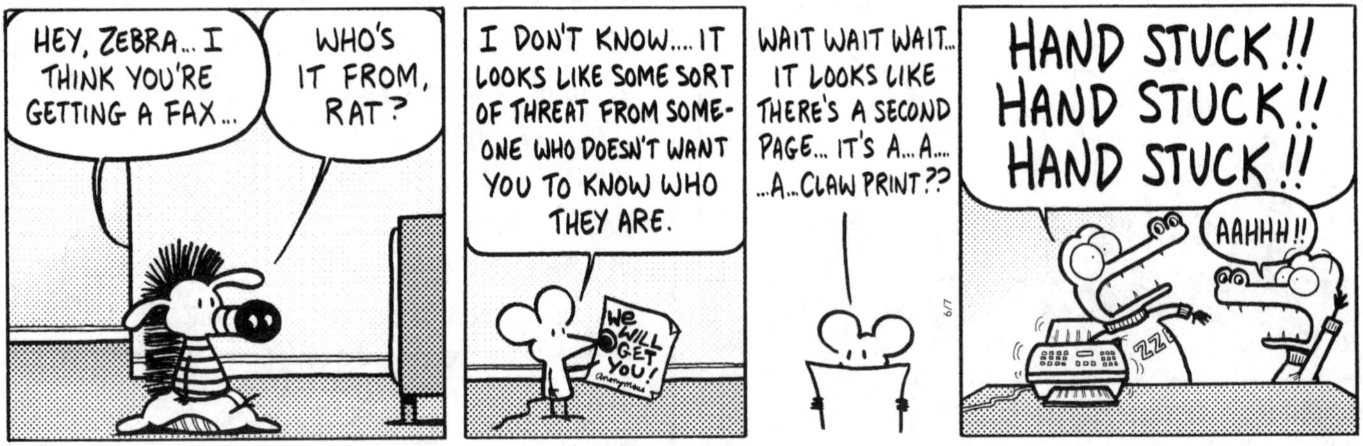
HEY, ZEBRA... I THINK YOU'RE GETTING A FAX...
WHO'S IT FROM, RAT?
I DON'T KNOW.... IT LOOKS LIKE SOME SORT OF THREAT FROM SOMEONE WHO DOESN'T WANT YOU TO KNOW WHO THEY ARE.
WE WILL GET YOU!
WAIT WAIT WAIT... IT LOOKS LIKE THERE'S A SECOND PAGE... IT'S A... A.... ...A...CLAW PRINT??
6/7
HAND STUCK!! HAND STUCK!! HAND STUCK!!
AAHHH!!
ZZZ

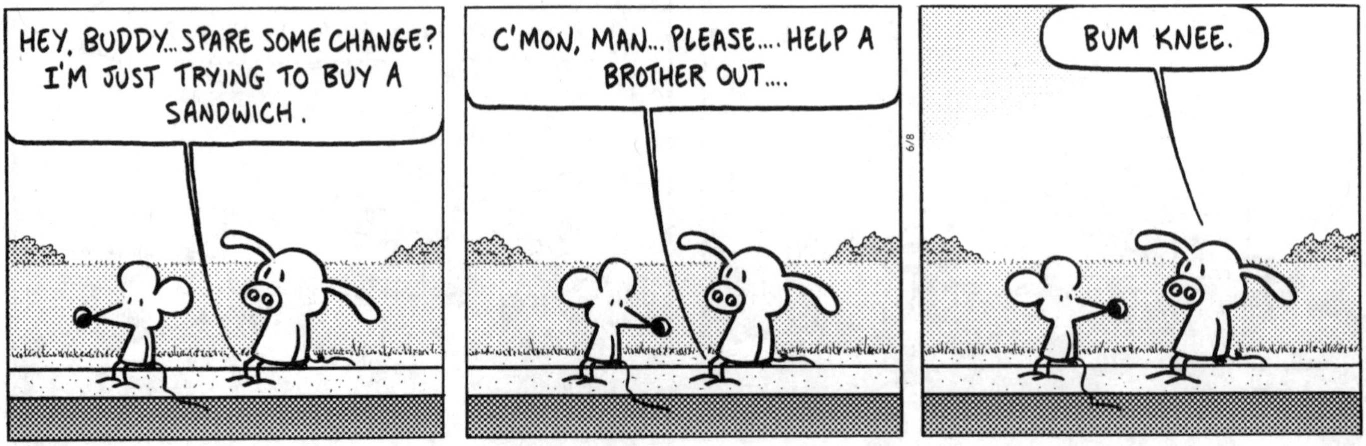
HEY, BUDDY... SPARE SOME CHANGE? I'M JUST TRYING TO BUY A SANDWICH.
C'MON, MAN... PLEASE.... HELP A BROTHER OUT....
6/8
BUM KNEE.

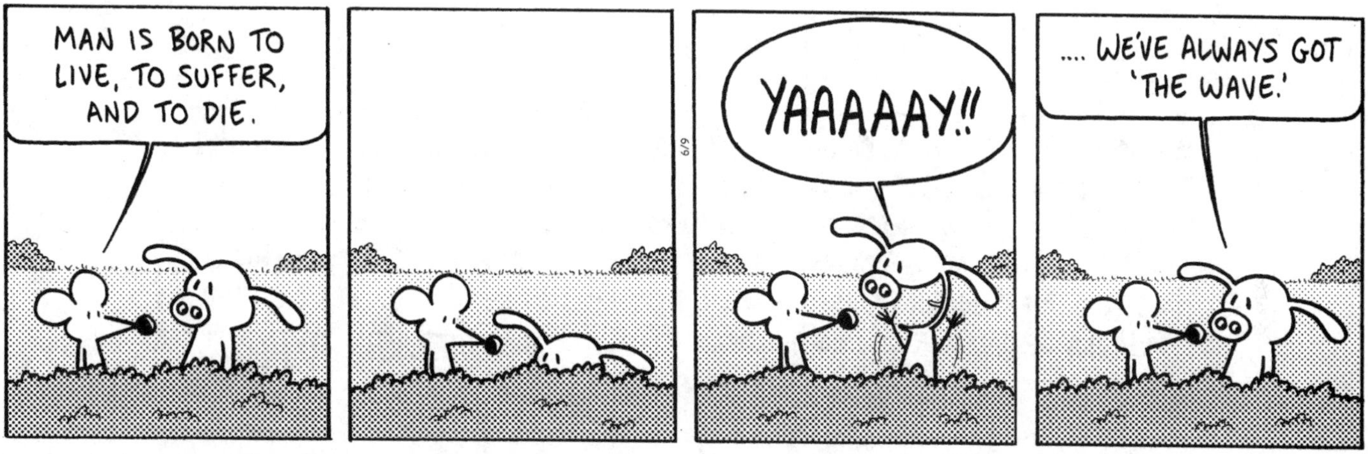
MAN IS BORN TO LIVE, TO SUFFER, AND TO DIE.
6/9
YAAAAAY!!
.... WE'VE ALWAYS GOT 'THE WAVE.'

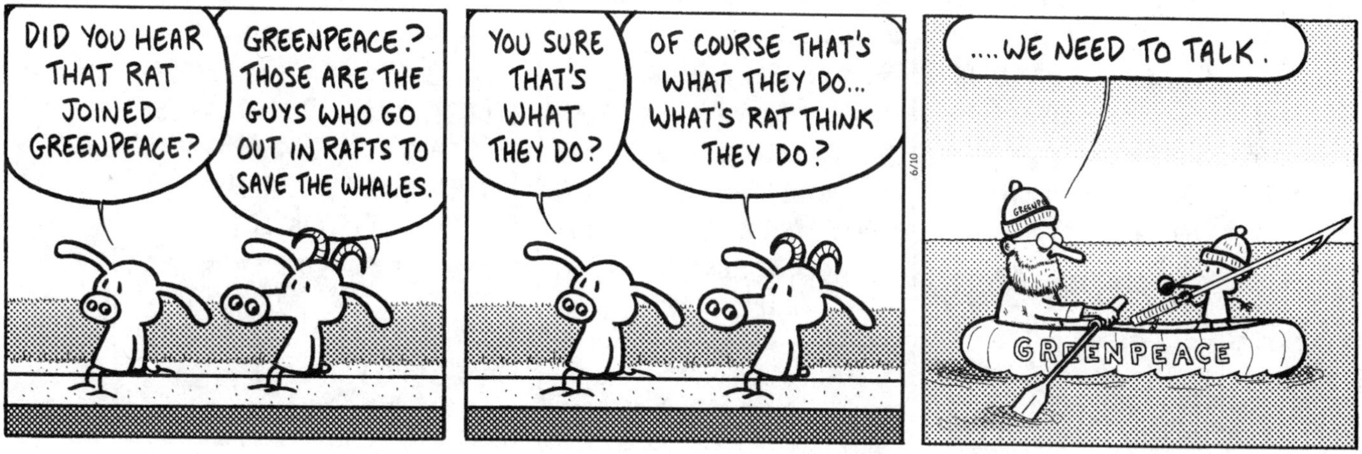
DID YOU HEAR THAT RAT JOINED GREENPEACE?
GREENPEACE? THOSE ARE THE GUYS WHO GO OUT IN RAFTS TO SAVE THE WHALES.
YOU SURE THAT'S WHAT THEY DO?
OF COURSE THAT'S WHAT THEY DO... WHAT'S RAT THINK THEY DO?
6/10
....WE NEED TO TALK.
GREENPEACE

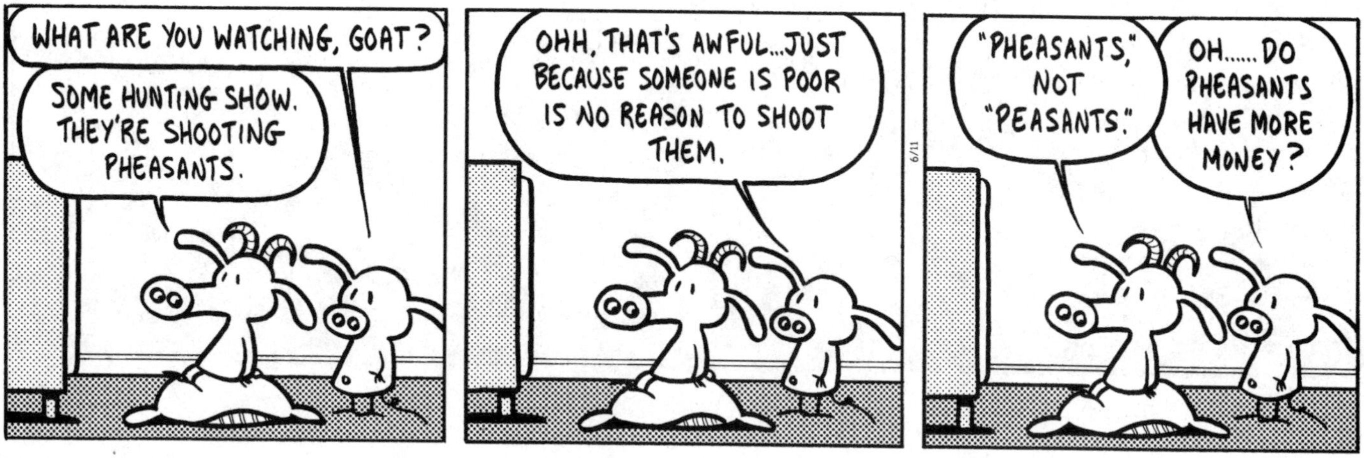
WHAT ARE YOU WATCHING, GOAT?
SOME HUNTING SHOW. THEY'RE SHOOTING PHEASANTS.
OHH, THAT'S AWFUL...JUST BECAUSE SOMEONE IS POOR IS NO REASON TO SHOOT THEM.
6/11
"PHEASANTS," NOT "PEASANTS."
OH...... DO PHEASANTS HAVE MORE MONEY?

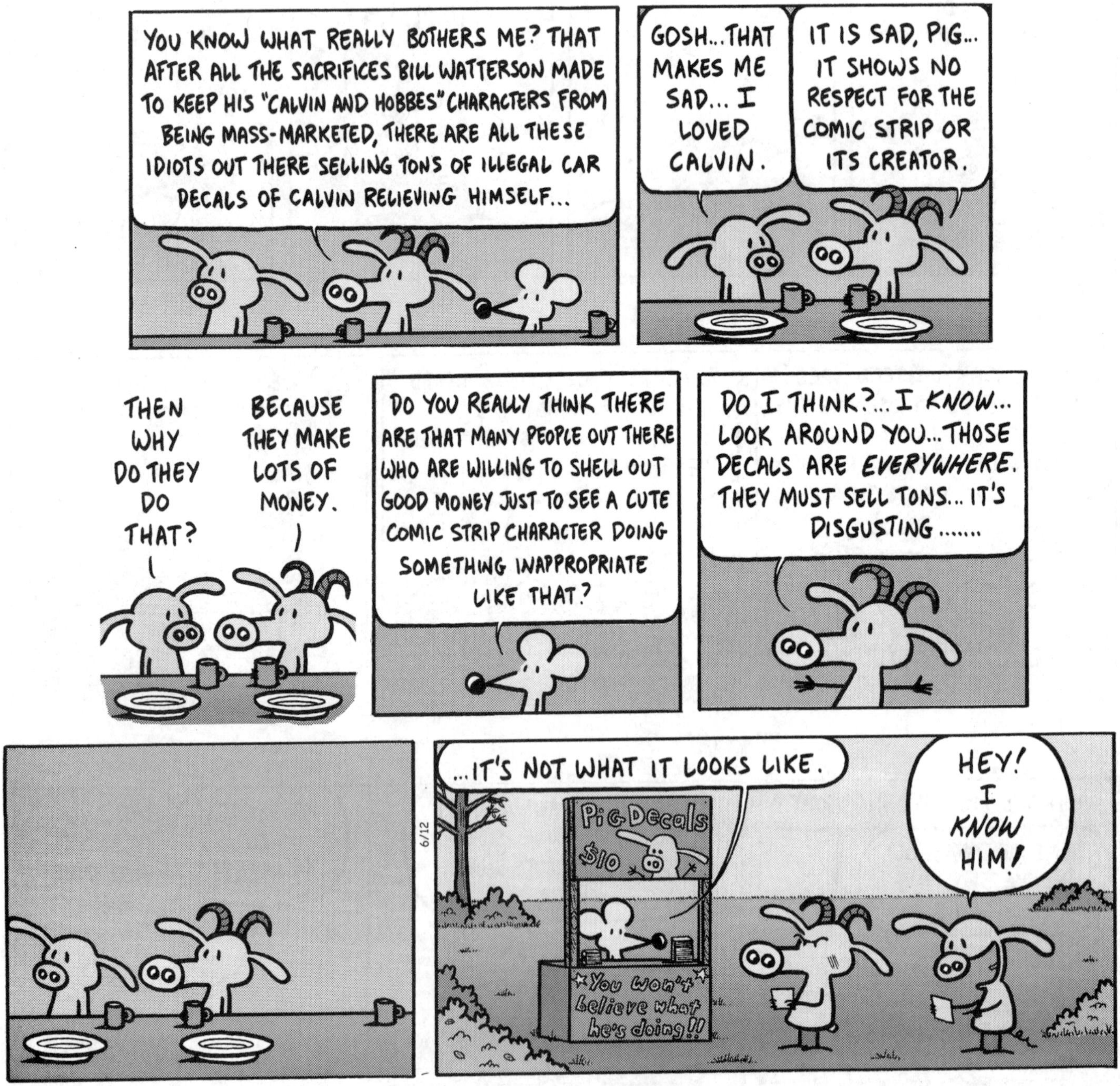
YOU KNOW WHAT REALLY BOTHERS ME? THAT AFTER ALL THE SACRIFICES BILL WATTERSON MADE TO KEEP HIS "CALVIN AND HOBBES" CHARACTERS FROM BEING MASS-MARKETED, THERE ARE ALL THESE IDIOTS OUT THERE SELLING TONS OF ILLEGAL CAR DECALS OF CALVIN RELIEVING HIMSELF...
GOSH...THAT MAKES ME SAD... I LOVED CALVIN.
IT IS SAD, PIG... IT SHOWS NO RESPECT FOR THE COMIC STRIP OR ITS CREATOR.
THEN WHY DO THEY DO THAT?
BECAUSE THEY MAKE LOTS OF MONEY.
DO YOU REALLY THINK THERE ARE THAT MANY PEOPLE OUT THERE WHO ARE WILLING TO SHELL OUT GOOD MONEY JUST TO SEE A CUTE COMIC STRIP CHARACTER DOING SOMETHING INAPPROPRIATE LIKE THAT?
DO I THINK?... I *KNOW*... LOOK AROUND YOU... THOSE DECALS ARE *EVERYWHERE*. THEY MUST SELL TONS... IT'S DISGUSTING.......
6/12
...IT'S NOT WHAT IT LOOKS LIKE.
Pig Decals
$10
You won't believe what he's doing!!
HEY! I *KNOW* HIM!

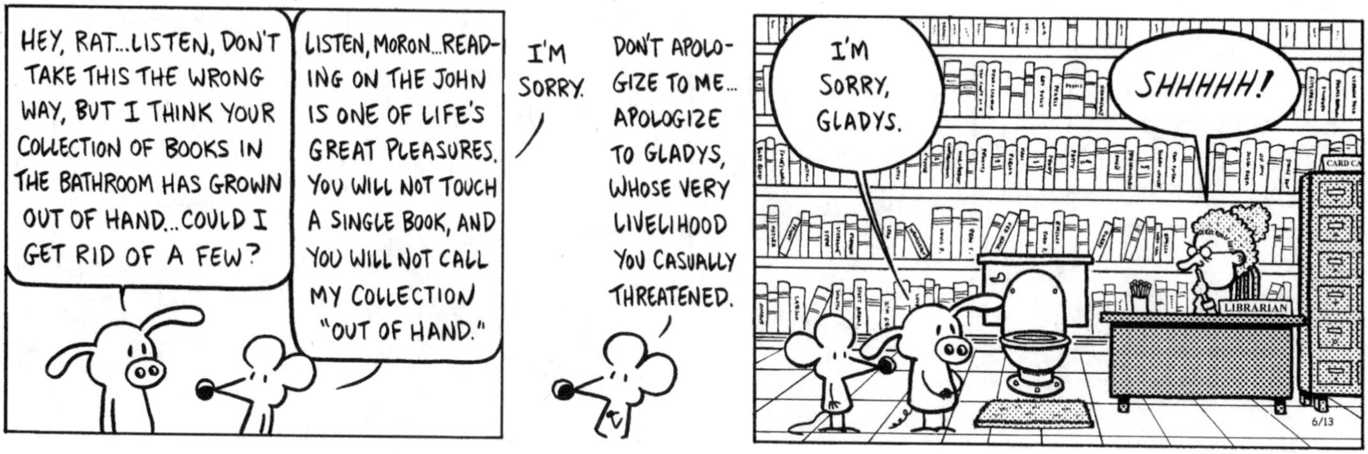
HEY, RAT...LISTEN, DON'T TAKE THIS THE WRONG WAY, BUT I THINK YOUR COLLECTION OF BOOKS IN THE BATHROOM HAS GROWN OUT OF HAND...COULD I GET RID OF A FEW?
LISTEN, MORON...READING ON THE JOHN IS ONE OF LIFE'S GREAT PLEASURES. YOU WILL NOT TOUCH A SINGLE BOOK, AND YOU WILL NOT CALL MY COLLECTION "OUT OF HAND."
I'M SORRY.
DON'T APOLOGIZE TO ME... APOLOGIZE TO GLADYS, WHOSE VERY LIVELIHOOD YOU CASUALLY THREATENED.
I'M SORRY, GLADYS.
SHHHHH!
LIBRARIAN
6/13

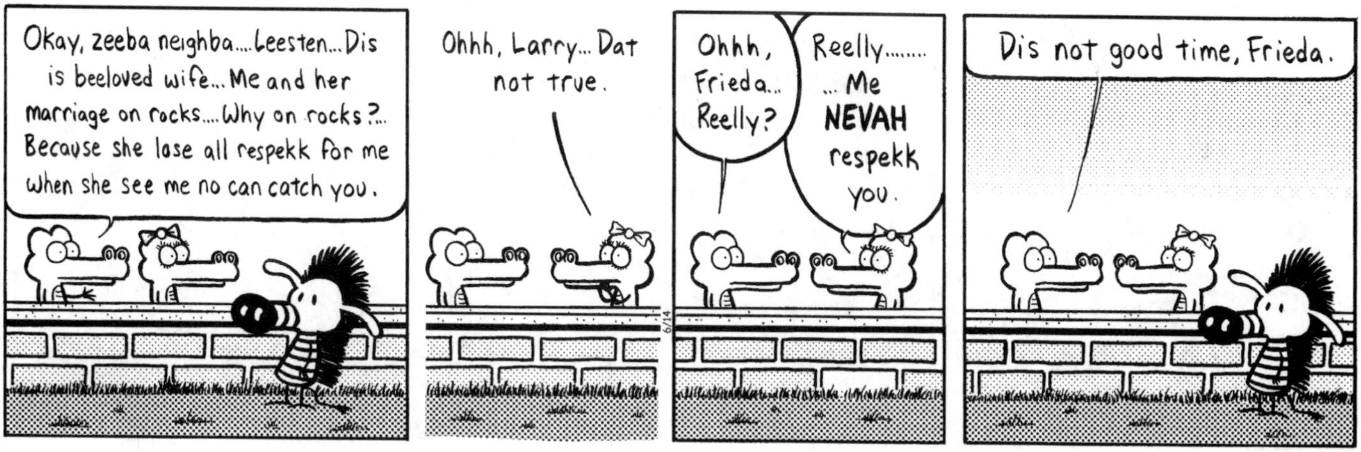
Okay, zeeba neighba.... Leesten... Dis is beeloved wife... Me and her marriage on rocks.... Why on rocks?... Because she lose all respekk for me when she see me no can catch you.
Ohhh, Larry... Dat not true.
6/14
Ohhh, Frieda... Reelly?
Reelly........ ... Me **NEVAH** respekk you.
Dis not good time, Frieda.

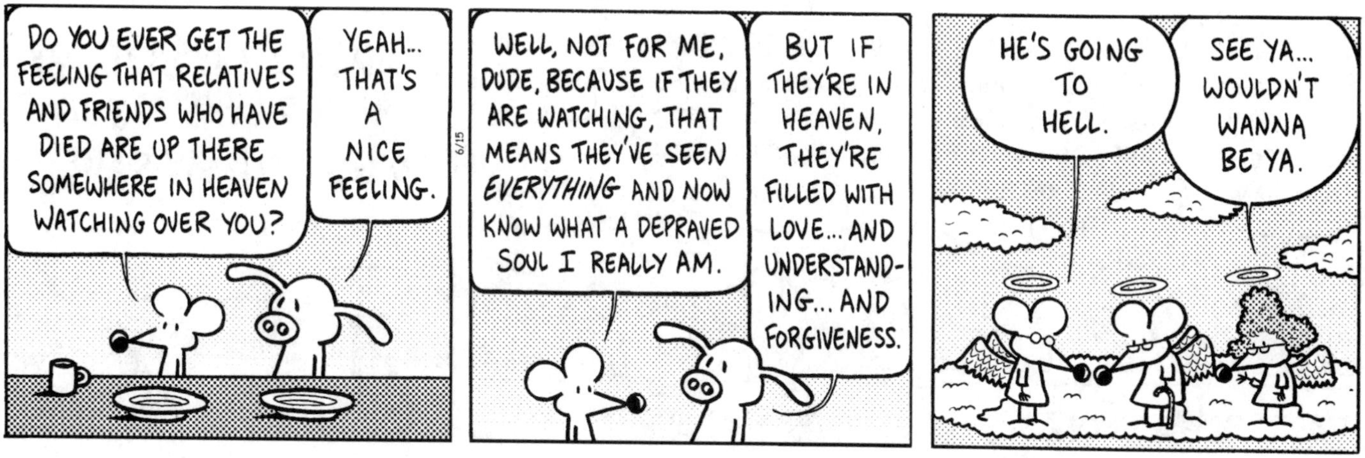
DO YOU EVER GET THE FEELING THAT RELATIVES AND FRIENDS WHO HAVE DIED ARE UP THERE SOMEWHERE IN HEAVEN WATCHING OVER YOU?
YEAH... THAT'S A NICE FEELING.
6/15
WELL, NOT FOR ME, DUDE, BECAUSE IF THEY ARE WATCHING, THAT MEANS THEY'VE SEEN *EVERYTHING* AND NOW KNOW WHAT A DEPRAVED SOUL I REALLY AM.
BUT IF THEY'RE IN HEAVEN, THEY'RE FILLED WITH LOVE... AND UNDERSTANDING... AND FORGIVENESS.
HE'S GOING TO HELL.
SEE YA... WOULDN'T WANNA BE YA.

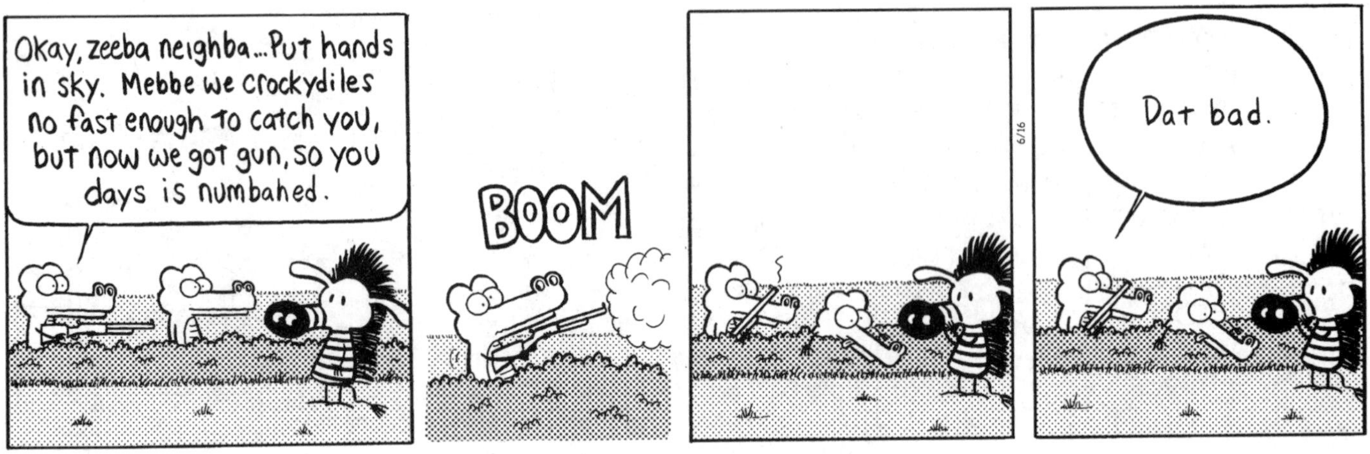
Okay, zeeba neighba... Put hands in sky. Mebbe we crockydiles no fast enough to catch you, but now we got gun, so you days is numbahed.
BOOM
Dat bad.

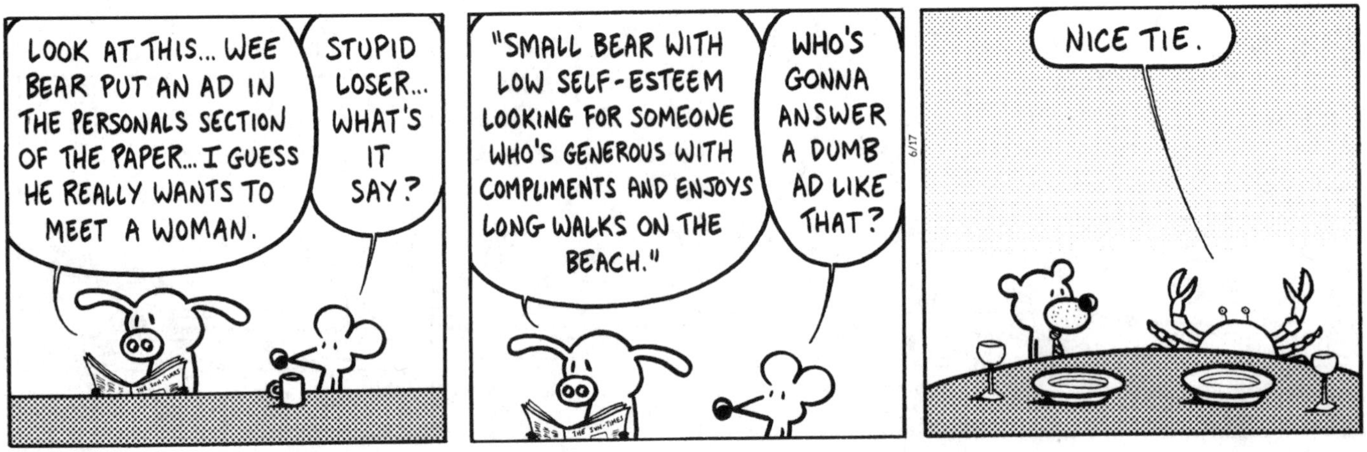
LOOK AT THIS... WEE BEAR PUT AN AD IN THE PERSONALS SECTION OF THE PAPER... I GUESS HE REALLY WANTS TO MEET A WOMAN.
STUPID LOSER... WHAT'S IT SAY?
"SMALL BEAR WITH LOW SELF-ESTEEM LOOKING FOR SOMEONE WHO'S GENEROUS WITH COMPLIMENTS AND ENJOYS LONG WALKS ON THE BEACH."
WHO'S GONNA ANSWER A DUMB AD LIKE THAT?
NICE TIE.

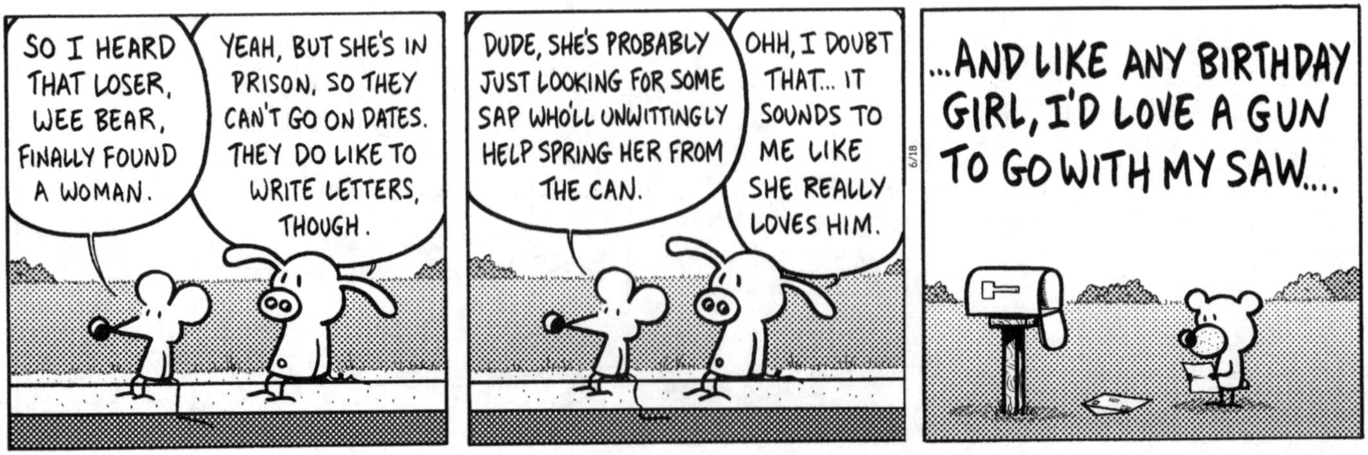
SO I HEARD THAT LOSER, WEE BEAR, FINALLY FOUND A WOMAN.
YEAH, BUT SHE'S IN PRISON, SO THEY CAN'T GO ON DATES. THEY DO LIKE TO WRITE LETTERS, THOUGH.
DUDE, SHE'S PROBABLY JUST LOOKING FOR SOME SAP WHO'LL UNWITTINGLY HELP SPRING HER FROM THE CAN.
OHH, I DOUBT THAT... IT SOUNDS TO ME LIKE SHE REALLY LOVES HIM.
...AND LIKE ANY BIRTHDAY GIRL, I'D LOVE A GUN TO GO WITH MY SAW....

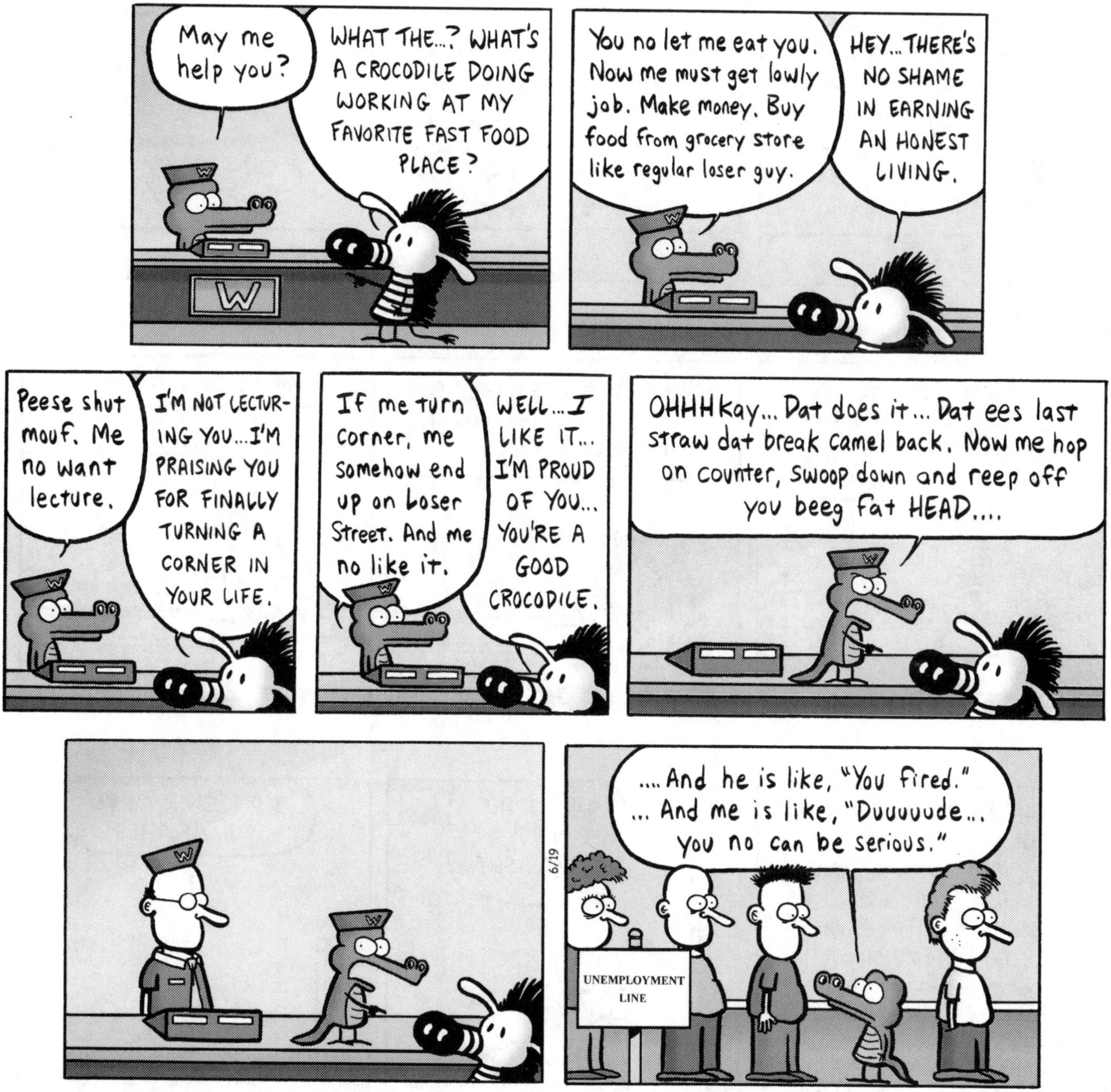
May me help you?
WHAT THE...? WHAT'S A CROCODILE DOING WORKING AT MY FAVORITE FAST FOOD PLACE?
You no let me eat you. Now me must get lowly job. Make money. Buy food from grocery store like regular loser guy.
HEY... THERE'S NO SHAME IN EARNING AN HONEST LIVING.
Peese shut mouf. Me no want lecture.
I'M NOT LECTURING YOU... I'M PRAISING YOU FOR FINALLY TURNING A CORNER IN YOUR LIFE.
If me turn corner, me somehow end up on Loser Street. And me no like it.
WELL... I LIKE IT... I'M PROUD OF YOU... YOU'RE A GOOD CROCODILE.
OHHHkay... Dat does it... Dat ees last straw dat break camel back. Now me hop on counter, swoop down and reep off you beeg fat HEAD....
6/19
....And he is like, "You fired." ... And me is like, "Duuuuude... you no can be serious."
UNEMPLOYMENT LINE

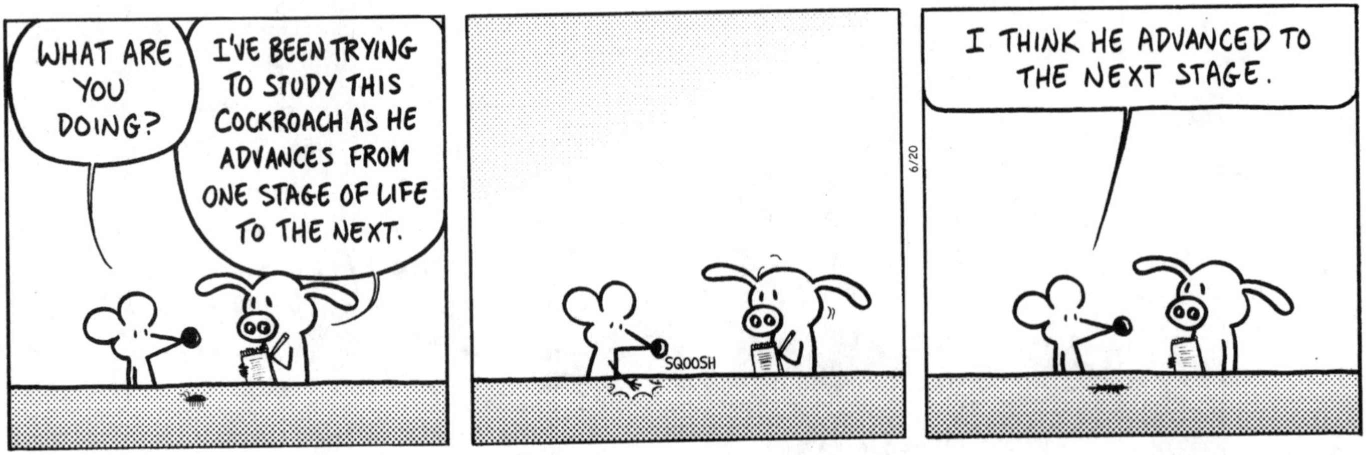
WHAT ARE YOU DOING?
I'VE BEEN TRYING TO STUDY THIS COCKROACH AS HE ADVANCES FROM ONE STAGE OF LIFE TO THE NEXT.
SQOOSH
I THINK HE ADVANCED TO THE NEXT STAGE.

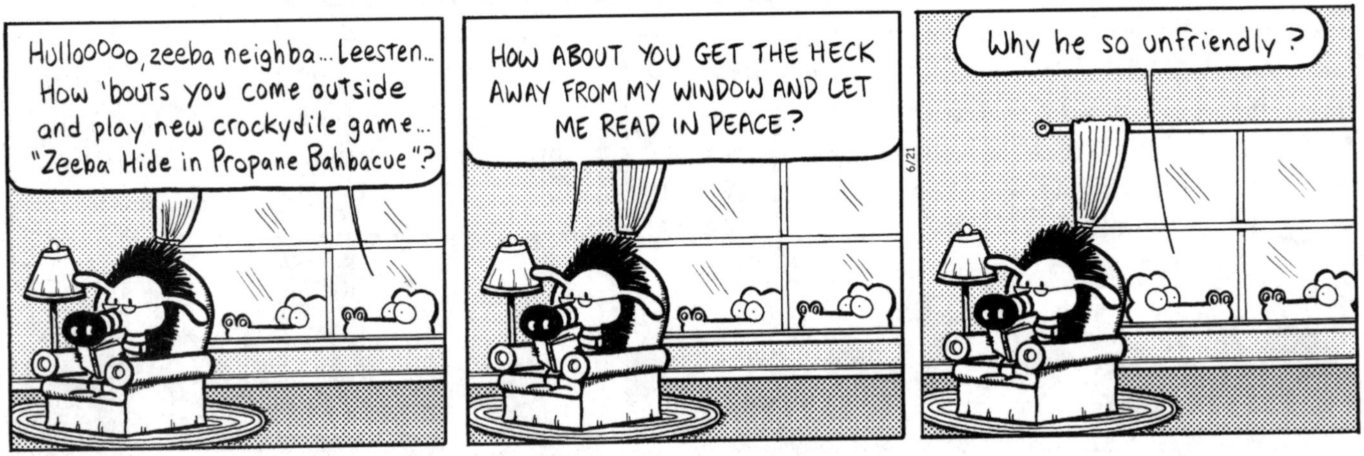
Hulloooo, zeeba neighba... Leesten.. How 'bouts you come outside and play new crockydile game... "Zeeba Hide in Propane Bahbacue"?
HOW ABOUT YOU GET THE HECK AWAY FROM MY WINDOW AND LET ME READ IN PEACE?
Why he so unfriendly?

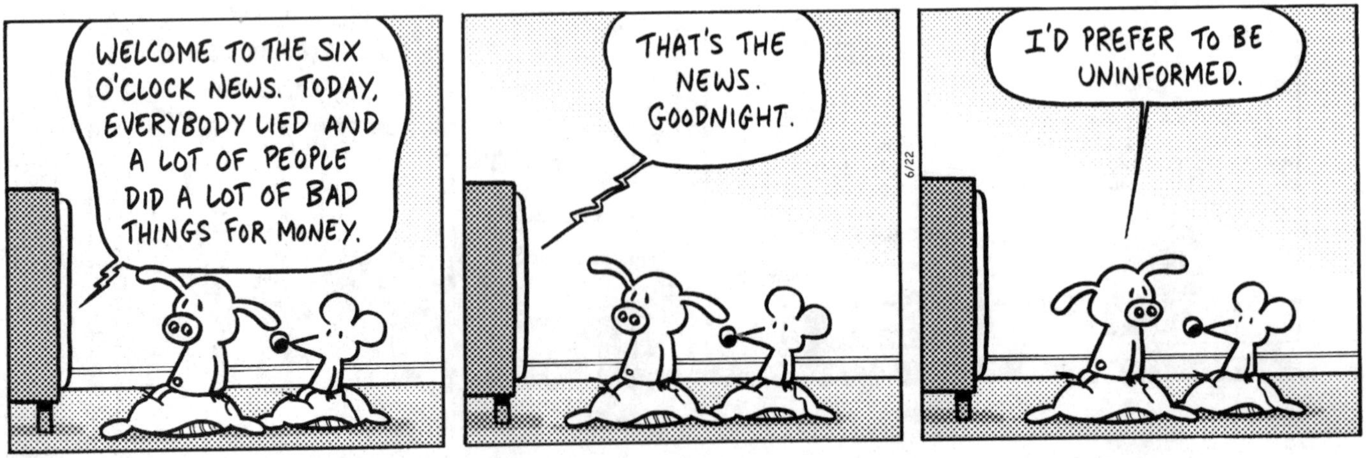
WELCOME TO THE SIX O'CLOCK NEWS. TODAY, EVERYBODY LIED AND A LOT OF PEOPLE DID A LOT OF BAD THINGS FOR MONEY.
THAT'S THE NEWS. GOODNIGHT.
I'D PREFER TO BE UNINFORMED.

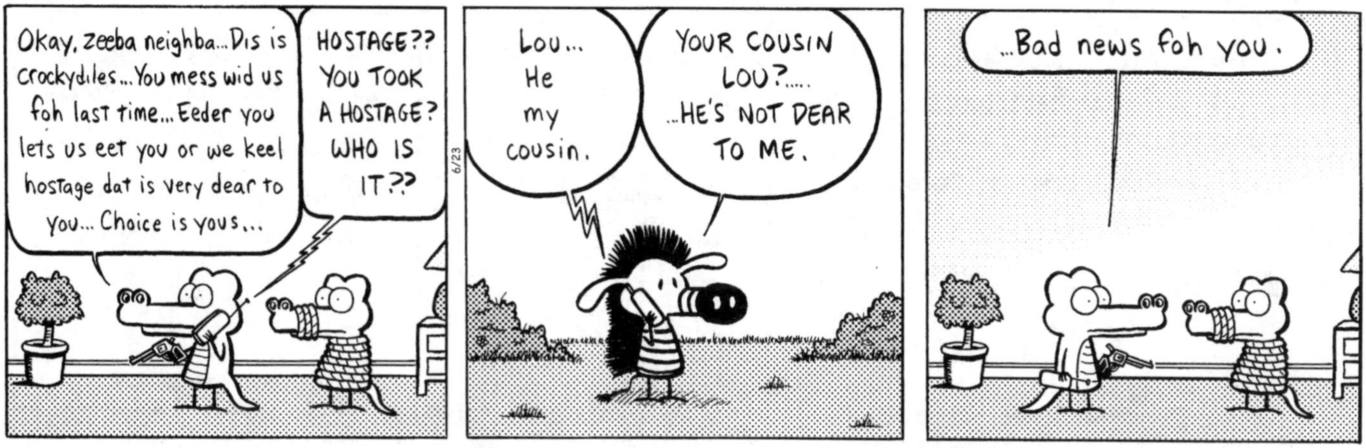
Okay, zeeba neighba... Dis is crockydiles... You mess wid us foh last time... Eeder you lets us eet you or we keel hostage dat is very dear to you... Choice is yous...
HOSTAGE?? YOU TOOK A HOSTAGE? WHO IS IT??
6/23
Lou... He my cousin.
YOUR COUSIN LOU?..... ..HE'S NOT DEAR TO ME.
...Bad news foh you.

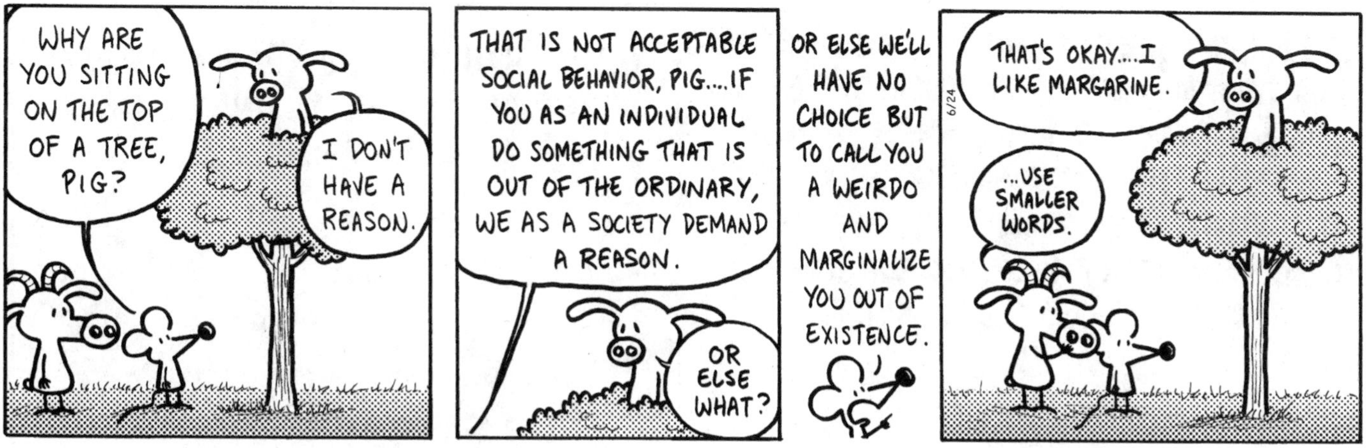
WHY ARE YOU SITTING ON THE TOP OF A TREE, PIG?
I DON'T HAVE A REASON.
THAT IS NOT ACCEPTABLE SOCIAL BEHAVIOR, PIG.... IF YOU AS AN INDIVIDUAL DO SOMETHING THAT IS OUT OF THE ORDINARY, WE AS A SOCIETY DEMAND A REASON.
OR ELSE WHAT?
OR ELSE WE'LL HAVE NO CHOICE BUT TO CALL YOU A WEIRDO AND MARGINALIZE YOU OUT OF EXISTENCE.
6/24
THAT'S OKAY.... I LIKE MARGARINE.
...USE SMALLER WORDS.

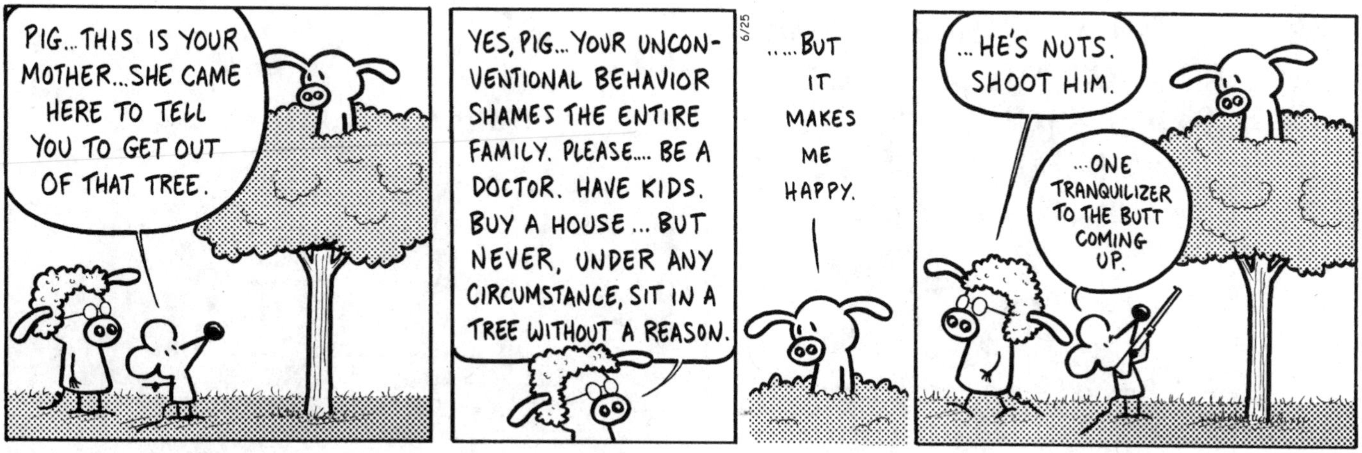
PIG... THIS IS YOUR MOTHER... SHE CAME HERE TO TELL YOU TO GET OUT OF THAT TREE.
YES, PIG... YOUR UNCONVENTIONAL BEHAVIOR SHAMES THE ENTIRE FAMILY. PLEASE.... BE A DOCTOR. HAVE KIDS. BUY A HOUSE... BUT NEVER, UNDER ANY CIRCUMSTANCE, SIT IN A TREE WITHOUT A REASON.
6/25
.....BUT IT MAKES ME HAPPY.
...HE'S NUTS. SHOOT HIM.
...ONE TRANQUILIZER TO THE BUTT COMING UP.

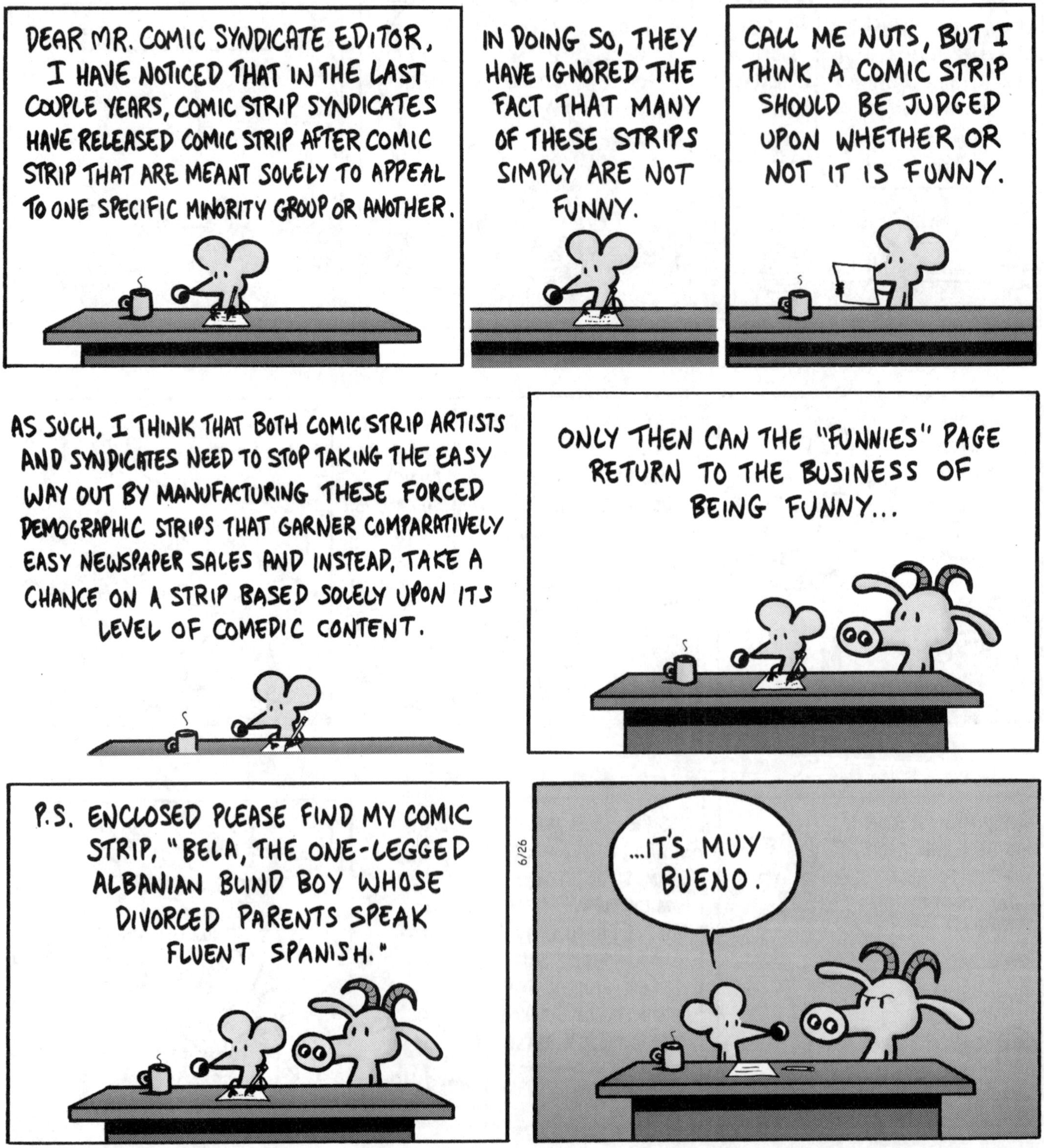
DEAR MR. COMIC SYNDICATE EDITOR, I HAVE NOTICED THAT IN THE LAST COUPLE YEARS, COMIC STRIP SYNDICATES HAVE RELEASED COMIC STRIP AFTER COMIC STRIP THAT ARE MEANT SOLELY TO APPEAL TO ONE SPECIFIC MINORITY GROUP OR ANOTHER.
IN DOING SO, THEY HAVE IGNORED THE FACT THAT MANY OF THESE STRIPS SIMPLY ARE NOT FUNNY.
CALL ME NUTS, BUT I THINK A COMIC STRIP SHOULD BE JUDGED UPON WHETHER OR NOT IT IS FUNNY.
AS SUCH, I THINK THAT BOTH COMIC STRIP ARTISTS AND SYNDICATES NEED TO STOP TAKING THE EASY WAY OUT BY MANUFACTURING THESE FORCED DEMOGRAPHIC STRIPS THAT GARNER COMPARATIVELY EASY NEWSPAPER SALES AND INSTEAD, TAKE A CHANCE ON A STRIP BASED SOLELY UPON ITS LEVEL OF COMEDIC CONTENT.
ONLY THEN CAN THE "FUNNIES" PAGE RETURN TO THE BUSINESS OF BEING FUNNY...
P.S. ENCLOSED PLEASE FIND MY COMIC STRIP, "BELA, THE ONE-LEGGED ALBANIAN BLIND BOY WHOSE DIVORCED PARENTS SPEAK FLUENT SPANISH."
6/26
...IT'S MUY BUENO.

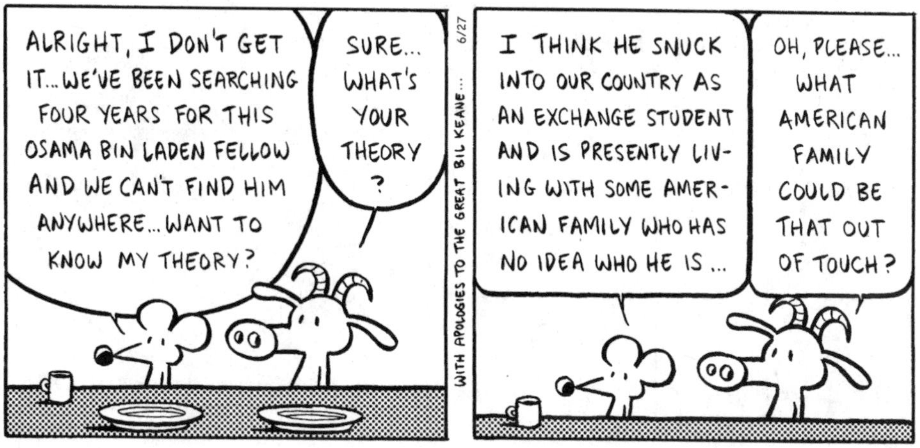
ALRIGHT, I DON'T GET IT... WE'VE BEEN SEARCHING FOUR YEARS FOR THIS OSAMA BIN LADEN FELLOW AND WE CAN'T FIND HIM ANYWHERE... WANT TO KNOW MY THEORY?
SURE... WHAT'S YOUR THEORY?
6/27
WITH APOLOGIES TO THE GREAT BIL KEANE...
I THINK HE SNUCK INTO OUR COUNTRY AS AN EXCHANGE STUDENT AND IS PRESENTLY LIVING WITH SOME AMERICAN FAMILY WHO HAS NO IDEA WHO HE IS...
OH, PLEASE... WHAT AMERICAN FAMILY COULD BE THAT OUT OF TOUCH?

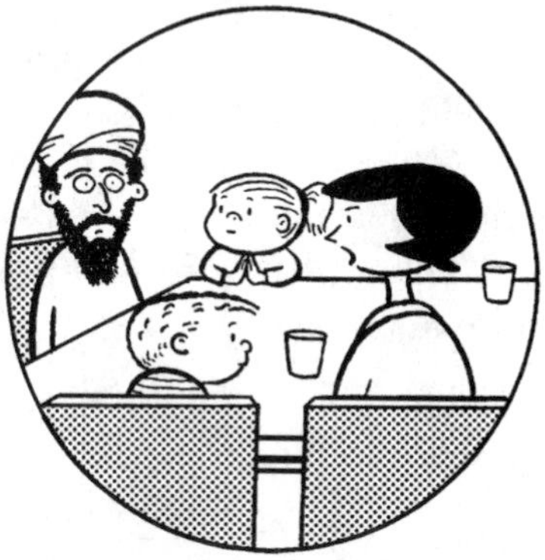

"I'm sorry, Osama, but at the end of grace, we say, 'Amen,' not 'Death to America.'"

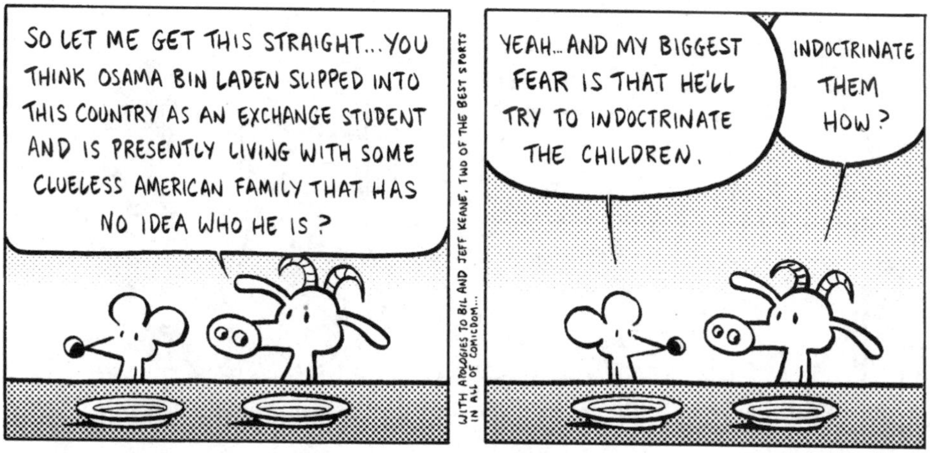
SO LET ME GET THIS STRAIGHT... YOU THINK OSAMA BIN LADEN SLIPPED INTO THIS COUNTRY AS AN EXCHANGE STUDENT AND IS PRESENTLY LIVING WITH SOME CLUELESS AMERICAN FAMILY THAT HAS NO IDEA WHO HE IS?
WITH APOLOGIES TO BIL AND JEFF KEANE, TWO OF THE BEST SPORTS IN ALL OF COMICDOM...
YEAH... AND MY BIGGEST FEAR IS THAT HE'LL TRY TO INDOCTRINATE THE CHILDREN.
INDOCTRINATE THEM HOW?
6/28

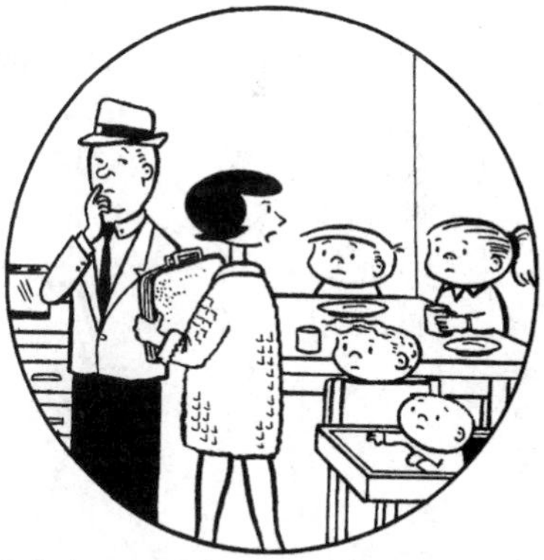

"...And when your father leaves for work, we give him hugs and kisses. We do not call him 'The Great Satan' and place a fatwa upon his head."

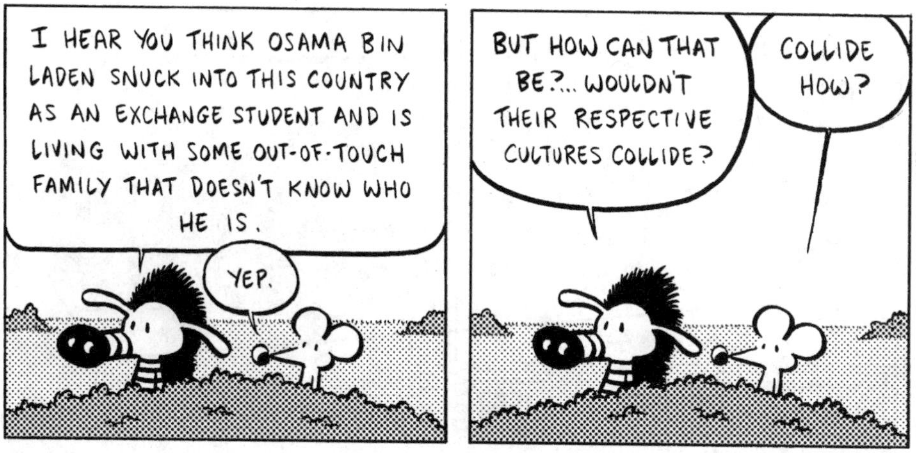
I HEAR YOU THINK OSAMA BIN LADEN SNUCK INTO THIS COUNTRY AS AN EXCHANGE STUDENT AND IS LIVING WITH SOME OUT-OF-TOUCH FAMILY THAT DOESN'T KNOW WHO HE IS.
YEP.
BUT HOW CAN THAT BE?... WOULDN'T THEIR RESPECTIVE CULTURES COLLIDE?
COLLIDE HOW?
6/29

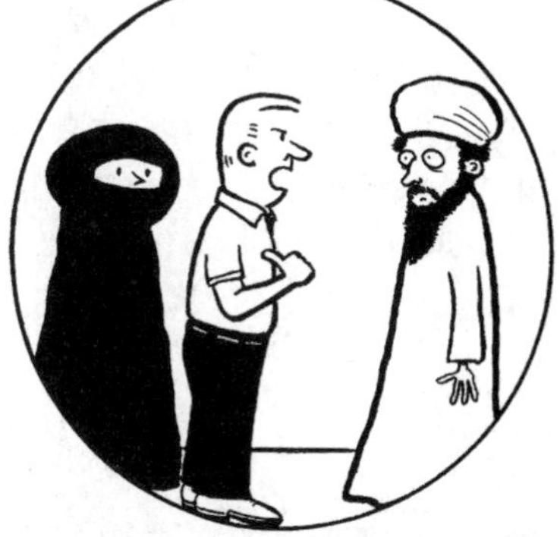

"...Culture *smulture,* you weirdo...My wife's got a bootylicious bod and DARN it, I want to see it."

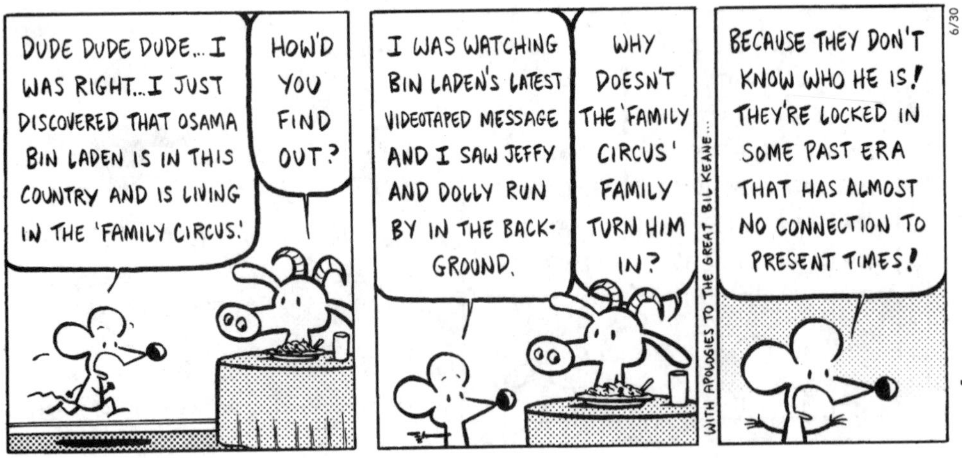
DUDE DUDE DUDE... I WAS RIGHT... I JUST DISCOVERED THAT OSAMA BIN LADEN IS IN THIS COUNTRY AND IS LIVING IN THE 'FAMILY CIRCUS.'
HOW'D YOU FIND OUT?
I WAS WATCHING BIN LADEN'S LATEST VIDEOTAPED MESSAGE AND I SAW JEFFY AND DOLLY RUN BY IN THE BACKGROUND.
WHY DOESN'T THE 'FAMILY CIRCUS' FAMILY TURN HIM IN?
WITH APOLOGIES TO THE GREAT BIL KEANE...
BECAUSE THEY DON'T KNOW WHO HE IS! THEY'RE LOCKED IN SOME PAST ERA THAT HAS ALMOST NO CONNECTION TO PRESENT TIMES!
6/30

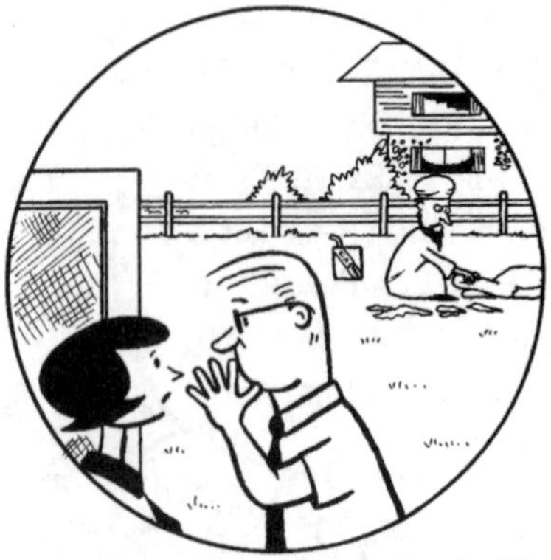

"He says he's gonna burn the president in effigy, but between you and me, it looks *nothing* like Eisenhower."

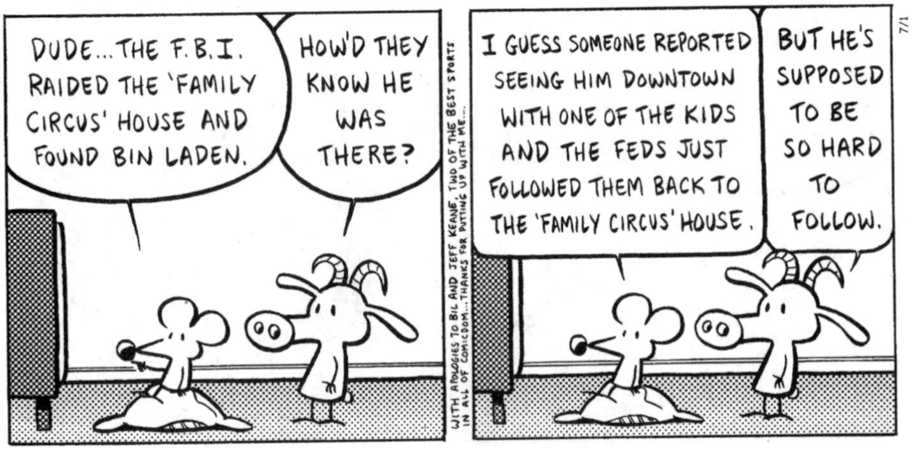
DUDE... THE F.B.I. RAIDED THE 'FAMILY CIRCUS' HOUSE AND FOUND BIN LADEN.
HOW'D THEY KNOW HE WAS THERE?
WITH APOLOGIES TO BIL AND JEFF KEANE, TWO OF THE BEST SPORTS IN ALL OF COMICDOM... THANKS FOR PUTTING UP WITH ME...
I GUESS SOMEONE REPORTED SEEING HIM DOWNTOWN WITH ONE OF THE KIDS AND THE FEDS JUST FOLLOWED THEM BACK TO THE 'FAMILY CIRCUS' HOUSE.
BUT HE'S SUPPOSED TO BE SO HARD TO FOLLOW.
7/1

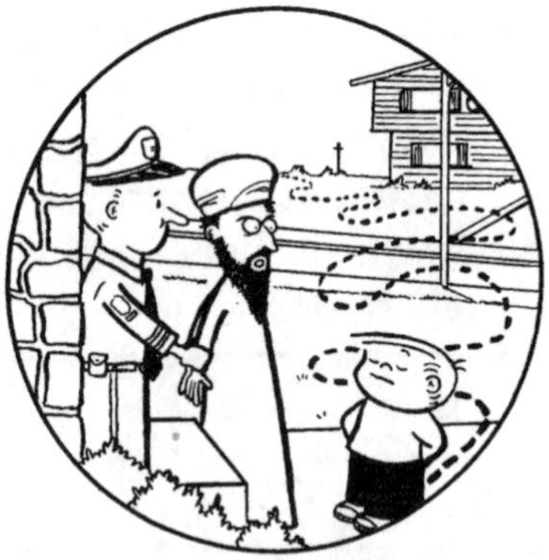

"Curse you, little Billy."

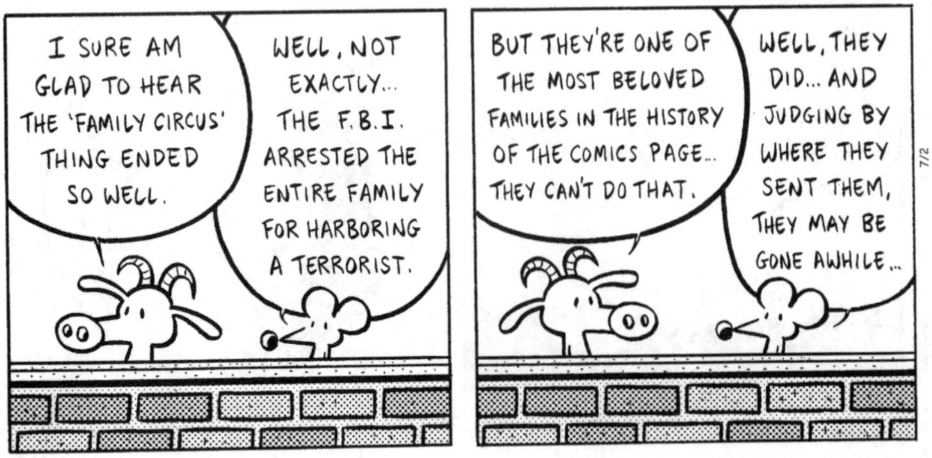
I SURE AM GLAD TO HEAR THE 'FAMILY CIRCUS' THING ENDED SO WELL.
WELL, NOT EXACTLY... THE F.B.I. ARRESTED THE ENTIRE FAMILY FOR HARBORING A TERRORIST.
BUT THEY'RE ONE OF THE MOST BELOVED FAMILIES IN THE HISTORY OF THE COMICS PAGE... THEY CAN'T DO THAT.
WELL, THEY DID... AND JUDGING BY WHERE THEY SENT THEM, THEY MAY BE GONE AWHILE...
7/2

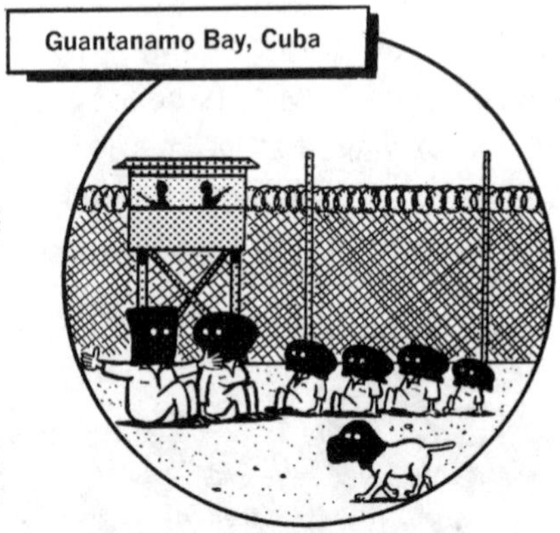
Guantanamo Bay, Cuba

"On a positive note, this should give us a whole BUNCH of new material."

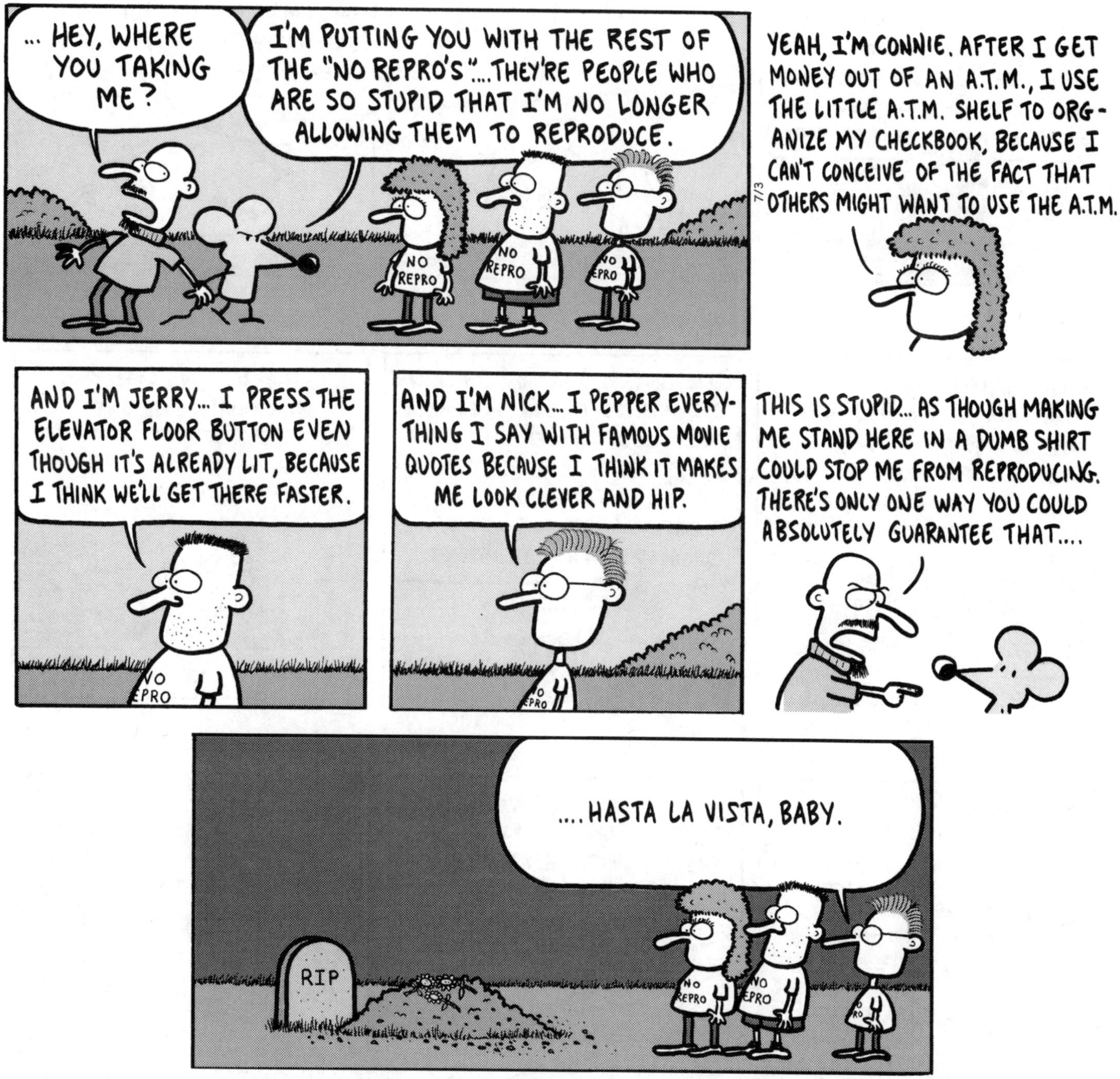
... HEY, WHERE YOU TAKING ME?
I'M PUTTING YOU WITH THE REST OF THE "NO REPRO'S"....THEY'RE PEOPLE WHO ARE SO STUPID THAT I'M NO LONGER ALLOWING THEM TO REPRODUCE.
NO REPRO
7/3
YEAH, I'M CONNIE. AFTER I GET MONEY OUT OF AN A.T.M., I USE THE LITTLE A.T.M. SHELF TO ORG-ANIZE MY CHECKBOOK, BECAUSE I CAN'T CONCEIVE OF THE FACT THAT OTHERS MIGHT WANT TO USE THE A.T.M.
AND I'M JERRY... I PRESS THE ELEVATOR FLOOR BUTTON EVEN THOUGH IT'S ALREADY LIT, BECAUSE I THINK WE'LL GET THERE FASTER.
AND I'M NICK... I PEPPER EVERY-THING I SAY WITH FAMOUS MOVIE QUOTES BECAUSE I THINK IT MAKES ME LOOK CLEVER AND HIP.
THIS IS STUPID... AS THOUGH MAKING ME STAND HERE IN A DUMB SHIRT COULD STOP ME FROM REPRODUCING. THERE'S ONLY ONE WAY YOU COULD ABSOLUTELY GUARANTEE THAT....
....HASTA LA VISTA, BABY.
RIP

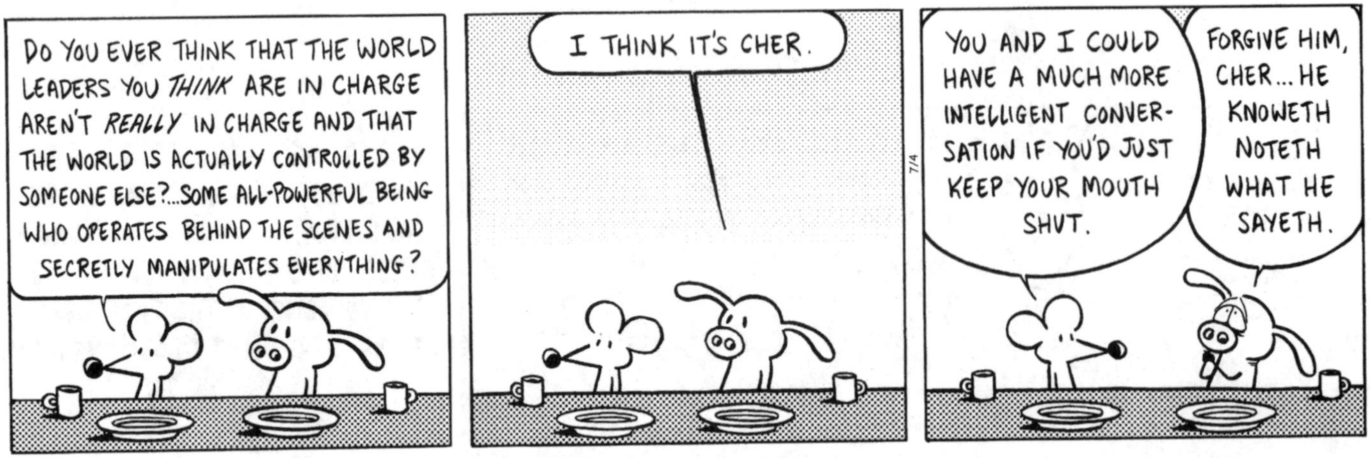
DO YOU EVER THINK THAT THE WORLD LEADERS YOU *THINK* ARE IN CHARGE AREN'T *REALLY* IN CHARGE AND THAT THE WORLD IS ACTUALLY CONTROLLED BY SOMEONE ELSE?...SOME ALL-POWERFUL BEING WHO OPERATES BEHIND THE SCENES AND SECRETLY MANIPULATES EVERYTHING?
I THINK IT'S CHER.
7/4
YOU AND I COULD HAVE A MUCH MORE INTELLIGENT CONVERSATION IF YOU'D JUST KEEP YOUR MOUTH SHUT.
FORGIVE HIM, CHER... HE KNOWETH NOTETH WHAT HE SAYETH.

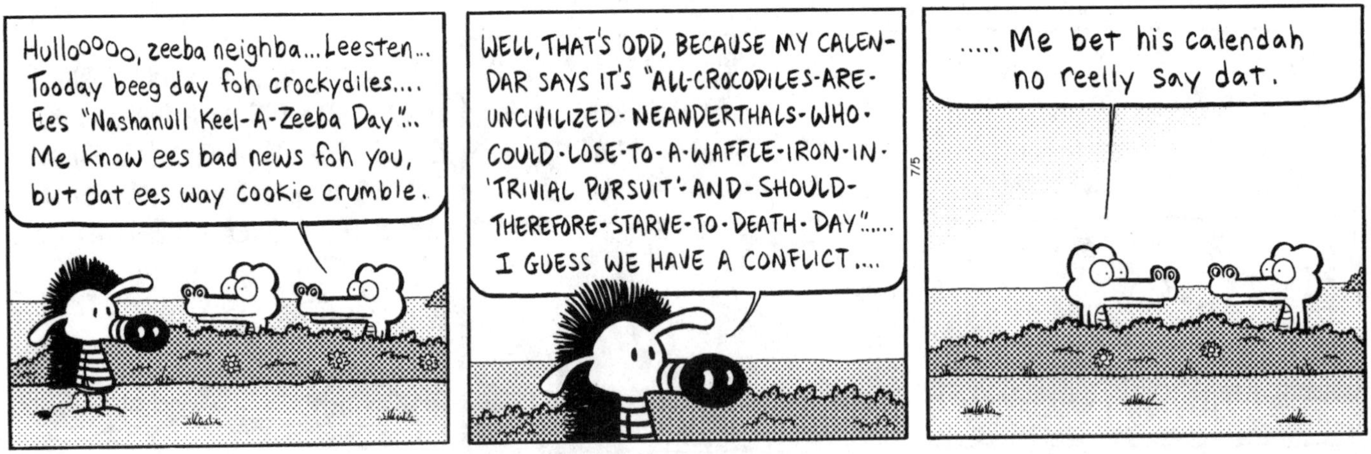
Hullooooo, zeeba neighba... Leesten... Tooday beeg day foh crockydiles.... Ees "Nashanull Keel-A-Zeeba Day"... Me know ees bad news foh you, but dat ees way cookie crumble.
WELL, THAT'S ODD, BECAUSE MY CALENDAR SAYS IT'S "ALL-CROCODILES-ARE-UNCIVILIZED-NEANDERTHALS-WHO-COULD-LOSE-TO-A-WAFFLE-IRON-IN-'TRIVIAL PURSUIT'-AND-SHOULD-THEREFORE-STARVE-TO-DEATH-DAY"..... I GUESS WE HAVE A CONFLICT....
7/5
..... Me bet his calendah no reelly say dat.

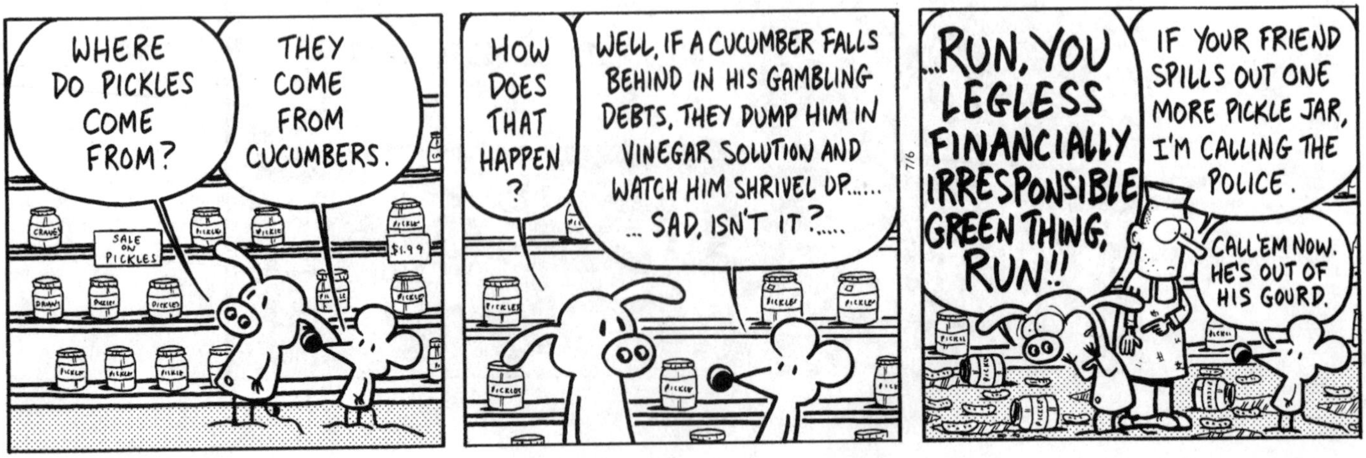
WHERE DO PICKLES COME FROM?
THEY COME FROM CUCUMBERS.
SALE ON PICKLES
$1.99
7/6
HOW DOES THAT HAPPEN?
WELL, IF A CUCUMBER FALLS BEHIND IN HIS GAMBLING DEBTS, THEY DUMP HIM IN VINEGAR SOLUTION AND WATCH HIM SHRIVEL UP..... ... SAD, ISN'T IT?.....
...RUN, YOU LEGLESS FINANCIALLY IRRESPONSIBLE GREEN THING, RUN!!
IF YOUR FRIEND SPILLS OUT ONE MORE PICKLE JAR, I'M CALLING THE POLICE.
CALL'EM NOW. HE'S OUT OF HIS GOURD.

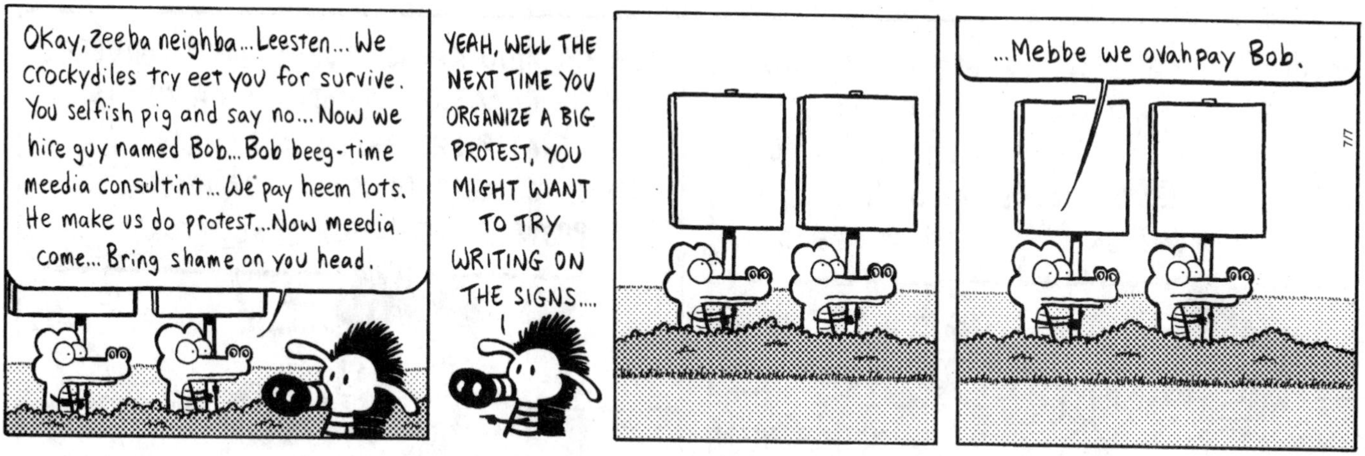
Okay, zeeba neighba... Leesten... We crockydiles try eet you for survive. You selfish pig and say no... Now we hire guy named Bob... Bob beeg-time meedia consultint... We pay heem lots. He make us do protest... Now meedia come... Bring shame on you head.
YEAH, WELL THE NEXT TIME YOU ORGANIZE A BIG PROTEST, YOU MIGHT WANT TO TRY WRITING ON THE SIGNS....
...Mebbe we ovahpay Bob.
7/7

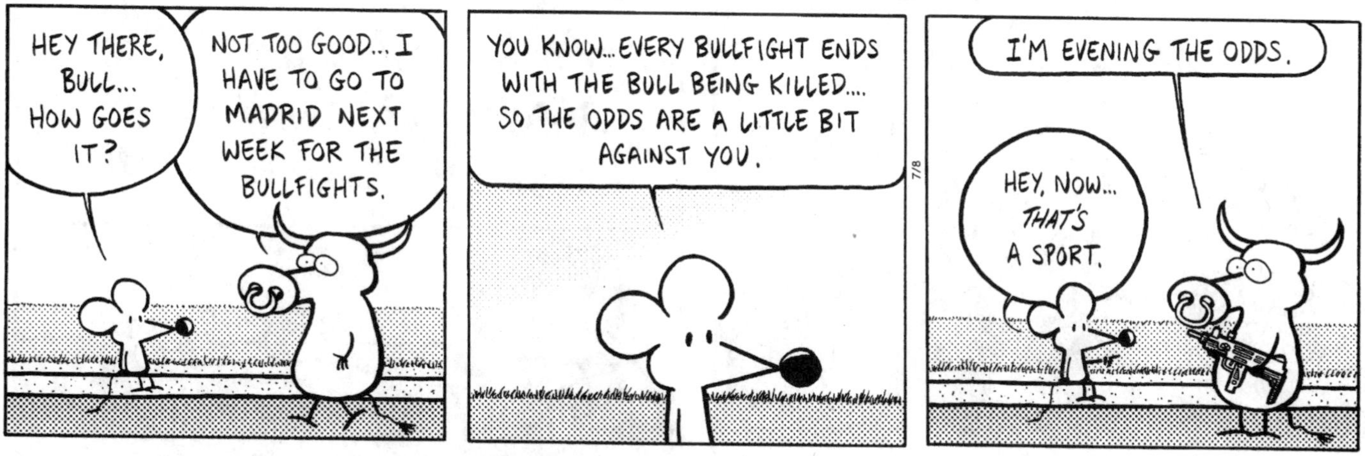
HEY THERE, BULL... HOW GOES IT?
NOT TOO GOOD... I HAVE TO GO TO MADRID NEXT WEEK FOR THE BULLFIGHTS.
YOU KNOW... EVERY BULLFIGHT ENDS WITH THE BULL BEING KILLED.... SO THE ODDS ARE A LITTLE BIT AGAINST YOU.
7/8
I'M EVENING THE ODDS.
HEY, NOW... THAT'S A SPORT.

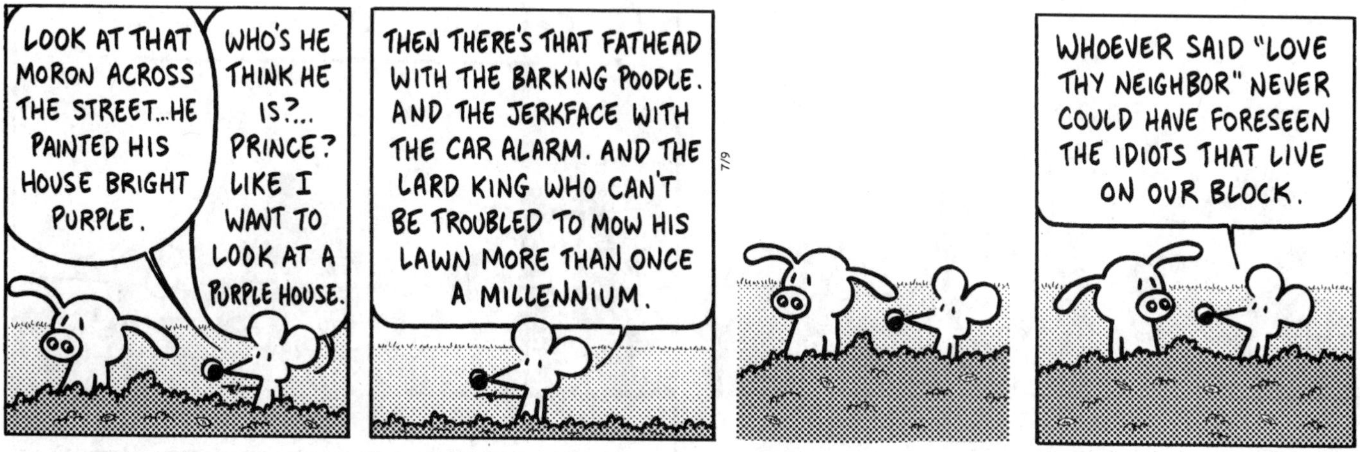
LOOK AT THAT MORON ACROSS THE STREET...HE PAINTED HIS HOUSE BRIGHT PURPLE.
WHO'S HE THINK HE IS?... PRINCE? LIKE I WANT TO LOOK AT A PURPLE HOUSE.
THEN THERE'S THAT FATHEAD WITH THE BARKING POODLE. AND THE JERKFACE WITH THE CAR ALARM. AND THE LARD KING WHO CAN'T BE TROUBLED TO MOW HIS LAWN MORE THAN ONCE A MILLENNIUM.
7/9
WHOEVER SAID "LOVE THY NEIGHBOR" NEVER COULD HAVE FORESEEN THE IDIOTS THAT LIVE ON OUR BLOCK.

Hullooºoo, zeeba neighba... Leesten... Me want you meet wife Debbie.... She a new crockydile mom wiff two keeds... Dis prove dat not all crockydiles ees destroyahs of life... Some ees gud moms dat love preshiss keeds....

HMMM... YOU KNOW, I'VE ALWAYS WONDERED SOMETHING ABOUT CROCODILE MOTHERS... IS IT TRUE THAT RIGHT AFTER YOUR CHILDREN ARE BORN, YOU KEEP THEM IN YOUR MOUTH TO PROTECT THEM FROM PREDATORS?

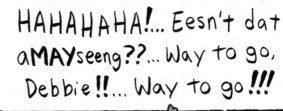

HAHAHAHA!... Eesn't dat aMAYseeng??... Way to go, Debbie!!... Way to go!!!

PAT PAT PAT PAT

☆GULP☆

Ees okay.... We make more.

80

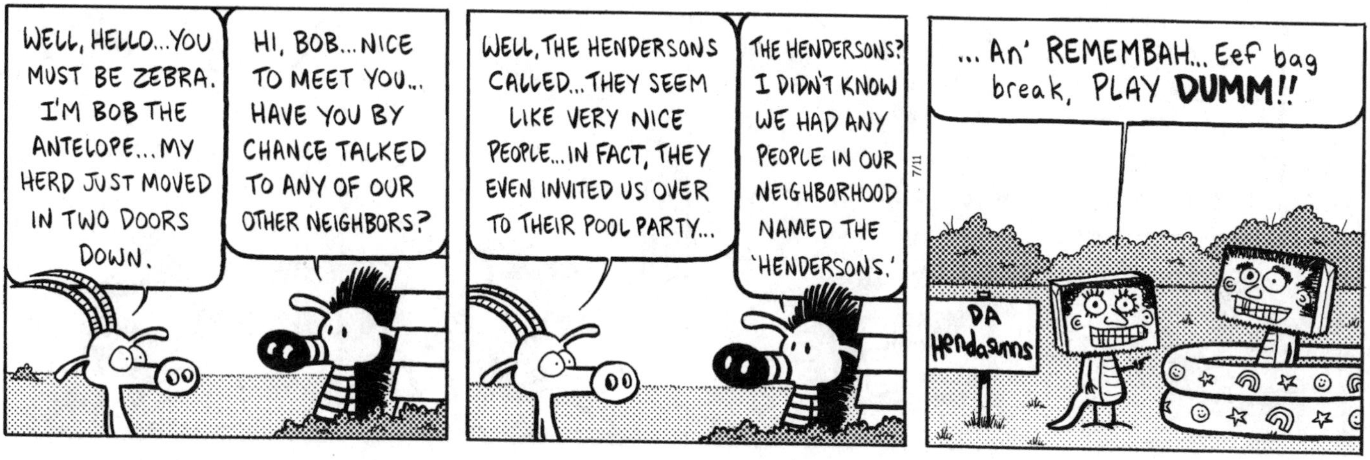
WELL, HELLO... YOU MUST BE ZEBRA. I'M BOB THE ANTELOPE... MY HERD JUST MOVED IN TWO DOORS DOWN.
HI, BOB... NICE TO MEET YOU... HAVE YOU BY CHANCE TALKED TO ANY OF OUR OTHER NEIGHBORS?
WELL, THE HENDERSONS CALLED... THEY SEEM LIKE VERY NICE PEOPLE... IN FACT, THEY EVEN INVITED US OVER TO THEIR POOL PARTY...
THE HENDERSONS? I DIDN'T KNOW WE HAD ANY PEOPLE IN OUR NEIGHBORHOOD NAMED THE 'HENDERSONS.'
7/11
... An' REMEMBAH... Eef bag break, PLAY **DUMM!!**
DA Hendasunns

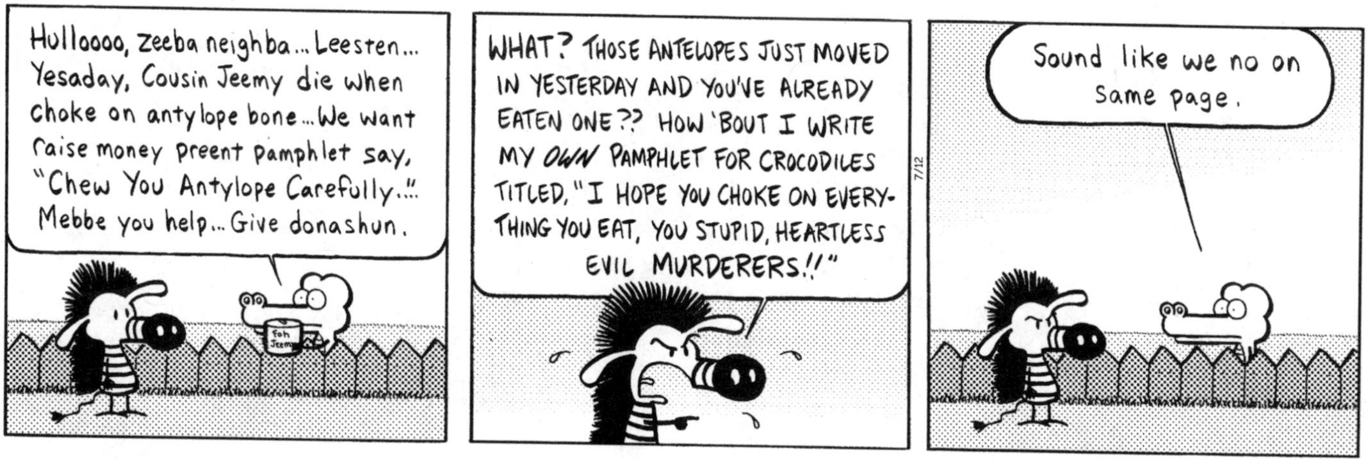
Hulloooo, zeeba neighba... Leesten... Yesaday, Cousin Jeemy die when choke on antylope bone... We want raise money preent pamphlet say, "Chew You Antylope Carefully..." Mebbe you help... Give donashun.
Foh Jeemy
WHAT? THOSE ANTELOPES JUST MOVED IN YESTERDAY AND YOU'VE ALREADY EATEN ONE?? HOW 'BOUT I WRITE MY *OWN* PAMPHLET FOR CROCODILES TITLED, "I HOPE YOU CHOKE ON EVERYTHING YOU EAT, YOU STUPID, HEARTLESS EVIL MURDERERS!!"
7/12
Sound like we no on same page.

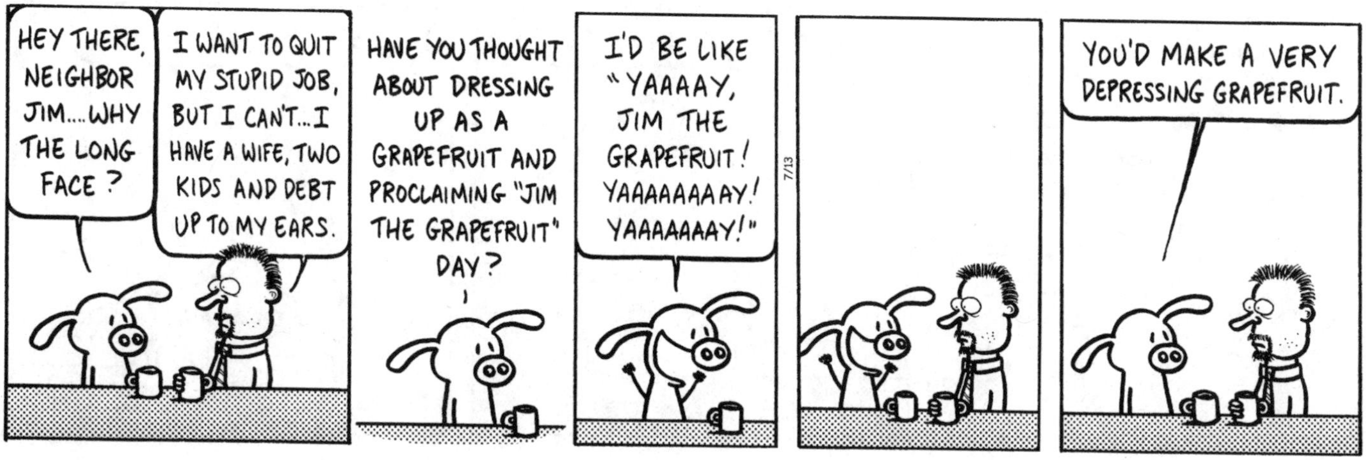
HEY THERE, NEIGHBOR JIM.... WHY THE LONG FACE?
I WANT TO QUIT MY STUPID JOB, BUT I CAN'T... I HAVE A WIFE, TWO KIDS AND DEBT UP TO MY EARS.
HAVE YOU THOUGHT ABOUT DRESSING UP AS A GRAPEFRUIT AND PROCLAIMING "JIM THE GRAPEFRUIT" DAY?
I'D BE LIKE "YAAAAY, JIM THE GRAPEFRUIT! YAAAAAAAAY! YAAAAAAAY!"
7/13
YOU'D MAKE A VERY DEPRESSING GRAPEFRUIT.

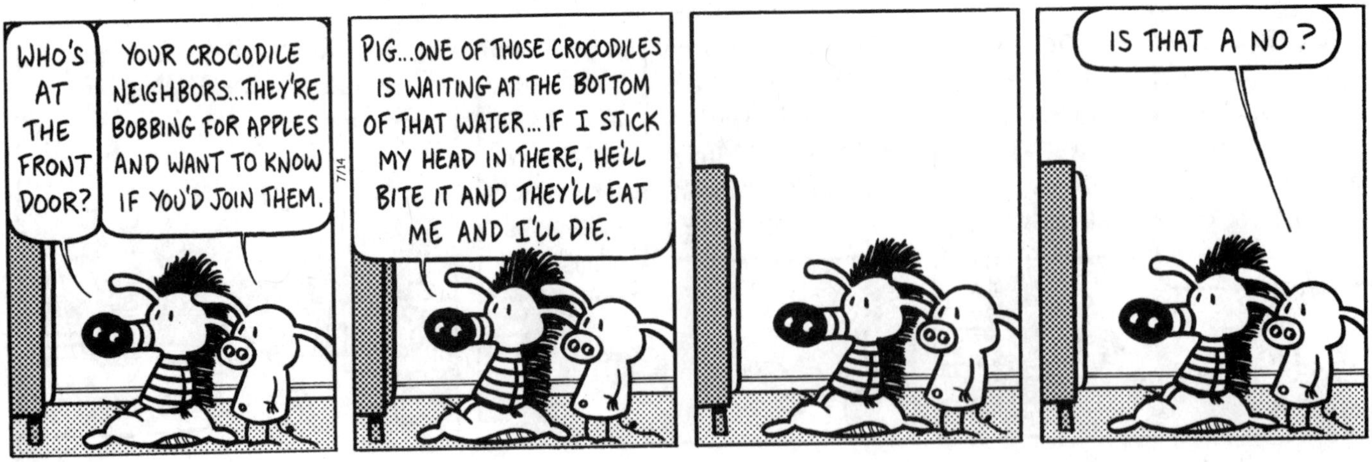
WHO'S AT THE FRONT DOOR?
YOUR CROCODILE NEIGHBORS...THEY'RE BOBBING FOR APPLES AND WANT TO KNOW IF YOU'D JOIN THEM.
7/14
PIG...ONE OF THOSE CROCODILES IS WAITING AT THE BOTTOM OF THAT WATER...IF I STICK MY HEAD IN THERE, HE'LL BITE IT AND THEY'LL EAT ME AND I'LL DIE.
IS THAT A NO?

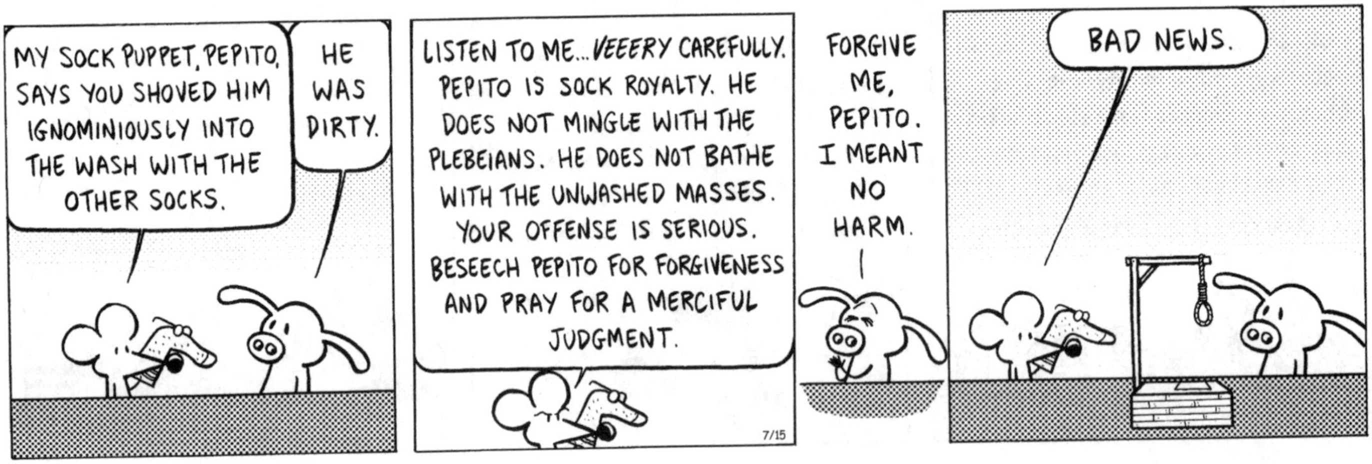
MY SOCK PUPPET, PEPITO, SAYS YOU SHOVED HIM IGNOMINIOUSLY INTO THE WASH WITH THE OTHER SOCKS.
HE WAS DIRTY.
LISTEN TO ME...VEEERY CAREFULLY. PEPITO IS SOCK ROYALTY. HE DOES NOT MINGLE WITH THE PLEBEIANS. HE DOES NOT BATHE WITH THE UNWASHED MASSES. YOUR OFFENSE IS SERIOUS. BESEECH PEPITO FOR FORGIVENESS AND PRAY FOR A MERCIFUL JUDGMENT.
7/15
FORGIVE ME, PEPITO. I MEANT NO HARM.
BAD NEWS.

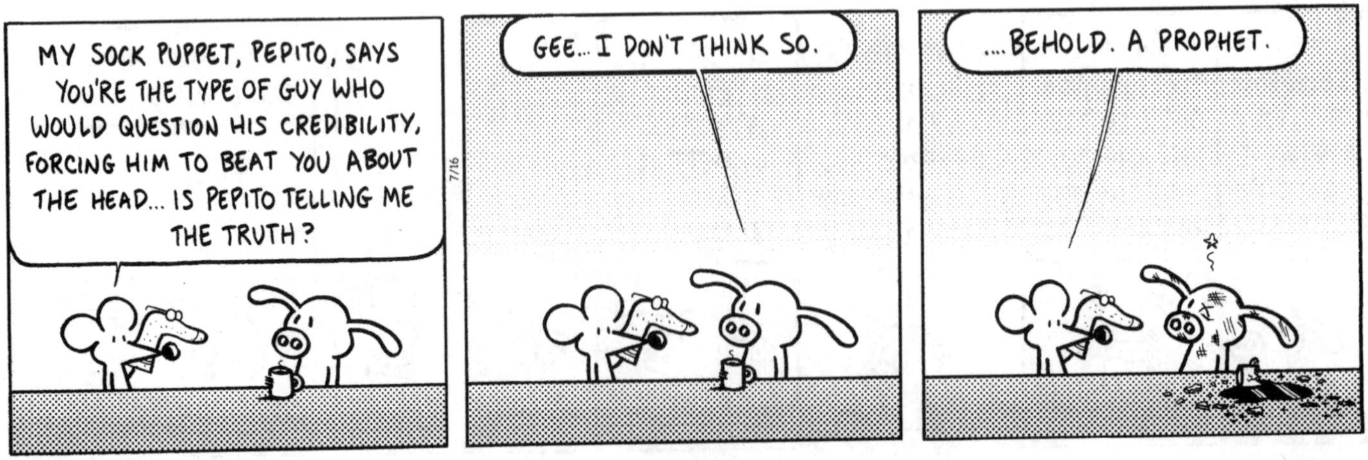
MY SOCK PUPPET, PEPITO, SAYS YOU'RE THE TYPE OF GUY WHO WOULD QUESTION HIS CREDIBILITY, FORCING HIM TO BEAT YOU ABOUT THE HEAD... IS PEPITO TELLING ME THE TRUTH?
7/16
GEE... I DON'T THINK SO.
....BEHOLD. A PROPHET.

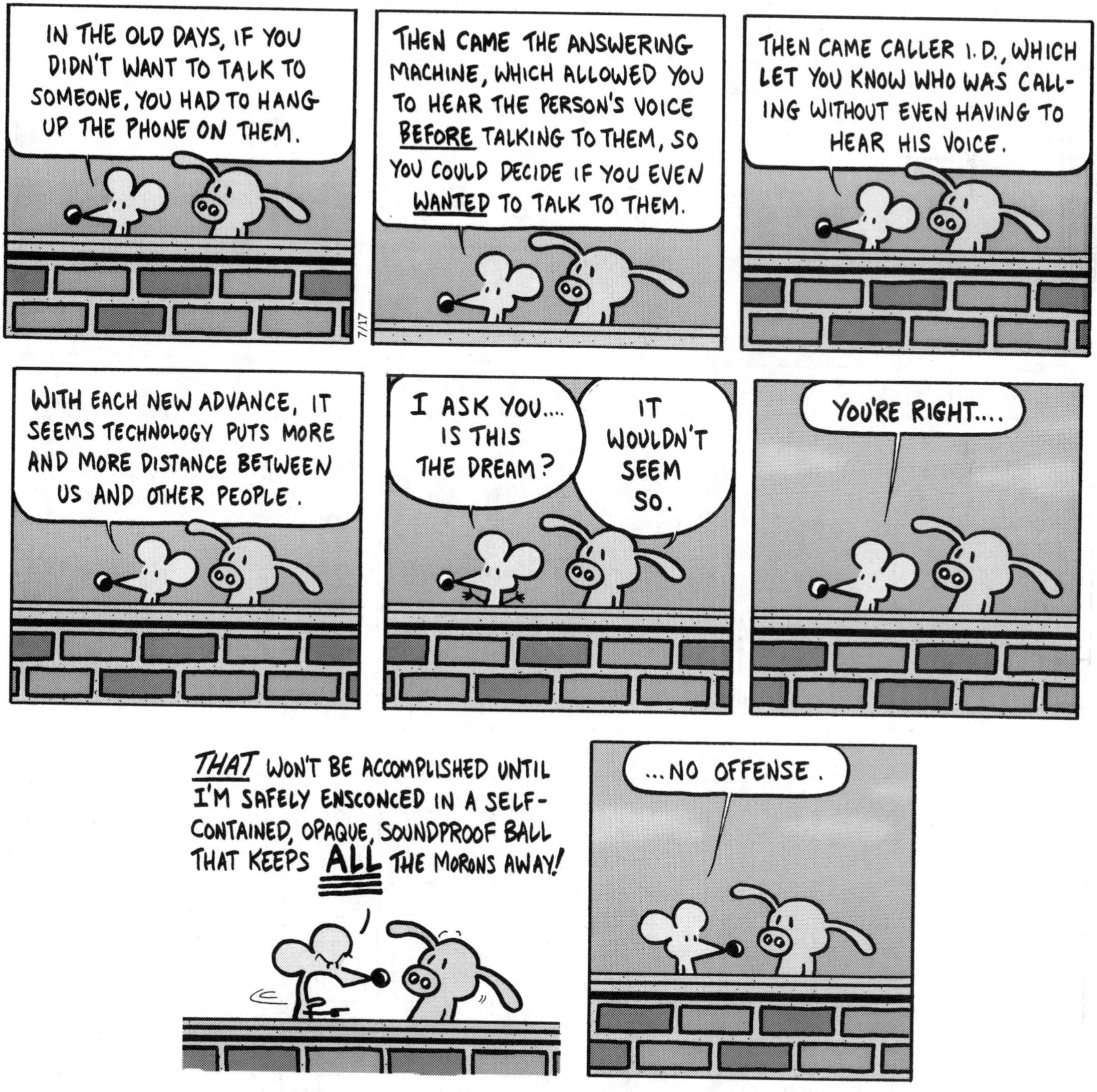
IN THE OLD DAYS, IF YOU DIDN'T WANT TO TALK TO SOMEONE, YOU HAD TO HANG UP THE PHONE ON THEM.
7/17
THEN CAME THE ANSWERING MACHINE, WHICH ALLOWED YOU TO HEAR THE PERSON'S VOICE BEFORE TALKING TO THEM, SO YOU COULD DECIDE IF YOU EVEN WANTED TO TALK TO THEM.
THEN CAME CALLER I.D., WHICH LET YOU KNOW WHO WAS CALLING WITHOUT EVEN HAVING TO HEAR HIS VOICE.
WITH EACH NEW ADVANCE, IT SEEMS TECHNOLOGY PUTS MORE AND MORE DISTANCE BETWEEN US AND OTHER PEOPLE.
I ASK YOU.... IS THIS THE DREAM?
IT WOULDN'T SEEM SO.
YOU'RE RIGHT....
THAT WON'T BE ACCOMPLISHED UNTIL I'M SAFELY ENSCONCED IN A SELF-CONTAINED, OPAQUE, SOUNDPROOF BALL THAT KEEPS ALL THE MORONS AWAY!
...NO OFFENSE.

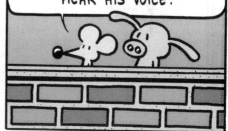

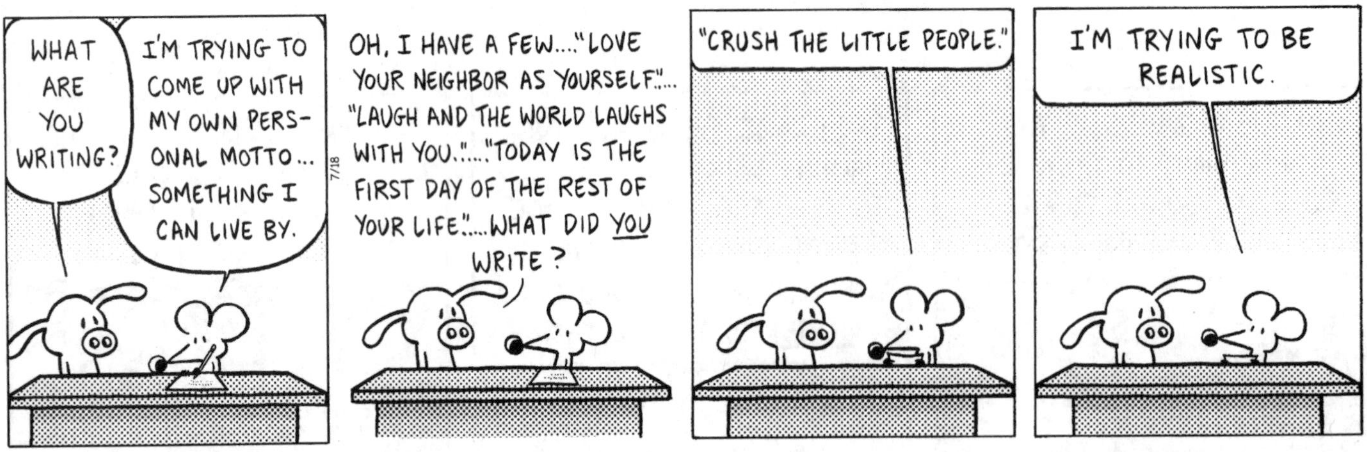
WHAT ARE YOU WRITING?
I'M TRYING TO COME UP WITH MY OWN PERSONAL MOTTO... SOMETHING I CAN LIVE BY.
OH, I HAVE A FEW...."LOVE YOUR NEIGHBOR AS YOURSELF."... "LAUGH AND THE WORLD LAUGHS WITH YOU."...."TODAY IS THE FIRST DAY OF THE REST OF YOUR LIFE."....WHAT DID YOU WRITE?
"CRUSH THE LITTLE PEOPLE."
I'M TRYING TO BE REALISTIC.

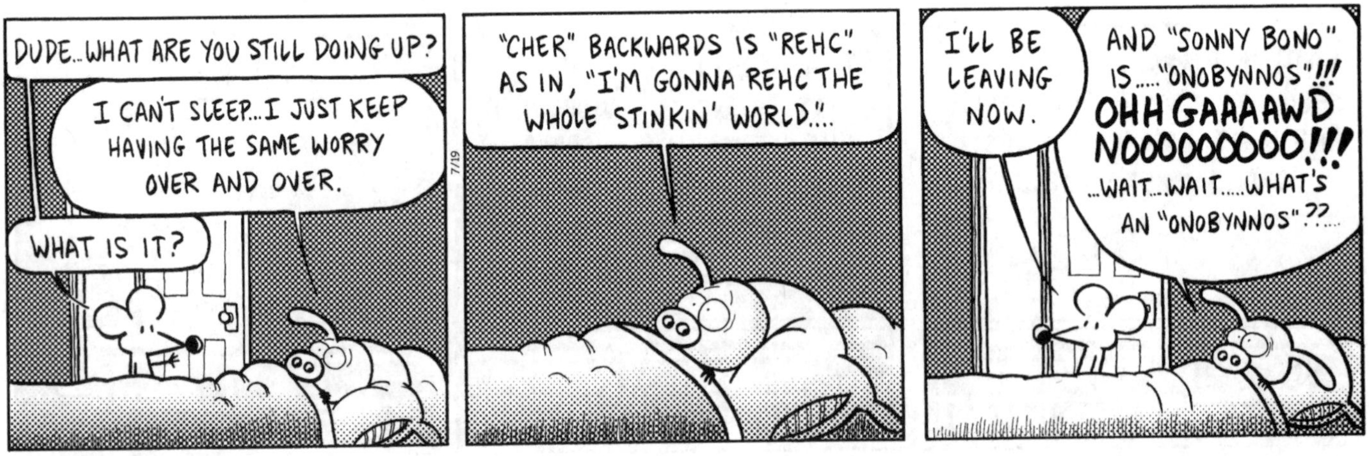
DUDE...WHAT ARE YOU STILL DOING UP?
I CAN'T SLEEP...I JUST KEEP HAVING THE SAME WORRY OVER AND OVER.
WHAT IS IT?
"CHER" BACKWARDS IS "REHC." AS IN, "I'M GONNA REHC THE WHOLE STINKIN' WORLD."...
I'LL BE LEAVING NOW.
AND "SONNY BONO" IS....."ONOBYNNOS"!!! OHH GAAAAWD NOOOOOOOOO!!! ...WAIT....WAIT.....WHAT'S AN "ONOBYNNOS"??...

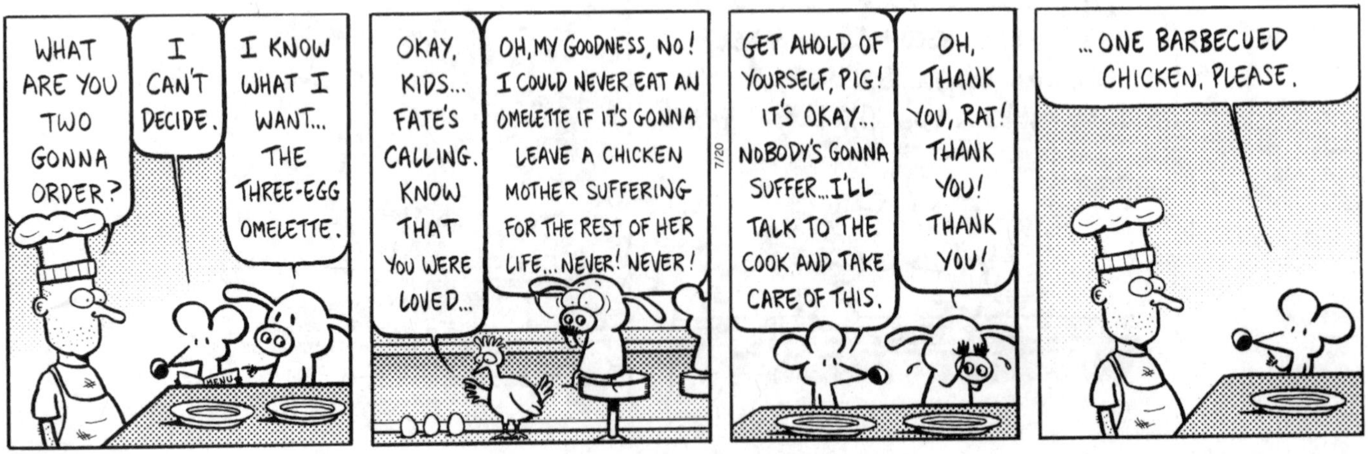
WHAT ARE YOU TWO GONNA ORDER?
I CAN'T DECIDE.
I KNOW WHAT I WANT... THE THREE-EGG OMELETTE.
MENU
OKAY, KIDS... FATE'S CALLING. KNOW THAT YOU WERE LOVED...
OH, MY GOODNESS, NO! I COULD NEVER EAT AN OMELETTE IF IT'S GONNA LEAVE A CHICKEN MOTHER SUFFERING FOR THE REST OF HER LIFE...NEVER! NEVER!
GET AHOLD OF YOURSELF, PIG! IT'S OKAY... NOBODY'S GONNA SUFFER...I'LL TALK TO THE COOK AND TAKE CARE OF THIS.
OH, THANK YOU, RAT! THANK YOU! THANK YOU!
...ONE BARBECUED CHICKEN, PLEASE.

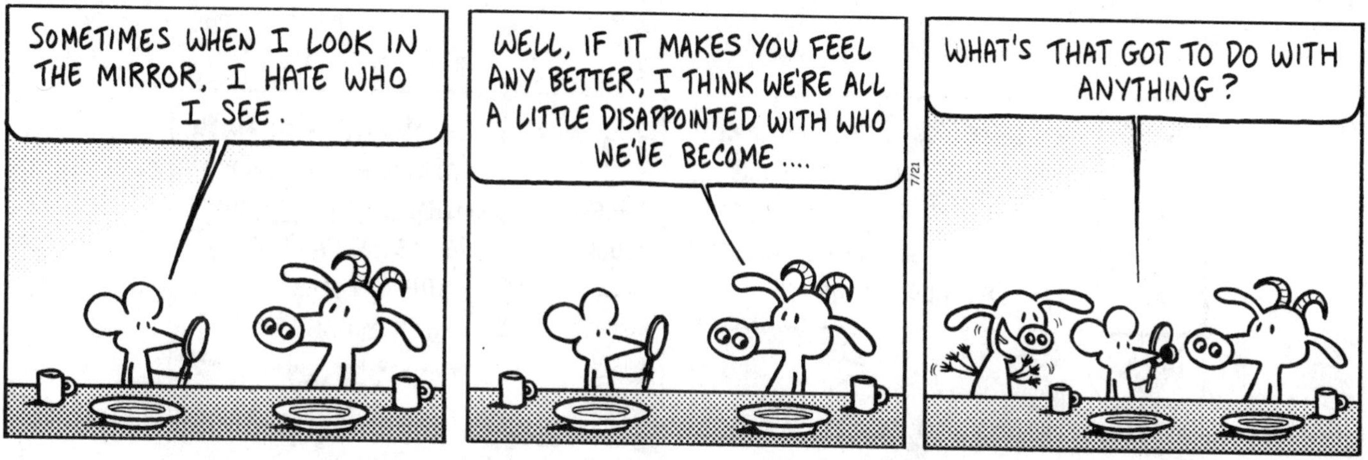
SOMETIMES WHEN I LOOK IN THE MIRROR, I HATE WHO I SEE.
WELL, IF IT MAKES YOU FEEL ANY BETTER, I THINK WE'RE ALL A LITTLE DISAPPOINTED WITH WHO WE'VE BECOME....
7/21
WHAT'S THAT GOT TO DO WITH ANYTHING?

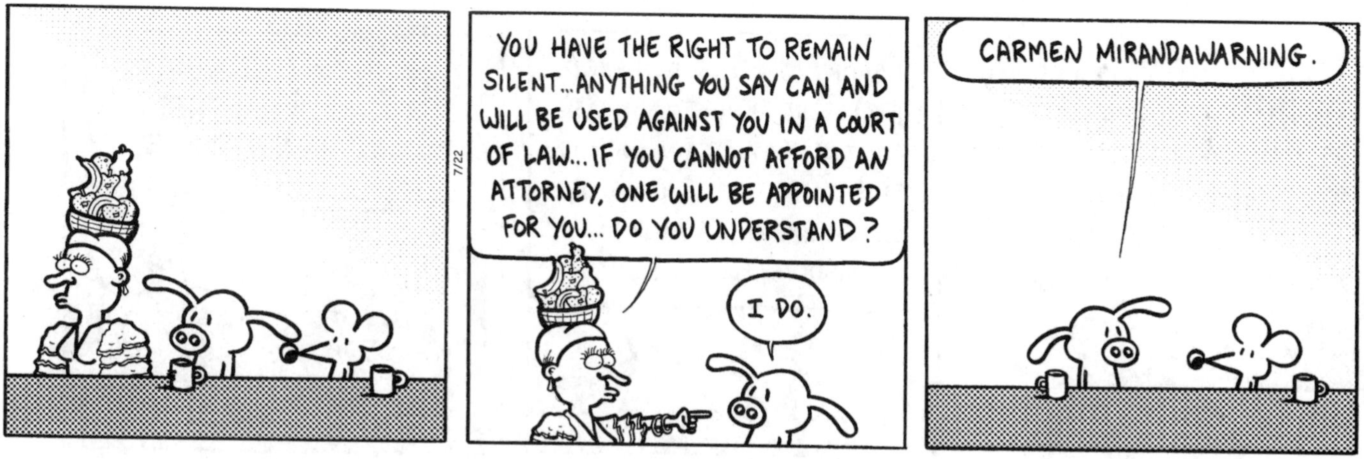
7/22
YOU HAVE THE RIGHT TO REMAIN SILENT... ANYTHING YOU SAY CAN AND WILL BE USED AGAINST YOU IN A COURT OF LAW... IF YOU CANNOT AFFORD AN ATTORNEY, ONE WILL BE APPOINTED FOR YOU... DO YOU UNDERSTAND?
I DO.
CARMEN MIRANDAWARNING.

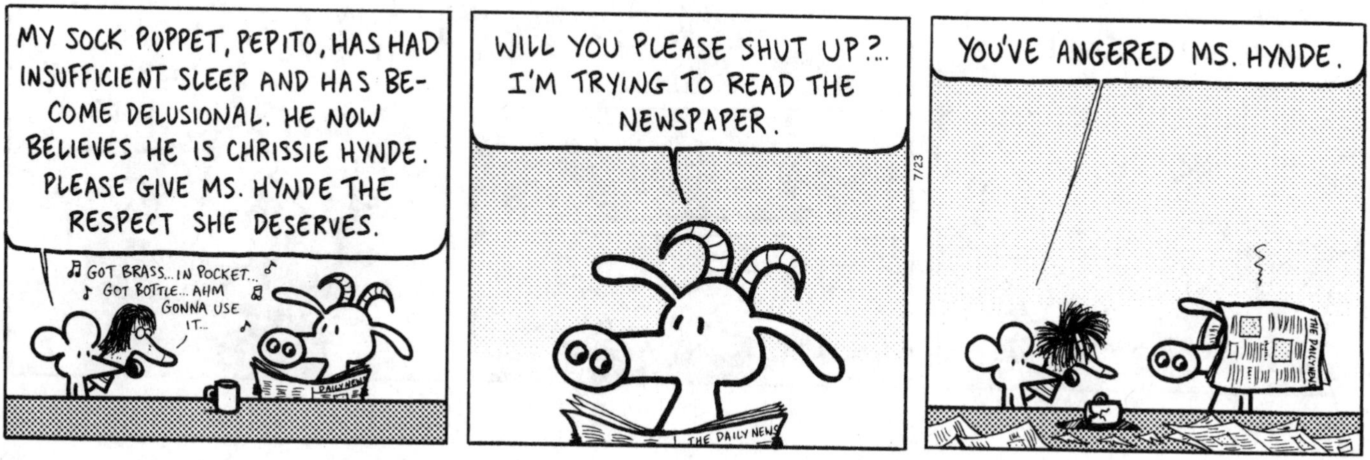
MY SOCK PUPPET, PEPITO, HAS HAD INSUFFICIENT SLEEP AND HAS BECOME DELUSIONAL. HE NOW BELIEVES HE IS CHRISSIE HYNDE. PLEASE GIVE MS. HYNDE THE RESPECT SHE DESERVES.
♫ GOT BRASS... IN POCKET... ♪ GOT BOTTLE... AHM GONNA USE IT...
DAILY NEWS
WILL YOU PLEASE SHUT UP?... I'M TRYING TO READ THE NEWSPAPER.
THE DAILY NEWS
7/23
YOU'VE ANGERED MS. HYNDE.
THE DAILY NEWS

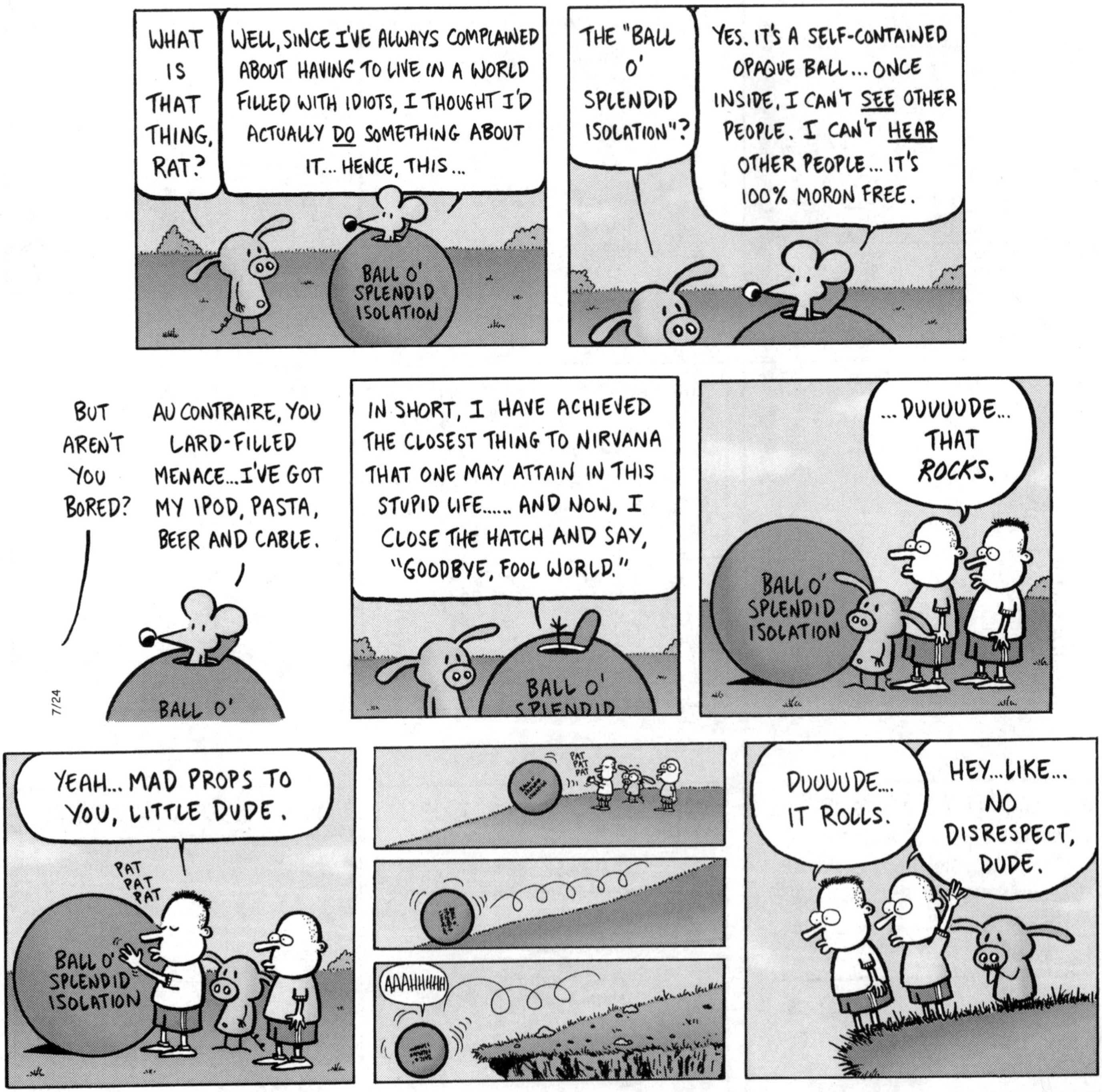
WHAT IS THAT THING, RAT?
WELL, SINCE I'VE ALWAYS COMPLAINED ABOUT HAVING TO LIVE IN A WORLD FILLED WITH IDIOTS, I THOUGHT I'D ACTUALLY DO SOMETHING ABOUT IT... HENCE, THIS...
BALL O' SPLENDID ISOLATION
THE "BALL O' SPLENDID ISOLATION"?
YES. IT'S A SELF-CONTAINED OPAQUE BALL... ONCE INSIDE, I CAN'T SEE OTHER PEOPLE. I CAN'T HEAR OTHER PEOPLE... IT'S 100% MORON FREE.
BUT AREN'T YOU BORED?
AU CONTRAIRE, YOU LARD-FILLED MENACE...I'VE GOT MY IPOD, PASTA, BEER AND CABLE.
BALL O'
7/24
IN SHORT, I HAVE ACHIEVED THE CLOSEST THING TO NIRVANA THAT ONE MAY ATTAIN IN THIS STUPID LIFE...... AND NOW, I CLOSE THE HATCH AND SAY, "GOODBYE, FOOL WORLD."
BALL O'
...DUUUUDE... THAT ROCKS.
BALL O' SPLENDID ISOLATION
YEAH... MAD PROPS TO YOU, LITTLE DUDE.
PAT PAT PAT
BALL O' SPLENDID ISOLATION
PAT PAT PAT
AAAHHHHHH
DUUUUDE.... IT ROLLS.
HEY...LIKE... NO DISRESPECT, DUDE.

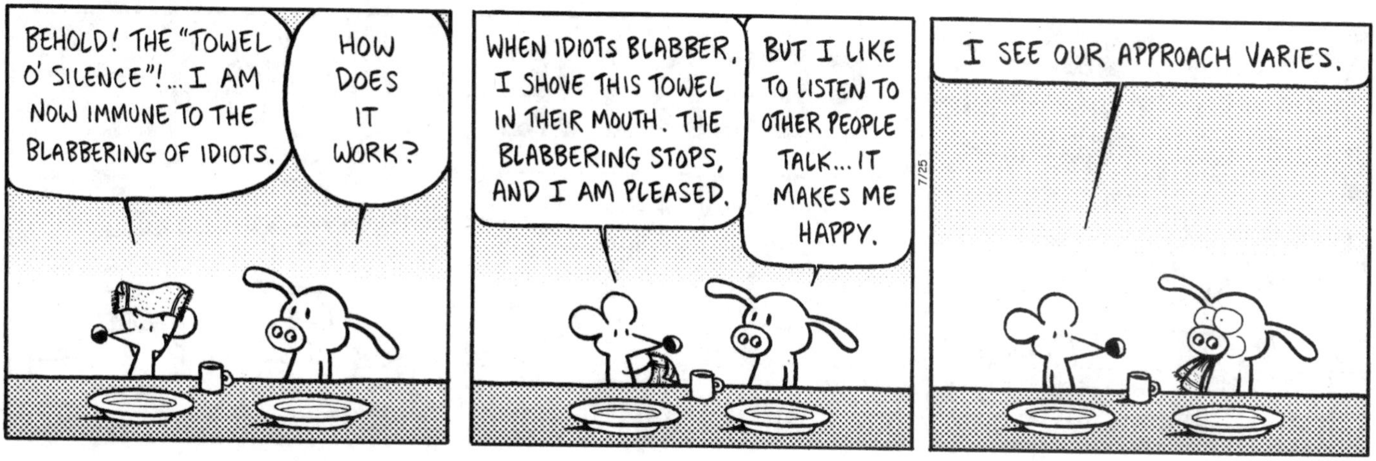

BEHOLD! THE "TOWEL O' SILENCE"!... I AM NOW IMMUNE TO THE BLABBERING OF IDIOTS.
HOW DOES IT WORK?
WHEN IDIOTS BLABBER, I SHOVE THIS TOWEL IN THEIR MOUTH. THE BLABBERING STOPS, AND I AM PLEASED.
BUT I LIKE TO LISTEN TO OTHER PEOPLE TALK... IT MAKES ME HAPPY.
7/25
I SEE OUR APPROACH VARIES.

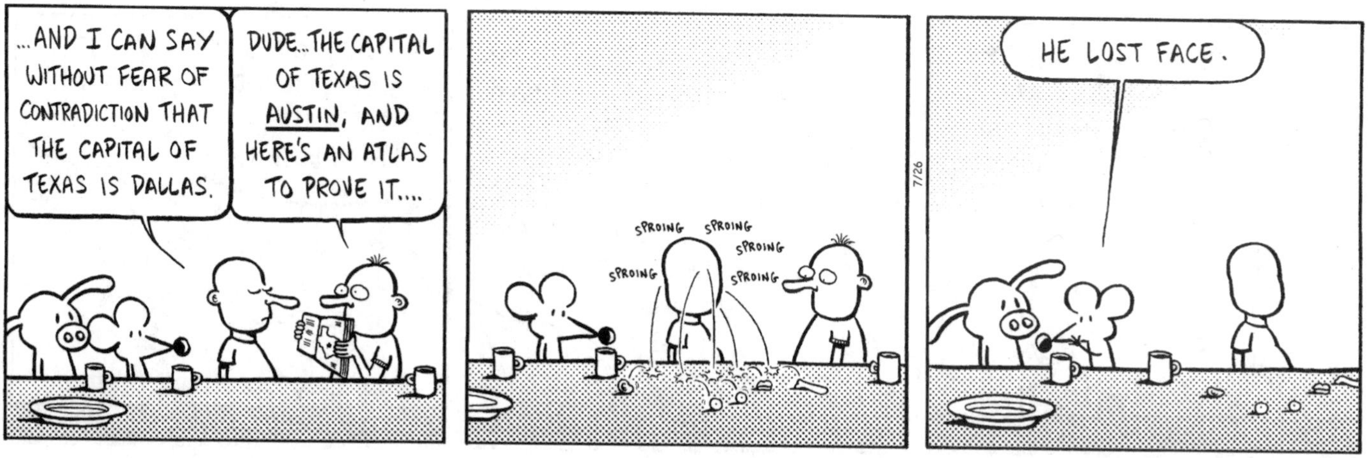

...AND I CAN SAY WITHOUT FEAR OF CONTRADICTION THAT THE CAPITAL OF TEXAS IS DALLAS.
DUDE... THE CAPITAL OF TEXAS IS AUSTIN, AND HERE'S AN ATLAS TO PROVE IT....
SPROING SPROING SPROING SPROING SPROING SPROING
7/26
HE LOST FACE.

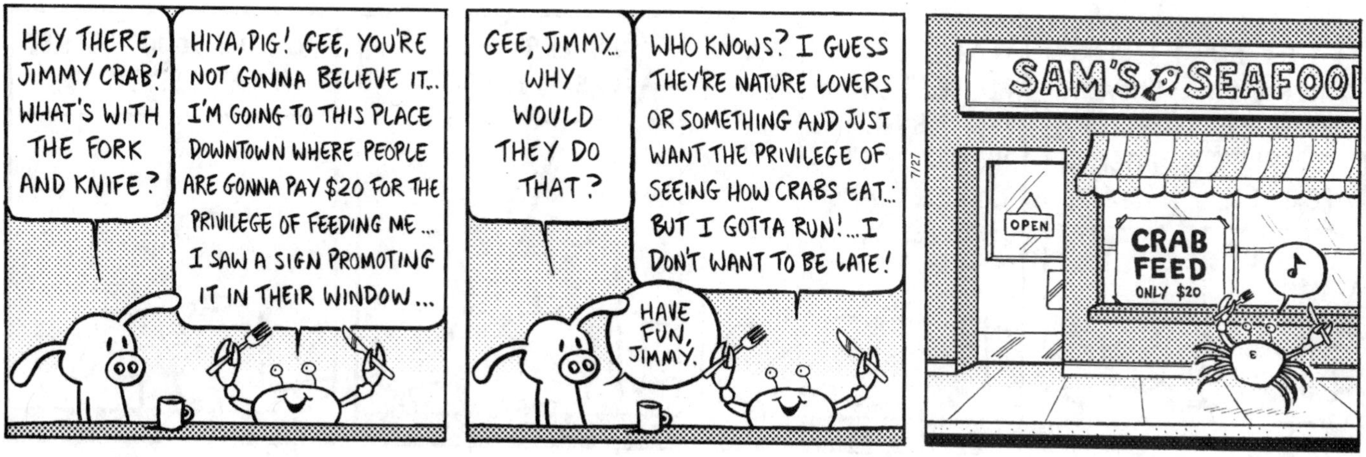

HEY THERE, JIMMY CRAB! WHAT'S WITH THE FORK AND KNIFE?
HIYA, PIG! GEE, YOU'RE NOT GONNA BELIEVE IT... I'M GOING TO THIS PLACE DOWNTOWN WHERE PEOPLE ARE GONNA PAY $20 FOR THE PRIVILEGE OF FEEDING ME... I SAW A SIGN PROMOTING IT IN THEIR WINDOW...
GEE, JIMMY... WHY WOULD THEY DO THAT?
WHO KNOWS? I GUESS THEY'RE NATURE LOVERS OR SOMETHING AND JUST WANT THE PRIVILEGE OF SEEING HOW CRABS EAT... BUT I GOTTA RUN!... I DON'T WANT TO BE LATE!
HAVE FUN, JIMMY.
7/27
SAM'S SEAFOO
OPEN
CRAB FEED
ONLY $20

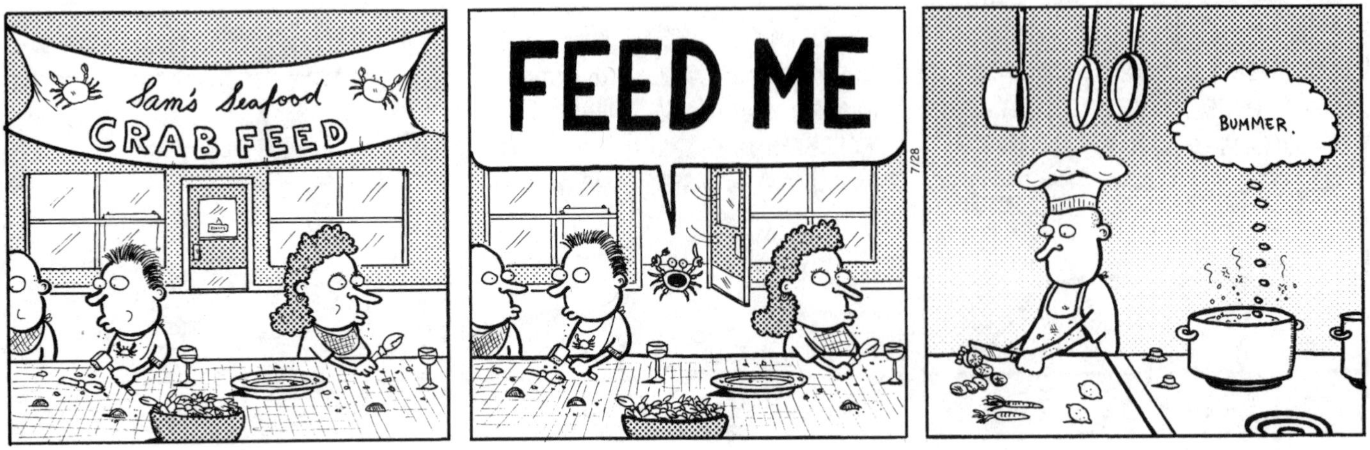
Sam's Seafood
CRAB FEED
FEED ME
7/28
BUMMER.

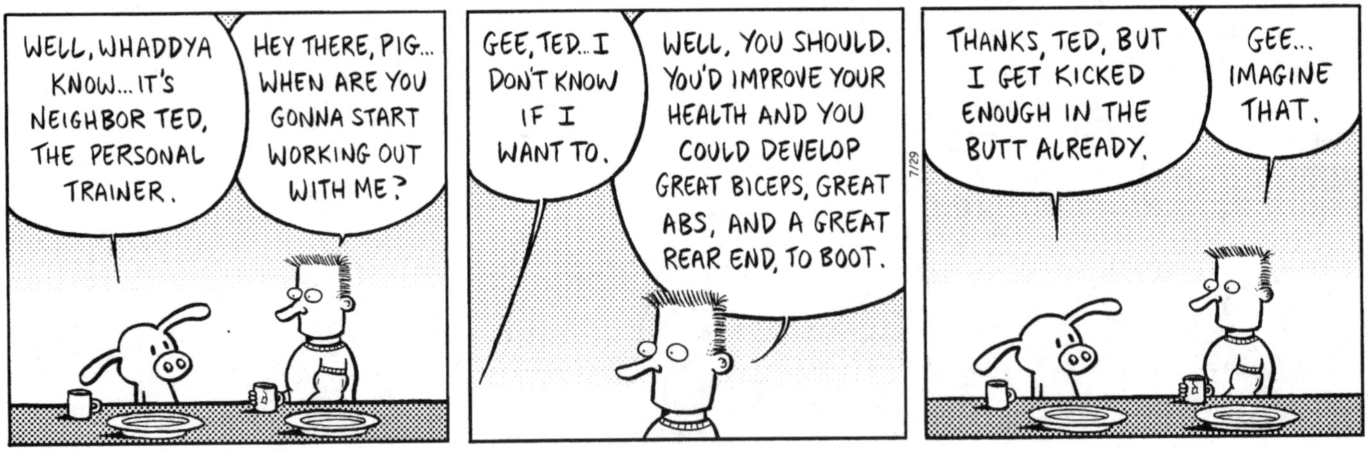
WELL, WHADDYA KNOW... IT'S NEIGHBOR TED, THE PERSONAL TRAINER.
HEY THERE, PIG... WHEN ARE YOU GONNA START WORKING OUT WITH ME?
GEE, TED... I DON'T KNOW IF I WANT TO.
WELL, YOU SHOULD. YOU'D IMPROVE YOUR HEALTH AND YOU COULD DEVELOP GREAT BICEPS, GREAT ABS, AND A GREAT REAR END, TO BOOT.
7/29
THANKS, TED, BUT I GET KICKED ENOUGH IN THE BUTT ALREADY.
GEE... IMAGINE THAT.

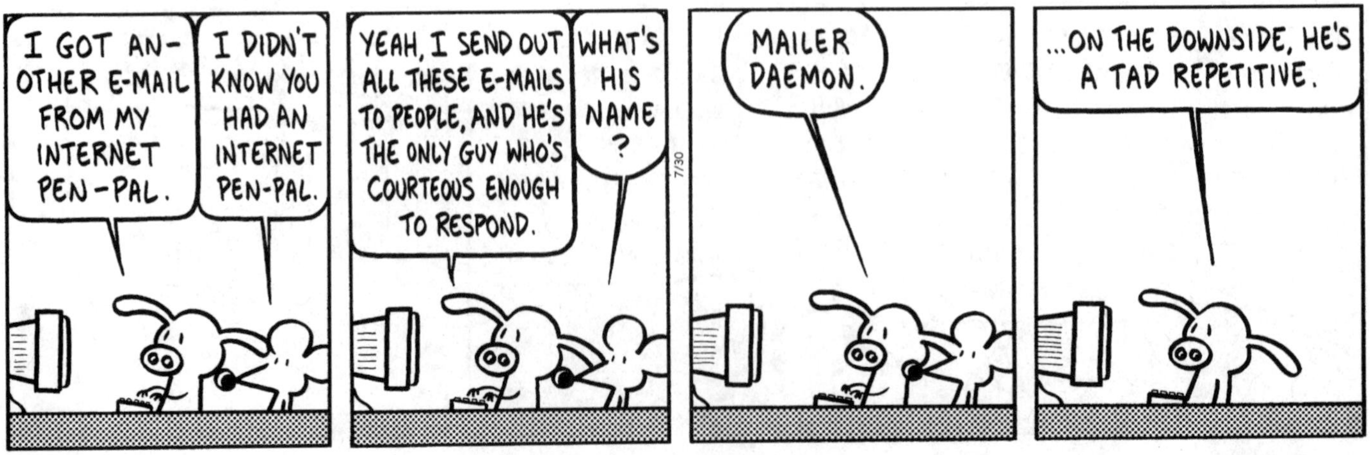
I GOT ANOTHER E-MAIL FROM MY INTERNET PEN-PAL.
I DIDN'T KNOW YOU HAD AN INTERNET PEN-PAL.
YEAH, I SEND OUT ALL THESE E-MAILS TO PEOPLE, AND HE'S THE ONLY GUY WHO'S COURTEOUS ENOUGH TO RESPOND.
WHAT'S HIS NAME?
7/30
MAILER DAEMON.
...ON THE DOWNSIDE, HE'S A TAD REPETITIVE.

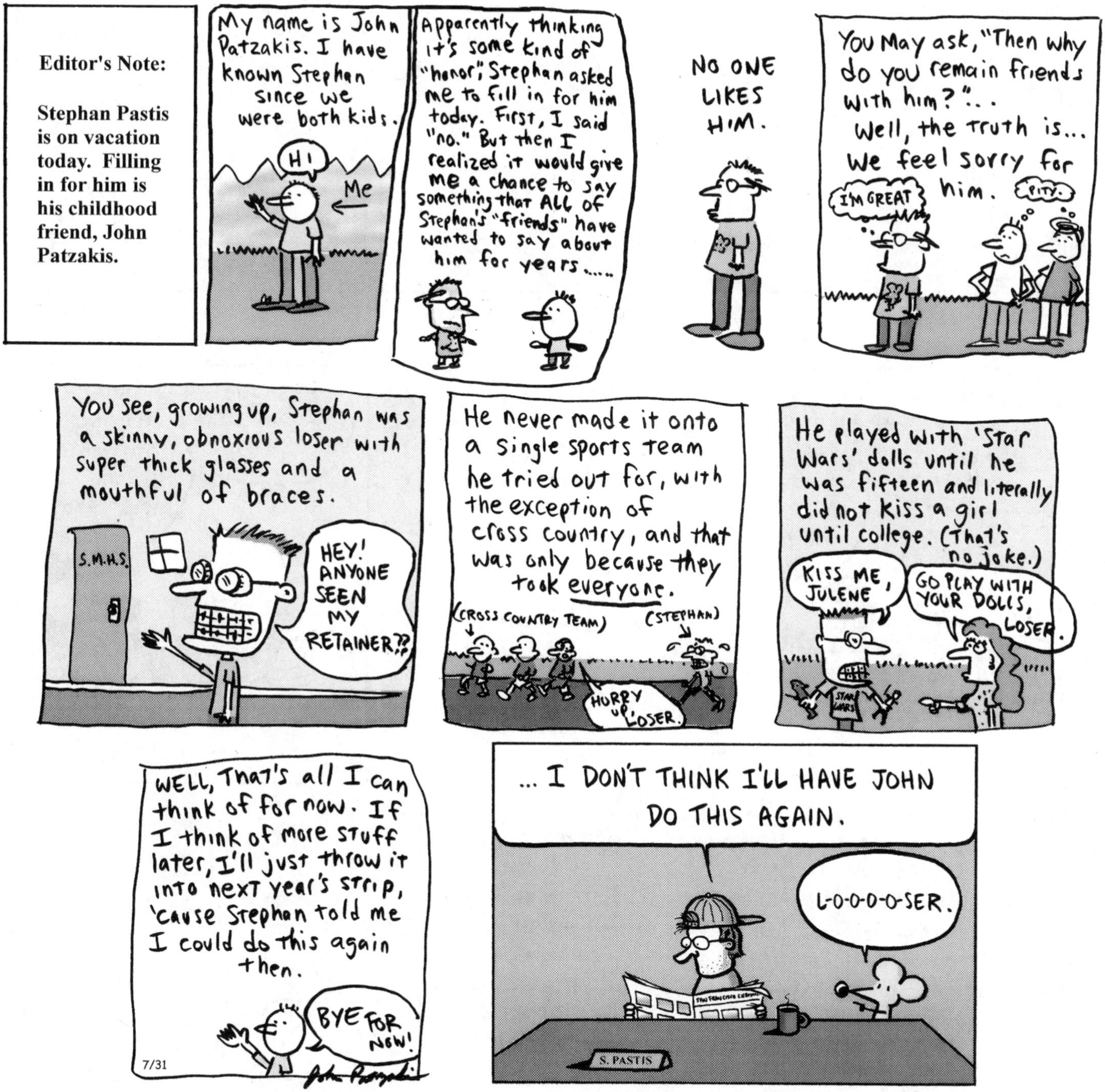

Editor's Note:
Stephan Pastis is on vacation today. Filling in for him is his childhood friend, John Patzakis.
My name is John Patzakis. I have known Stephan since we were both kids.
HI
Me
Apparently thinking it's some kind of "honor," Stephan asked me to fill in for him today. First, I said "no." But then I realized it would give me a chance to say something that ALL of Stephan's "friends" have wanted to say about him for years.....
NO ONE LIKES HIM.
You May ask, "Then why do you remain friends with him?"... Well, the truth is... We feel sorry for him.
I'M GREAT
PITY.
You see, growing up, Stephan was a skinny, obnoxious loser with super thick glasses and a mouthful of braces.
S.M.H.S.
HEY! ANYONE SEEN MY RETAINER??
He never made it onto a single sports team he tried out for, with the exception of cross country, and that was only because they took everyone.
(CROSS COUNTRY TEAM)
(STEPHAN)
HURRY UP, LOSER.
He played with 'Star Wars' dolls until he was fifteen and literally did not kiss a girl until college. (That's no joke.)
KISS ME, JULENE
GO PLAY WITH YOUR DOLLS, LOSER.
STAR WARS
WELL, That's all I can think of for now. If I think of more stuff later, I'll just throw it into next year's strip, 'cause Stephan told me I could do this again then.
BYE FOR NOW!
7/31
John Patzakis
... I DON'T THINK I'LL HAVE JOHN DO THIS AGAIN.
L-O-O-O-O-SER.
S. PASTIS

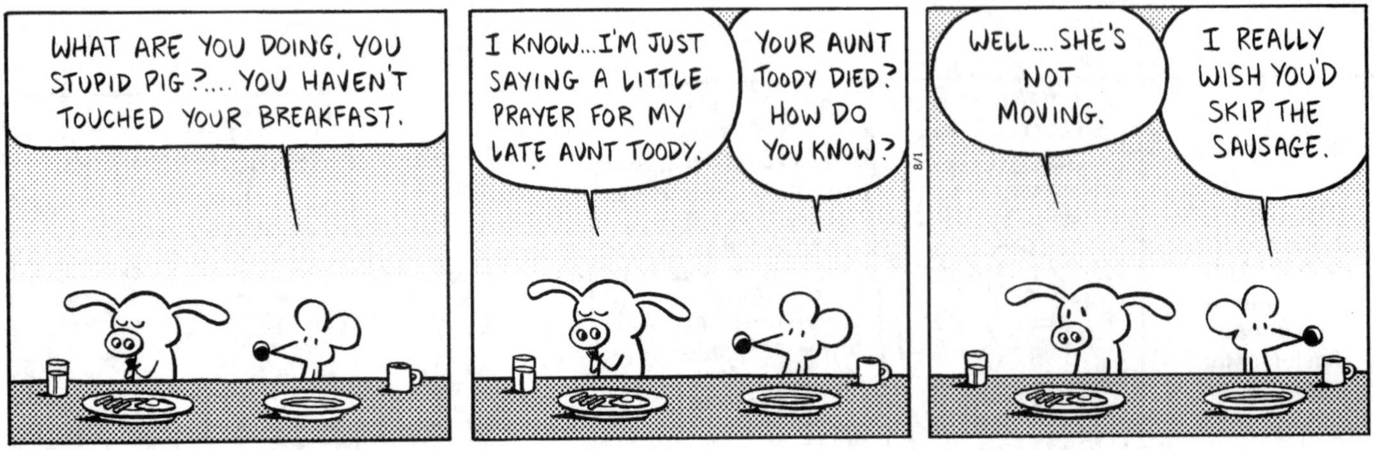
WHAT ARE YOU DOING, YOU STUPID PIG?.... YOU HAVEN'T TOUCHED YOUR BREAKFAST.
I KNOW...I'M JUST SAYING A LITTLE PRAYER FOR MY LATE AUNT TOODY.
YOUR AUNT TOODY DIED? HOW DO YOU KNOW?
8/1
WELL.... SHE'S NOT MOVING.
I REALLY WISH YOU'D SKIP THE SAUSAGE.

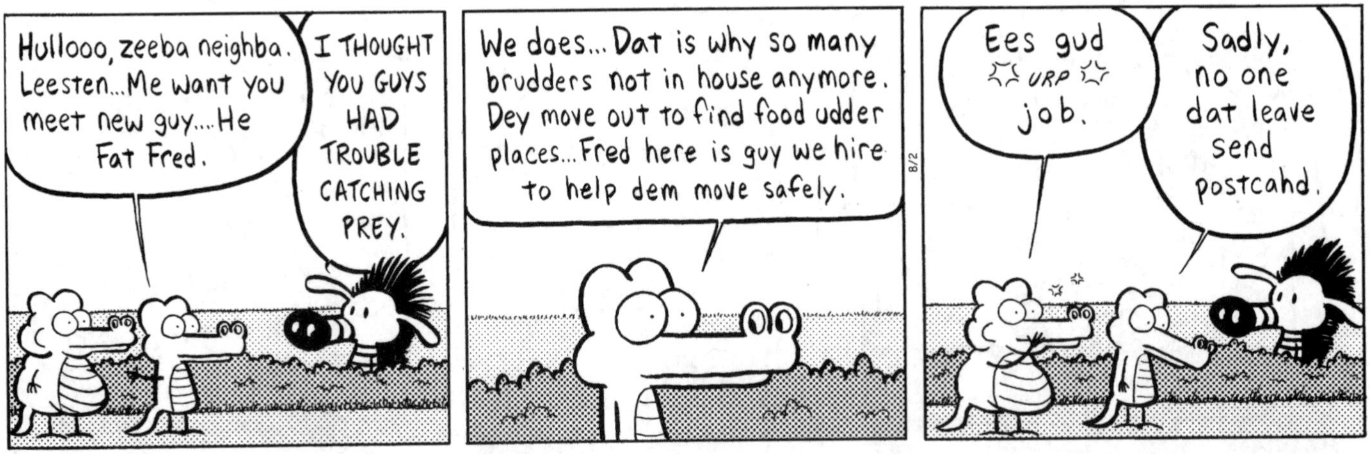
Hullooo, zeeba neighba. Leesten...Me want you meet new guy....He Fat Fred.
I THOUGHT YOU GUYS HAD TROUBLE CATCHING PREY.
We does... Dat is why so many brudders not in house anymore. Dey move out to find food udder places...Fred here is guy we hire to help dem move safely.
8/2
Ees gud URP job.
Sadly, no one dat leave send postcahd.

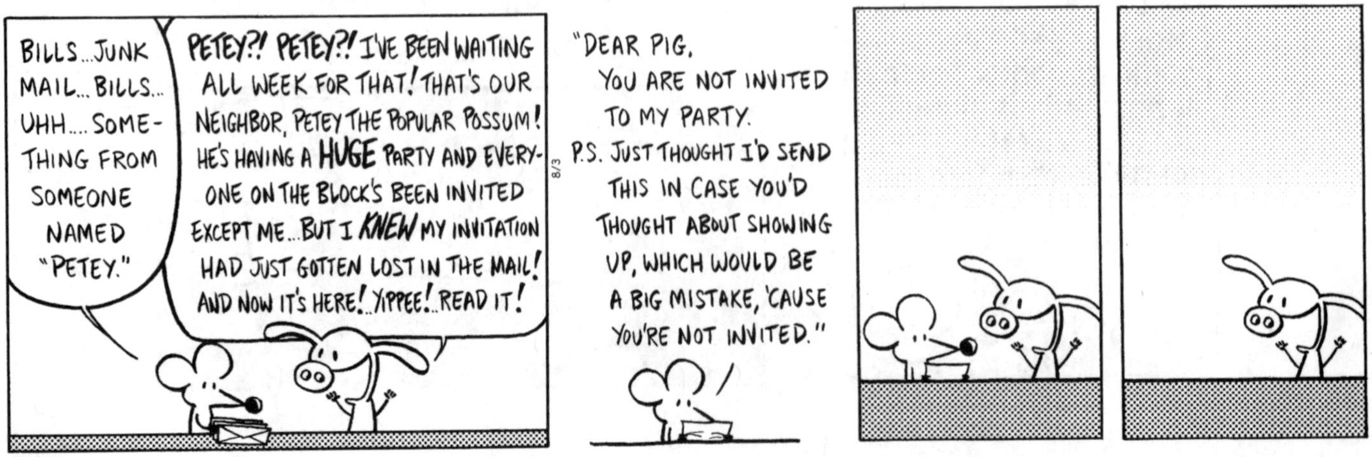
BILLS...JUNK MAIL...BILLS... UHH.... SOMETHING FROM SOMEONE NAMED "PETEY."
PETEY?! PETEY?! I'VE BEEN WAITING ALL WEEK FOR THAT! THAT'S OUR NEIGHBOR, PETEY THE POPULAR POSSUM! HE'S HAVING A HUGE PARTY AND EVERYONE ON THE BLOCK'S BEEN INVITED EXCEPT ME...BUT I KNEW MY INVITATION HAD JUST GOTTEN LOST IN THE MAIL! AND NOW IT'S HERE! YIPPEE! READ IT!
8/3
"DEAR PIG, YOU ARE NOT INVITED TO MY PARTY. P.S. JUST THOUGHT I'D SEND THIS IN CASE YOU'D THOUGHT ABOUT SHOWING UP, WHICH WOULD BE A BIG MISTAKE, 'CAUSE YOU'RE NOT INVITED."

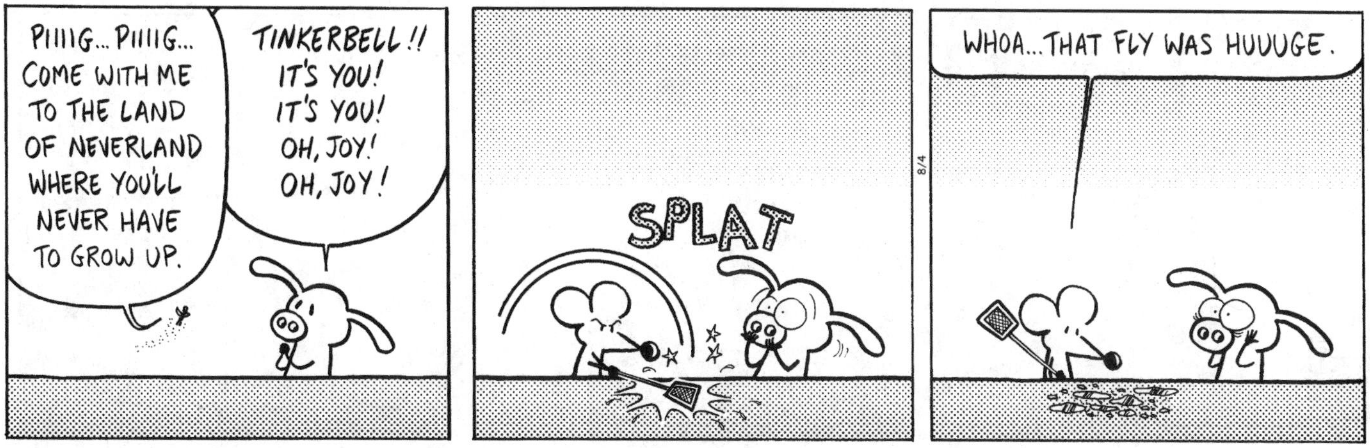
PIIIIG... PIIIIG... COME WITH ME TO THE LAND OF NEVERLAND WHERE YOU'LL NEVER HAVE TO GROW UP.
TINKERBELL!! IT'S YOU! IT'S YOU! OH, JOY! OH, JOY!
SPLAT
8/4
WHOA...THAT FLY WAS HUUUGE.

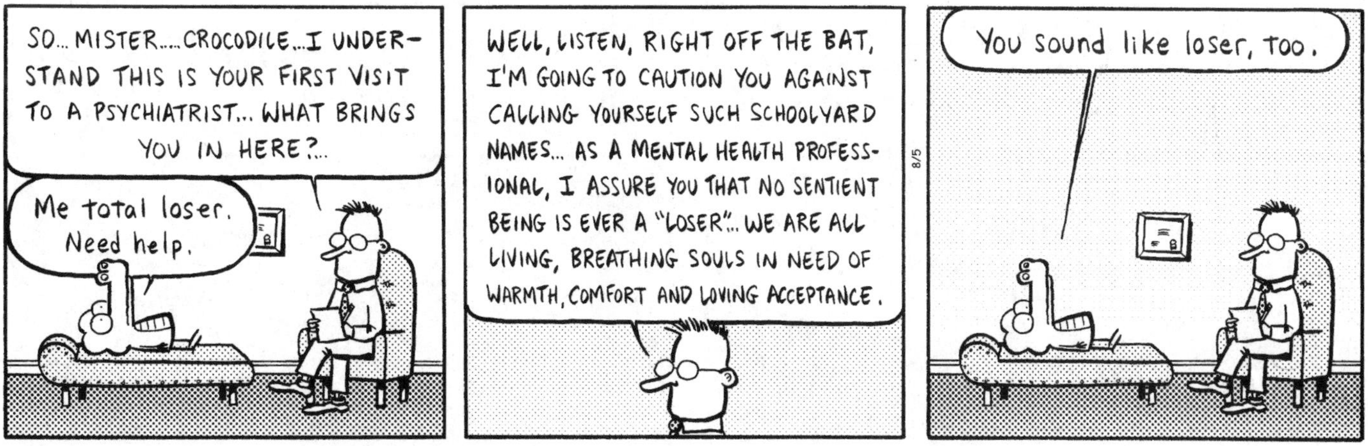
SO... MISTER.....CROCODILE...I UNDERSTAND THIS IS YOUR FIRST VISIT TO A PSYCHIATRIST... WHAT BRINGS YOU IN HERE?...
Me total loser. Need help.
WELL, LISTEN, RIGHT OFF THE BAT, I'M GOING TO CAUTION YOU AGAINST CALLING YOURSELF SUCH SCHOOLYARD NAMES... AS A MENTAL HEALTH PROFESSIONAL, I ASSURE YOU THAT NO SENTIENT BEING IS EVER A "LOSER"... WE ARE ALL LIVING, BREATHING SOULS IN NEED OF WARMTH, COMFORT AND LOVING ACCEPTANCE.
8/5
You sound like loser, too.

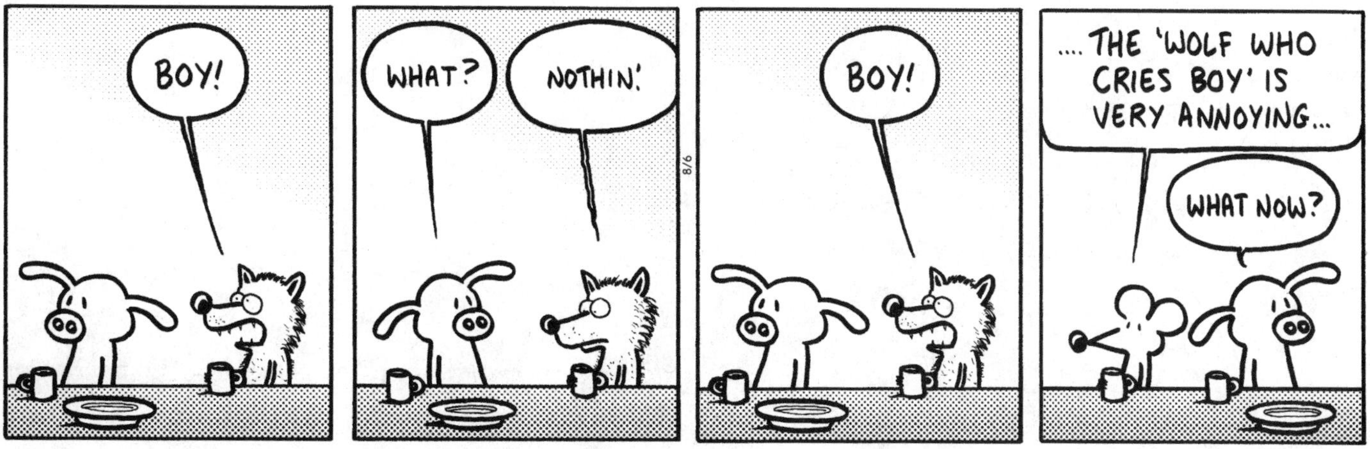
BOY!
WHAT?
NOTHIN'.
8/6
BOY!
.... THE 'WOLF WHO CRIES BOY' IS VERY ANNOYING...
WHAT NOW?

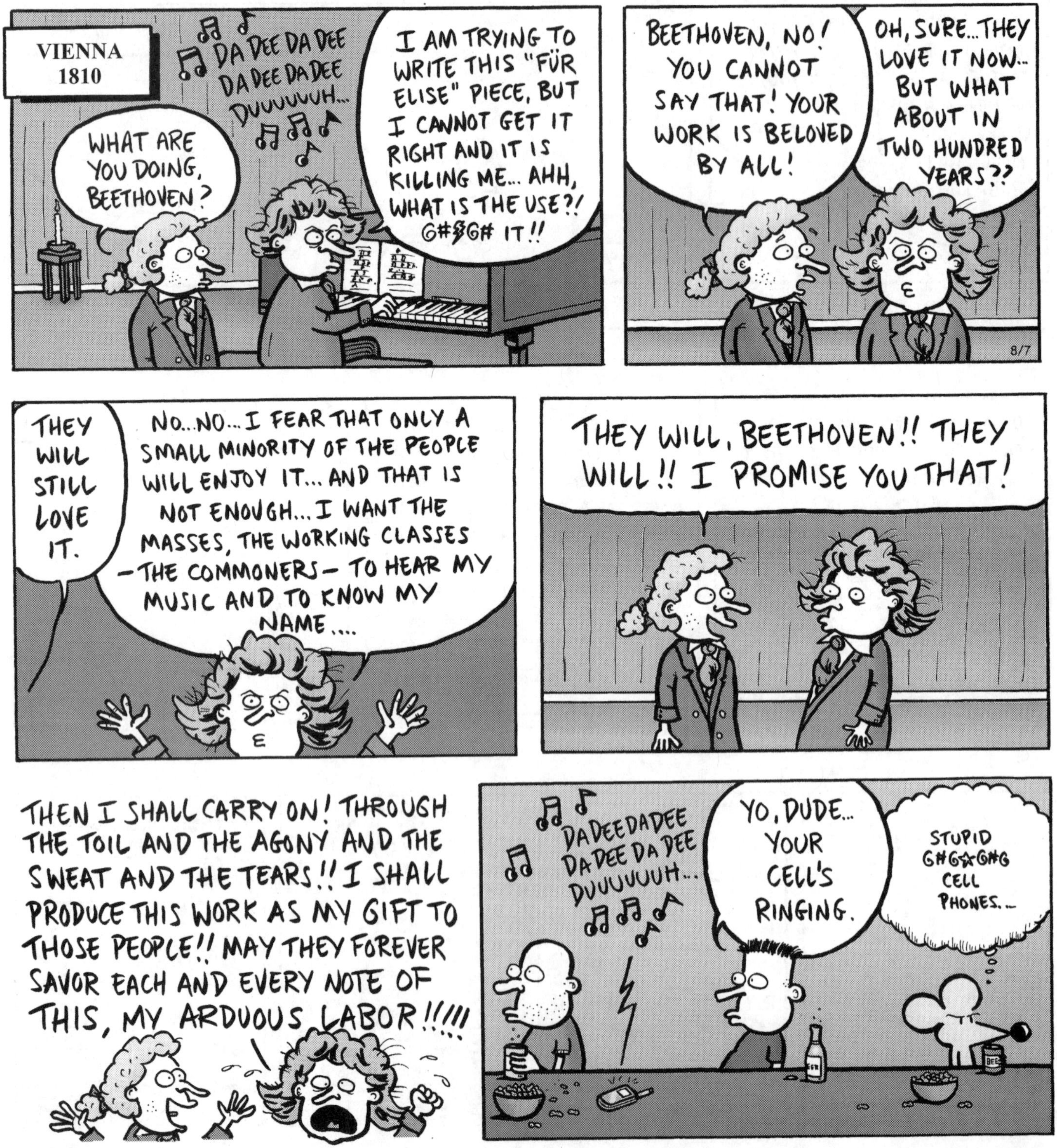
VIENNA 1810
DA DEE DA DEE DA DEE DA DEE DUUUUUUH...
WHAT ARE YOU DOING, BEETHOVEN?
I AM TRYING TO WRITE THIS "FÜR ELISE" PIECE, BUT I CANNOT GET IT RIGHT AND IT IS KILLING ME... AHH, WHAT IS THE USE?! G#$G# IT!!
BEETHOVEN, NO! YOU CANNOT SAY THAT! YOUR WORK IS BELOVED BY ALL!
OH, SURE... THEY LOVE IT NOW... BUT WHAT ABOUT IN TWO HUNDRED YEARS??
8/7
THEY WILL STILL LOVE IT.
NO... NO... I FEAR THAT ONLY A SMALL MINORITY OF THE PEOPLE WILL ENJOY IT... AND THAT IS NOT ENOUGH... I WANT THE MASSES, THE WORKING CLASSES —THE COMMONERS— TO HEAR MY MUSIC AND TO KNOW MY NAME....
THEY WILL, BEETHOVEN!! THEY WILL!! I PROMISE YOU THAT!
THEN I SHALL CARRY ON! THROUGH THE TOIL AND THE AGONY AND THE SWEAT AND THE TEARS!! I SHALL PRODUCE THIS WORK AS MY GIFT TO THOSE PEOPLE!! MAY THEY FOREVER SAVOR EACH AND EVERY NOTE OF THIS, MY ARDUOUS LABOR!!!!!
DA DEE DA DEE DA DEE DA DEE DUUUUUUH...
YO, DUDE... YOUR CELL'S RINGING.
STUPID G#G☆G#G CELL PHONES...

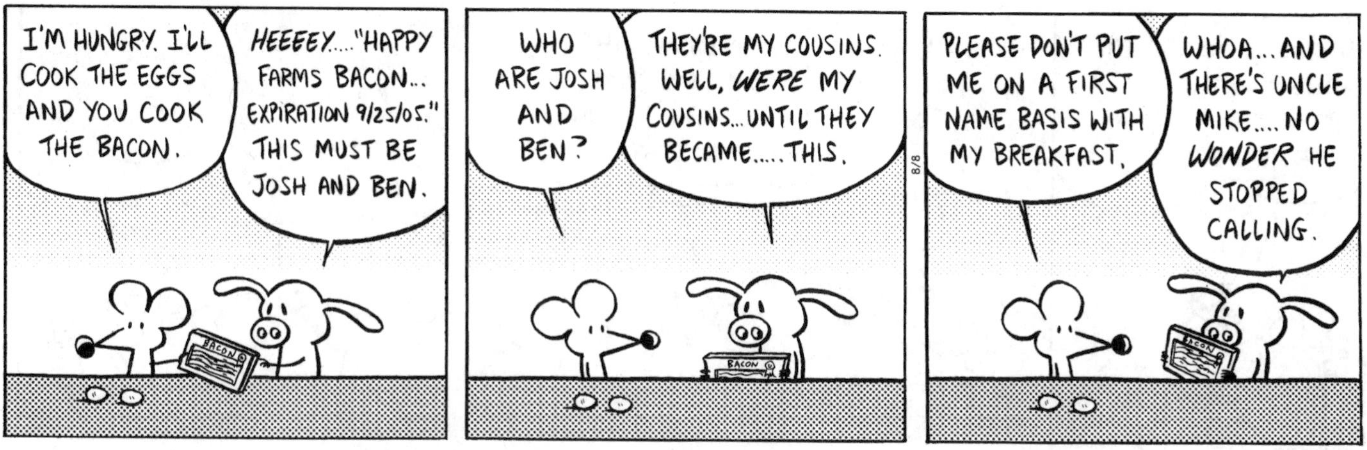
I'M HUNGRY. I'LL COOK THE EGGS AND YOU COOK THE BACON.
HEEEEY...."HAPPY FARMS BACON... EXPIRATION 9/25/05." THIS MUST BE JOSH AND BEN.
BACON
WHO ARE JOSH AND BEN?
THEY'RE MY COUSINS. WELL, WERE MY COUSINS...UNTIL THEY BECAME.....THIS.
BACON
8/8
PLEASE DON'T PUT ME ON A FIRST NAME BASIS WITH MY BREAKFAST.
WHOA...AND THERE'S UNCLE MIKE....NO WONDER HE STOPPED CALLING.
BACON

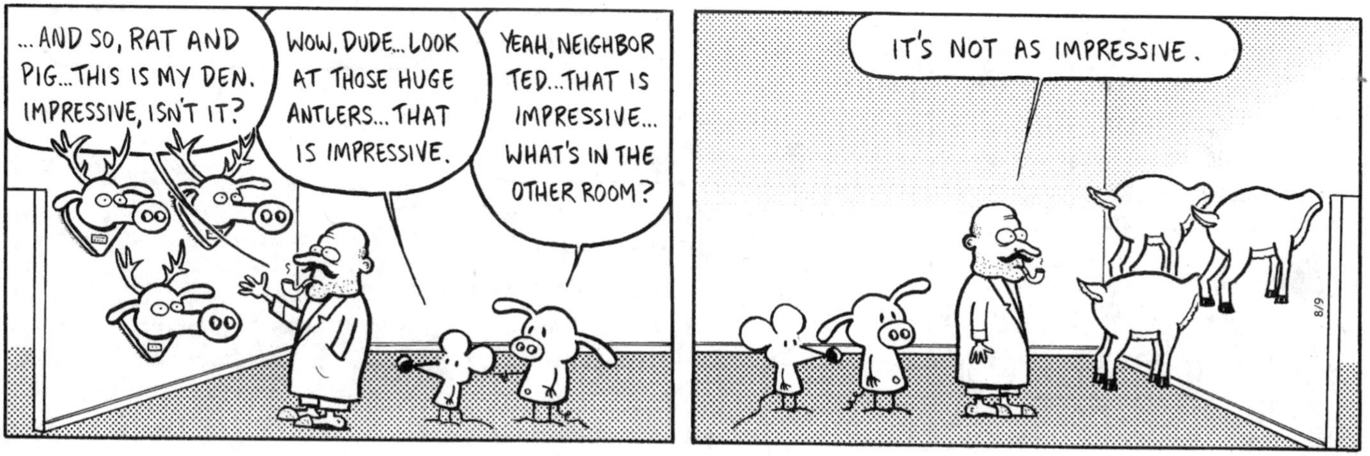
...AND SO, RAT AND PIG...THIS IS MY DEN. IMPRESSIVE, ISN'T IT?
WOW, DUDE...LOOK AT THOSE HUGE ANTLERS...THAT IS IMPRESSIVE.
YEAH, NEIGHBOR TED...THAT IS IMPRESSIVE... WHAT'S IN THE OTHER ROOM?
IT'S NOT AS IMPRESSIVE.
8/9

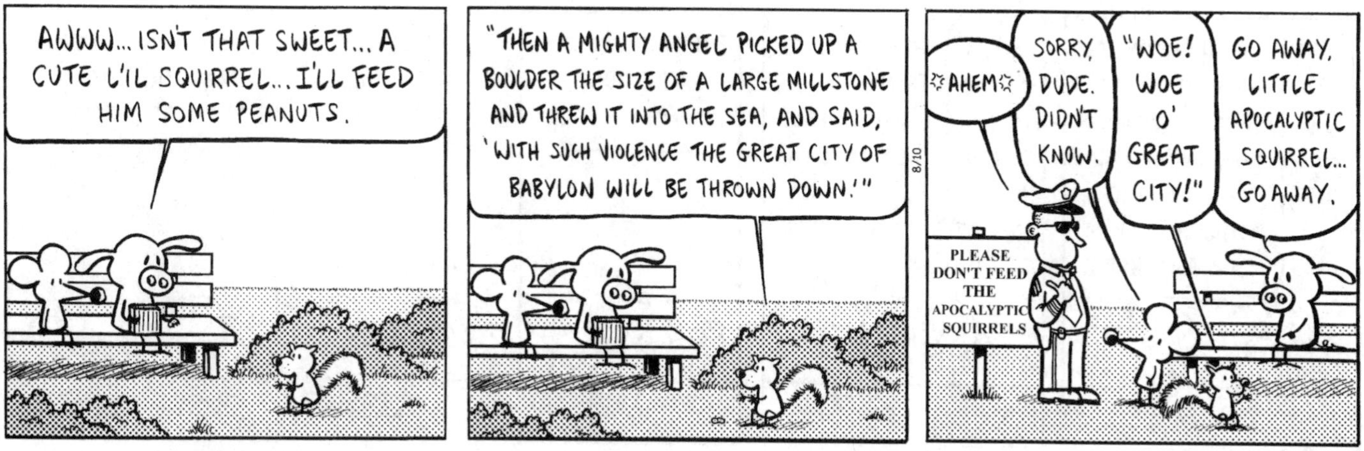
AWWW... ISN'T THAT SWEET... A CUTE L'IL SQUIRREL... I'LL FEED HIM SOME PEANUTS.
8/10
"THEN A MIGHTY ANGEL PICKED UP A BOULDER THE SIZE OF A LARGE MILLSTONE AND THREW IT INTO THE SEA, AND SAID, 'WITH SUCH VIOLENCE THE GREAT CITY OF BABYLON WILL BE THROWN DOWN.'"
AHEM
SORRY, DUDE. DIDN'T KNOW.
"WOE! WOE O' GREAT CITY!"
GO AWAY, LITTLE APOCALYPTIC SQUIRREL... GO AWAY.
PLEASE DON'T FEED THE APOCALYPTIC SQUIRRELS

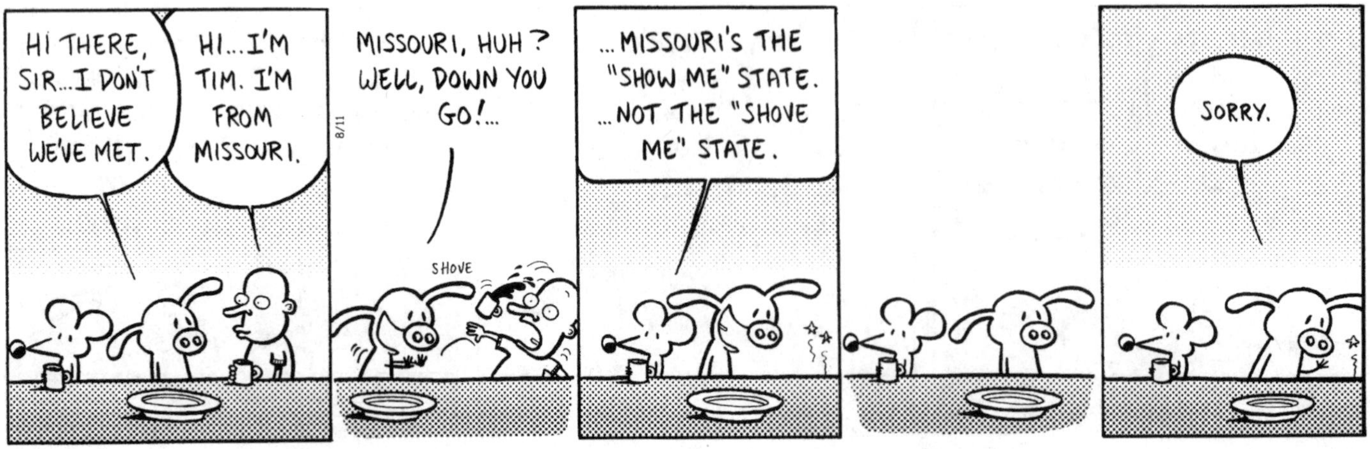
HI THERE, SIR...I DON'T BELIEVE WE'VE MET.
HI...I'M TIM. I'M FROM MISSOURI.
8/11
MISSOURI, HUH? WELL, DOWN YOU GO!...
SHOVE
...MISSOURI'S THE "SHOW ME" STATE. ...NOT THE "SHOVE ME" STATE.
SORRY.

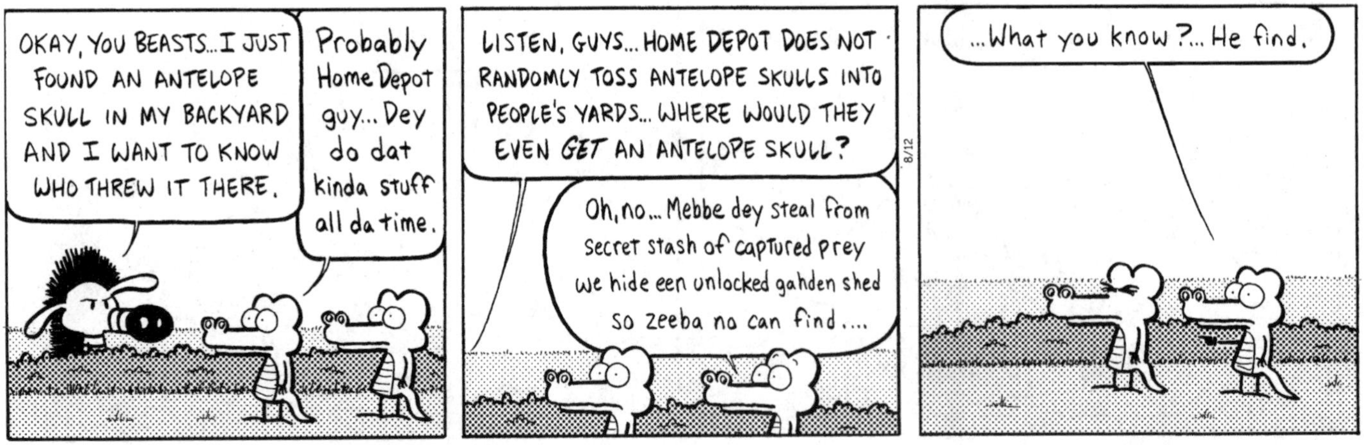
OKAY, YOU BEASTS...I JUST FOUND AN ANTELOPE SKULL IN MY BACKYARD AND I WANT TO KNOW WHO THREW IT THERE.
Probably Home Depot guy... Dey do dat kinda stuff all da time.
LISTEN, GUYS... HOME DEPOT DOES NOT RANDOMLY TOSS ANTELOPE SKULLS INTO PEOPLE'S YARDS... WHERE WOULD THEY EVEN GET AN ANTELOPE SKULL?
Oh, no... Mebbe dey steal from secret stash of captured prey we hide een unlocked gahden shed so zeeba no can find....
8/12
...What you know?... He find.

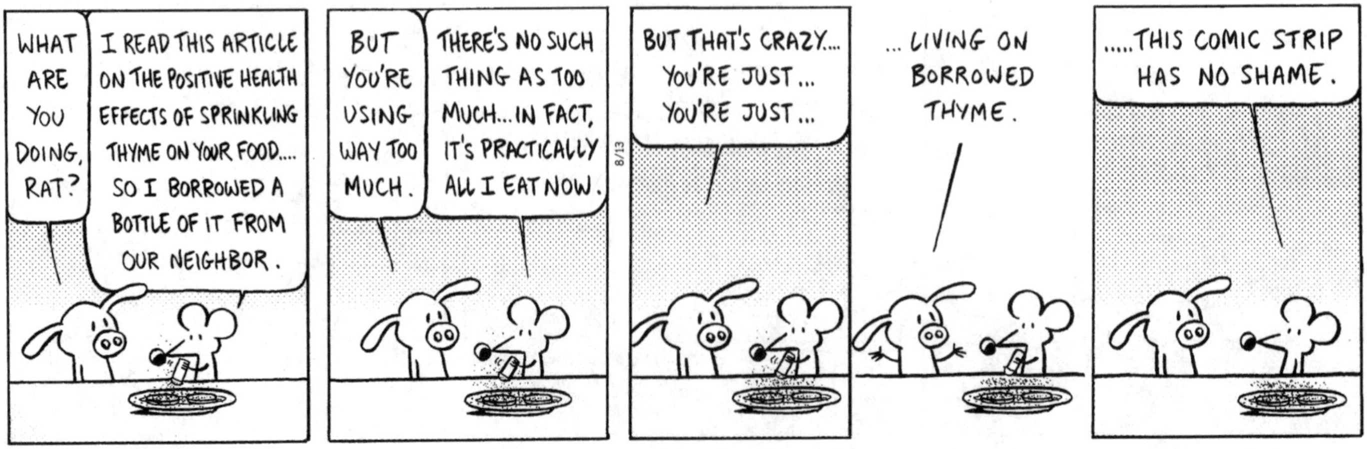
WHAT ARE YOU DOING, RAT?
I READ THIS ARTICLE ON THE POSITIVE HEALTH EFFECTS OF SPRINKLING THYME ON YOUR FOOD.... SO I BORROWED A BOTTLE OF IT FROM OUR NEIGHBOR.
BUT YOU'RE USING WAY TOO MUCH.
THERE'S NO SUCH THING AS TOO MUCH...IN FACT, IT'S PRACTICALLY ALL I EAT NOW.
8/13
BUT THAT'S CRAZY... YOU'RE JUST... YOU'RE JUST...
...LIVING ON BORROWED THYME.
.....THIS COMIC STRIP HAS NO SHAME.

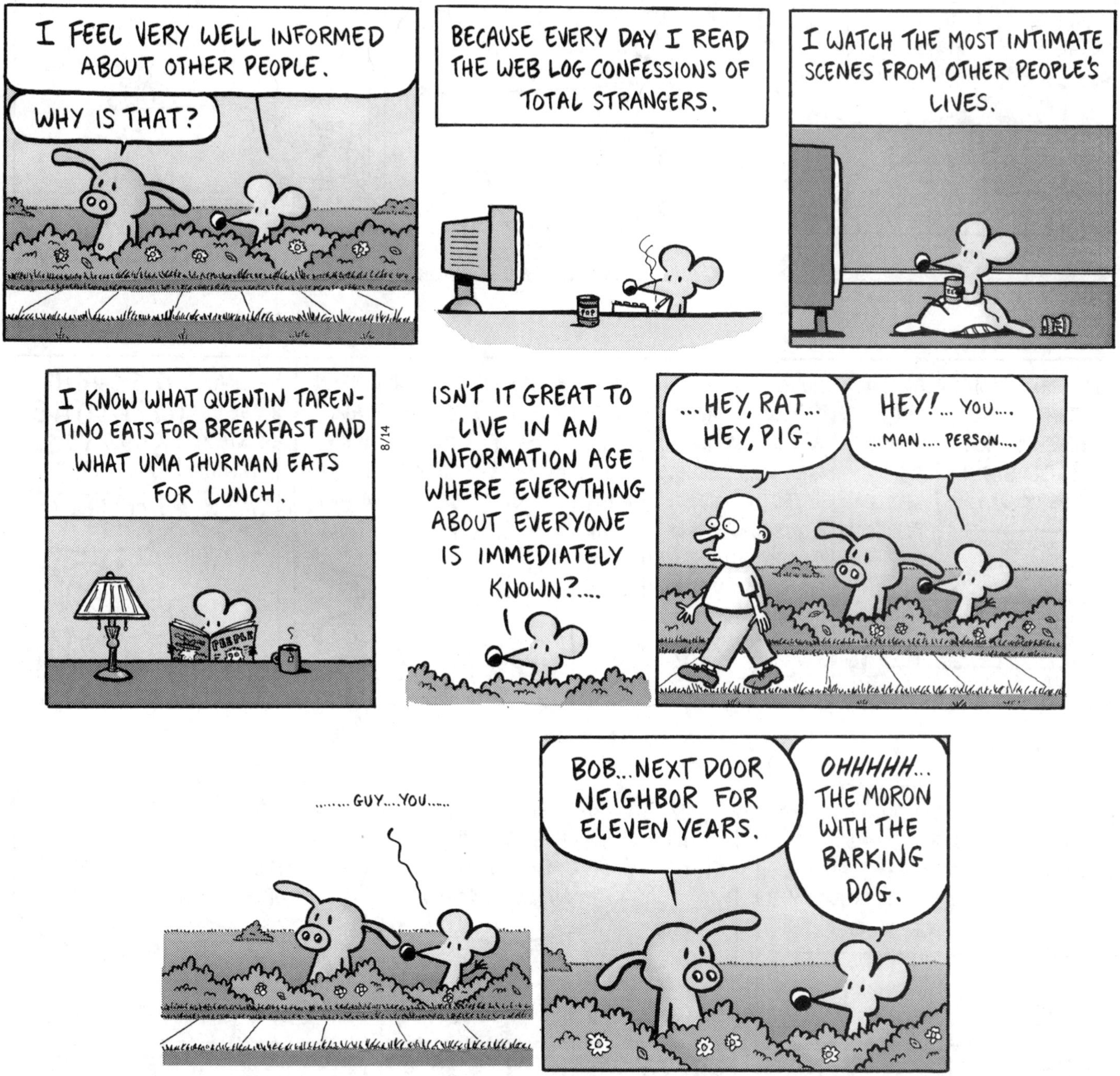
I FEEL VERY WELL INFORMED ABOUT OTHER PEOPLE.
WHY IS THAT?
BECAUSE EVERY DAY I READ THE WEB LOG CONFESSIONS OF TOTAL STRANGERS.
I WATCH THE MOST INTIMATE SCENES FROM OTHER PEOPLE'S LIVES.
I KNOW WHAT QUENTIN TARENTINO EATS FOR BREAKFAST AND WHAT UMA THURMAN EATS FOR LUNCH.
8/14
ISN'T IT GREAT TO LIVE IN AN INFORMATION AGE WHERE EVERYTHING ABOUT EVERYONE IS IMMEDIATELY KNOWN?....
...HEY, RAT... HEY, PIG.
HEY!... YOU.... ...MAN.... PERSON....
........GUY....YOU......
BOB...NEXT DOOR NEIGHBOR FOR ELEVEN YEARS.
OHHHHH... THE MORON WITH THE BARKING DOG.

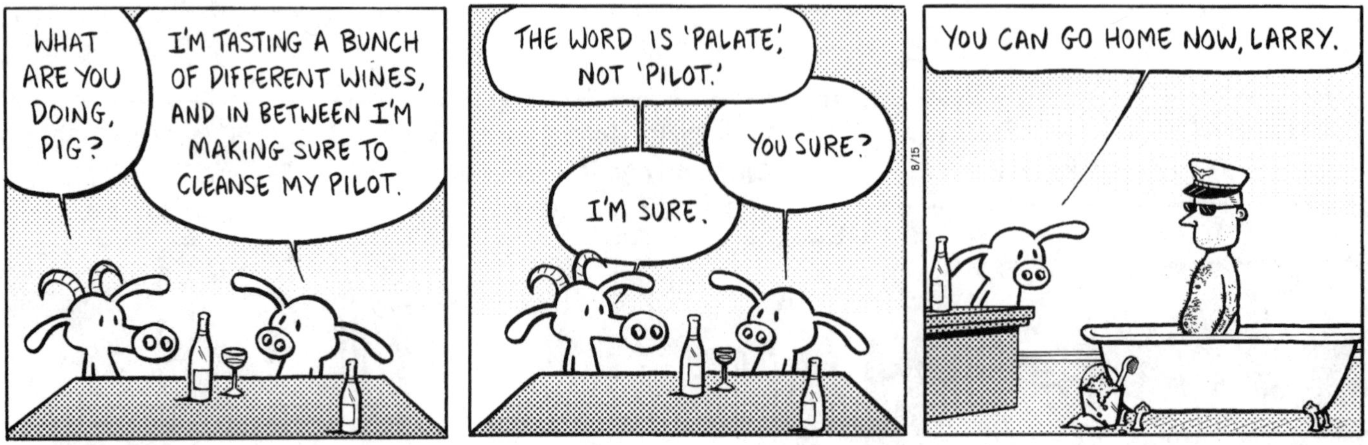
WHAT ARE YOU DOING, PIG?
I'M TASTING A BUNCH OF DIFFERENT WINES, AND IN BETWEEN I'M MAKING SURE TO CLEANSE MY PILOT.
THE WORD IS 'PALATE,' NOT 'PILOT.'
YOU SURE?
I'M SURE.
8/15
YOU CAN GO HOME NOW, LARRY.

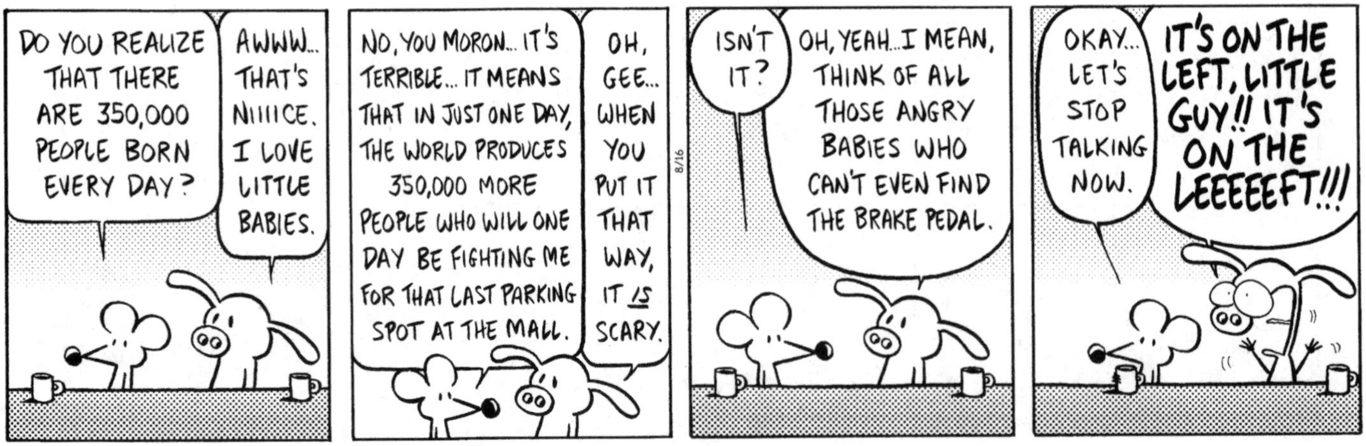
DO YOU REALIZE THAT THERE ARE 350,000 PEOPLE BORN EVERY DAY?
AWWW... THAT'S NIIIICE. I LOVE LITTLE BABIES.
NO, YOU MORON... IT'S TERRIBLE... IT MEANS THAT IN JUST ONE DAY, THE WORLD PRODUCES 350,000 MORE PEOPLE WHO WILL ONE DAY BE FIGHTING ME FOR THAT LAST PARKING SPOT AT THE MALL.
OH, GEE... WHEN YOU PUT IT THAT WAY, IT IS SCARY.
8/16
ISN'T IT?
OH, YEAH... I MEAN, THINK OF ALL THOSE ANGRY BABIES WHO CAN'T EVEN FIND THE BRAKE PEDAL.
OKAY... LET'S STOP TALKING NOW.
IT'S ON THE LEFT, LITTLE GUY!! IT'S ON THE LEEEEEFT!!!

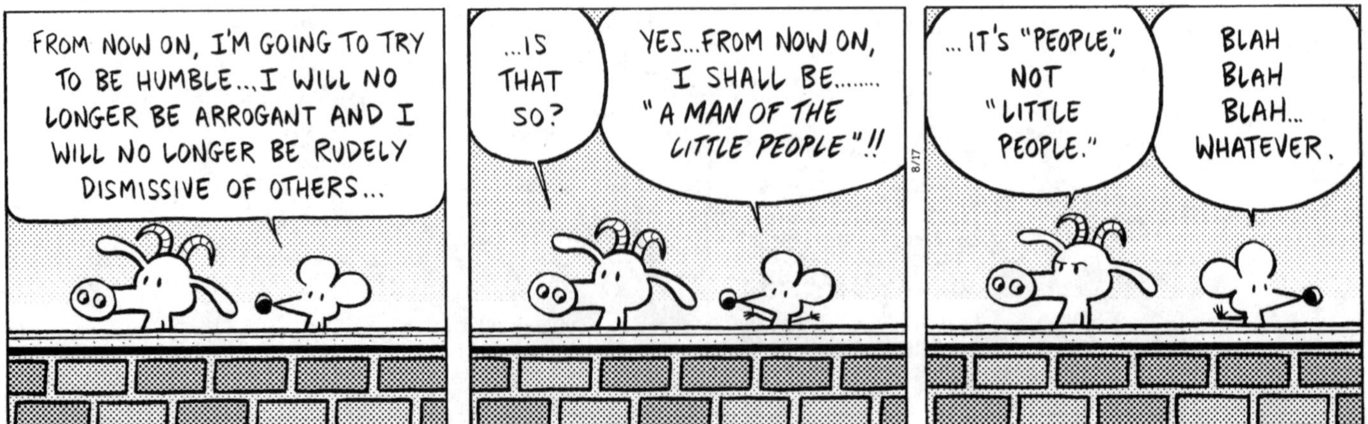
FROM NOW ON, I'M GOING TO TRY TO BE HUMBLE... I WILL NO LONGER BE ARROGANT AND I WILL NO LONGER BE RUDELY DISMISSIVE OF OTHERS...
...IS THAT SO?
YES... FROM NOW ON, I SHALL BE....... "A MAN OF THE LITTLE PEOPLE"!!
8/17
...IT'S "PEOPLE," NOT "LITTLE PEOPLE."
BLAH BLAH BLAH... WHATEVER.

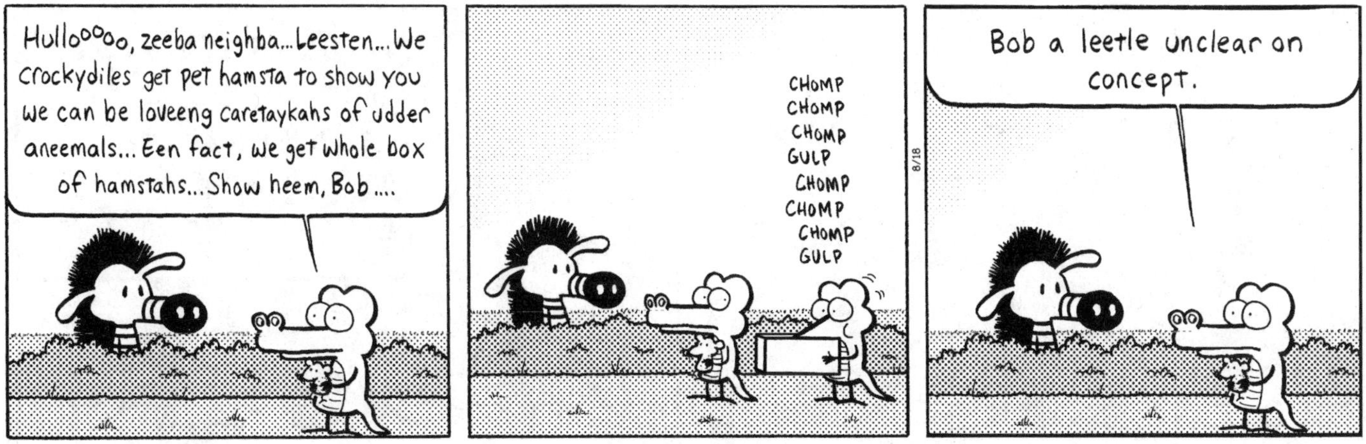
Hulloooo, zeeba neighba...Leesten...We crockydiles get pet hamsta to show you we can be loveeng caretaykahs of udder aneemals... Een fact, we get whole box of hamstahs...Show heem, Bob....
CHOMP CHOMP CHOMP GULP CHOMP CHOMP CHOMP GULP
8/18
Bob a leetle unclear on concept.

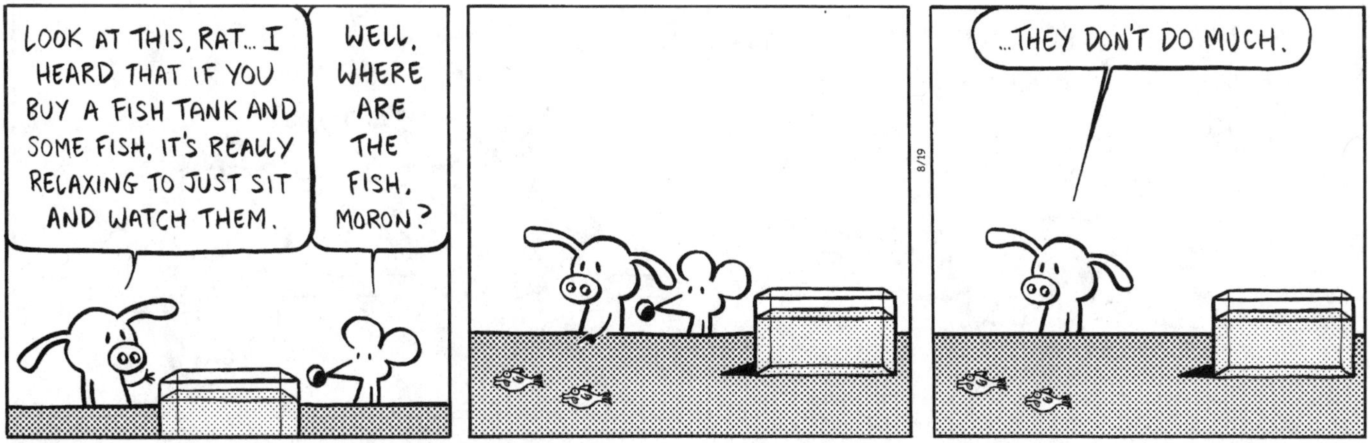
LOOK AT THIS, RAT... I HEARD THAT IF YOU BUY A FISH TANK AND SOME FISH, IT'S REALLY RELAXING TO JUST SIT AND WATCH THEM.
WELL, WHERE ARE THE FISH, MORON?
8/19
...THEY DON'T DO MUCH.

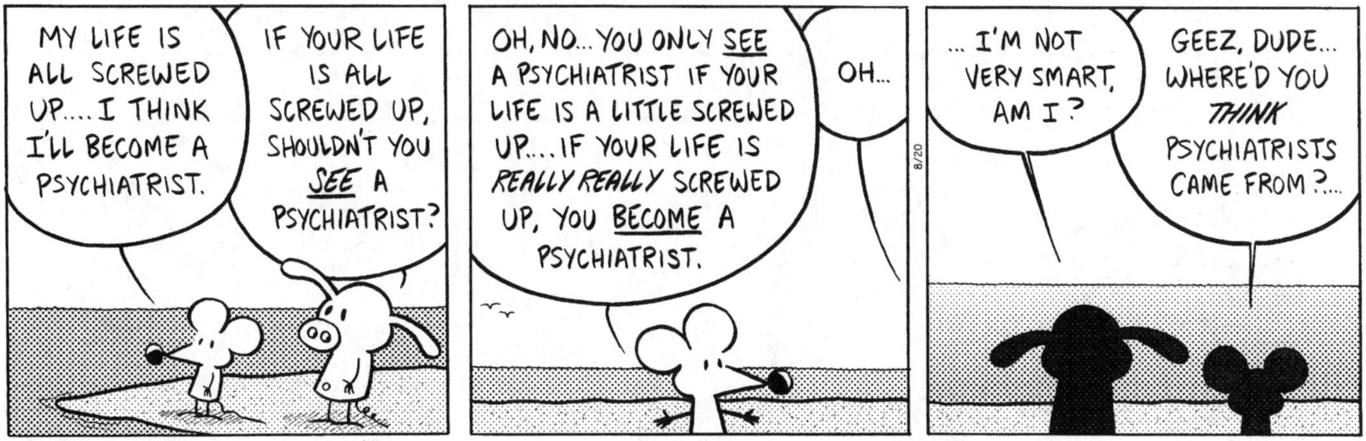
MY LIFE IS ALL SCREWED UP.... I THINK I'LL BECOME A PSYCHIATRIST.
IF YOUR LIFE IS ALL SCREWED UP, SHOULDN'T YOU SEE A PSYCHIATRIST?
OH, NO... YOU ONLY SEE A PSYCHIATRIST IF YOUR LIFE IS A LITTLE SCREWED UP.... IF YOUR LIFE IS REALLY REALLY SCREWED UP, YOU BECOME A PSYCHIATRIST.
OH...
8/20
... I'M NOT VERY SMART, AM I?
GEEZ, DUDE... WHERE'D YOU THINK PSYCHIATRISTS CAME FROM?...

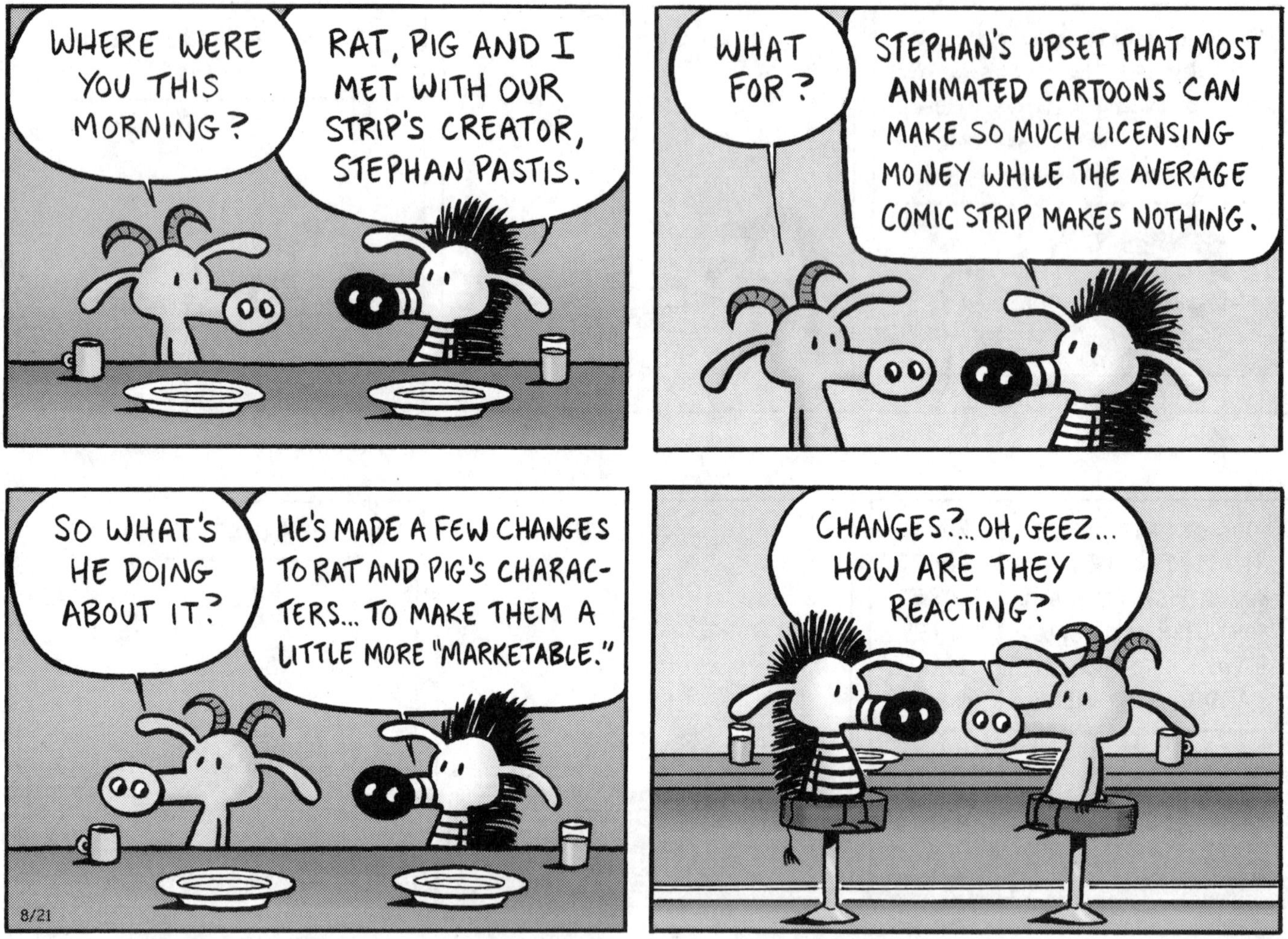
WHERE WERE YOU THIS MORNING?
RAT, PIG AND I MET WITH OUR STRIP'S CREATOR, STEPHAN PASTIS.
WHAT FOR?
STEPHAN'S UPSET THAT MOST ANIMATED CARTOONS CAN MAKE SO MUCH LICENSING MONEY WHILE THE AVERAGE COMIC STRIP MAKES NOTHING.
SO WHAT'S HE DOING ABOUT IT?
HE'S MADE A FEW CHANGES TO RAT AND PIG'S CHARACTERS... TO MAKE THEM A LITTLE MORE "MARKETABLE."
8/21
CHANGES?... OH, GEEZ... HOW ARE THEY REACTING?

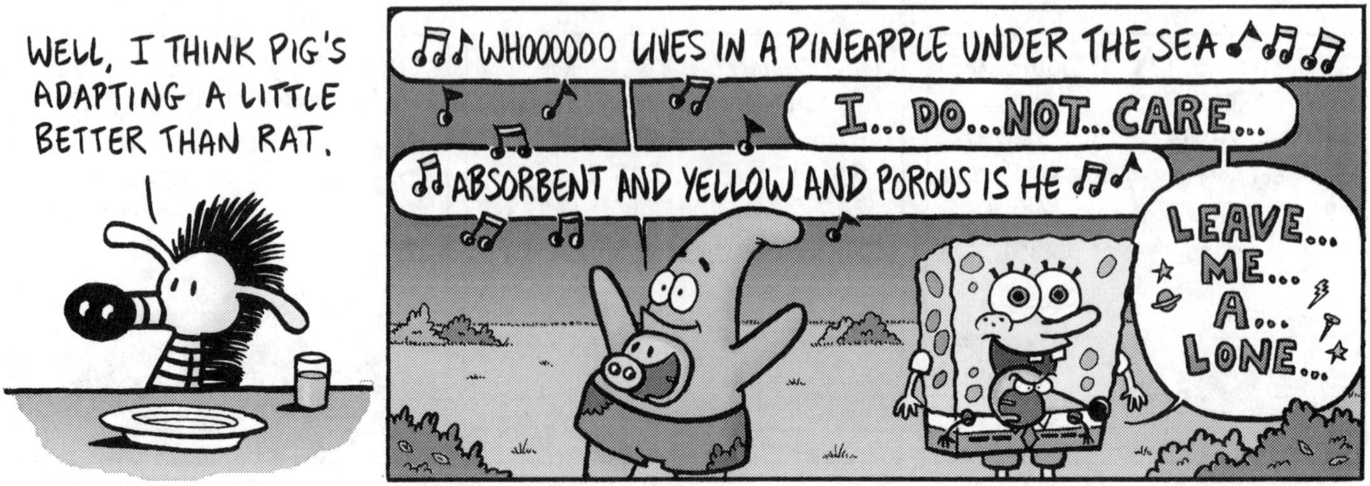
WELL, I THINK PIG'S ADAPTING A LITTLE BETTER THAN RAT.
♫♫♪ WHOOOOOOO LIVES IN A PINEAPPLE UNDER THE SEA ♪♫♫
I... DO... NOT... CARE...
♫ ABSORBENT AND YELLOW AND POROUS IS HE ♫♪
LEAVE... ME... A... LONE...

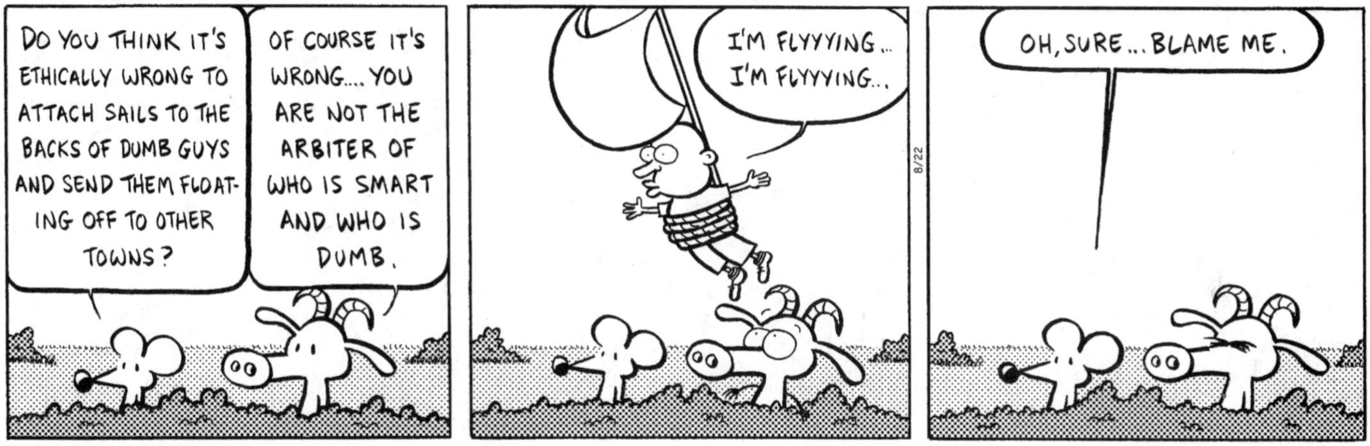
DO YOU THINK IT'S ETHICALLY WRONG TO ATTACH SAILS TO THE BACKS OF DUMB GUYS AND SEND THEM FLOATING OFF TO OTHER TOWNS?
OF COURSE IT'S WRONG.... YOU ARE NOT THE ARBITER OF WHO IS SMART AND WHO IS DUMB.
I'M FLYYYING... I'M FLYYYING...
8/22
OH, SURE... BLAME ME.

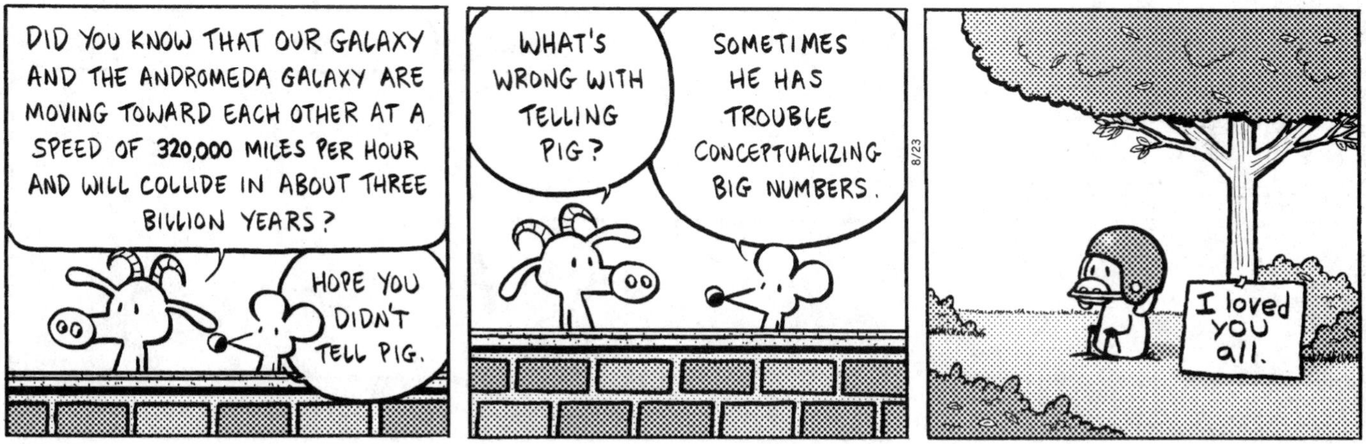
DID YOU KNOW THAT OUR GALAXY AND THE ANDROMEDA GALAXY ARE MOVING TOWARD EACH OTHER AT A SPEED OF 320,000 MILES PER HOUR AND WILL COLLIDE IN ABOUT THREE BILLION YEARS?
HOPE YOU DIDN'T TELL PIG.
WHAT'S WRONG WITH TELLING PIG?
SOMETIMES HE HAS TROUBLE CONCEPTUALIZING BIG NUMBERS.
8/23
I loved you all.

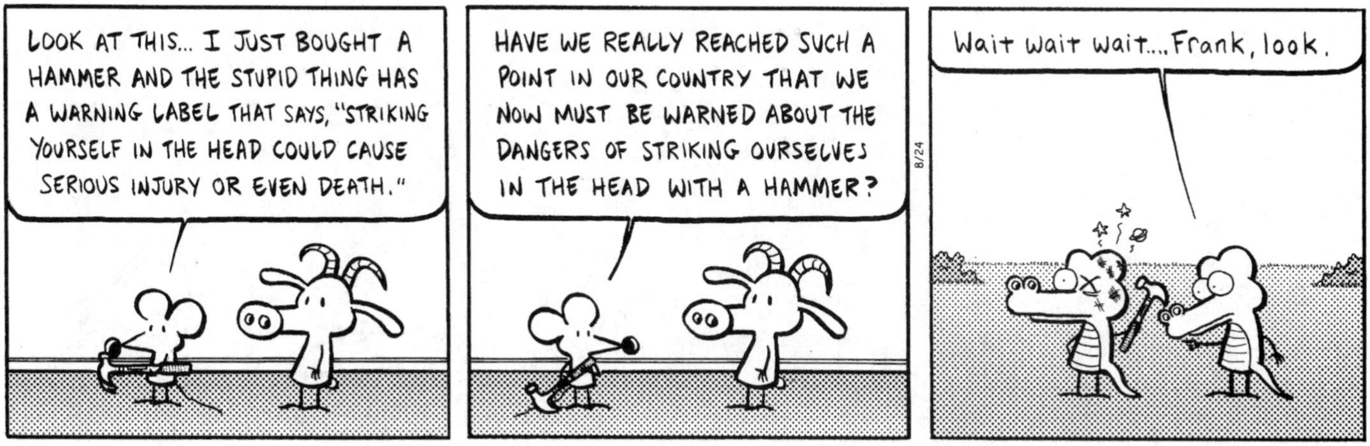
LOOK AT THIS... I JUST BOUGHT A HAMMER AND THE STUPID THING HAS A WARNING LABEL THAT SAYS, "STRIKING YOURSELF IN THE HEAD COULD CAUSE SERIOUS INJURY OR EVEN DEATH."
HAVE WE REALLY REACHED SUCH A POINT IN OUR COUNTRY THAT WE NOW MUST BE WARNED ABOUT THE DANGERS OF STRIKING OURSELVES IN THE HEAD WITH A HAMMER?
8/24
Wait wait wait.... Frank, look.

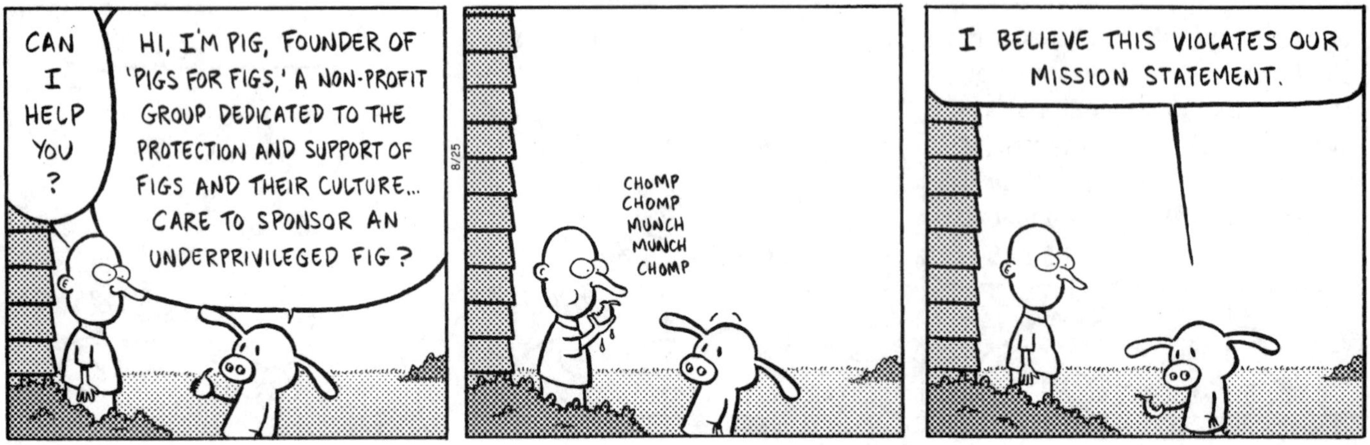
CAN I HELP YOU ?
HI, I'M PIG, FOUNDER OF 'PIGS FOR FIGS,' A NON-PROFIT GROUP DEDICATED TO THE PROTECTION AND SUPPORT OF FIGS AND THEIR CULTURE... CARE TO SPONSOR AN UNDERPRIVILEGED FIG ?
8/25
CHOMP CHOMP MUNCH MUNCH CHOMP
I BELIEVE THIS VIOLATES OUR MISSION STATEMENT.

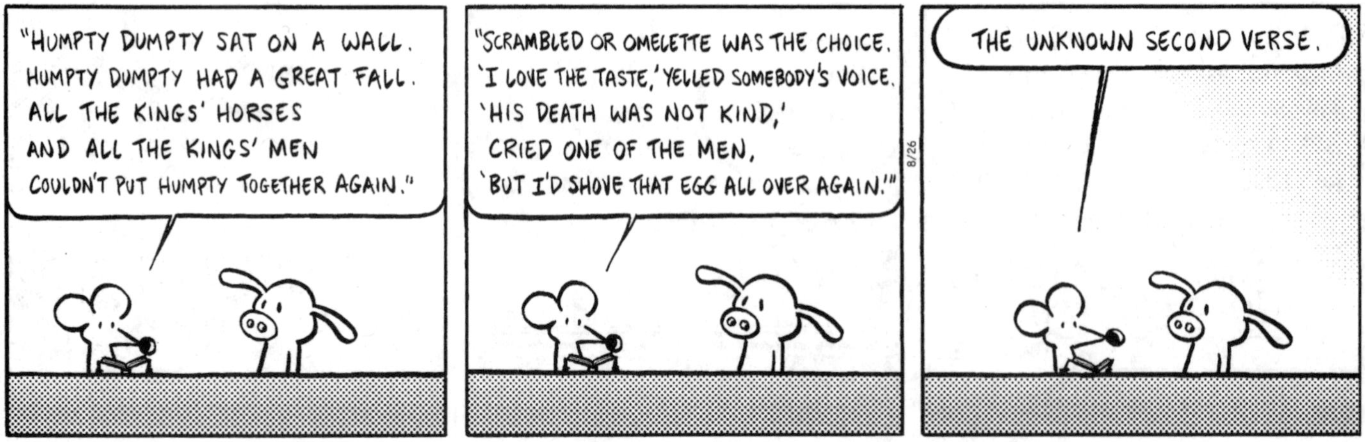
"HUMPTY DUMPTY SAT ON A WALL. HUMPTY DUMPTY HAD A GREAT FALL. ALL THE KINGS' HORSES AND ALL THE KINGS' MEN COULDN'T PUT HUMPTY TOGETHER AGAIN."
"SCRAMBLED OR OMELETTE WAS THE CHOICE. 'I LOVE THE TASTE,' YELLED SOMEBODY'S VOICE. 'HIS DEATH WAS NOT KIND,' CRIED ONE OF THE MEN, 'BUT I'D SHOVE THAT EGG ALL OVER AGAIN.'"
8/26
THE UNKNOWN SECOND VERSE.

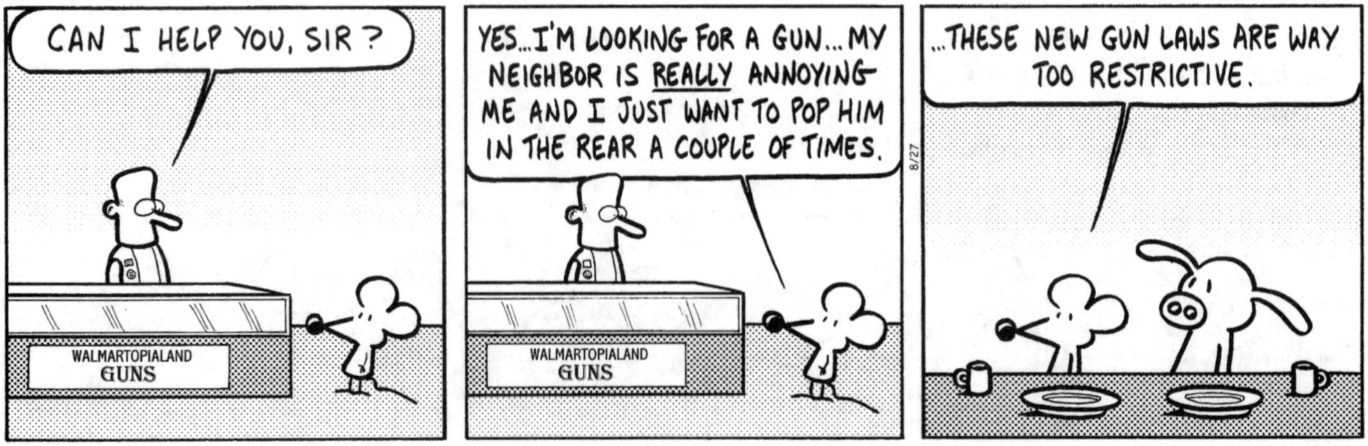
CAN I HELP YOU, SIR ?
WALMARTOPIALAND GUNS
YES...I'M LOOKING FOR A GUN... MY NEIGHBOR IS REALLY ANNOYING ME AND I JUST WANT TO POP HIM IN THE REAR A COUPLE OF TIMES.
WALMARTOPIALAND GUNS
8/27
...THESE NEW GUN LAWS ARE WAY TOO RESTRICTIVE.

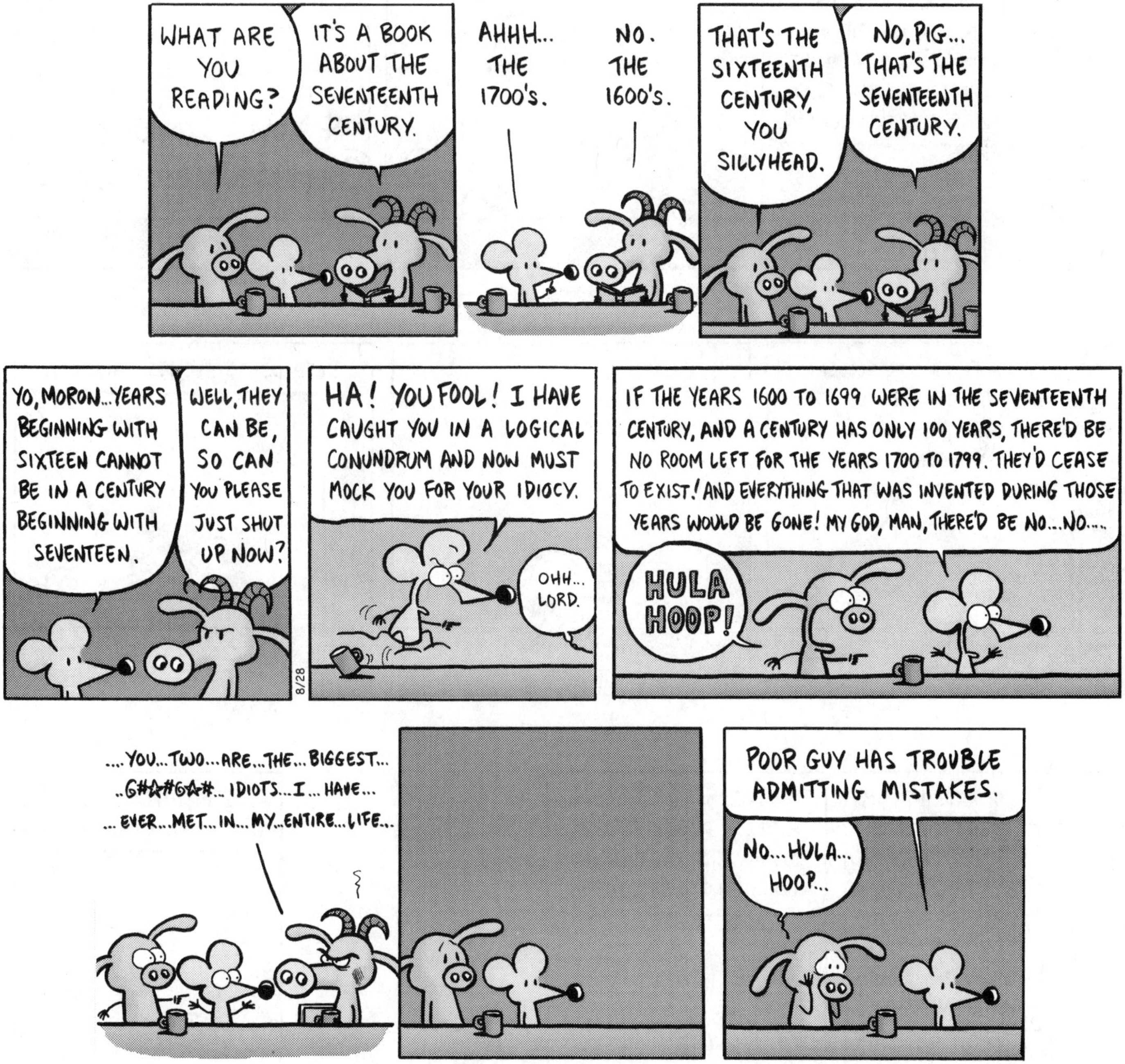
WHAT ARE YOU READING?
IT'S A BOOK ABOUT THE SEVENTEENTH CENTURY.
AHHH... THE 1700's.
NO. THE 1600's.
THAT'S THE SIXTEENTH CENTURY, YOU SILLYHEAD.
NO, PIG... THAT'S THE SEVENTEENTH CENTURY.
YO, MORON... YEARS BEGINNING WITH SIXTEEN CANNOT BE IN A CENTURY BEGINNING WITH SEVENTEEN.
WELL, THEY CAN BE, SO CAN YOU PLEASE JUST SHUT UP NOW?
8/28
HA! YOU FOOL! I HAVE CAUGHT YOU IN A LOGICAL CONUNDRUM AND NOW MUST MOCK YOU FOR YOUR IDIOCY.
OHH... LORD.
IF THE YEARS 1600 TO 1699 WERE IN THE SEVENTEENTH CENTURY, AND A CENTURY HAS ONLY 100 YEARS, THERE'D BE NO ROOM LEFT FOR THE YEARS 1700 TO 1799. THEY'D CEASE TO EXIST! AND EVERYTHING THAT WAS INVENTED DURING THOSE YEARS WOULD BE GONE! MY GOD, MAN, THERE'D BE NO...NO....
HULA HOOP!
....YOU...TWO...ARE...THE...BIGGEST... ..G#☆#G☆#.. IDIOTS...I...HAVE... ...EVER...MET...IN...MY...ENTIRE...LIFE...
POOR GUY HAS TROUBLE ADMITTING MISTAKES.
NO...HULA... HOOP...

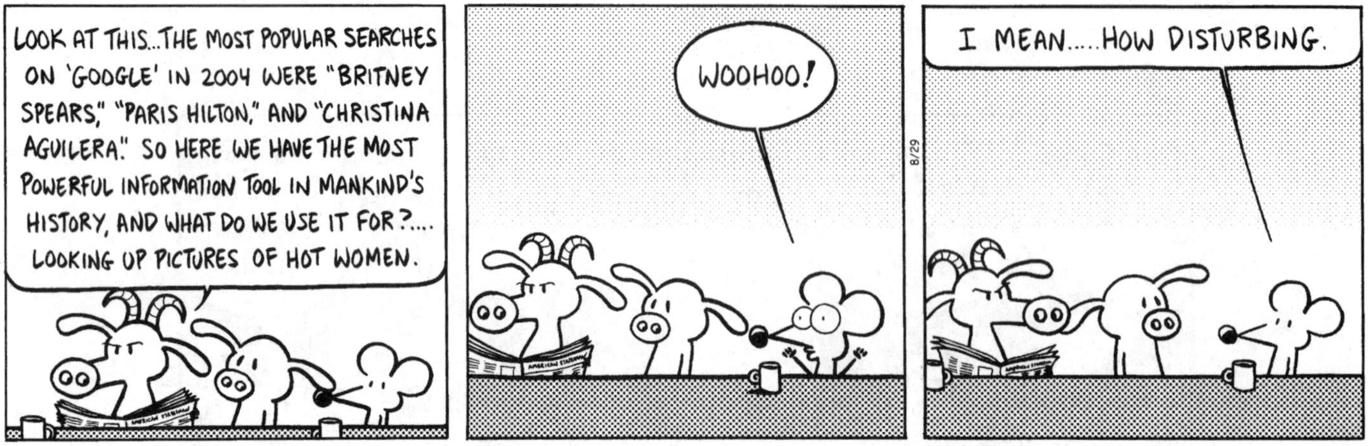
LOOK AT THIS...THE MOST POPULAR SEARCHES ON 'GOOGLE' IN 2004 WERE "BRITNEY SPEARS," "PARIS HILTON," AND "CHRISTINA AGUILERA." SO HERE WE HAVE THE MOST POWERFUL INFORMATION TOOL IN MANKIND'S HISTORY, AND WHAT DO WE USE IT FOR?.... LOOKING UP PICTURES OF HOT WOMEN.
WOOHOO!
8/29
I MEAN.....HOW DISTURBING.

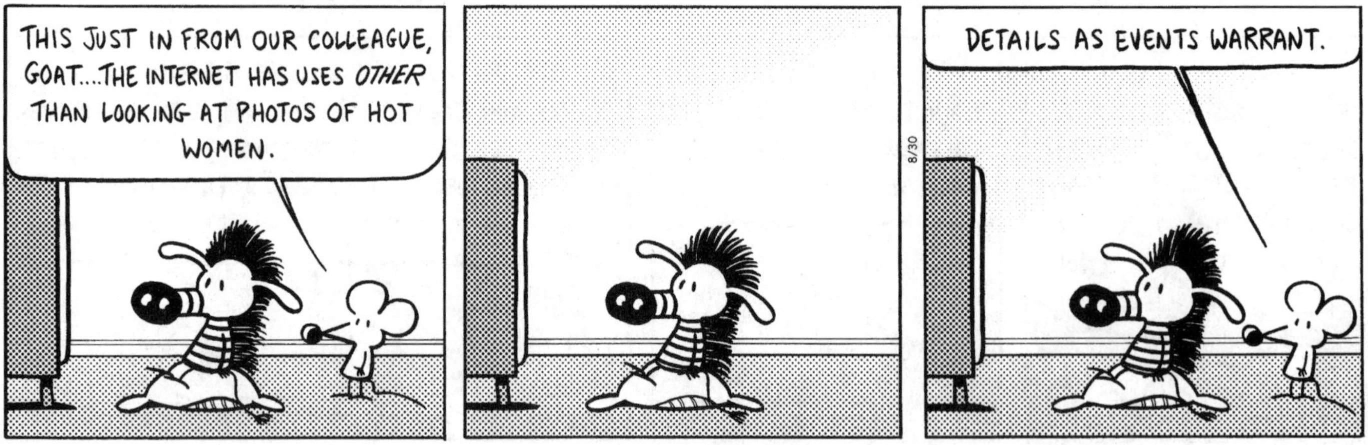
THIS JUST IN FROM OUR COLLEAGUE, GOAT....THE INTERNET HAS USES *OTHER* THAN LOOKING AT PHOTOS OF HOT WOMEN.
8/30
DETAILS AS EVENTS WARRANT.

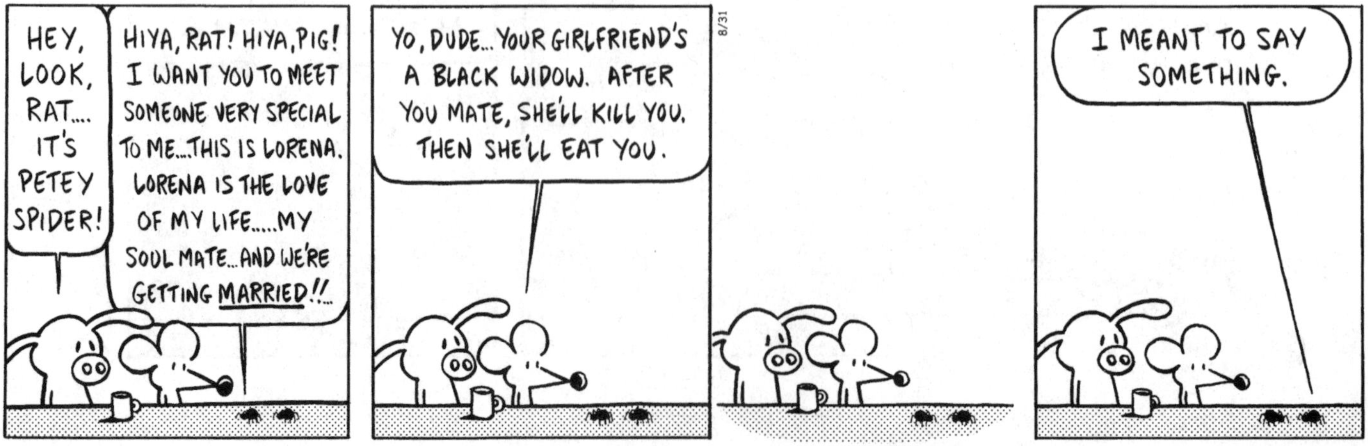
HEY, LOOK, RAT.... IT'S PETEY SPIDER!
HIYA, RAT! HIYA, PIG! I WANT YOU TO MEET SOMEONE VERY SPECIAL TO ME...THIS IS LORENA. LORENA IS THE LOVE OF MY LIFE.....MY SOUL MATE...AND WE'RE GETTING MARRIED!!...
YO, DUDE... YOUR GIRLFRIEND'S A BLACK WIDOW. AFTER YOU MATE, SHE'LL KILL YOU. THEN SHE'LL EAT YOU.
8/31
I MEANT TO SAY SOMETHING.

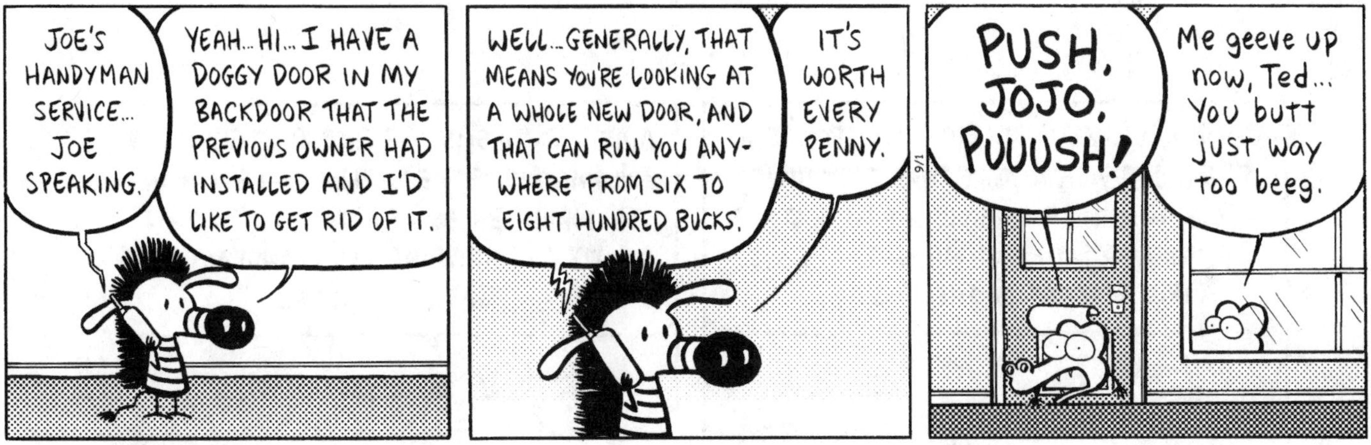
JOE'S HANDYMAN SERVICE... JOE SPEAKING.
YEAH... HI... I HAVE A DOGGY DOOR IN MY BACKDOOR THAT THE PREVIOUS OWNER HAD INSTALLED AND I'D LIKE TO GET RID OF IT.
WELL... GENERALLY, THAT MEANS YOU'RE LOOKING AT A WHOLE NEW DOOR, AND THAT CAN RUN YOU ANY-WHERE FROM SIX TO EIGHT HUNDRED BUCKS.
IT'S WORTH EVERY PENNY.
9/1
PUSH, JOJO, PUUUSH!
Me geeve up now, Ted... You butt just way too beeg.

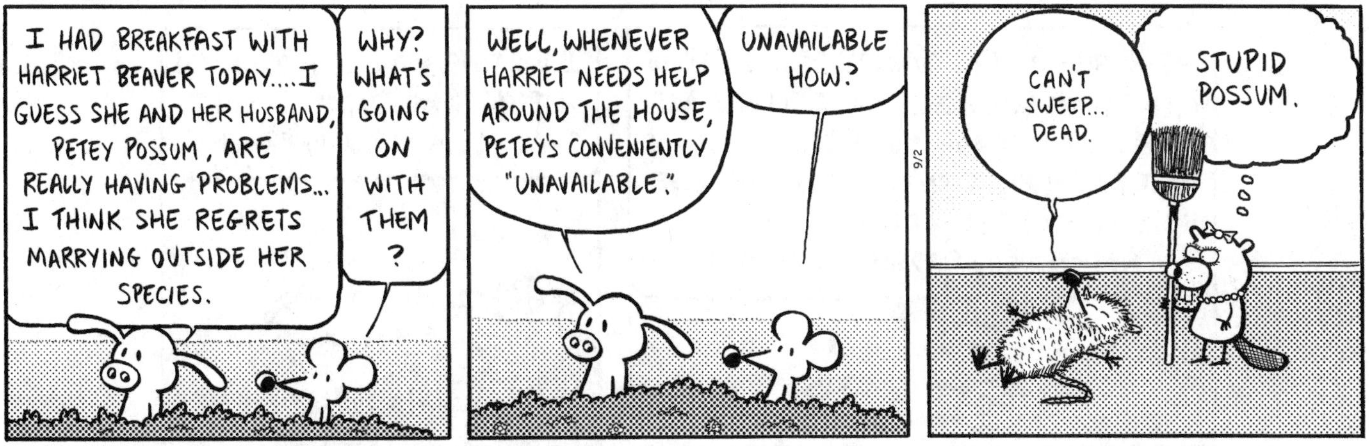
I HAD BREAKFAST WITH HARRIET BEAVER TODAY.... I GUESS SHE AND HER HUSBAND, PETEY POSSUM, ARE REALLY HAVING PROBLEMS... I THINK SHE REGRETS MARRYING OUTSIDE HER SPECIES.
WHY? WHAT'S GOING ON WITH THEM?
WELL, WHENEVER HARRIET NEEDS HELP AROUND THE HOUSE, PETEY'S CONVENIENTLY "UNAVAILABLE."
UNAVAILABLE HOW?
9/2
CAN'T SWEEP... DEAD.
STUPID POSSUM.

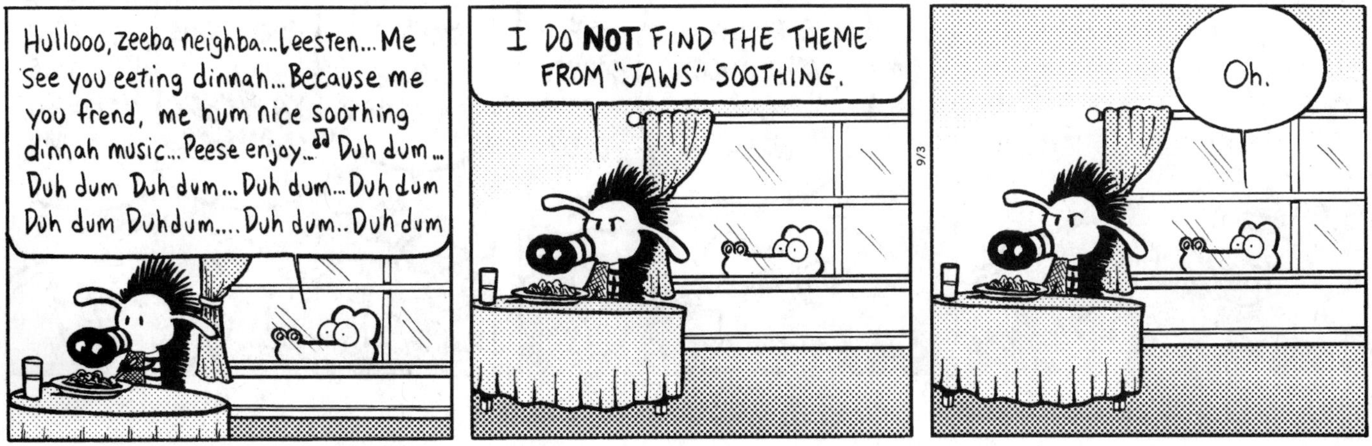
Hullooo, zeeba neighba... Leesten... Me see you eeting dinnah... Because me you frend, me hum nice soothing dinnah music... Peese enjoy... ♫ Duh dum... Duh dum Duh dum... Duh dum... Duh dum Duh dum Duhdum.... Duh dum.. Duh dum
I DO **NOT** FIND THE THEME FROM "JAWS" SOOTHING.
9/3
Oh.

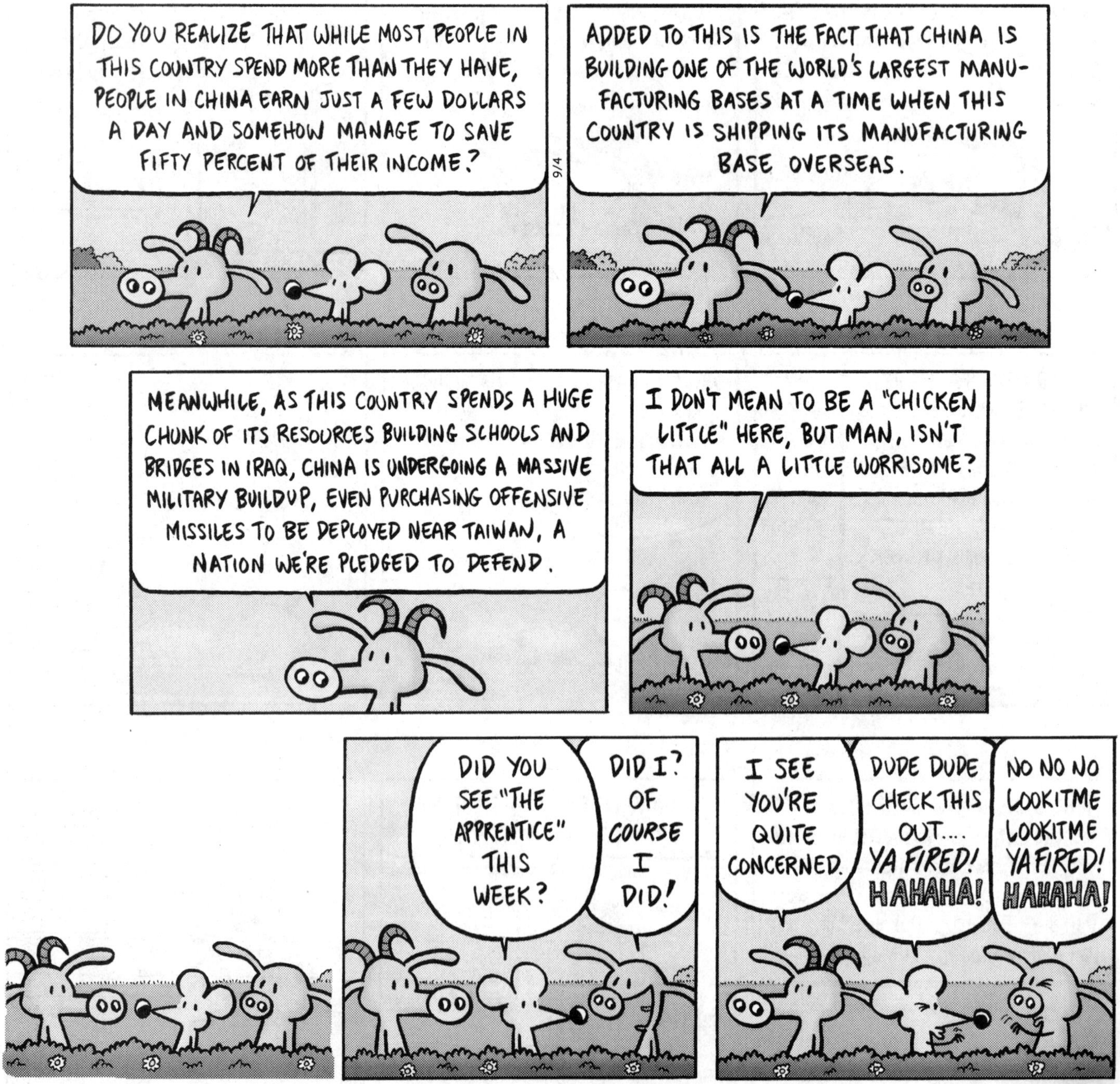
DO YOU REALIZE THAT WHILE MOST PEOPLE IN THIS COUNTRY SPEND MORE THAN THEY HAVE, PEOPLE IN CHINA EARN JUST A FEW DOLLARS A DAY AND SOMEHOW MANAGE TO SAVE FIFTY PERCENT OF THEIR INCOME?
9/4
ADDED TO THIS IS THE FACT THAT CHINA IS BUILDING ONE OF THE WORLD'S LARGEST MANU-FACTURING BASES AT A TIME WHEN THIS COUNTRY IS SHIPPING ITS MANUFACTURING BASE OVERSEAS.
MEANWHILE, AS THIS COUNTRY SPENDS A HUGE CHUNK OF ITS RESOURCES BUILDING SCHOOLS AND BRIDGES IN IRAQ, CHINA IS UNDERGOING A MASSIVE MILITARY BUILDUP, EVEN PURCHASING OFFENSIVE MISSILES TO BE DEPLOYED NEAR TAIWAN, A NATION WE'RE PLEDGED TO DEFEND.
I DON'T MEAN TO BE A "CHICKEN LITTLE" HERE, BUT MAN, ISN'T THAT ALL A LITTLE WORRISOME?
DID YOU SEE "THE APPRENTICE" THIS WEEK?
DID I? OF COURSE I DID!
I SEE YOU'RE QUITE CONCERNED.
DUDE DUDE CHECK THIS OUT.... YA FIRED! HAHAHA!
NO NO NO LOOKITME LOOKITME YA FIRED! HAHAHA!

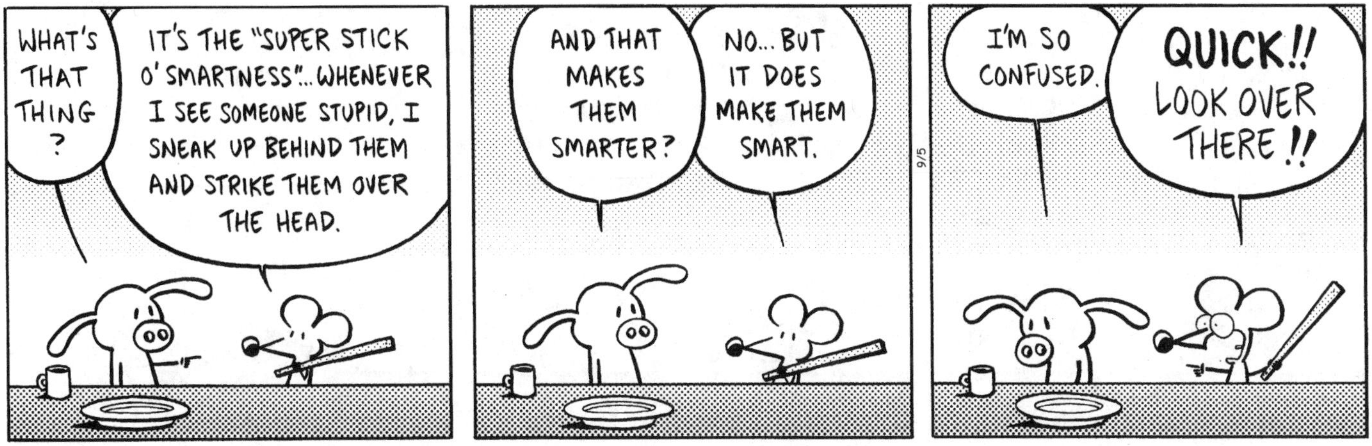
WHAT'S THAT THING?
IT'S THE "SUPER STICK O' SMARTNESS"... WHENEVER I SEE SOMEONE STUPID, I SNEAK UP BEHIND THEM AND STRIKE THEM OVER THE HEAD.
AND THAT MAKES THEM SMARTER?
NO... BUT IT DOES MAKE THEM SMART.
9/5
I'M SO CONFUSED.
QUICK!! LOOK OVER THERE!!

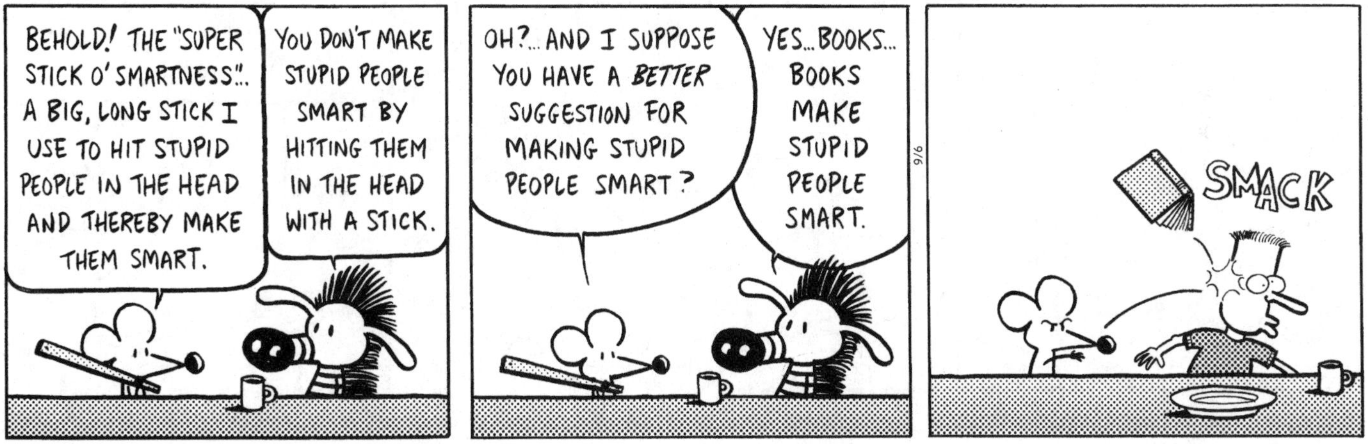
BEHOLD! THE "SUPER STICK O' SMARTNESS"... A BIG, LONG STICK I USE TO HIT STUPID PEOPLE IN THE HEAD AND THEREBY MAKE THEM SMART.
YOU DON'T MAKE STUPID PEOPLE SMART BY HITTING THEM IN THE HEAD WITH A STICK.
OH?... AND I SUPPOSE YOU HAVE A *BETTER* SUGGESTION FOR MAKING STUPID PEOPLE SMART?
YES... BOOKS... BOOKS MAKE STUPID PEOPLE SMART.
9/6
SMACK

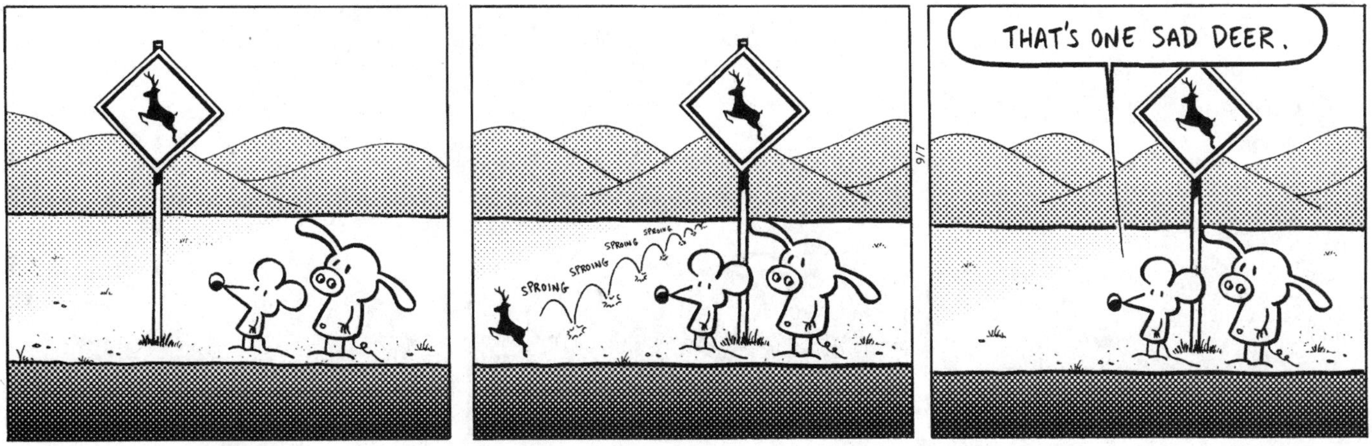
9/7
SPROING
SPROING
SPROING
SPROING
THAT'S ONE SAD DEER.

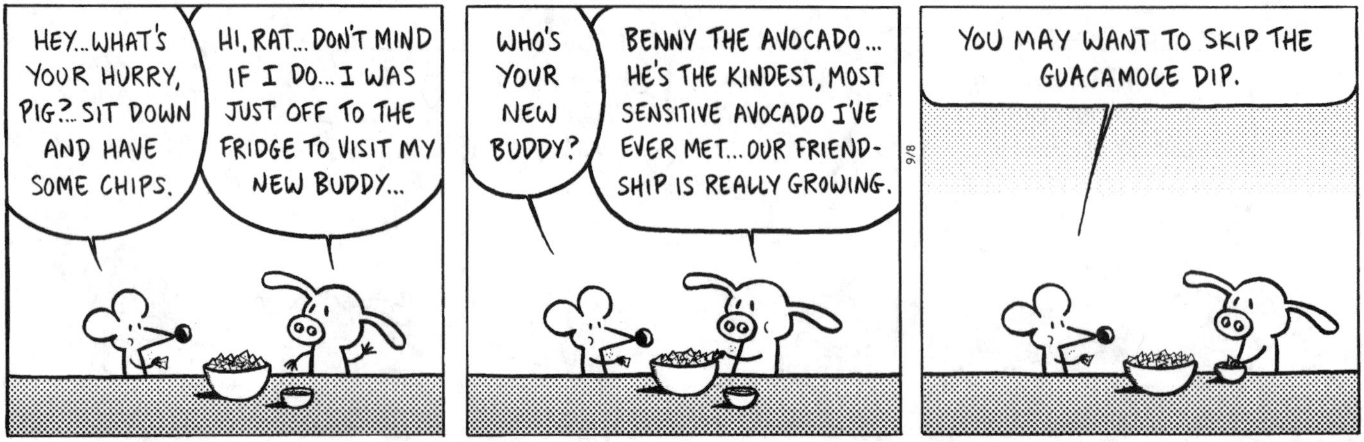
HEY...WHAT'S YOUR HURRY, PIG?...SIT DOWN AND HAVE SOME CHIPS.
HI, RAT...DON'T MIND IF I DO...I WAS JUST OFF TO THE FRIDGE TO VISIT MY NEW BUDDY...
WHO'S YOUR NEW BUDDY?
BENNY THE AVOCADO... HE'S THE KINDEST, MOST SENSITIVE AVOCADO I'VE EVER MET...OUR FRIENDSHIP IS REALLY GROWING.
9/8
YOU MAY WANT TO SKIP THE GUACAMOLE DIP.

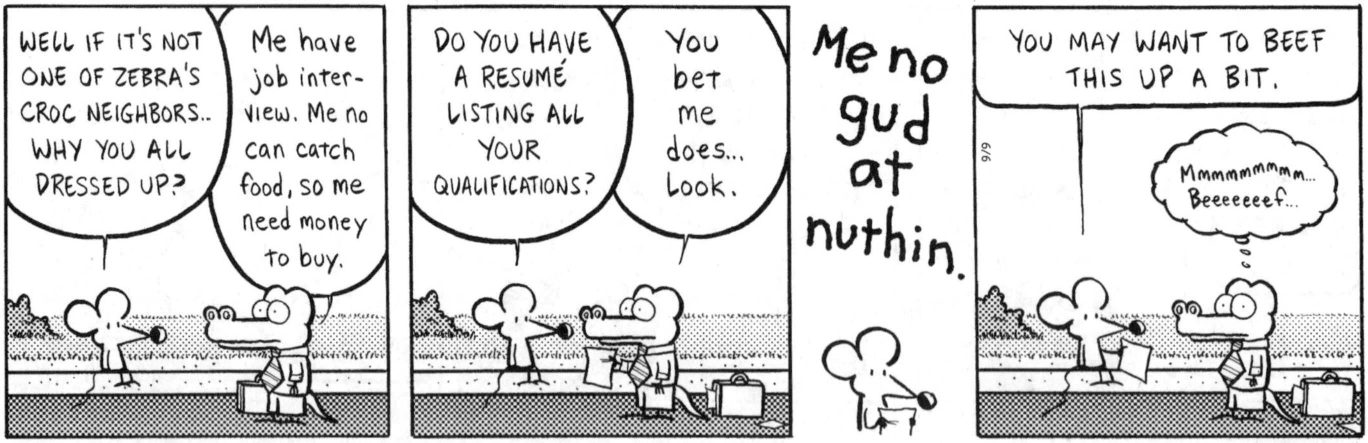
WELL IF IT'S NOT ONE OF ZEBRA'S CROC NEIGHBORS.. WHY YOU ALL DRESSED UP?
Me have job interview. Me no can catch food, so me need money to buy.
DO YOU HAVE A RESUMÉ LISTING ALL YOUR QUALIFICATIONS?
You bet me does... Look.
Me no gud at nuthin.
9/9
YOU MAY WANT TO BEEF THIS UP A BIT.
Mmmmmmmm... Beeeeeeef...

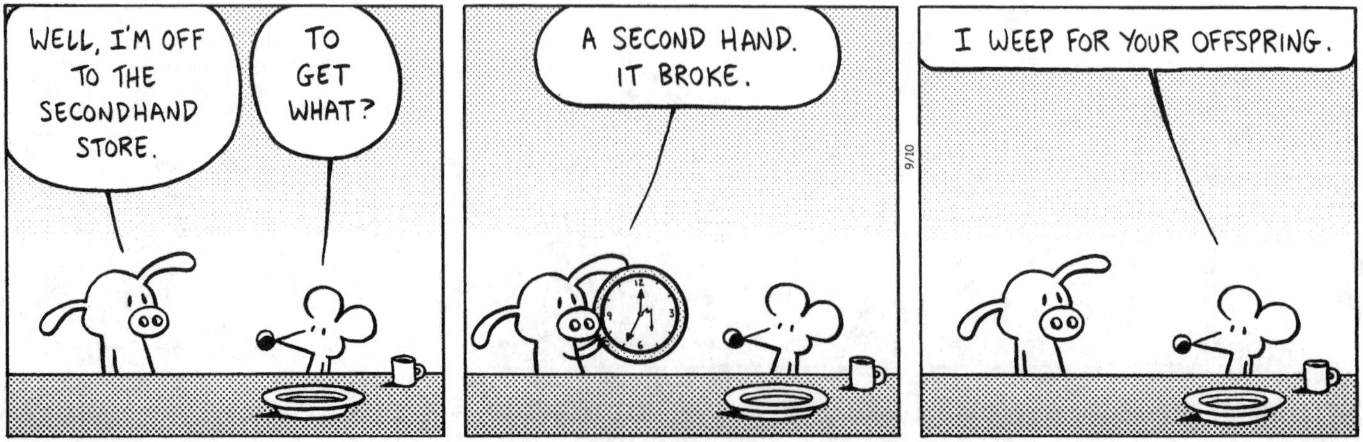
WELL, I'M OFF TO THE SECONDHAND STORE.
TO GET WHAT?
A SECOND HAND. IT BROKE.
9/10
I WEEP FOR YOUR OFFSPRING.

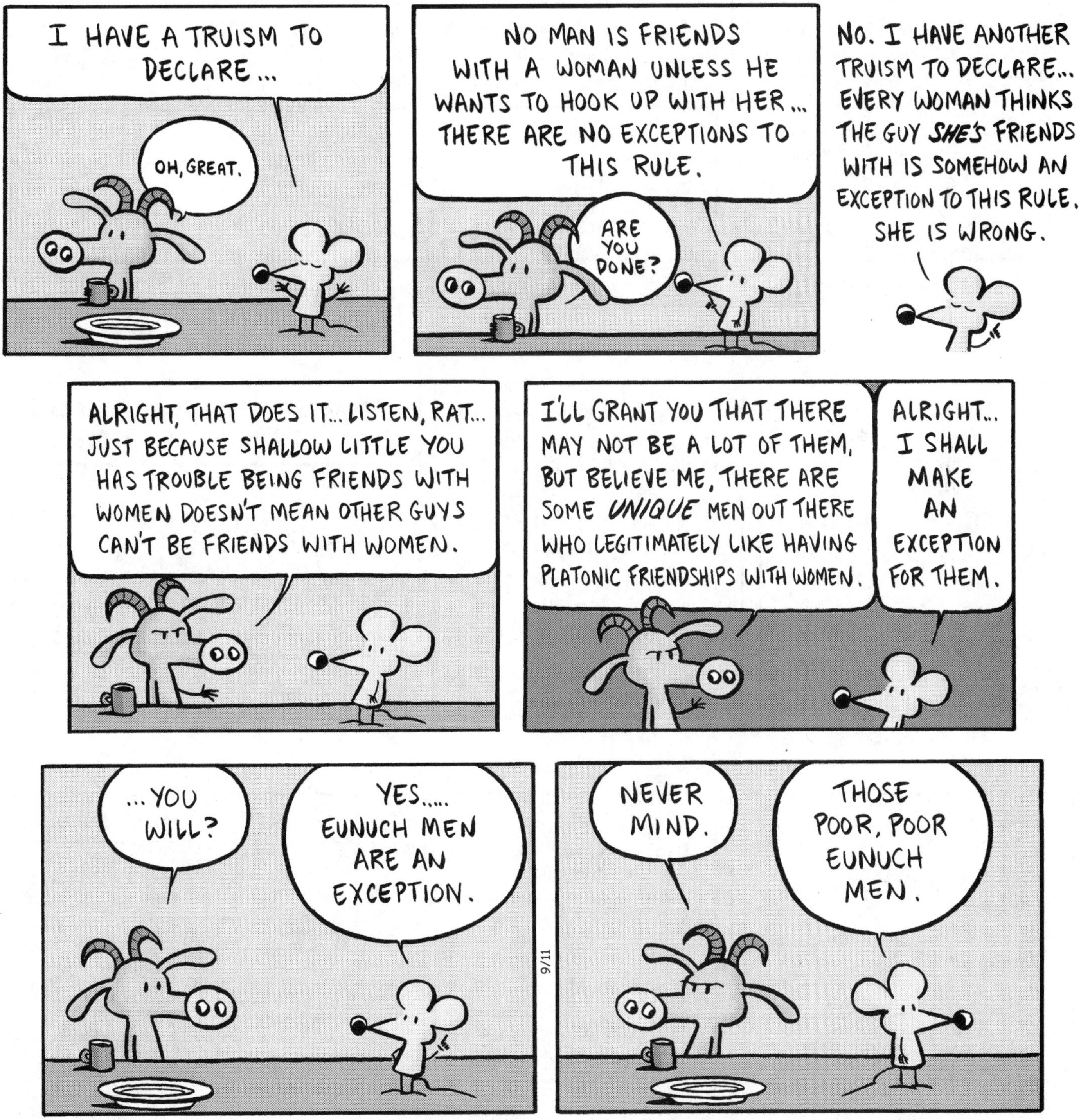

I HAVE A TRUISM TO DECLARE...
OH, GREAT.
NO MAN IS FRIENDS WITH A WOMAN UNLESS HE WANTS TO HOOK UP WITH HER... THERE ARE NO EXCEPTIONS TO THIS RULE.
ARE YOU DONE?
NO. I HAVE ANOTHER TRUISM TO DECLARE... EVERY WOMAN THINKS THE GUY *SHE'S* FRIENDS WITH IS SOMEHOW AN EXCEPTION TO THIS RULE. SHE IS WRONG.
ALRIGHT, THAT DOES IT... LISTEN, RAT... JUST BECAUSE SHALLOW LITTLE YOU HAS TROUBLE BEING FRIENDS WITH WOMEN DOESN'T MEAN OTHER GUYS CAN'T BE FRIENDS WITH WOMEN.
I'LL GRANT YOU THAT THERE MAY NOT BE A LOT OF THEM, BUT BELIEVE ME, THERE ARE SOME *UNIQUE* MEN OUT THERE WHO LEGITIMATELY LIKE HAVING PLATONIC FRIENDSHIPS WITH WOMEN.
ALRIGHT... I SHALL MAKE AN EXCEPTION FOR THEM.
...YOU WILL?
YES..... EUNUCH MEN ARE AN EXCEPTION.
9/11
NEVER MIND.
THOSE POOR, POOR EUNUCH MEN.

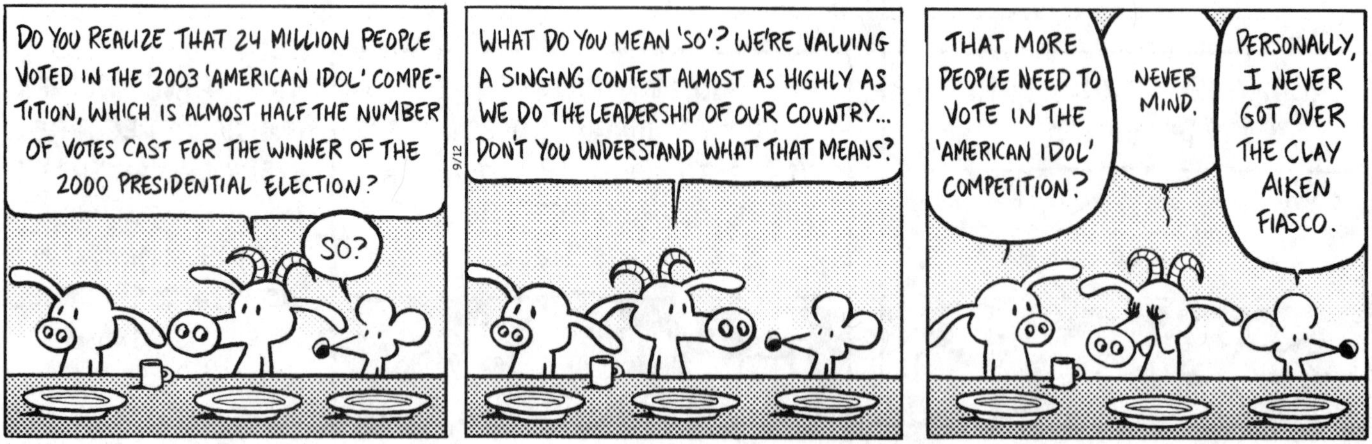
DO YOU REALIZE THAT 24 MILLION PEOPLE VOTED IN THE 2003 'AMERICAN IDOL' COMPETITION, WHICH IS ALMOST HALF THE NUMBER OF VOTES CAST FOR THE WINNER OF THE 2000 PRESIDENTIAL ELECTION?
SO?
9/12
WHAT DO YOU MEAN 'SO'? WE'RE VALUING A SINGING CONTEST ALMOST AS HIGHLY AS WE DO THE LEADERSHIP OF OUR COUNTRY... DON'T YOU UNDERSTAND WHAT THAT MEANS?
THAT MORE PEOPLE NEED TO VOTE IN THE 'AMERICAN IDOL' COMPETITION?
NEVER MIND.
PERSONALLY, I NEVER GOT OVER THE CLAY AIKEN FIASCO.

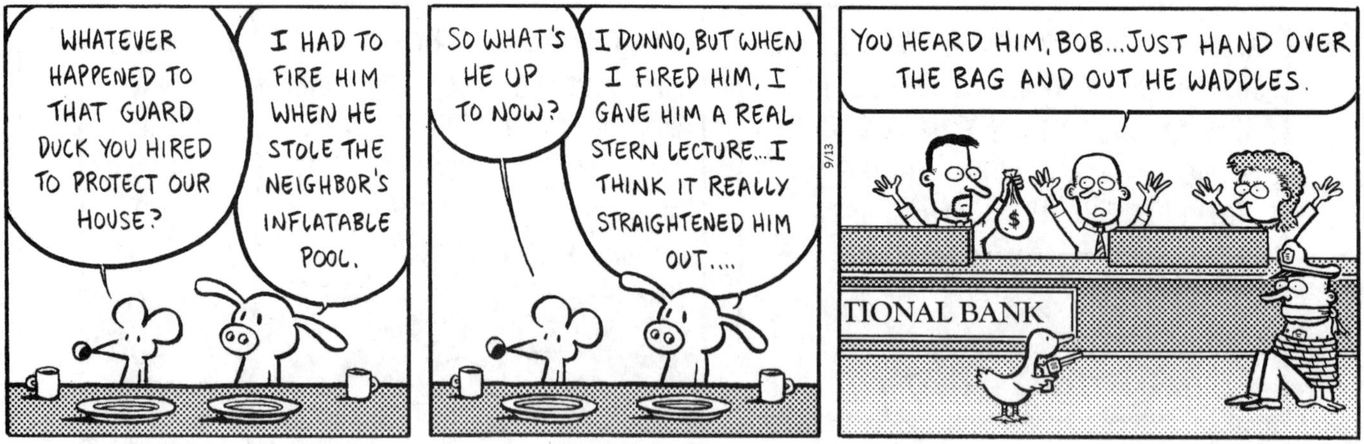
WHATEVER HAPPENED TO THAT GUARD DUCK YOU HIRED TO PROTECT OUR HOUSE?
I HAD TO FIRE HIM WHEN HE STOLE THE NEIGHBOR'S INFLATABLE POOL.
SO WHAT'S HE UP TO NOW?
I DUNNO, BUT WHEN I FIRED HIM, I GAVE HIM A REAL STERN LECTURE... I THINK IT REALLY STRAIGHTENED HIM OUT....
9/13
YOU HEARD HIM, BOB...JUST HAND OVER THE BAG AND OUT HE WADDLES.
TIONAL BANK

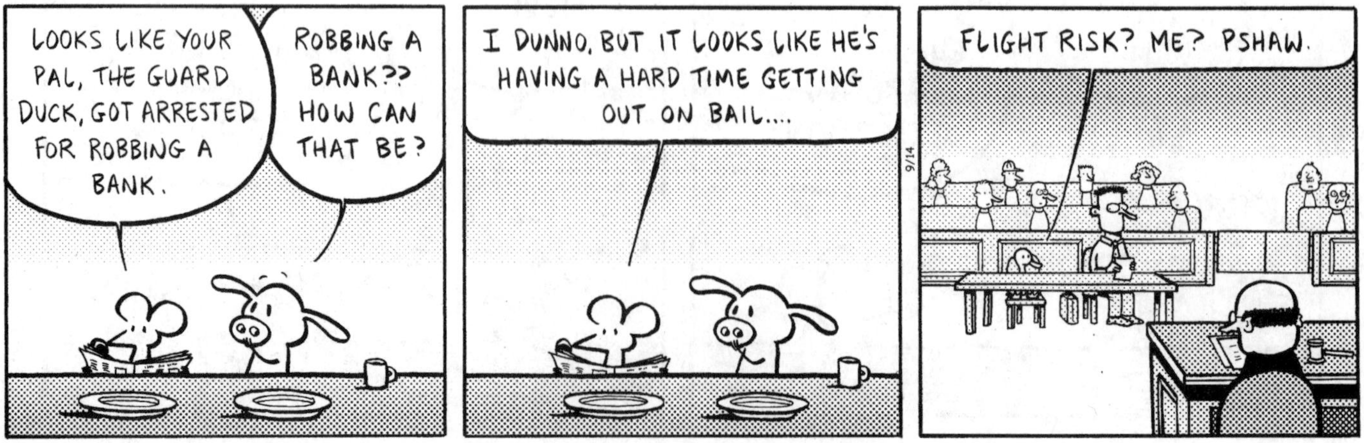
LOOKS LIKE YOUR PAL, THE GUARD DUCK, GOT ARRESTED FOR ROBBING A BANK.
ROBBING A BANK?? HOW CAN THAT BE?
I DUNNO, BUT IT LOOKS LIKE HE'S HAVING A HARD TIME GETTING OUT ON BAIL....
9/14
FLIGHT RISK? ME? PSHAW.

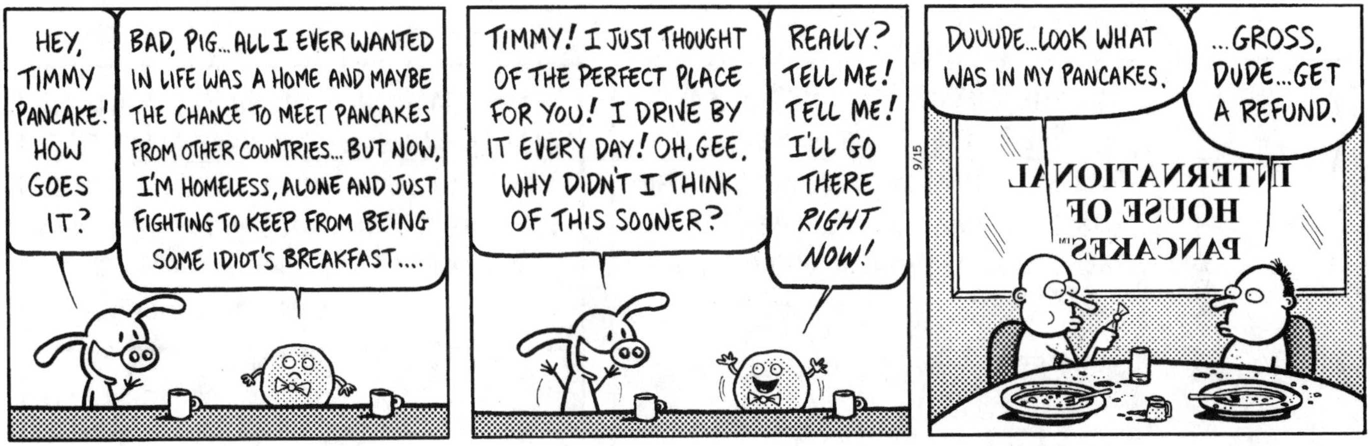
HEY, TIMMY PANCAKE! HOW GOES IT?
BAD, PIG... ALL I EVER WANTED IN LIFE WAS A HOME AND MAYBE THE CHANCE TO MEET PANCAKES FROM OTHER COUNTRIES... BUT NOW, I'M HOMELESS, ALONE AND JUST FIGHTING TO KEEP FROM BEING SOME IDIOT'S BREAKFAST....
TIMMY! I JUST THOUGHT OF THE PERFECT PLACE FOR YOU! I DRIVE BY IT EVERY DAY! OH, GEE. WHY DIDN'T I THINK OF THIS SOONER?
REALLY? TELL ME! TELL ME! I'LL GO THERE *RIGHT NOW!*
9/15
DUUUDE... LOOK WHAT WAS IN MY PANCAKES.
...GROSS, DUDE... GET A REFUND.
INTERNATIONAL HOUSE OF PANCAKES™

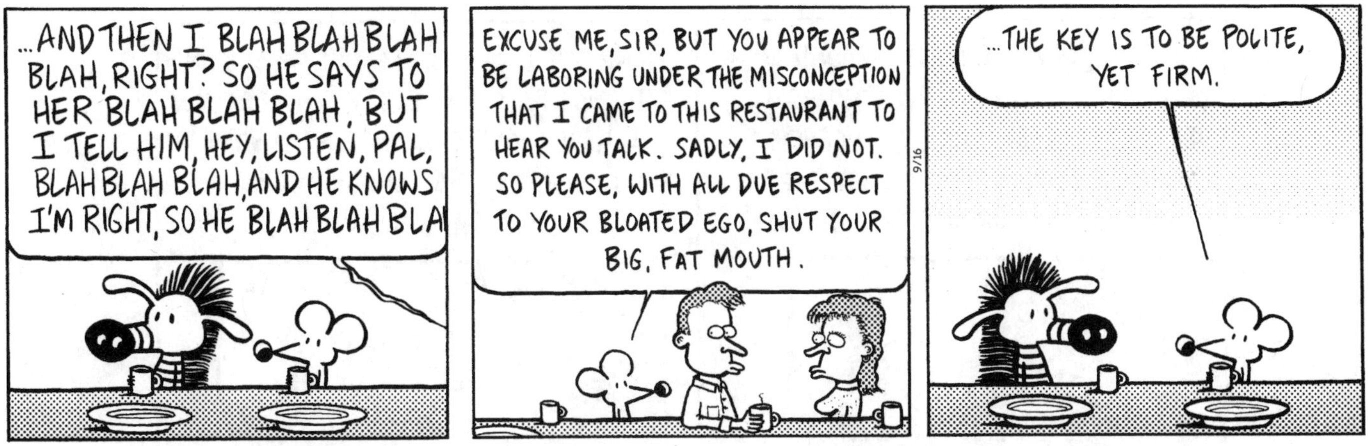
...AND THEN I BLAH BLAH BLAH BLAH, RIGHT? SO HE SAYS TO HER BLAH BLAH BLAH. BUT I TELL HIM, HEY, LISTEN, PAL, BLAH BLAH BLAH, AND HE KNOWS I'M RIGHT, SO HE BLAH BLAH BLA
EXCUSE ME, SIR, BUT YOU APPEAR TO BE LABORING UNDER THE MISCONCEPTION THAT I CAME TO THIS RESTAURANT TO HEAR YOU TALK. SADLY, I DID NOT. SO PLEASE, WITH ALL DUE RESPECT TO YOUR BLOATED EGO, SHUT YOUR BIG, FAT MOUTH.
9/16
...THE KEY IS TO BE POLITE, YET FIRM.

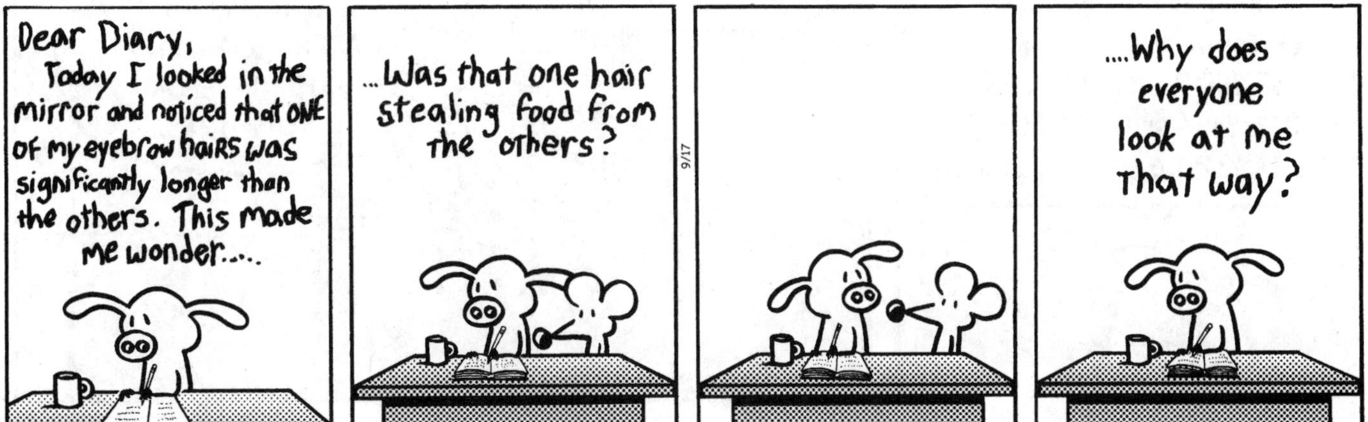
Dear Diary, Today I looked in the mirror and noticed that ONE of my eyebrow hairs was significantly longer than the others. This made me wonder.....
...Was that one hair stealing food from the others?
9/17
....Why does everyone look at me that way?

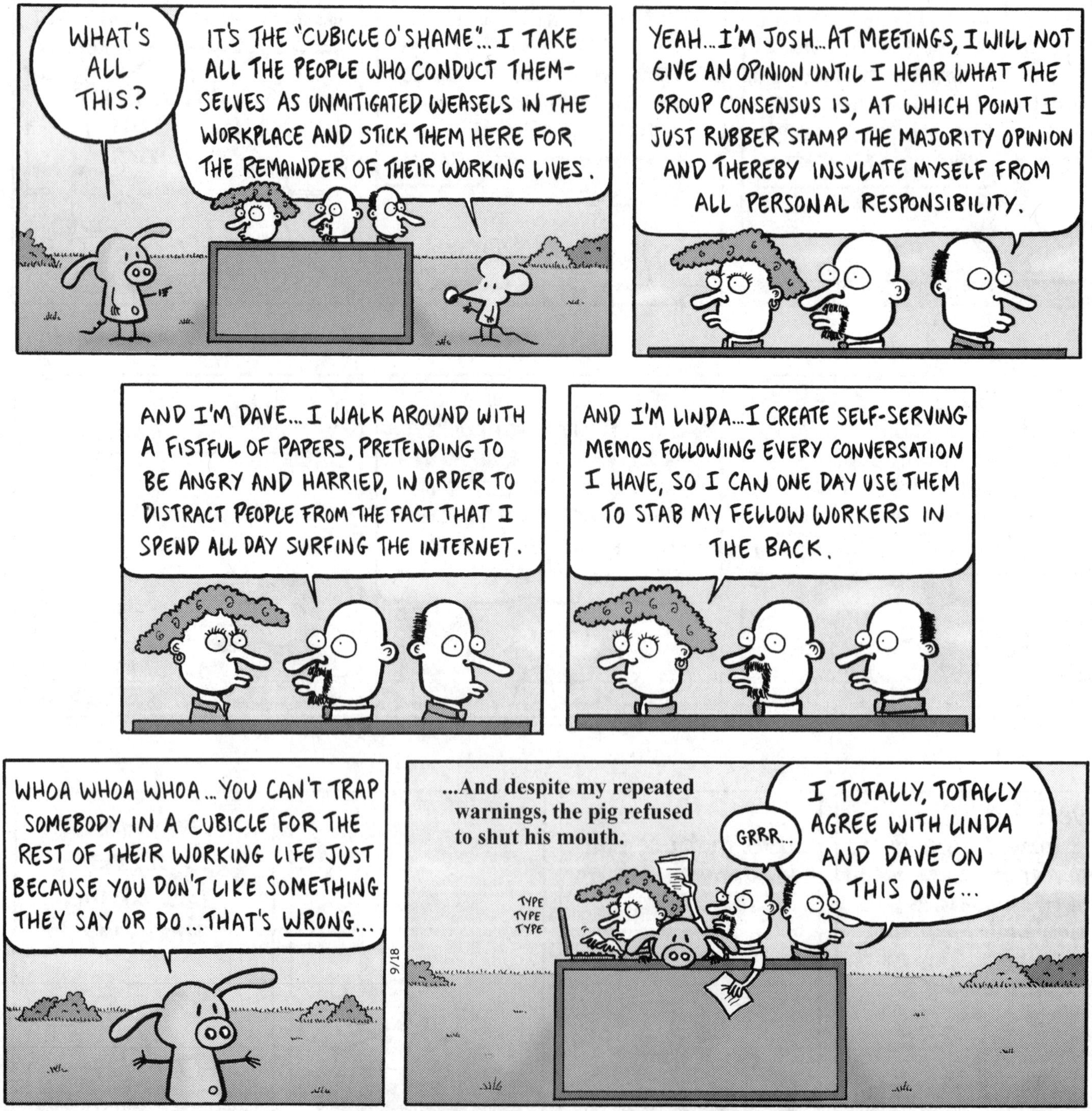
WHAT'S ALL THIS?
IT'S THE "CUBICLE O' SHAME"... I TAKE ALL THE PEOPLE WHO CONDUCT THEMSELVES AS UNMITIGATED WEASELS IN THE WORKPLACE AND STICK THEM HERE FOR THE REMAINDER OF THEIR WORKING LIVES.
YEAH... I'M JOSH... AT MEETINGS, I WILL NOT GIVE AN OPINION UNTIL I HEAR WHAT THE GROUP CONSENSUS IS, AT WHICH POINT I JUST RUBBER STAMP THE MAJORITY OPINION AND THEREBY INSULATE MYSELF FROM ALL PERSONAL RESPONSIBILITY.
AND I'M DAVE... I WALK AROUND WITH A FISTFUL OF PAPERS, PRETENDING TO BE ANGRY AND HARRIED, IN ORDER TO DISTRACT PEOPLE FROM THE FACT THAT I SPEND ALL DAY SURFING THE INTERNET.
AND I'M LINDA... I CREATE SELF-SERVING MEMOS FOLLOWING EVERY CONVERSATION I HAVE, SO I CAN ONE DAY USE THEM TO STAB MY FELLOW WORKERS IN THE BACK.
WHOA WHOA WHOA... YOU CAN'T TRAP SOMEBODY IN A CUBICLE FOR THE REST OF THEIR WORKING LIFE JUST BECAUSE YOU DON'T LIKE SOMETHING THEY SAY OR DO... THAT'S WRONG...
9/18
...And despite my repeated warnings, the pig refused to shut his mouth.
TYPE TYPE TYPE
GRRR...
I TOTALLY, TOTALLY AGREE WITH LINDA AND DAVE ON THIS ONE...

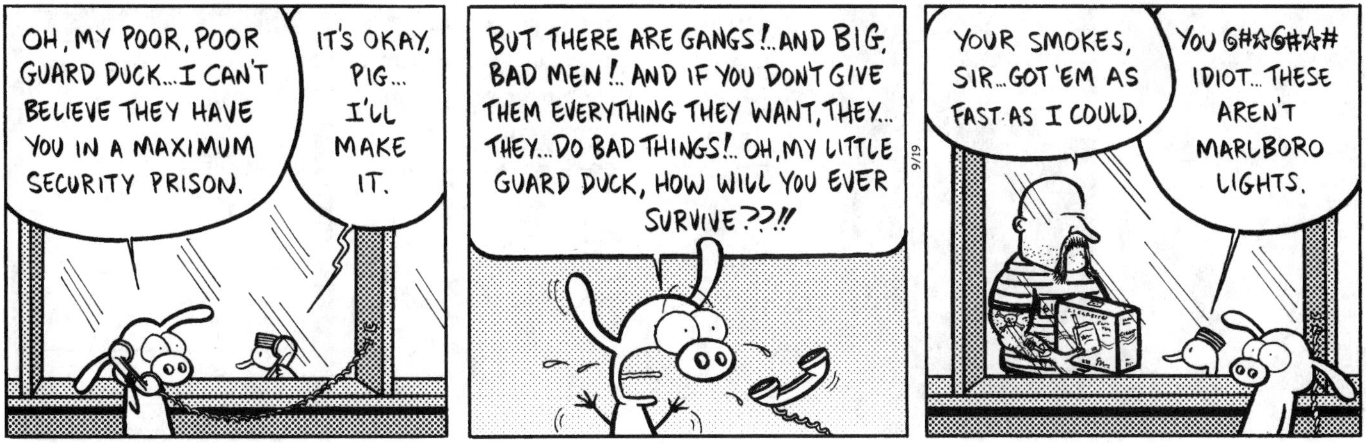
OH, MY POOR, POOR GUARD DUCK...I CAN'T BELIEVE THEY HAVE YOU IN A MAXIMUM SECURITY PRISON.
IT'S OKAY, PIG... I'LL MAKE IT.
BUT THERE ARE GANGS!..AND BIG, BAD MEN!..AND IF YOU DON'T GIVE THEM EVERYTHING THEY WANT, THEY... THEY...DO BAD THINGS!..OH, MY LITTLE GUARD DUCK, HOW WILL YOU EVER SURVIVE??!!
9/19
YOUR SMOKES, SIR...GOT 'EM AS FAST AS I COULD.
YOU G#☆G#☆# IDIOT...THESE AREN'T MARLBORO LIGHTS.

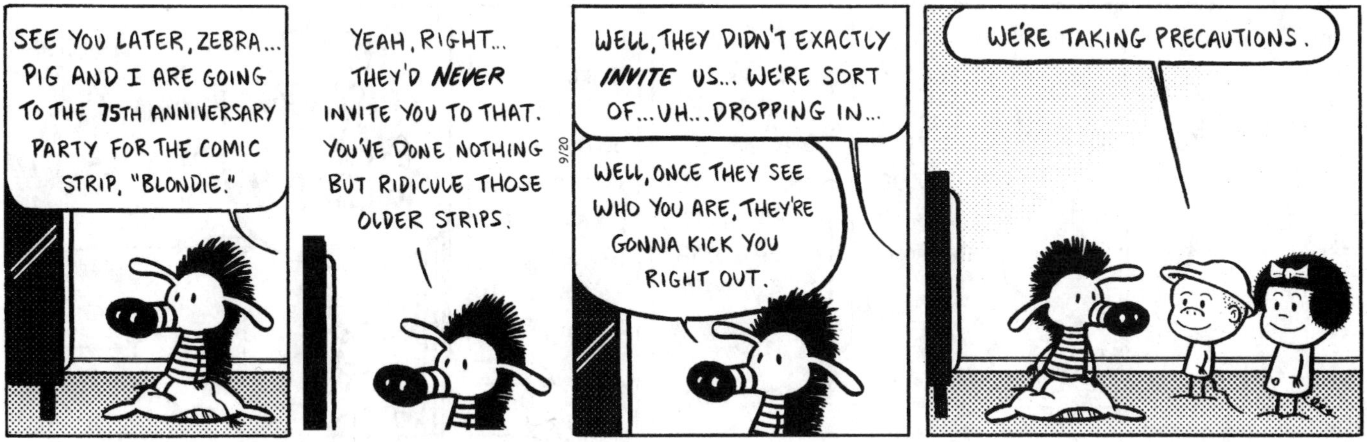
SEE YOU LATER, ZEBRA... PIG AND I ARE GOING TO THE 75TH ANNIVERSARY PARTY FOR THE COMIC STRIP, "BLONDIE."
YEAH, RIGHT... THEY'D NEVER INVITE YOU TO THAT. YOU'VE DONE NOTHING BUT RIDICULE THOSE OLDER STRIPS.
9/20
WELL, THEY DIDN'T EXACTLY INVITE US... WE'RE SORT OF...UH...DROPPING IN...
WELL, ONCE THEY SEE WHO YOU ARE, THEY'RE GONNA KICK YOU RIGHT OUT.
WE'RE TAKING PRECAUTIONS.

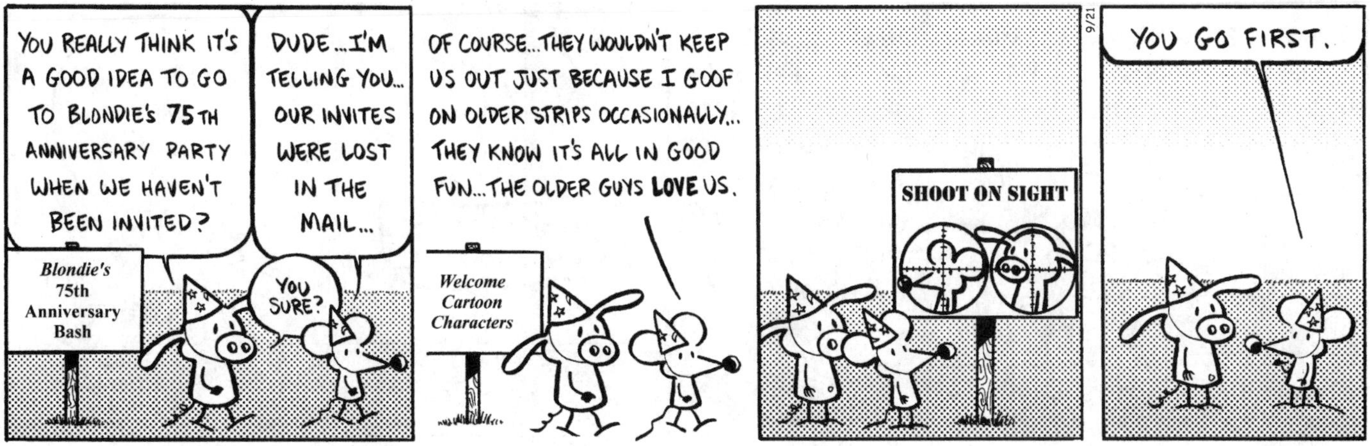
YOU REALLY THINK IT'S A GOOD IDEA TO GO TO BLONDIE'S 75TH ANNIVERSARY PARTY WHEN WE HAVEN'T BEEN INVITED?
DUDE...I'M TELLING YOU... OUR INVITES WERE LOST IN THE MAIL...
Blondie's 75th Anniversary Bash
YOU SURE?
OF COURSE...THEY WOULDN'T KEEP US OUT JUST BECAUSE I GOOF ON OLDER STRIPS OCCASIONALLY... THEY KNOW IT'S ALL IN GOOD FUN...THE OLDER GUYS LOVE US.
Welcome Cartoon Characters
SHOOT ON SIGHT
9/21
YOU GO FIRST.

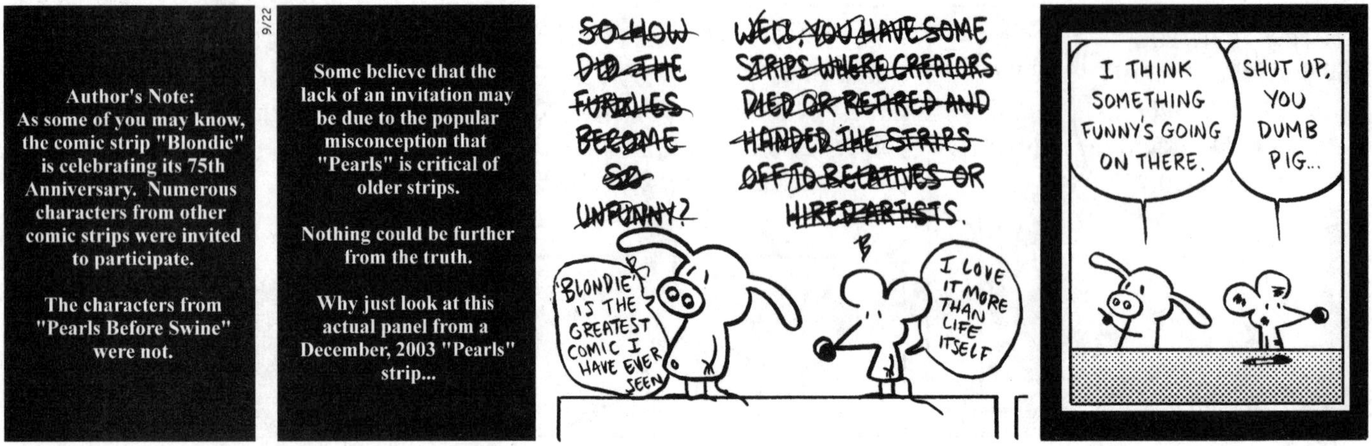
9/22
Author's Note:
As some of you may know, the comic strip "Blondie" is celebrating its 75th Anniversary. Numerous characters from other comic strips were invited to participate.
The characters from "Pearls Before Swine" were not.
Some believe that the lack of an invitation may be due to the popular misconception that "Pearls" is critical of older strips.
Nothing could be further from the truth.
Why just look at this actual panel from a December, 2003 "Pearls" strip...
~~SO HOW DID THE FUNNIES BECOME SO UNFUNNY?~~
~~WELL, YOU HAVE SOME STRIPS WHERE CREATORS DIED OR RETIRED AND HANDED THE STRIPS OFF TO RELATIVES OR HIRED ARTISTS~~.
'BLONDIE' IS THE GREATEST COMIC I HAVE EVER SEEN
I LOVE IT MORE THAN LIFE ITSELF
I THINK SOMETHING FUNNY'S GOING ON THERE.
SHUT UP, YOU DUMB PIG...

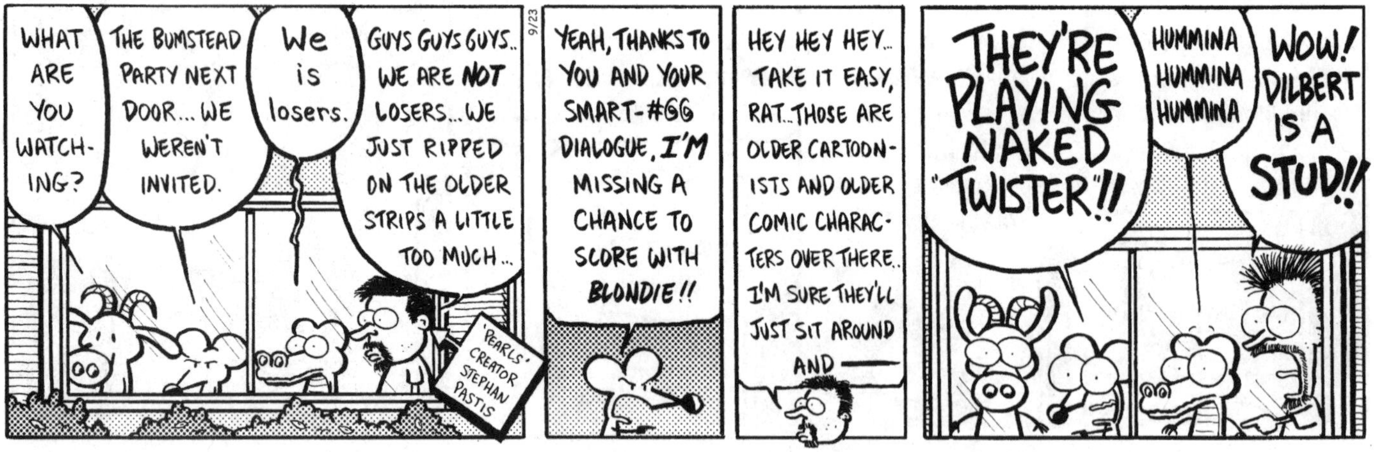
WHAT ARE YOU WATCH-ING?
THE BUMSTEAD PARTY NEXT DOOR... WE WEREN'T INVITED.
We is losers.
GUYS GUYS GUYS.. WE ARE NOT LOSERS... WE JUST RIPPED ON THE OLDER STRIPS A LITTLE TOO MUCH...
'PEARLS' CREATOR STEPHAN PASTIS
9/23
YEAH, THANKS TO YOU AND YOUR SMART-#@ DIALOGUE, I'M MISSING A CHANCE TO SCORE WITH BLONDIE!!
HEY HEY HEY... TAKE IT EASY, RAT... THOSE ARE OLDER CARTOON-ISTS AND OLDER COMIC CHARAC-TERS OVER THERE.. I'M SURE THEY'LL JUST SIT AROUND AND ——
THEY'RE PLAYING NAKED "TWISTER"!!
HUMMINA HUMMINA HUMMINA
WOW! DILBERT IS A STUD!!

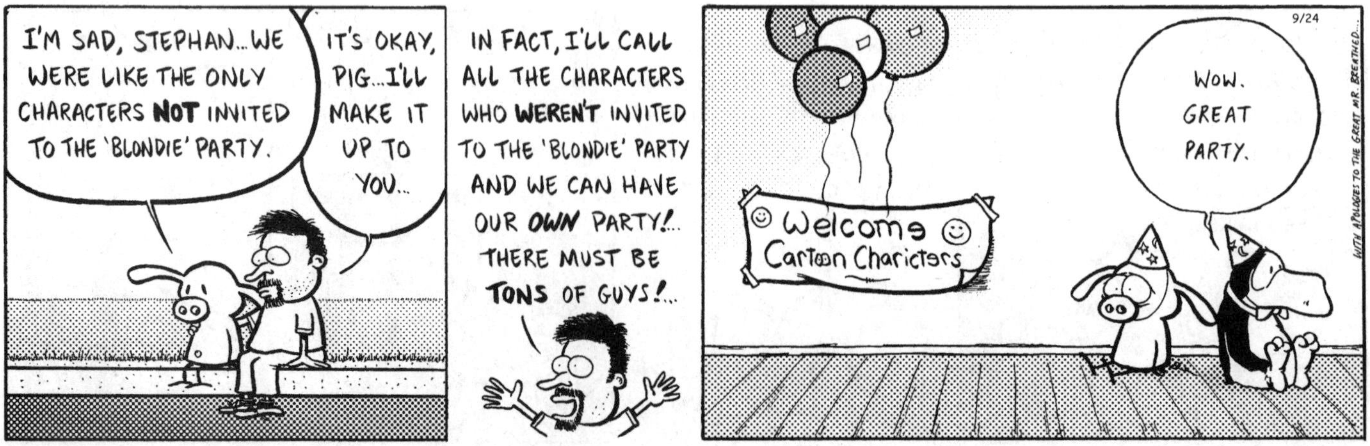
I'M SAD, STEPHAN... WE WERE LIKE THE ONLY CHARACTERS NOT INVITED TO THE 'BLONDIE' PARTY.
IT'S OKAY, PIG... I'LL MAKE IT UP TO YOU...
IN FACT, I'LL CALL ALL THE CHARACTERS WHO WEREN'T INVITED TO THE 'BLONDIE' PARTY AND WE CAN HAVE OUR OWN PARTY!... THERE MUST BE TONS OF GUYS!...
9/24
Welcome Cartoon Charicters
WOW. GREAT PARTY.
WITH APOLOGIES TO THE GREAT MR. BREATHED...

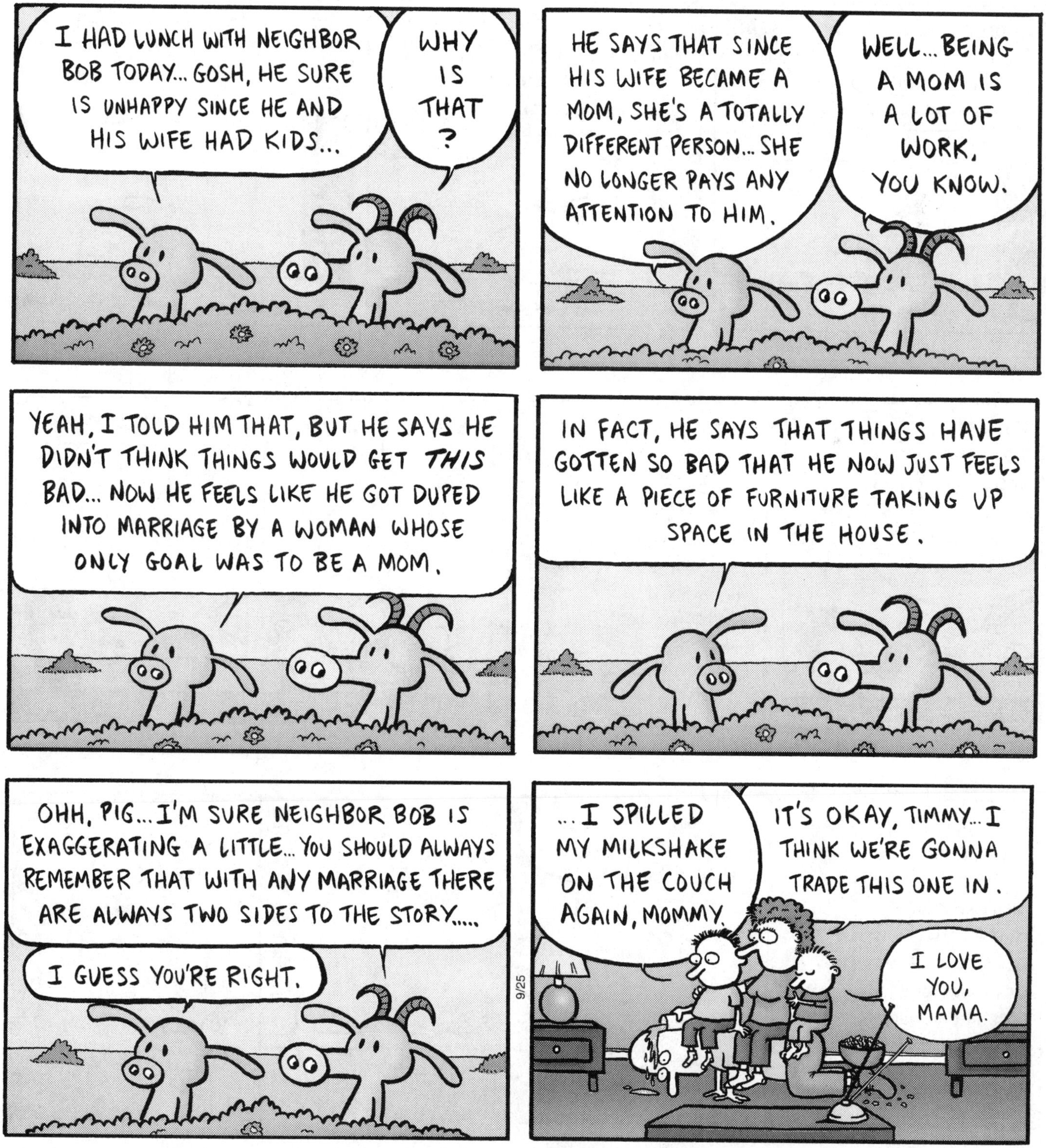
I HAD LUNCH WITH NEIGHBOR BOB TODAY... GOSH, HE SURE IS UNHAPPY SINCE HE AND HIS WIFE HAD KIDS...
WHY IS THAT?
HE SAYS THAT SINCE HIS WIFE BECAME A MOM, SHE'S A TOTALLY DIFFERENT PERSON... SHE NO LONGER PAYS ANY ATTENTION TO HIM.
WELL... BEING A MOM IS A LOT OF WORK, YOU KNOW.
YEAH, I TOLD HIM THAT, BUT HE SAYS HE DIDN'T THINK THINGS WOULD GET *THIS* BAD... NOW HE FEELS LIKE HE GOT DUPED INTO MARRIAGE BY A WOMAN WHOSE ONLY GOAL WAS TO BE A MOM.
IN FACT, HE SAYS THAT THINGS HAVE GOTTEN SO BAD THAT HE NOW JUST FEELS LIKE A PIECE OF FURNITURE TAKING UP SPACE IN THE HOUSE.
OHH, PIG... I'M SURE NEIGHBOR BOB IS EXAGGERATING A LITTLE... YOU SHOULD ALWAYS REMEMBER THAT WITH ANY MARRIAGE THERE ARE ALWAYS TWO SIDES TO THE STORY.....
I GUESS YOU'RE RIGHT.
9/25
...I SPILLED MY MILKSHAKE ON THE COUCH AGAIN, MOMMY.
IT'S OKAY, TIMMY... I THINK WE'RE GONNA TRADE THIS ONE IN.
I LOVE YOU, MAMA.

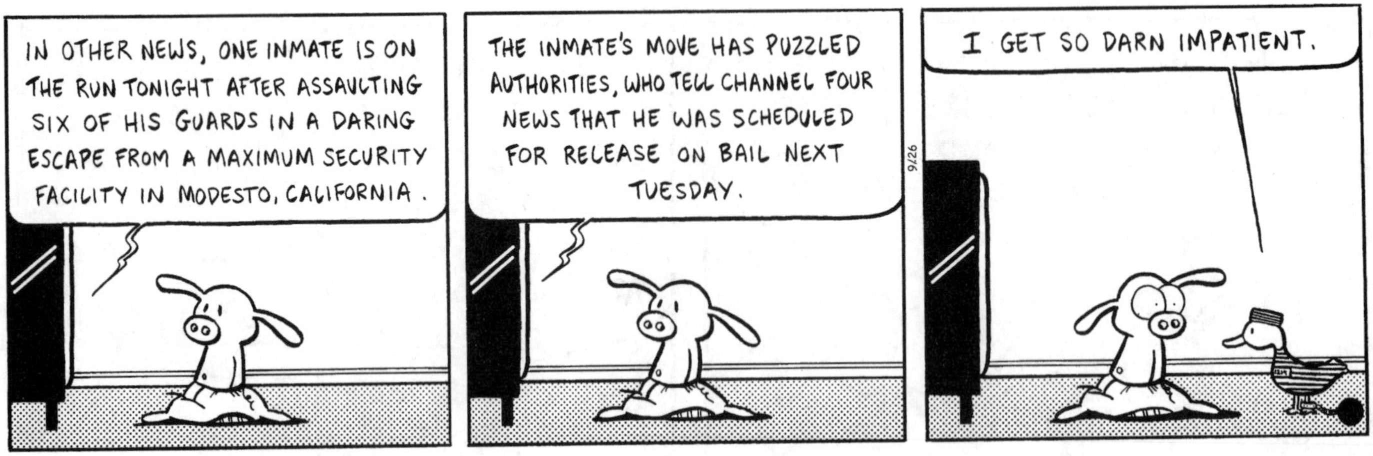
IN OTHER NEWS, ONE INMATE IS ON THE RUN TONIGHT AFTER ASSAULTING SIX OF HIS GUARDS IN A DARING ESCAPE FROM A MAXIMUM SECURITY FACILITY IN MODESTO, CALIFORNIA.
THE INMATE'S MOVE HAS PUZZLED AUTHORITIES, WHO TELL CHANNEL FOUR NEWS THAT HE WAS SCHEDULED FOR RELEASE ON BAIL NEXT TUESDAY.
9/26
I GET SO DARN IMPATIENT.

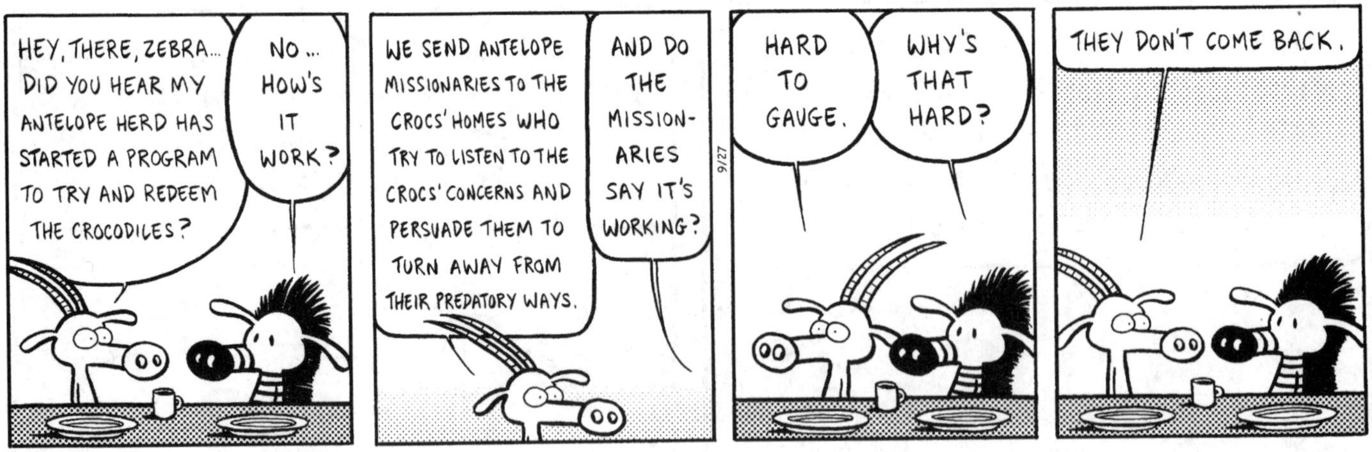
HEY, THERE, ZEBRA... DID YOU HEAR MY ANTELOPE HERD HAS STARTED A PROGRAM TO TRY AND REDEEM THE CROCODILES?
NO... HOW'S IT WORK?
WE SEND ANTELOPE MISSIONARIES TO THE CROCS' HOMES WHO TRY TO LISTEN TO THE CROCS' CONCERNS AND PERSUADE THEM TO TURN AWAY FROM THEIR PREDATORY WAYS.
AND DO THE MISSION-ARIES SAY IT'S WORKING?
9/27
HARD TO GAUGE.
WHY'S THAT HARD?
THEY DON'T COME BACK.

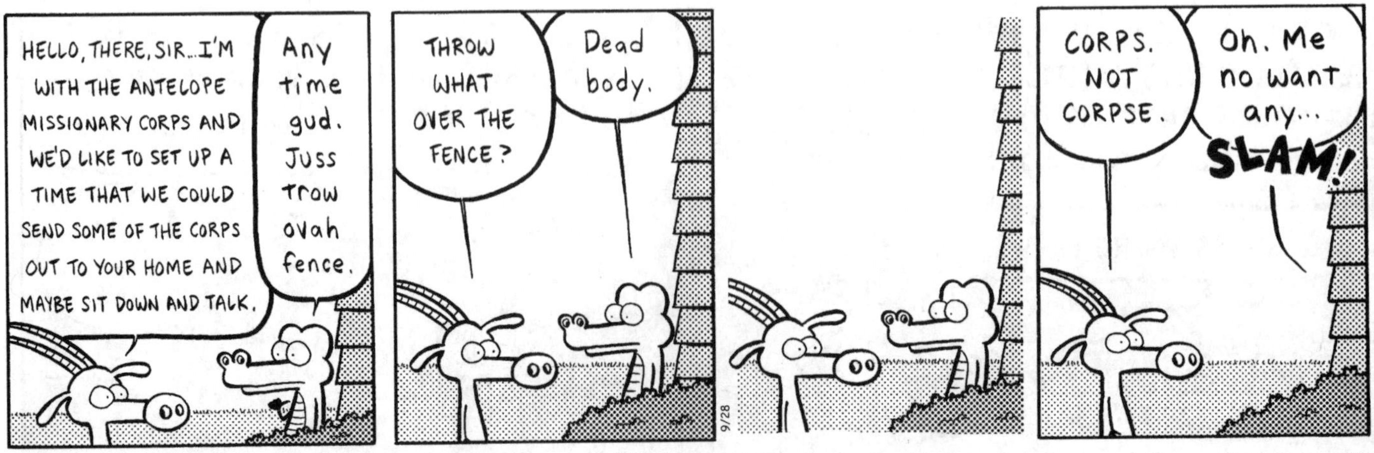
HELLO, THERE, SIR...I'M WITH THE ANTELOPE MISSIONARY CORPS AND WE'D LIKE TO SET UP A TIME THAT WE COULD SEND SOME OF THE CORPS OUT TO YOUR HOME AND MAYBE SIT DOWN AND TALK.
Any time gud. Juss trow ovah fence.
THROW WHAT OVER THE FENCE?
Dead body.
9/28
CORPS. NOT CORPSE.
Oh. Me no want any...
SLAM!

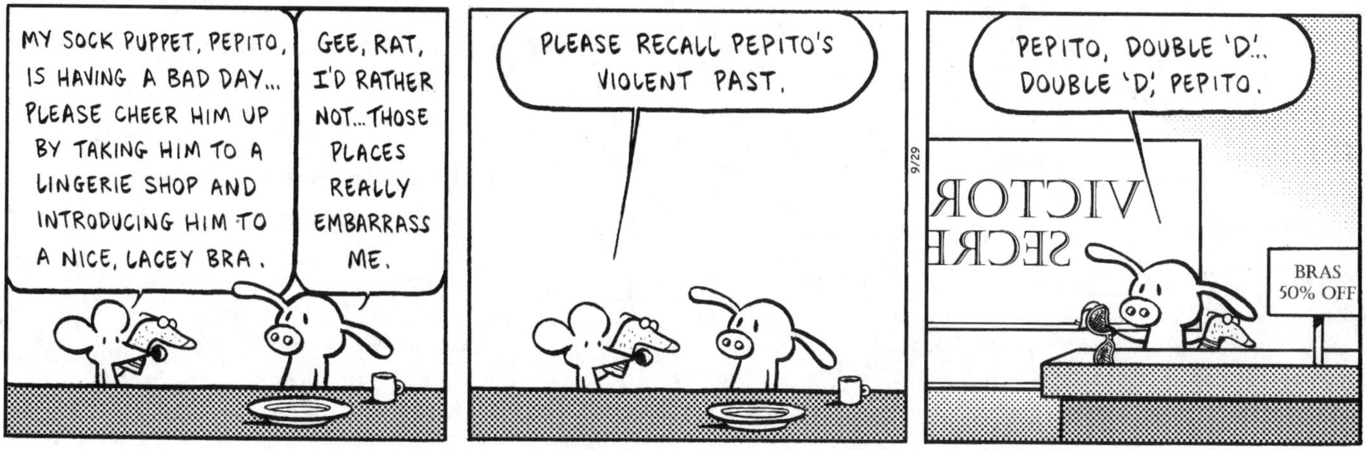
MY SOCK PUPPET, PEPITO, IS HAVING A BAD DAY... PLEASE CHEER HIM UP BY TAKING HIM TO A LINGERIE SHOP AND INTRODUCING HIM TO A NICE, LACEY BRA.
GEE, RAT, I'D RATHER NOT... THOSE PLACES REALLY EMBARRASS ME.
PLEASE RECALL PEPITO'S VIOLENT PAST.
9/29
PEPITO, DOUBLE 'D'.. DOUBLE 'D,' PEPITO.
BRAS 50% OFF

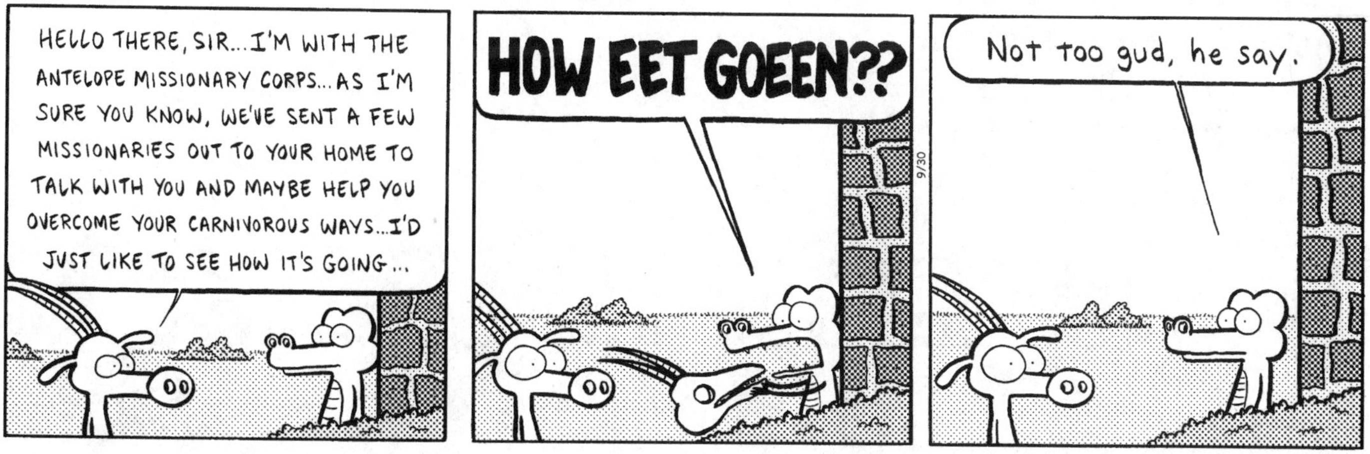
HELLO THERE, SIR... I'M WITH THE ANTELOPE MISSIONARY CORPS... AS I'M SURE YOU KNOW, WE'VE SENT A FEW MISSIONARIES OUT TO YOUR HOME TO TALK WITH YOU AND MAYBE HELP YOU OVERCOME YOUR CARNIVOROUS WAYS... I'D JUST LIKE TO SEE HOW IT'S GOING...
HOW EET GOEEN??
9/30
Not too gud, he say.

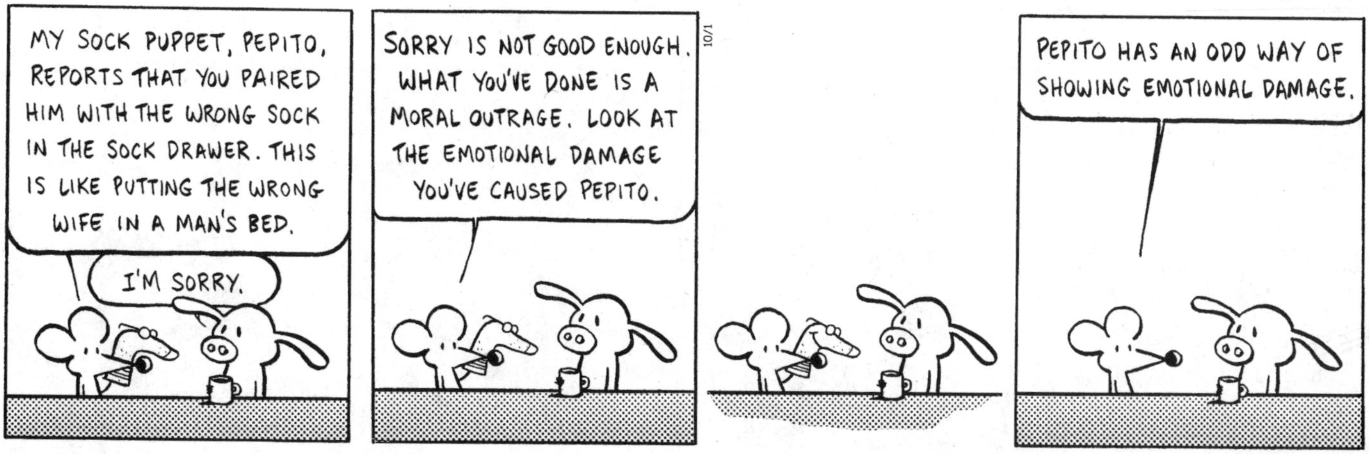
MY SOCK PUPPET, PEPITO, REPORTS THAT YOU PAIRED HIM WITH THE WRONG SOCK IN THE SOCK DRAWER. THIS IS LIKE PUTTING THE WRONG WIFE IN A MAN'S BED.
I'M SORRY.
SORRY IS NOT GOOD ENOUGH. WHAT YOU'VE DONE IS A MORAL OUTRAGE. LOOK AT THE EMOTIONAL DAMAGE YOU'VE CAUSED PEPITO.
10/1
PEPITO HAS AN ODD WAY OF SHOWING EMOTIONAL DAMAGE.

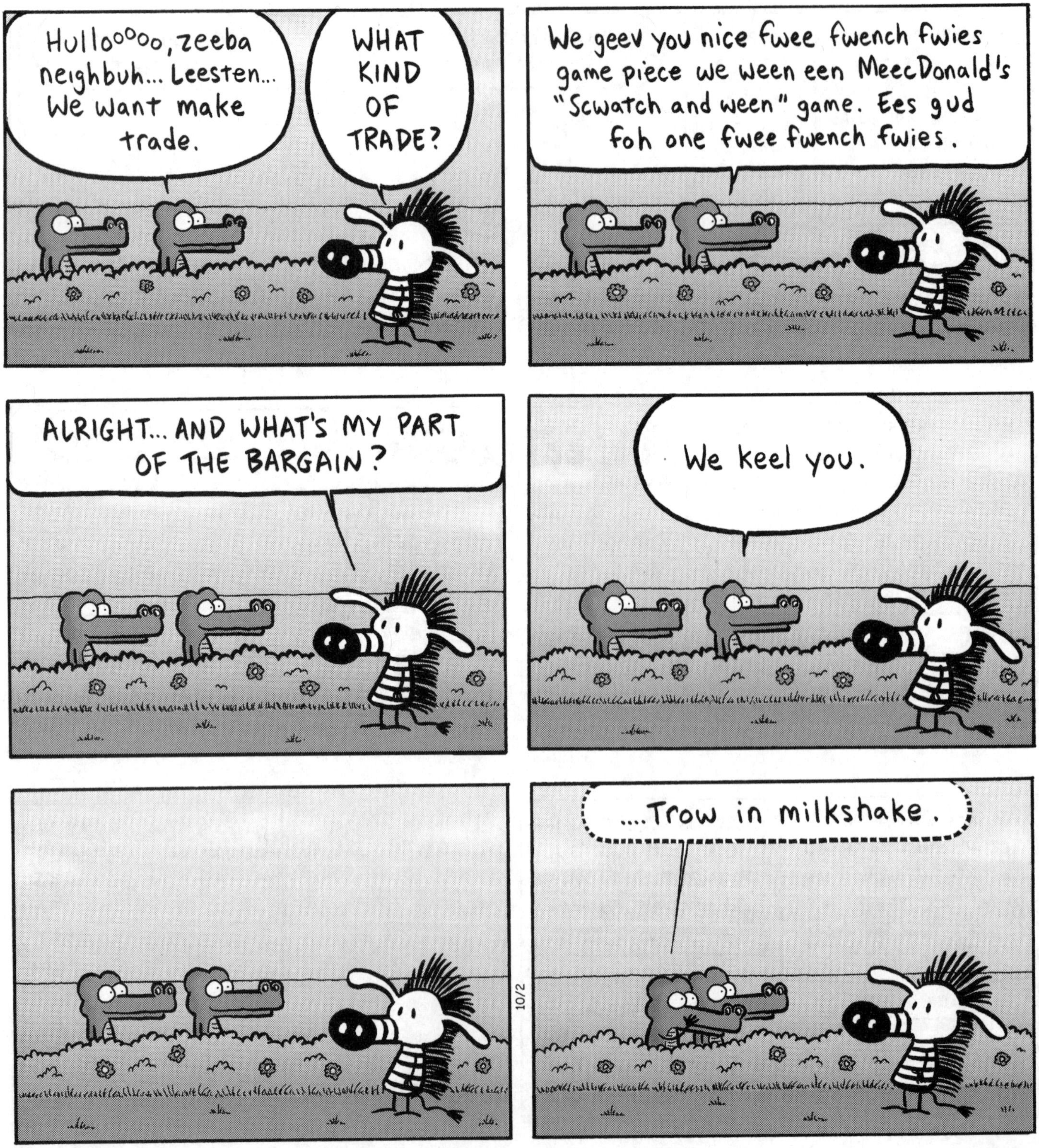
Hulloooo, zeeba neighbuh... Leesten... We want make trade.
WHAT KIND OF TRADE?
We geev you nice fwee fwench fwies game piece we ween een MeecDonald's "Scwatch and ween" game. Ees gud foh one fwee fwench fwies.
ALRIGHT... AND WHAT'S MY PART OF THE BARGAIN?
We keel you.
10/2
....Trow in milkshake.

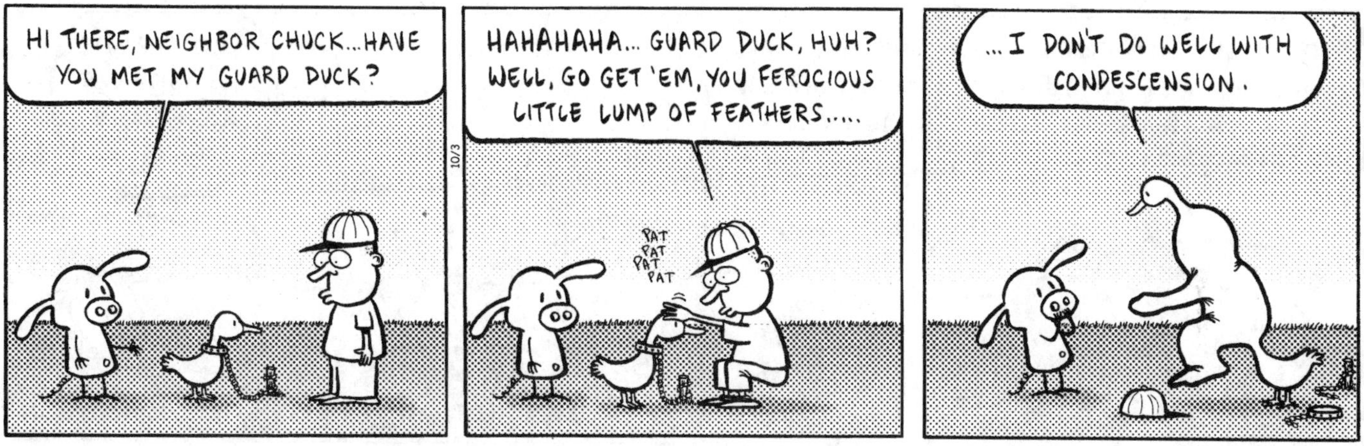
HI THERE, NEIGHBOR CHUCK...HAVE YOU MET MY GUARD DUCK?
10/3
HAHAHAHA... GUARD DUCK, HUH? WELL, GO GET 'EM, YOU FEROCIOUS LITTLE LUMP OF FEATHERS.....
PAT PAT PAT PAT
...I DON'T DO WELL WITH CONDESCENSION.

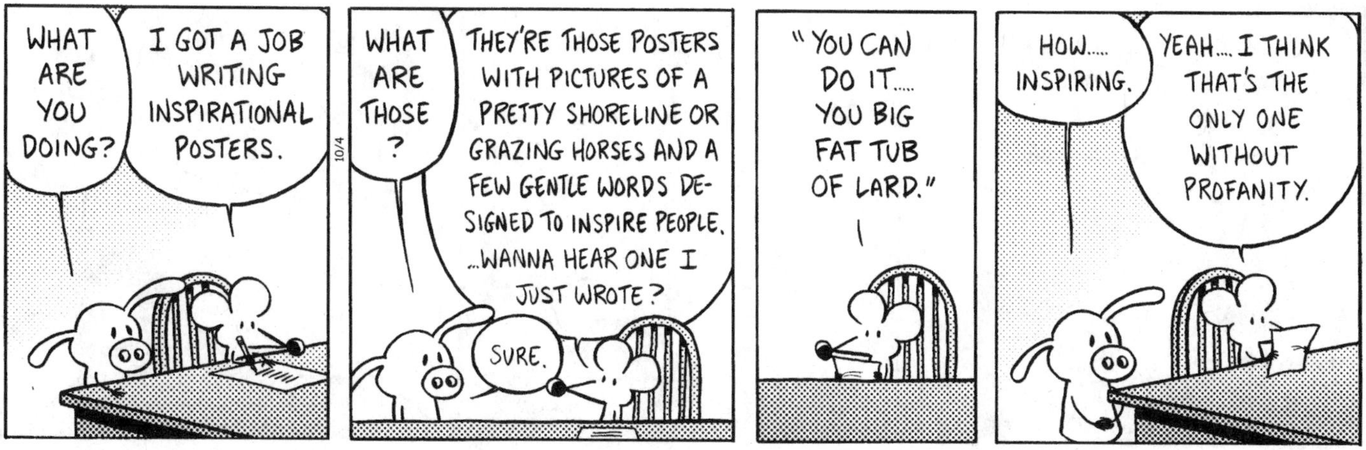
WHAT ARE YOU DOING?
I GOT A JOB WRITING INSPIRATIONAL POSTERS.
10/4
WHAT ARE THOSE?
THEY'RE THOSE POSTERS WITH PICTURES OF A PRETTY SHORELINE OR GRAZING HORSES AND A FEW GENTLE WORDS DESIGNED TO INSPIRE PEOPLE. ...WANNA HEAR ONE I JUST WROTE?
SURE.
"YOU CAN DO IT..... YOU BIG FAT TUB OF LARD."
HOW..... INSPIRING.
YEAH.... I THINK THAT'S THE ONLY ONE WITHOUT PROFANITY.

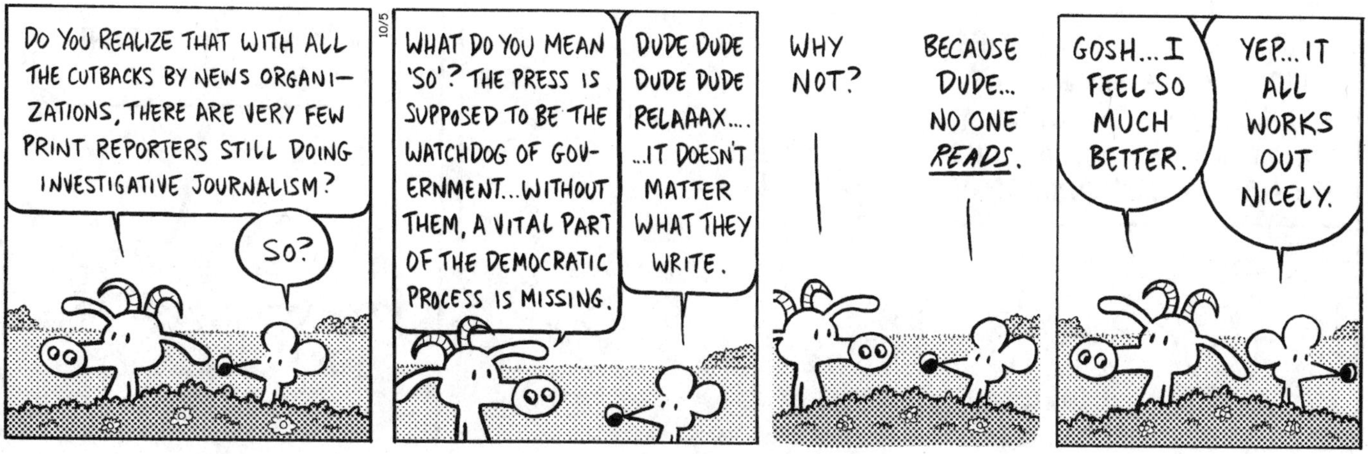
DO YOU REALIZE THAT WITH ALL THE CUTBACKS BY NEWS ORGANIZATIONS, THERE ARE VERY FEW PRINT REPORTERS STILL DOING INVESTIGATIVE JOURNALISM?
SO?
10/5
WHAT DO YOU MEAN 'SO'? THE PRESS IS SUPPOSED TO BE THE WATCHDOG OF GOVERNMENT...WITHOUT THEM, A VITAL PART OF THE DEMOCRATIC PROCESS IS MISSING.
DUDE DUDE DUDE DUDE RELAAAX.... ...IT DOESN'T MATTER WHAT THEY WRITE.
WHY NOT?
BECAUSE DUDE... NO ONE READS.
GOSH... I FEEL SO MUCH BETTER.
YEP... IT ALL WORKS OUT NICELY.

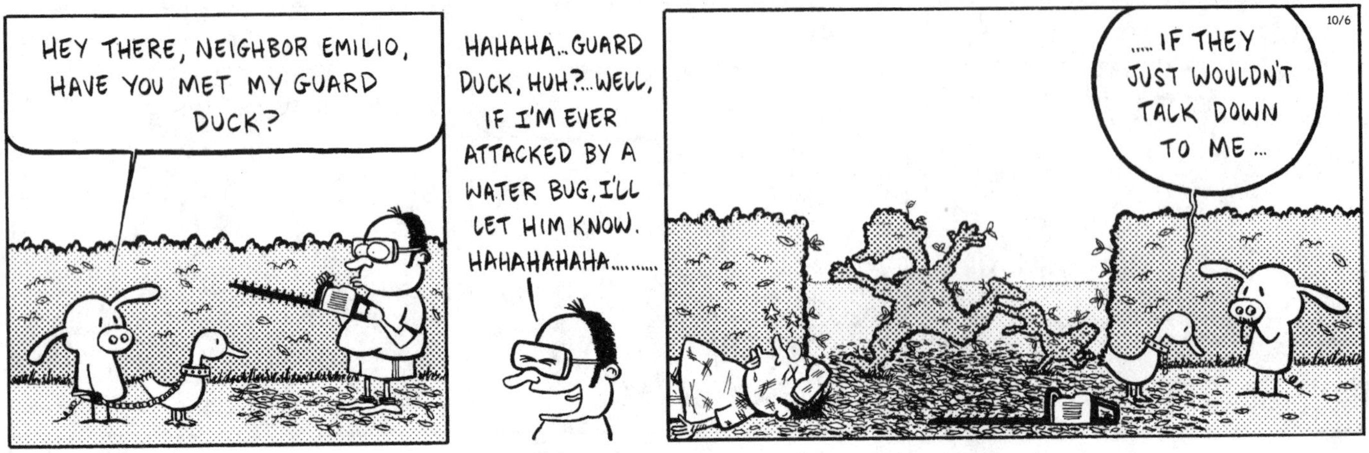
HEY THERE, NEIGHBOR EMILIO, HAVE YOU MET MY GUARD DUCK?
HAHAHA... GUARD DUCK, HUH?... WELL, IF I'M EVER ATTACKED BY A WATER BUG, I'LL LET HIM KNOW. HAHAHAHAHA.........
10/6
..... IF THEY JUST WOULDN'T TALK DOWN TO ME ...

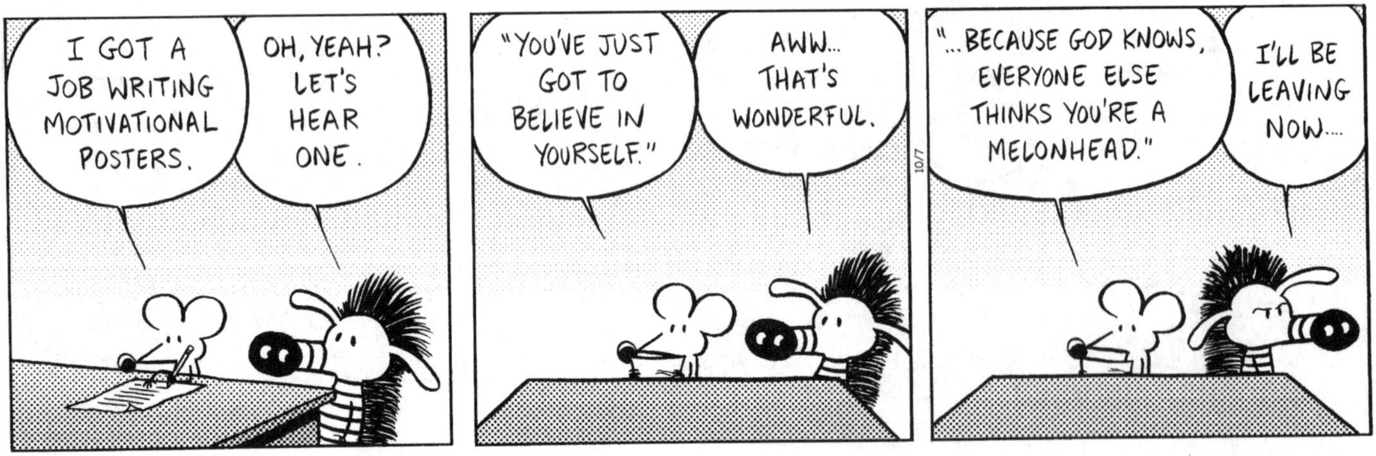
I GOT A JOB WRITING MOTIVATIONAL POSTERS.
OH, YEAH? LET'S HEAR ONE.
"YOU'VE JUST GOT TO BELIEVE IN YOURSELF."
AWW... THAT'S WONDERFUL.
10/7
"... BECAUSE GOD KNOWS, EVERYONE ELSE THINKS YOU'RE A MELONHEAD."
I'LL BE LEAVING NOW....

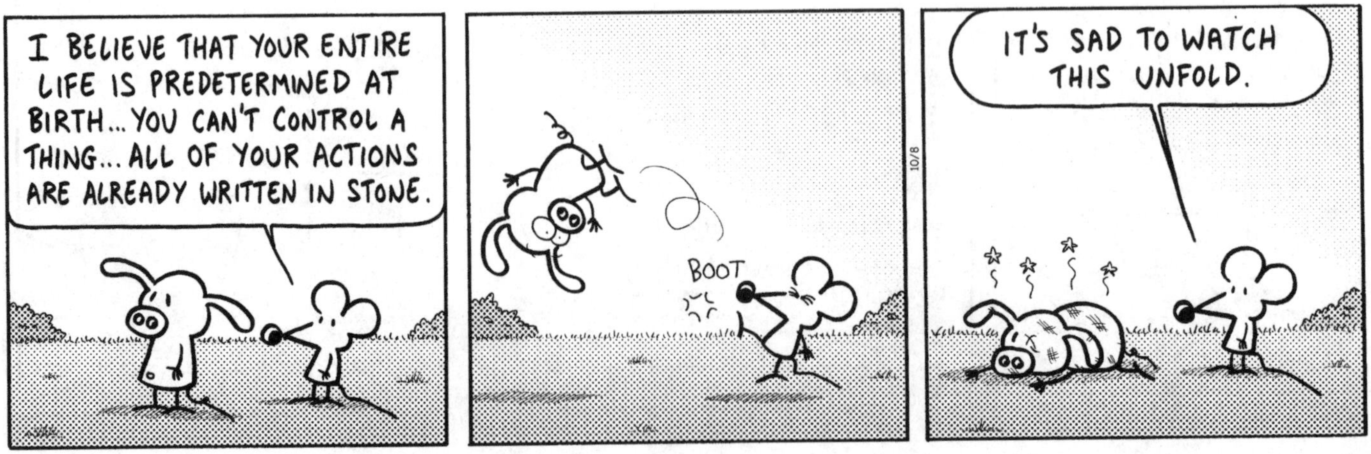
I BELIEVE THAT YOUR ENTIRE LIFE IS PREDETERMINED AT BIRTH... YOU CAN'T CONTROL A THING... ALL OF YOUR ACTIONS ARE ALREADY WRITTEN IN STONE.
BOOT
10/8
IT'S SAD TO WATCH THIS UNFOLD.

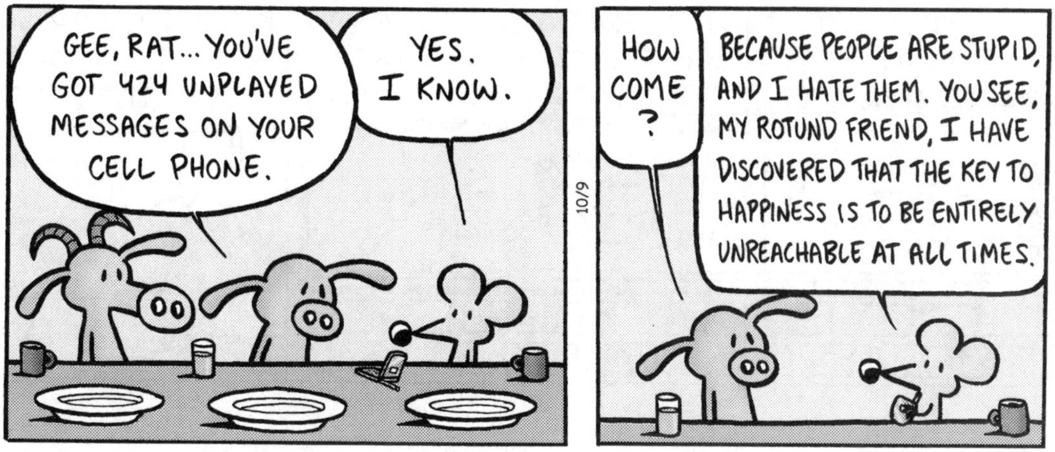
GEE, RAT... YOU'VE GOT 424 UNPLAYED MESSAGES ON YOUR CELL PHONE.
YES. I KNOW.
10/9
HOW COME ?
BECAUSE PEOPLE ARE STUPID, AND I HATE THEM. YOU SEE, MY ROTUND FRIEND, I HAVE DISCOVERED THAT THE KEY TO HAPPINESS IS TO BE ENTIRELY UNREACHABLE AT ALL TIMES.

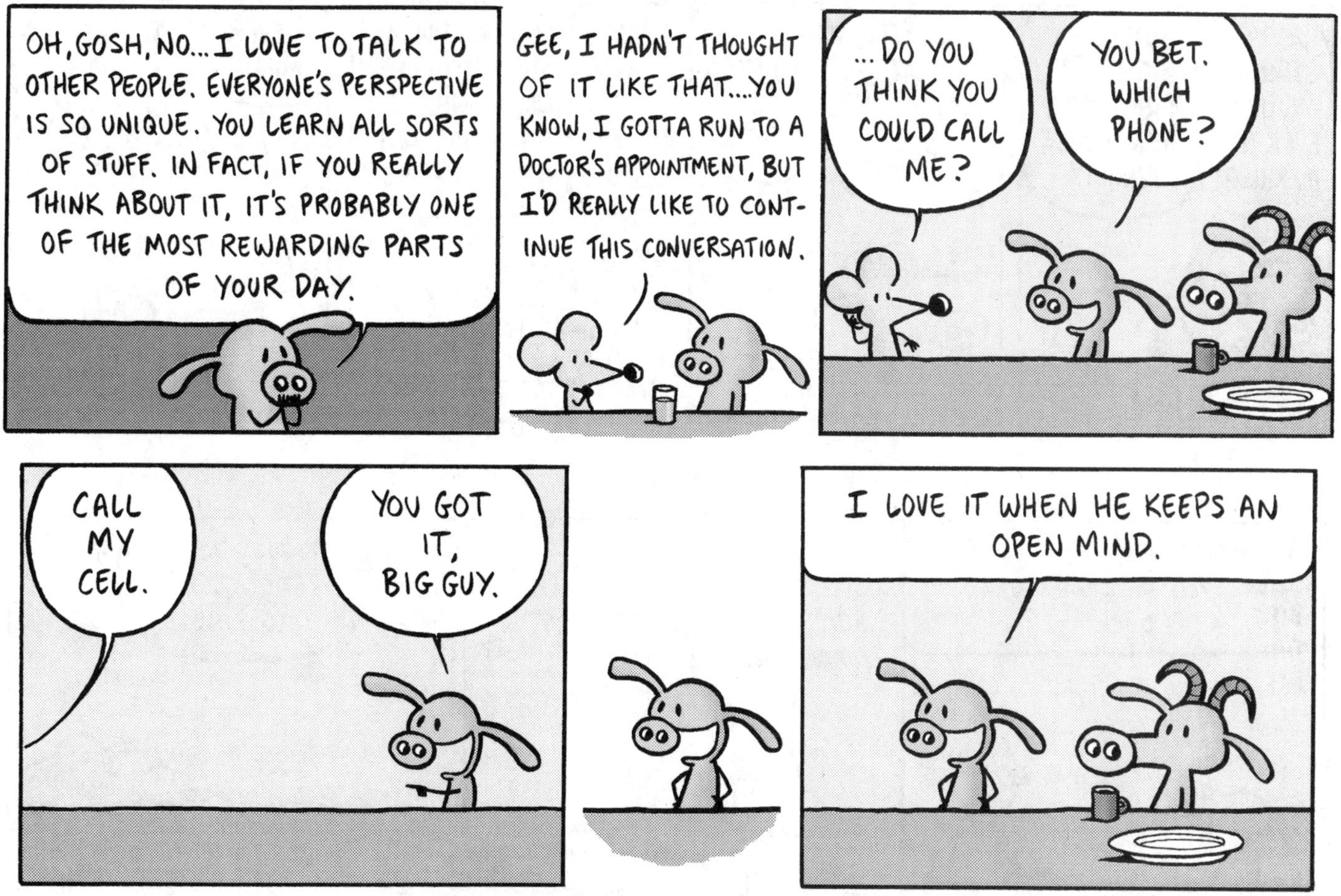
OH, GOSH, NO... I LOVE TO TALK TO OTHER PEOPLE. EVERYONE'S PERSPECTIVE IS SO UNIQUE. YOU LEARN ALL SORTS OF STUFF. IN FACT, IF YOU REALLY THINK ABOUT IT, IT'S PROBABLY ONE OF THE MOST REWARDING PARTS OF YOUR DAY.
GEE, I HADN'T THOUGHT OF IT LIKE THAT....YOU KNOW, I GOTTA RUN TO A DOCTOR'S APPOINTMENT, BUT I'D REALLY LIKE TO CONTINUE THIS CONVERSATION.
... DO YOU THINK YOU COULD CALL ME?
YOU BET. WHICH PHONE?
CALL MY CELL.
YOU GOT IT, BIG GUY.
I LOVE IT WHEN HE KEEPS AN OPEN MIND.

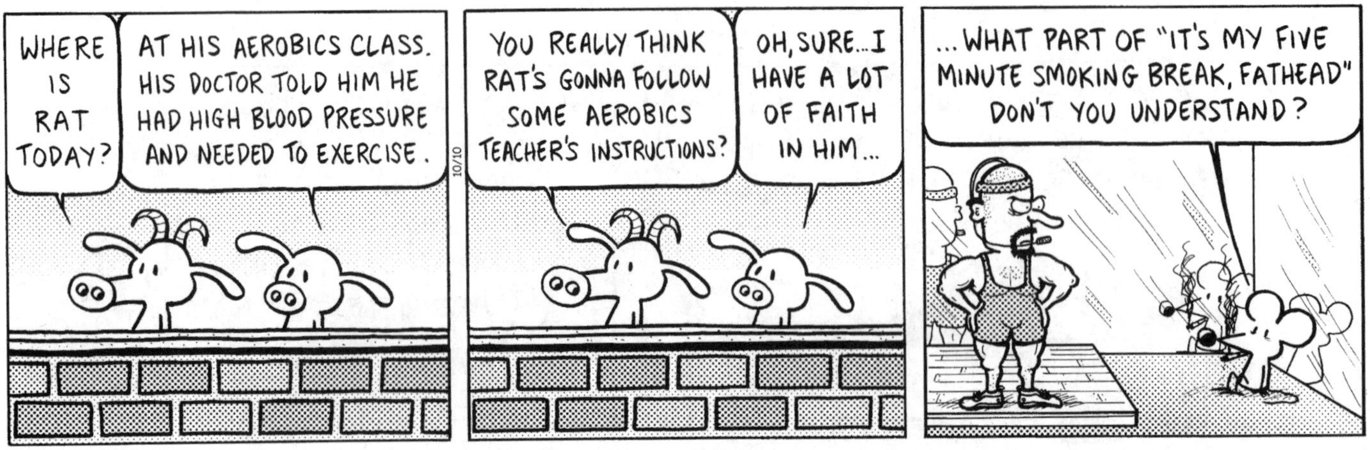
WHERE IS RAT TODAY?
AT HIS AEROBICS CLASS. HIS DOCTOR TOLD HIM HE HAD HIGH BLOOD PRESSURE AND NEEDED TO EXERCISE.
10/10
YOU REALLY THINK RAT'S GONNA FOLLOW SOME AEROBICS TEACHER'S INSTRUCTIONS?
OH, SURE...I HAVE A LOT OF FAITH IN HIM...
...WHAT PART OF "IT'S MY FIVE MINUTE SMOKING BREAK, FATHEAD" DON'T YOU UNDERSTAND?

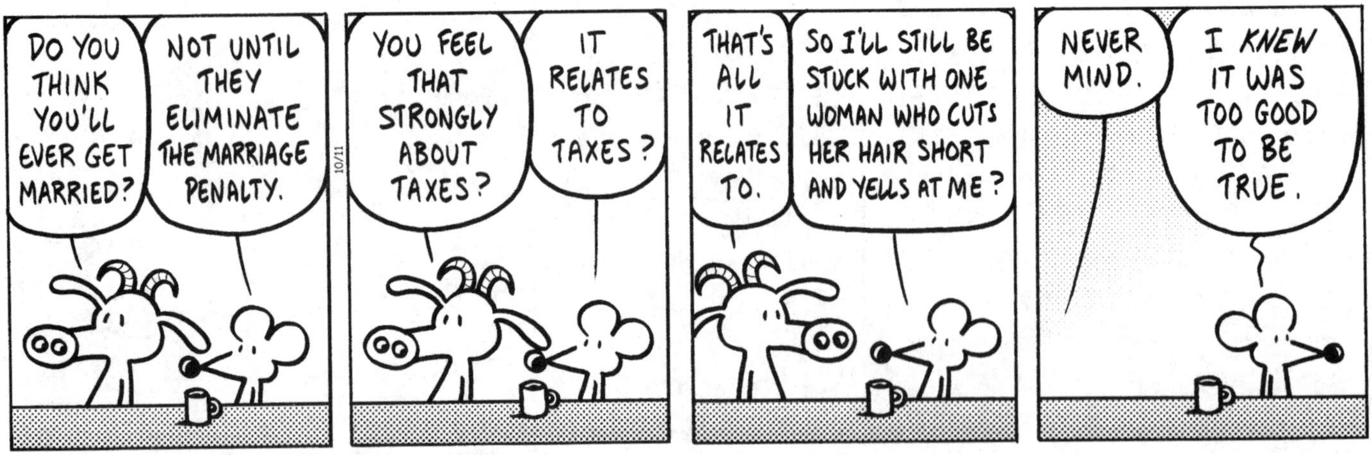
DO YOU THINK YOU'LL EVER GET MARRIED?
NOT UNTIL THEY ELIMINATE THE MARRIAGE PENALTY.
10/11
YOU FEEL THAT STRONGLY ABOUT TAXES?
IT RELATES TO TAXES?
THAT'S ALL IT RELATES TO.
SO I'LL STILL BE STUCK WITH ONE WOMAN WHO CUTS HER HAIR SHORT AND YELLS AT ME?
NEVER MIND.
I KNEW IT WAS TOO GOOD TO BE TRUE.

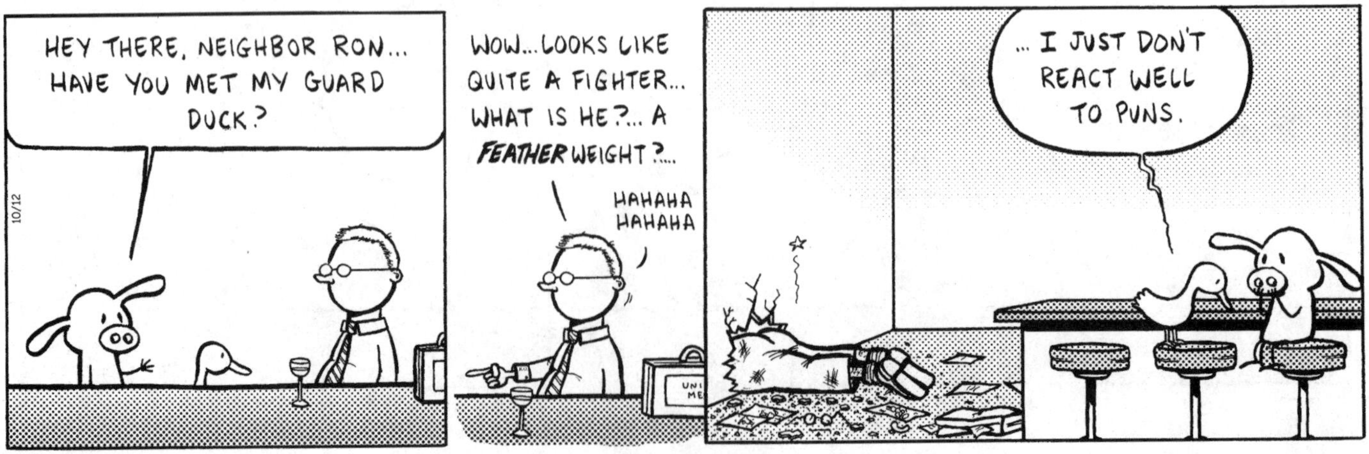
10/12
HEY THERE, NEIGHBOR RON... HAVE YOU MET MY GUARD DUCK?
WOW...LOOKS LIKE QUITE A FIGHTER... WHAT IS HE?... A FEATHER WEIGHT?....
HAHAHA HAHAHA
...I JUST DON'T REACT WELL TO PUNS.

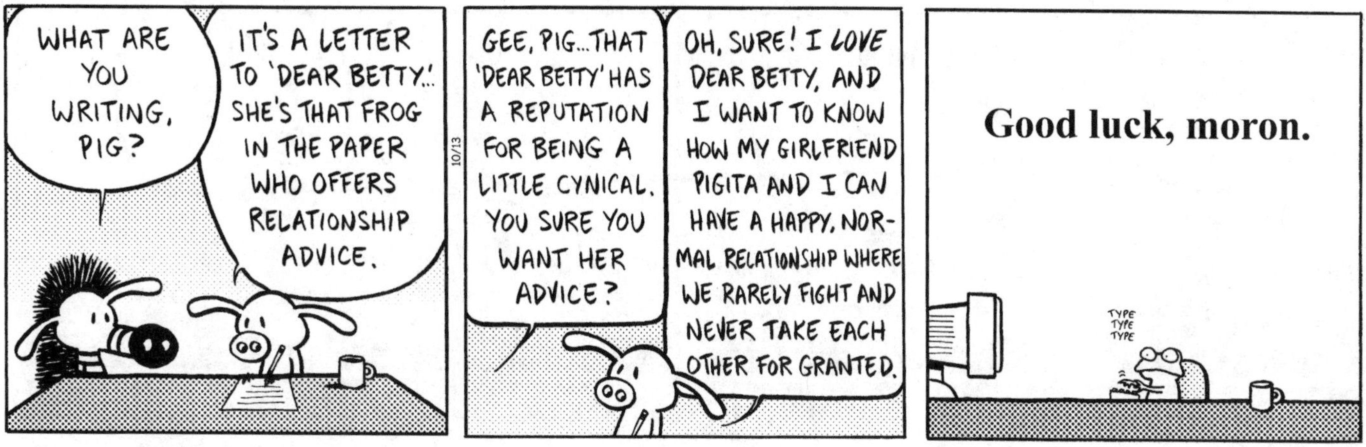
WHAT ARE YOU WRITING, PIG?
IT'S A LETTER TO 'DEAR BETTY.'... SHE'S THAT FROG IN THE PAPER WHO OFFERS RELATIONSHIP ADVICE.
10/13
GEE, PIG... THAT 'DEAR BETTY' HAS A REPUTATION FOR BEING A LITTLE CYNICAL. YOU SURE YOU WANT HER ADVICE?
OH, SURE! I LOVE DEAR BETTY, AND I WANT TO KNOW HOW MY GIRLFRIEND PIGITA AND I CAN HAVE A HAPPY, NORMAL RELATIONSHIP WHERE WE RARELY FIGHT AND NEVER TAKE EACH OTHER FOR GRANTED.
Good luck, moron.
TYPE TYPE TYPE

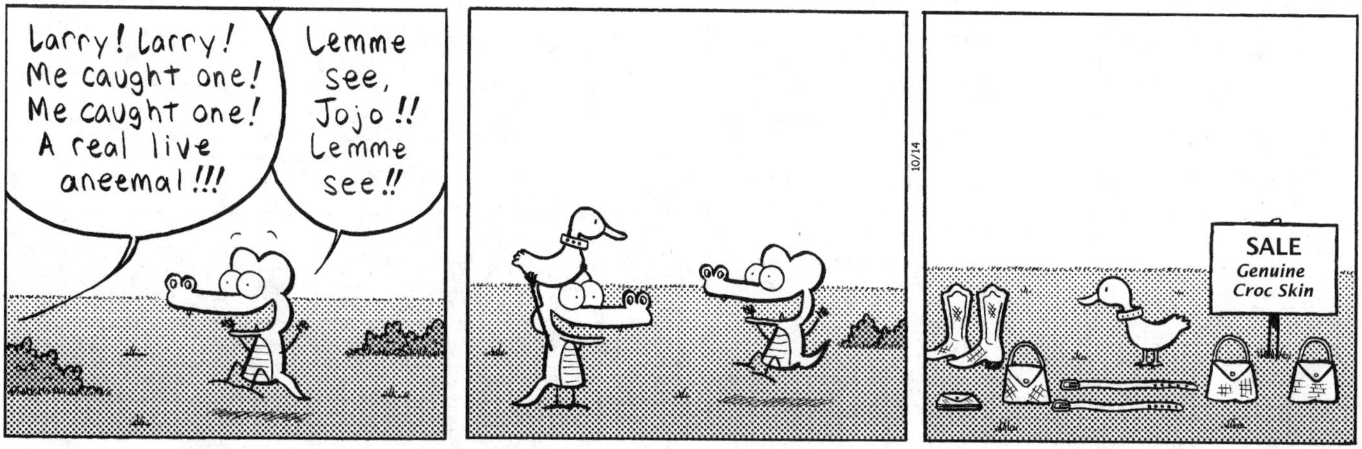
Larry! Larry! Me caught one! Me caught one! A real live aneemal!!!
Lemme see, Jojo!! Lemme see!!
10/14
SALE
Genuine Croc Skin

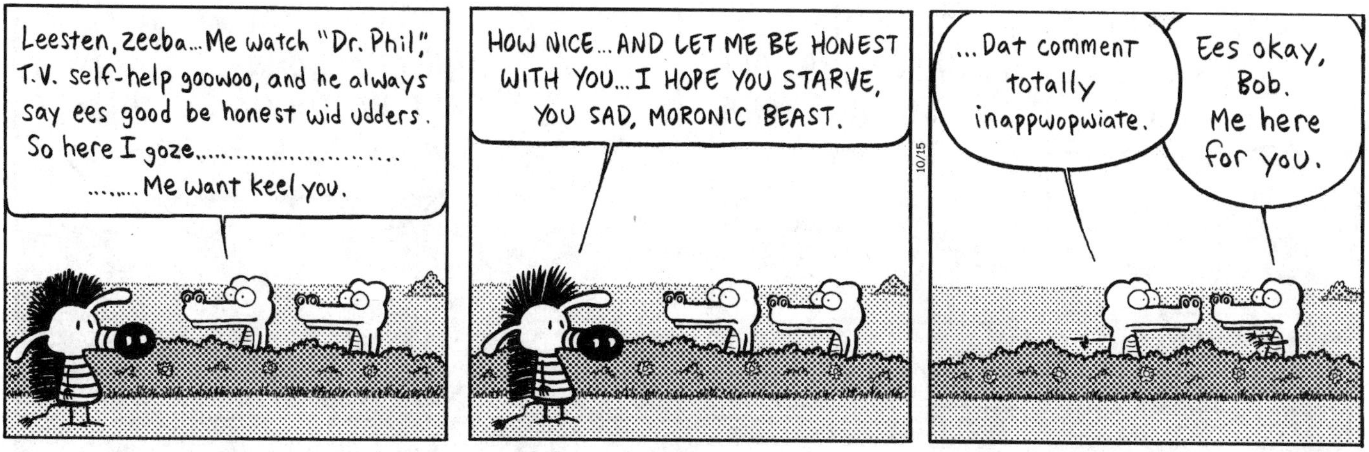
Leesten, zeeba... Me watch "Dr. Phil," T.V. self-help goowoo, and he always say ees good be honest wid udders. So here I goze.............................. ....Me want keel you.
HOW NICE... AND LET ME BE HONEST WITH YOU... I HOPE YOU STARVE, YOU SAD, MORONIC BEAST.
10/15
...Dat comment totally inappwopwiate.
Ees okay, Bob. Me here for you.

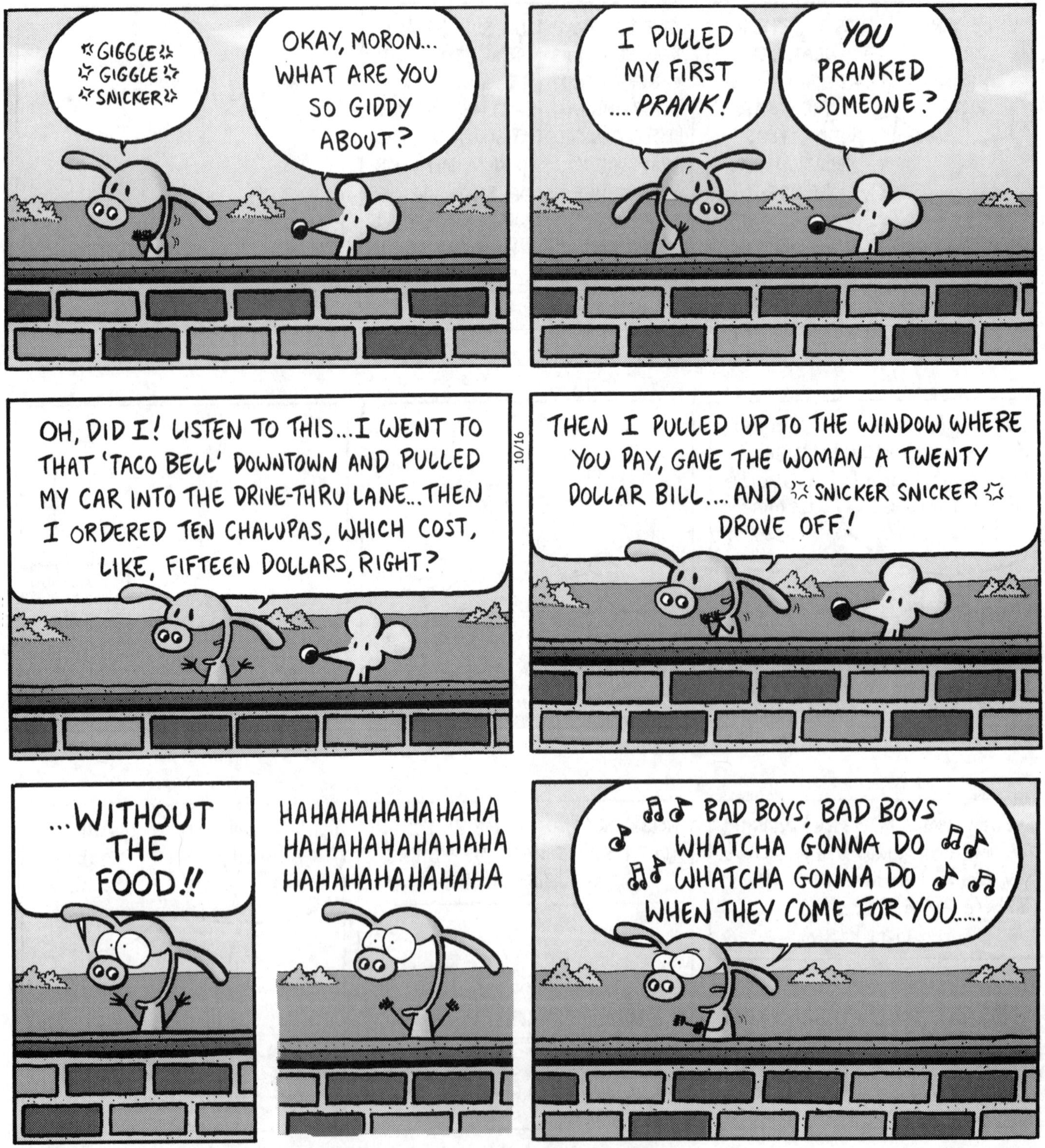
GIGGLE GIGGLE SNICKER
OKAY, MORON... WHAT ARE YOU SO GIDDY ABOUT?
I PULLED MY FIRST ....PRANK!
YOU PRANKED SOMEONE?
OH, DID I! LISTEN TO THIS...I WENT TO THAT 'TACO BELL' DOWNTOWN AND PULLED MY CAR INTO THE DRIVE-THRU LANE...THEN I ORDERED TEN CHALUPAS, WHICH COST, LIKE, FIFTEEN DOLLARS, RIGHT?
10/16
THEN I PULLED UP TO THE WINDOW WHERE YOU PAY, GAVE THE WOMAN A TWENTY DOLLAR BILL.... AND SNICKER SNICKER DROVE OFF!
...WITHOUT THE FOOD!!
HAHAHAHAHAHAHA HAHAHAHAHAHAHA HAHAHAHAHAHAHA
BAD BOYS, BAD BOYS WHATCHA GONNA DO WHATCHA GONNA DO WHEN THEY COME FOR YOU.....

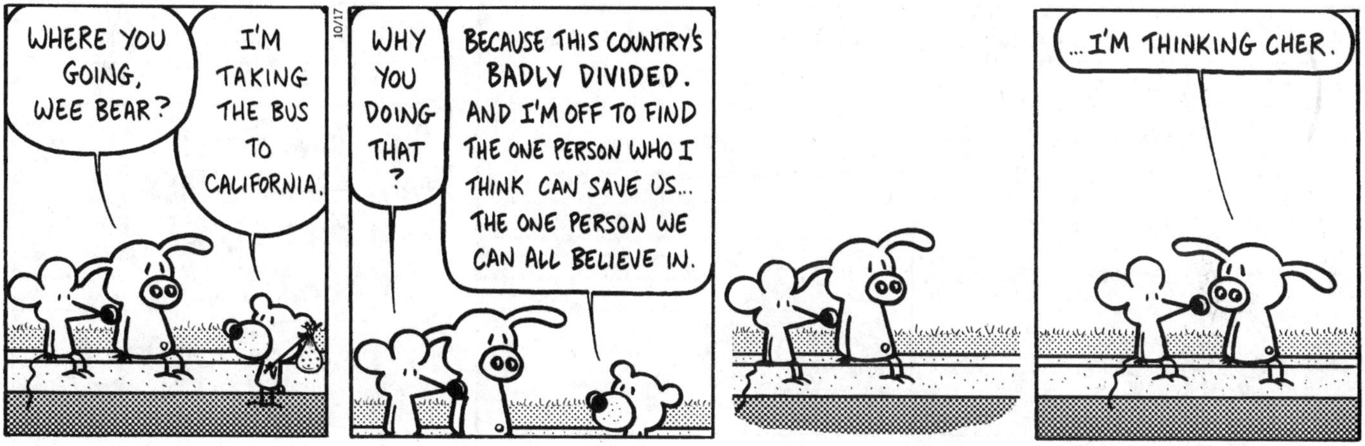
WHERE YOU GOING, WEE BEAR?
I'M TAKING THE BUS TO CALIFORNIA.
WHY YOU DOING THAT?
BECAUSE THIS COUNTRY'S BADLY DIVIDED. AND I'M OFF TO FIND THE ONE PERSON WHO I THINK CAN SAVE US... THE ONE PERSON WE CAN ALL BELIEVE IN.
...I'M THINKING CHER.

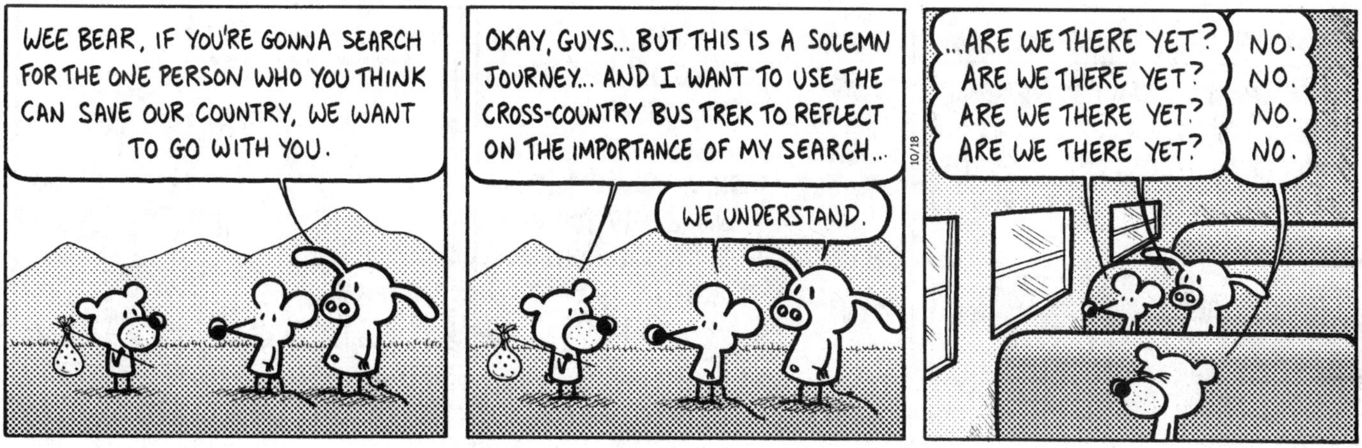
WEE BEAR, IF YOU'RE GONNA SEARCH FOR THE ONE PERSON WHO YOU THINK CAN SAVE OUR COUNTRY, WE WANT TO GO WITH YOU.
OKAY, GUYS... BUT THIS IS A SOLEMN JOURNEY... AND I WANT TO USE THE CROSS-COUNTRY BUS TREK TO REFLECT ON THE IMPORTANCE OF MY SEARCH...
WE UNDERSTAND.
...ARE WE THERE YET? ARE WE THERE YET? ARE WE THERE YET? ARE WE THERE YET?
NO. NO. NO. NO.

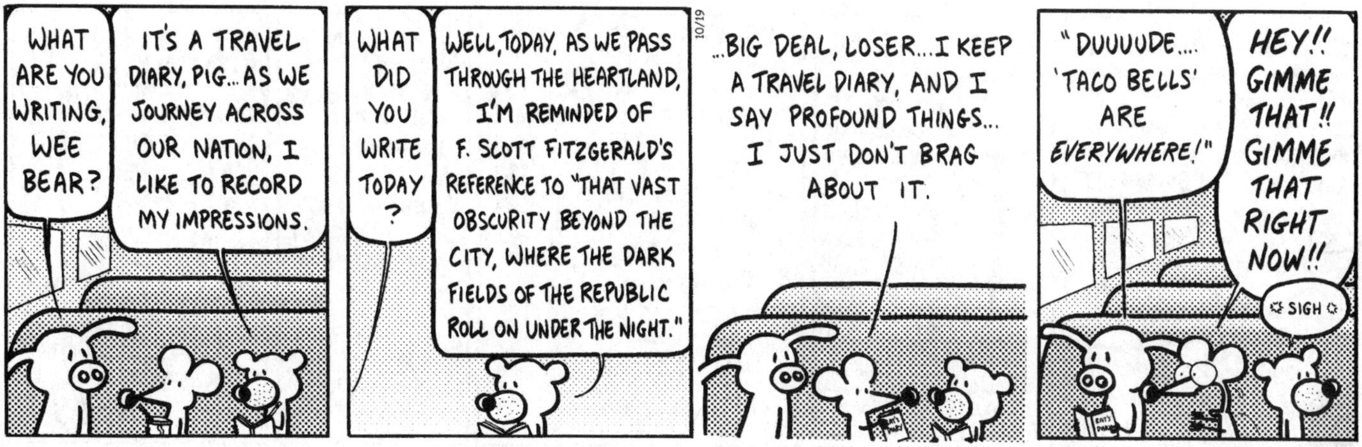
WHAT ARE YOU WRITING, WEE BEAR?
IT'S A TRAVEL DIARY, PIG... AS WE JOURNEY ACROSS OUR NATION, I LIKE TO RECORD MY IMPRESSIONS.
WHAT DID YOU WRITE TODAY?
WELL, TODAY, AS WE PASS THROUGH THE HEARTLAND, I'M REMINDED OF F. SCOTT FITZGERALD'S REFERENCE TO "THAT VAST OBSCURITY BEYOND THE CITY, WHERE THE DARK FIELDS OF THE REPUBLIC ROLL ON UNDER THE NIGHT."
...BIG DEAL, LOSER... I KEEP A TRAVEL DIARY, AND I SAY PROFOUND THINGS... I JUST DON'T BRAG ABOUT IT.
"DUUUUDE.... 'TACO BELLS' ARE *EVERYWHERE!*"
HEY!! GIMME THAT!! GIMME THAT RIGHT NOW!!
SIGH

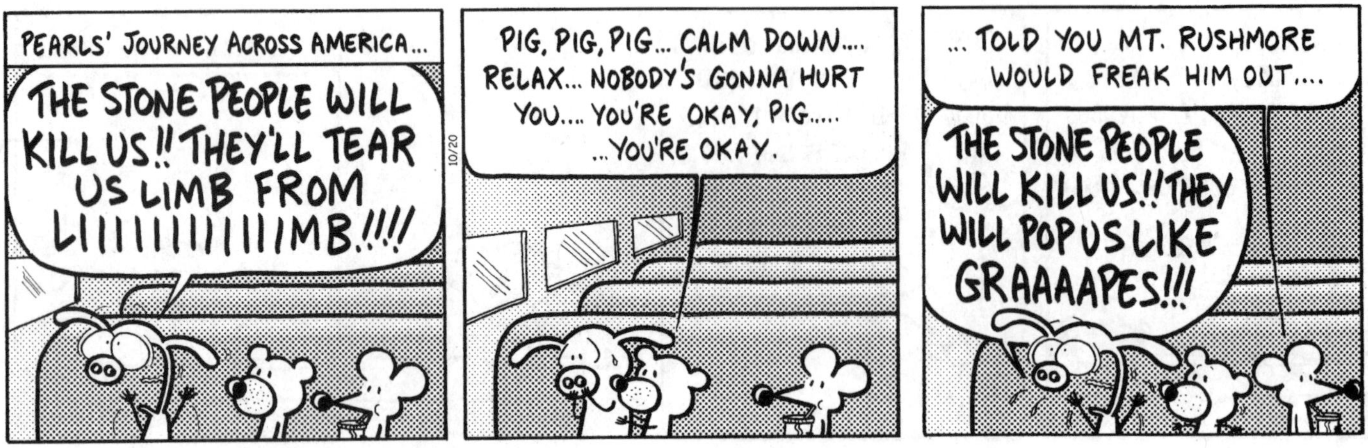
PEARLS' JOURNEY ACROSS AMERICA...
THE STONE PEOPLE WILL KILL US!! THEY'LL TEAR US LIMB FROM LIIIIIIIIIIIMB!!!!
10/20
PIG, PIG, PIG... CALM DOWN.... RELAX... NOBODY'S GONNA HURT YOU.... YOU'RE OKAY, PIG..... ...YOU'RE OKAY.
... TOLD YOU MT. RUSHMORE WOULD FREAK HIM OUT....
THE STONE PEOPLE WILL KILL US!! THEY WILL POP US LIKE GRAAAAPES!!!

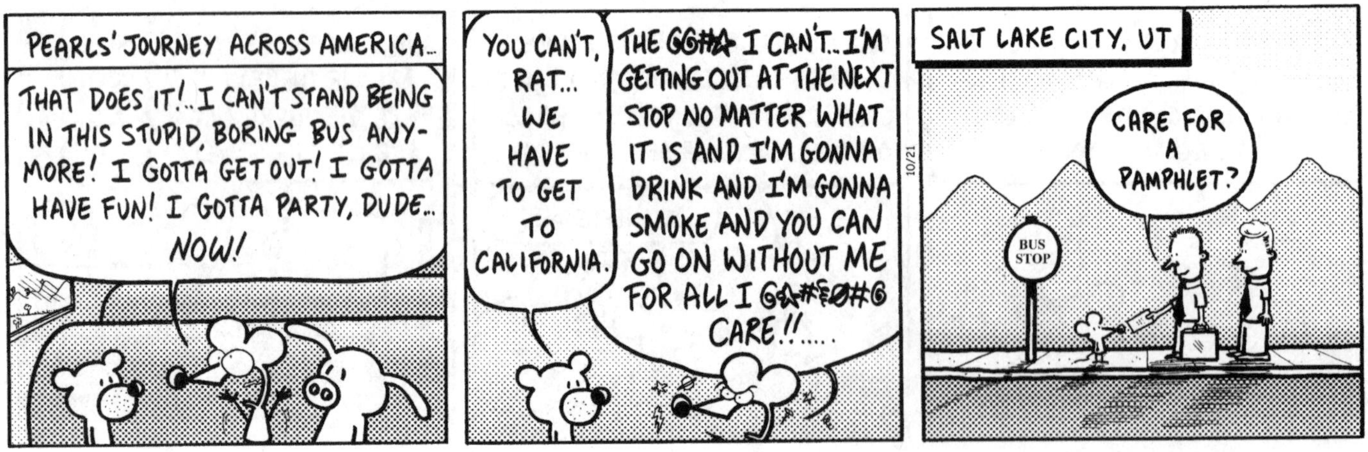
PEARLS' JOURNEY ACROSS AMERICA...
THAT DOES IT!.. I CAN'T STAND BEING IN THIS STUPID, BORING BUS ANYMORE! I GOTTA GET OUT! I GOTTA HAVE FUN! I GOTTA PARTY, DUDE... NOW!
YOU CAN'T, RAT... WE HAVE TO GET TO CALIFORNIA.
THE G@#& I CAN'T.. I'M GETTING OUT AT THE NEXT STOP NO MATTER WHAT IT IS AND I'M GONNA DRINK AND I'M GONNA SMOKE AND YOU CAN GO ON WITHOUT ME FOR ALL I G@#$@# CARE!!.....
10/21
SALT LAKE CITY, UT
CARE FOR A PAMPHLET?
BUS STOP

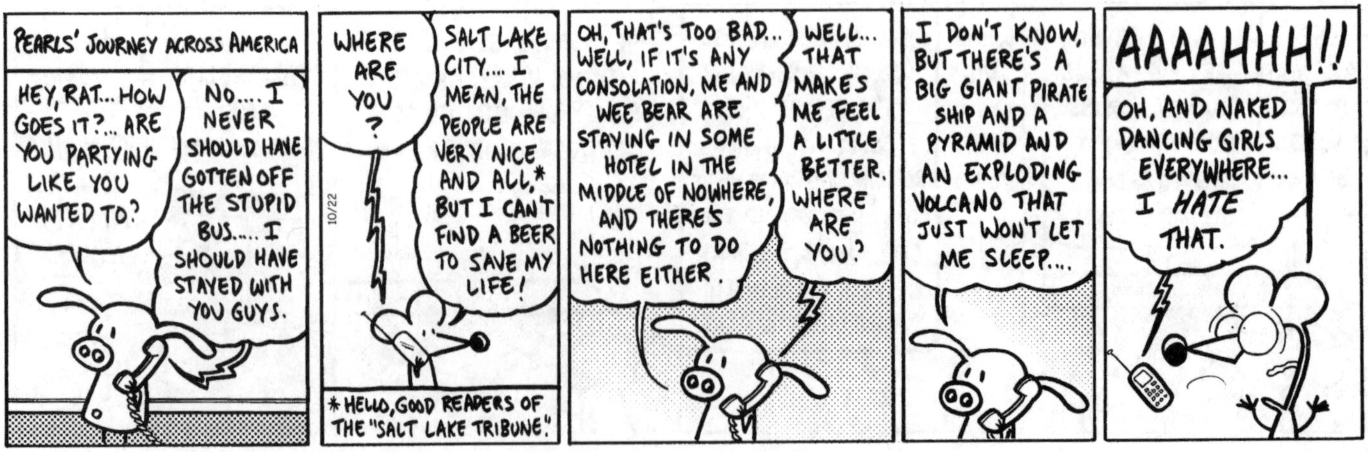
PEARLS' JOURNEY ACROSS AMERICA
HEY, RAT... HOW GOES IT?... ARE YOU PARTYING LIKE YOU WANTED TO?
NO.... I NEVER SHOULD HAVE GOTTEN OFF THE STUPID BUS..... I SHOULD HAVE STAYED WITH YOU GUYS.
10/22
WHERE ARE YOU ?
SALT LAKE CITY.... I MEAN, THE PEOPLE ARE VERY NICE AND ALL,* BUT I CAN'T FIND A BEER TO SAVE MY LIFE!
* HELLO, GOOD READERS OF THE "SALT LAKE TRIBUNE."
OH, THAT'S TOO BAD... WELL, IF IT'S ANY CONSOLATION, ME AND WEE BEAR ARE STAYING IN SOME HOTEL IN THE MIDDLE OF NOWHERE, AND THERE'S NOTHING TO DO HERE EITHER.
WELL... THAT MAKES ME FEEL A LITTLE BETTER. WHERE ARE YOU?
I DON'T KNOW, BUT THERE'S A BIG GIANT PIRATE SHIP AND A PYRAMID AND AN EXPLODING VOLCANO THAT JUST WON'T LET ME SLEEP....
AAAAHHH!!
OH, AND NAKED DANCING GIRLS EVERYWHERE... I *HATE* THAT.

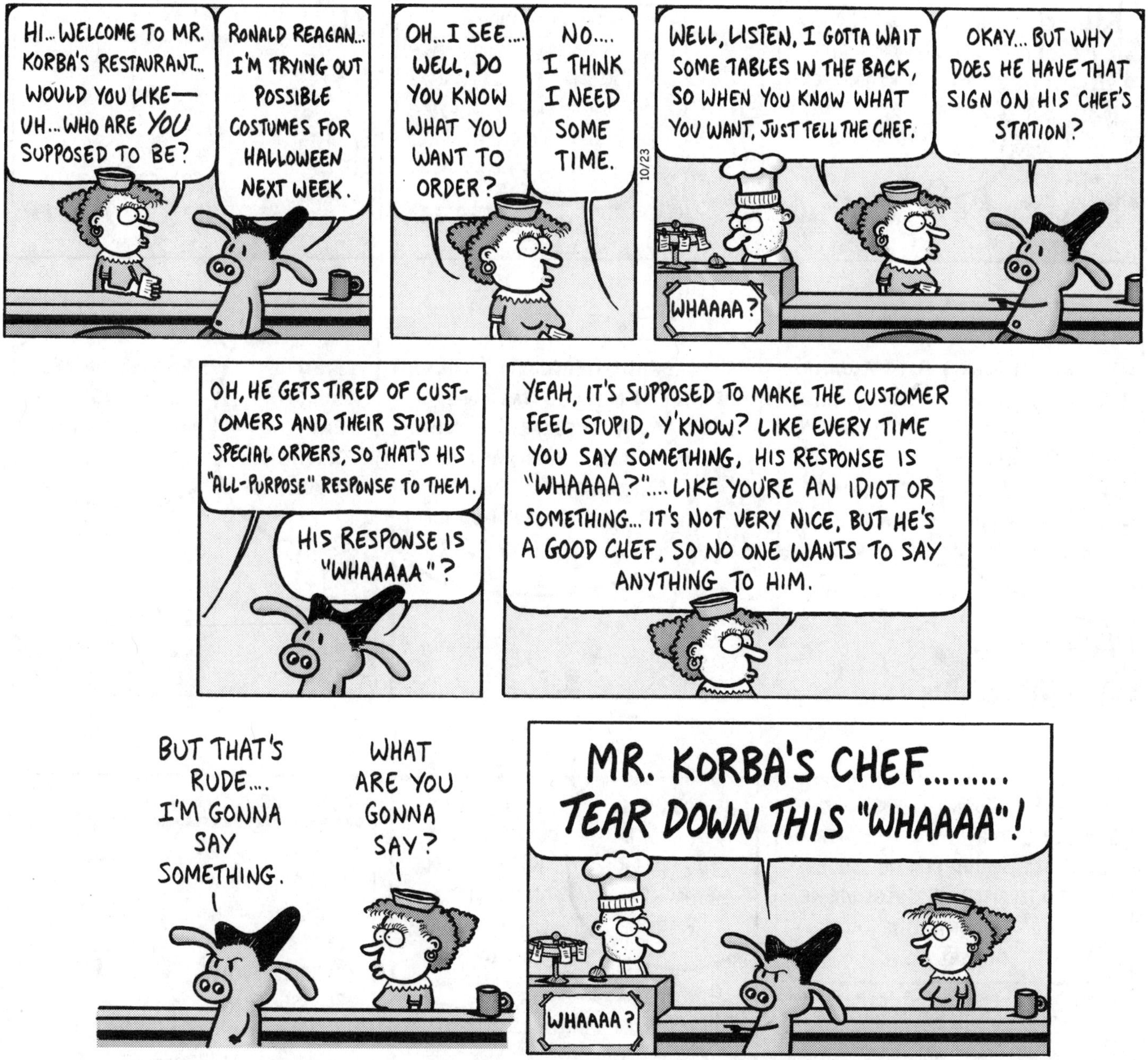

HI... WELCOME TO MR. KORBA'S RESTAURANT... WOULD YOU LIKE— UH... WHO ARE *YOU* SUPPOSED TO BE?
RONALD REAGAN... I'M TRYING OUT POSSIBLE COSTUMES FOR HALLOWEEN NEXT WEEK.
OH... I SEE.... WELL, DO YOU KNOW WHAT YOU WANT TO ORDER?
NO.... I THINK I NEED SOME TIME.
10/23
WELL, LISTEN, I GOTTA WAIT SOME TABLES IN THE BACK, SO WHEN YOU KNOW WHAT YOU WANT, JUST TELL THE CHEF.
OKAY... BUT WHY DOES HE HAVE THAT SIGN ON HIS CHEF'S STATION?
WHAAAA?
OH, HE GETS TIRED OF CUSTOMERS AND THEIR STUPID SPECIAL ORDERS, SO THAT'S HIS "ALL-PURPOSE" RESPONSE TO THEM.
HIS RESPONSE IS "WHAAAAA"?
YEAH, IT'S SUPPOSED TO MAKE THE CUSTOMER FEEL STUPID, Y'KNOW? LIKE EVERY TIME YOU SAY SOMETHING, HIS RESPONSE IS "WHAAAA?".... LIKE YOU'RE AN IDIOT OR SOMETHING... IT'S NOT VERY NICE, BUT HE'S A GOOD CHEF, SO NO ONE WANTS TO SAY ANYTHING TO HIM.
BUT THAT'S RUDE.... I'M GONNA SAY SOMETHING.
WHAT ARE YOU GONNA SAY?
MR. KORBA'S CHEF........ TEAR DOWN THIS "WHAAAA"!
WHAAAA?

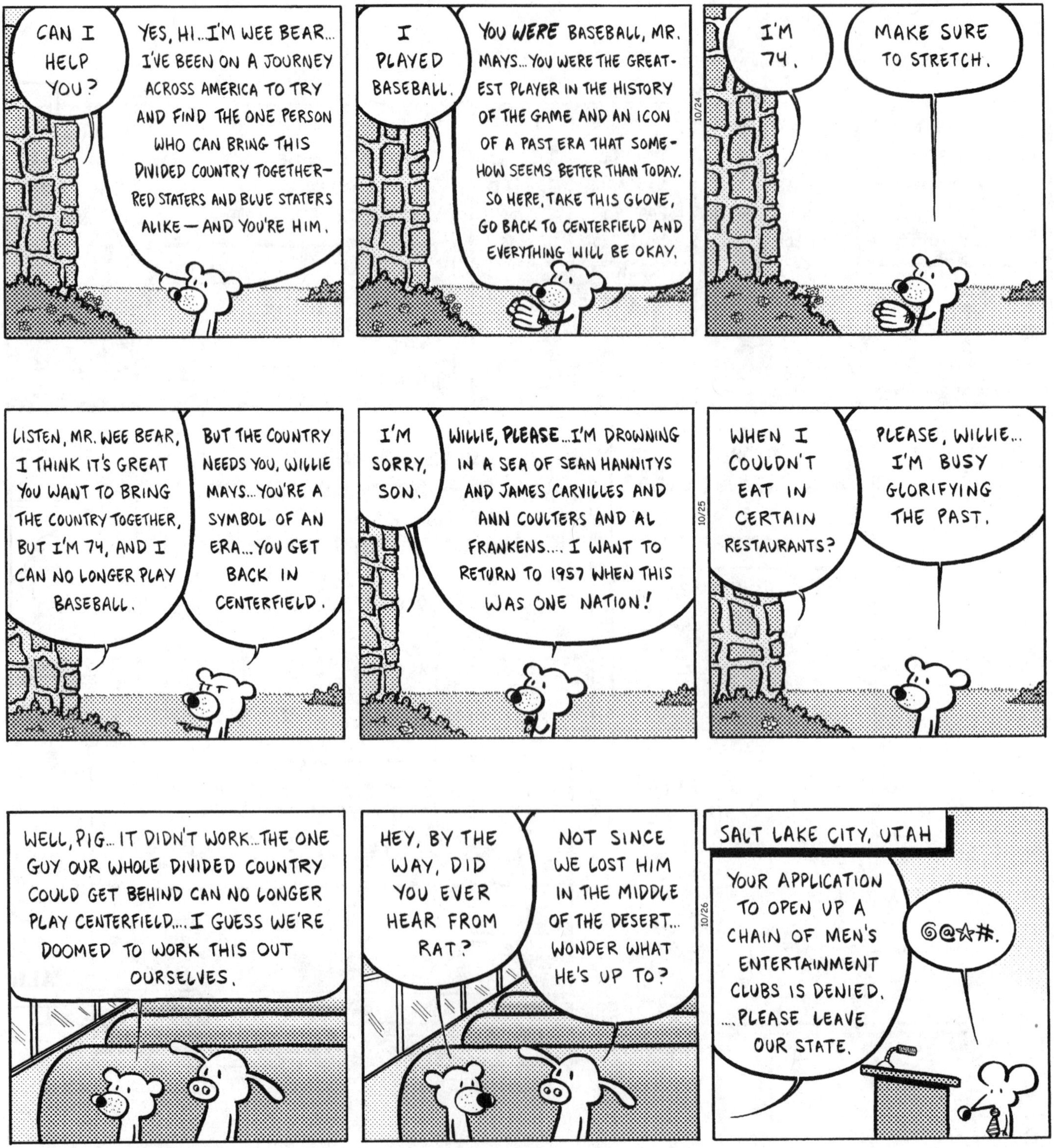
CAN I HELP YOU?
YES, HI...I'M WEE BEAR...I'VE BEEN ON A JOURNEY ACROSS AMERICA TO TRY AND FIND THE ONE PERSON WHO CAN BRING THIS DIVIDED COUNTRY TOGETHER—RED STATERS AND BLUE STATERS ALIKE—AND YOU'RE HIM.
I PLAYED BASEBALL.
YOU **WERE** BASEBALL, MR. MAYS...YOU WERE THE GREATEST PLAYER IN THE HISTORY OF THE GAME AND AN ICON OF A PAST ERA THAT SOMEHOW SEEMS BETTER THAN TODAY. SO HERE, TAKE THIS GLOVE, GO BACK TO CENTERFIELD AND EVERYTHING WILL BE OKAY.
10/24
I'M 74.
MAKE SURE TO STRETCH.
LISTEN, MR. WEE BEAR, I THINK IT'S GREAT YOU WANT TO BRING THE COUNTRY TOGETHER, BUT I'M 74, AND I CAN NO LONGER PLAY BASEBALL.
BUT THE COUNTRY NEEDS YOU, WILLIE MAYS...YOU'RE A SYMBOL OF AN ERA...YOU GET BACK IN CENTERFIELD.
I'M SORRY, SON.
WILLIE, **PLEASE**...I'M DROWNING IN A SEA OF SEAN HANNITYS AND JAMES CARVILLES AND ANN COULTERS AND AL FRANKENS.... I WANT TO RETURN TO 1957 WHEN THIS WAS ONE NATION!
10/25
WHEN I COULDN'T EAT IN CERTAIN RESTAURANTS?
PLEASE, WILLIE... I'M BUSY GLORIFYING THE PAST.
WELL, PIG... IT DIDN'T WORK...THE ONE GUY OUR WHOLE DIVIDED COUNTRY COULD GET BEHIND CAN NO LONGER PLAY CENTERFIELD....I GUESS WE'RE DOOMED TO WORK THIS OUT OURSELVES.
HEY, BY THE WAY, DID YOU EVER HEAR FROM RAT?
NOT SINCE WE LOST HIM IN THE MIDDLE OF THE DESERT... WONDER WHAT HE'S UP TO?
10/26
SALT LAKE CITY, UTAH
YOUR APPLICATION TO OPEN UP A CHAIN OF MEN'S ENTERTAINMENT CLUBS IS DENIED. ...PLEASE LEAVE OUR STATE.
@@☆#.

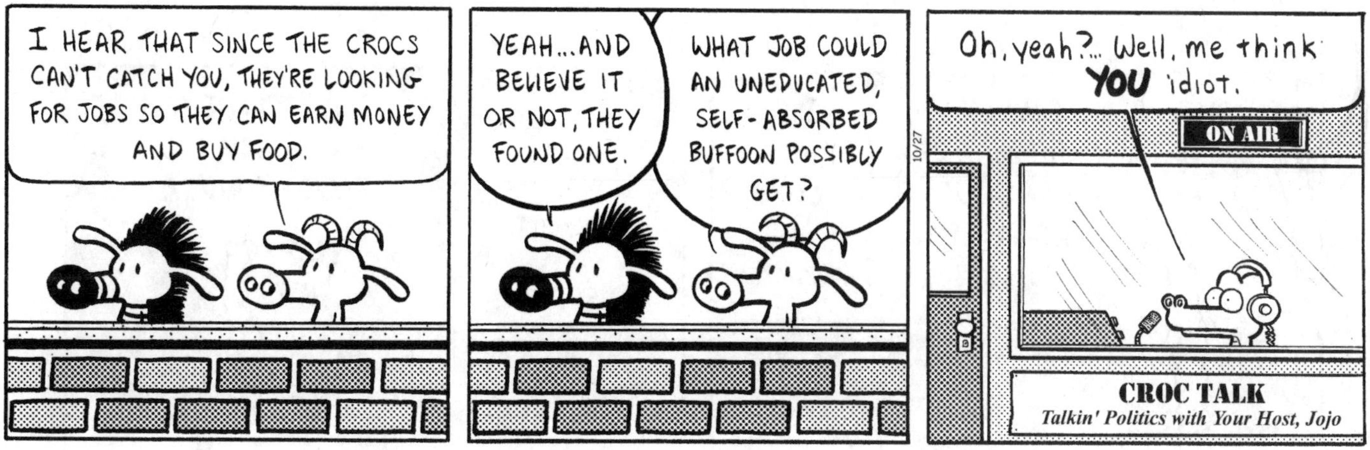
I HEAR THAT SINCE THE CROCS CAN'T CATCH YOU, THEY'RE LOOKING FOR JOBS SO THEY CAN EARN MONEY AND BUY FOOD.
YEAH...AND BELIEVE IT OR NOT, THEY FOUND ONE.
WHAT JOB COULD AN UNEDUCATED, SELF-ABSORBED BUFFOON POSSIBLY GET?
10/27
Oh, yeah?... Well, me think **YOU** idiot.
ON AIR
CROC TALK
Talkin' Politics with Your Host, Jojo

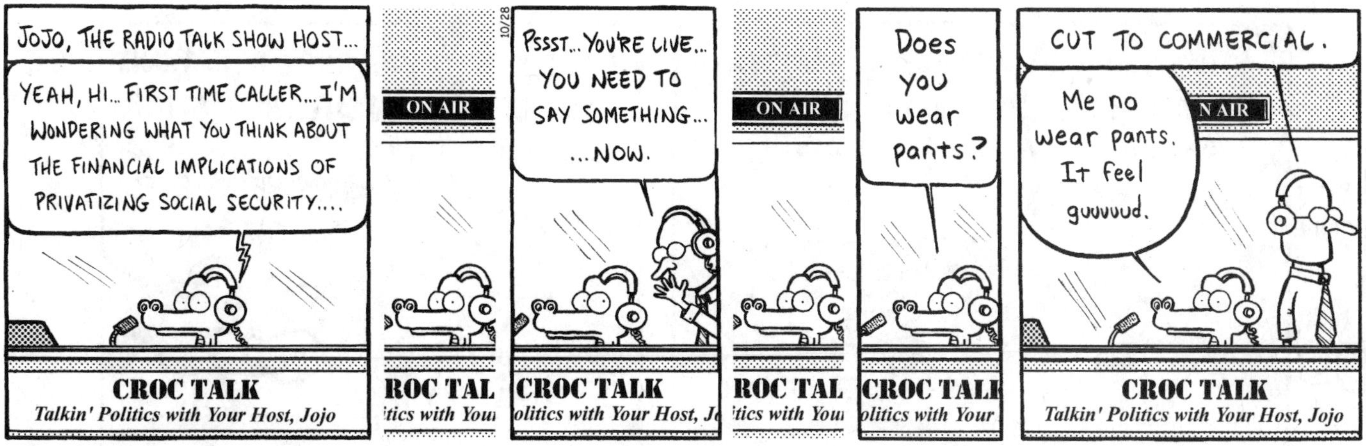
JOJO, THE RADIO TALK SHOW HOST...
YEAH, HI... FIRST TIME CALLER... I'M WONDERING WHAT YOU THINK ABOUT THE FINANCIAL IMPLICATIONS OF PRIVATIZING SOCIAL SECURITY....
CROC TALK
Talkin' Politics with Your Host, Jojo
ON AIR
10/28
PSSST... YOU'RE LIVE... YOU NEED TO SAY SOMETHING... ...NOW.
ON AIR
Does you wear pants?
CUT TO COMMERCIAL.
Me no wear pants. It feel guuuuud.
CROC TALK
Talkin' Politics with Your Host, Jojo

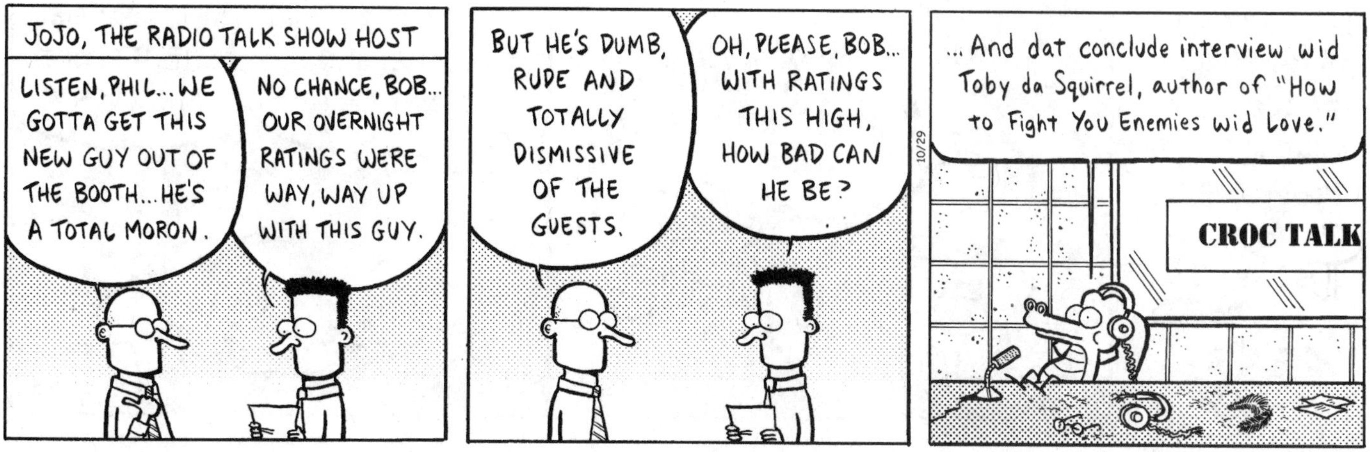
JOJO, THE RADIO TALK SHOW HOST
LISTEN, PHIL... WE GOTTA GET THIS NEW GUY OUT OF THE BOOTH... HE'S A TOTAL MORON.
NO CHANCE, BOB... OUR OVERNIGHT RATINGS WERE WAY, WAY UP WITH THIS GUY.
BUT HE'S DUMB, RUDE AND TOTALLY DISMISSIVE OF THE GUESTS.
OH, PLEASE, BOB... WITH RATINGS THIS HIGH, HOW BAD CAN HE BE?
10/29
... And dat conclude interview wid Toby da Squirrel, author of "How to Fight You Enemies wid Love."
CROC TALK

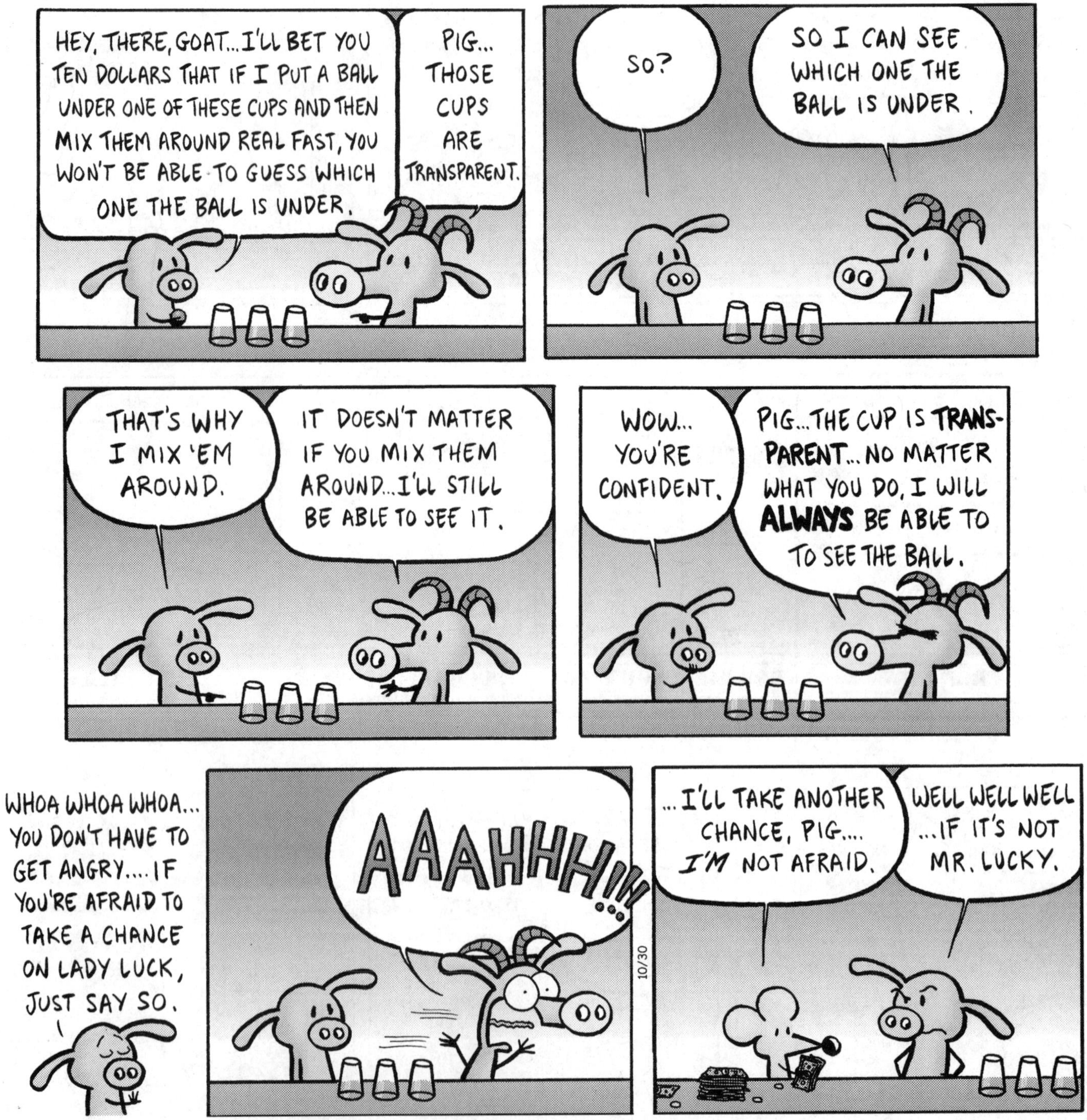
HEY, THERE, GOAT... I'LL BET YOU TEN DOLLARS THAT IF I PUT A BALL UNDER ONE OF THESE CUPS AND THEN MIX THEM AROUND REAL FAST, YOU WON'T BE ABLE TO GUESS WHICH ONE THE BALL IS UNDER.
PIG... THOSE CUPS ARE TRANSPARENT.
SO?
SO I CAN SEE WHICH ONE THE BALL IS UNDER.
THAT'S WHY I MIX 'EM AROUND.
IT DOESN'T MATTER IF YOU MIX THEM AROUND... I'LL STILL BE ABLE TO SEE IT.
WOW... YOU'RE CONFIDENT.
PIG... THE CUP IS **TRANSPARENT**... NO MATTER WHAT YOU DO, I WILL **ALWAYS** BE ABLE TO TO SEE THE BALL.
WHOA WHOA WHOA... YOU DON'T HAVE TO GET ANGRY.... IF YOU'RE AFRAID TO TAKE A CHANCE ON LADY LUCK, JUST SAY SO.
AAAHHH!!!
10/30
...I'LL TAKE ANOTHER CHANCE, PIG.... *I'M* NOT AFRAID.
WELL WELL WELL ...IF IT'S NOT MR. LUCKY.